CIVIL SOCIETY
BEFORE DEMOCRACY

CIVIL SOCIETY BEFORE DEMOCRACY

Lessons from Nineteenth-Century Europe

NANCY BERMEO AND PHILIP NORD

ROWMAN & LITTLEFIELD PUBLISHERS, INC.
Lanham • Boulder • New York • Oxford

ROWMAN & LITTLEFIELD PUBLISHERS, INC.

Published in the United States of America
by Rowman & Littlefield Publishers, Inc.
4720 Boston Way, Lanham, Maryland 20706
http://www.rowmanlittlefield.com

12 Hid's Copse Road
Cumnor Hill, Oxford OX2 9JJ, England

British Library Cataloging in Publication Information Available

Library of Congress Cataloging-in-Publication Data

Civil society before democracy : lessons from nineteenth-century Europe / edited by
Nancy Bermeo and Philip Nord.
    p. cm.
    Includes bibliographical references and index.
    ISBN 0-8476-9549-2 (cloth : alk. paper)—ISBN 0-8476-9550-6 (pbk. : alk. paper)
        1. Civil society—Europe—History—19th century. 2. Democracy—Europe—
History—19th century. 3. Europe—Politics and government—19th century. I.
Bermeo, Nancy Gina, 1951-II. Nord, Philip G., 1950–

JC337 .C553 2000
320.94'09'034—dc21
                                                                        00-038268

Printed in the United States of America

∞™ The paper used in this publication meets the minimum requirements of
American National Standard for Information Sciences—Permanence of Paper for
Printed Library Materials, ANSI/NISO Z39.48-1992.

To Eleanor Bermeo, who taught me all about civility.

—Nancy Bermeo

To Arno Mayer and Robert Paxton, who taught me that politics
and history do mix.

—Philip Nord

CONTENTS

ACKNOWLEDGMENTS

A first thanks is owed to the Social Science Research Council—to Peter Hall, Peter Lange, and Kent Worcester in particular—which supplied the seed money that got this project off the ground. The Council for European Studies in New York and its executive director Ioannis Sinanoglou came to our aid at a critical moment. Additional funding was provided by the Luso-American Development Foundation and, closer to home, by a trio of Princeton bodies: the Council on Regional Studies, the Committee for European Studies, and the Center of International Studies. We are grateful to Rui Machete, Gil Rozman, and Ezra Suleiman who made these grants possible.

The present volume grew out of a pair of conferences that met at Princeton. We are indebted to a number of colleagues who helped to organize these events or participated in them: Douglas Chalmers, Gerhard Haupt, Kenneth Maxwell, Philippe Schmitter, and Mark Von Hagen. Portions of this manuscript were read by Sheri Berman, Jürgen Kocka, Atul Kohli, Steven Kotkin, Arno Mayer, Frank Trentmann, Hans-Ulrich Wehler, and Deborah Yashar. We are appreciative of their efforts to save us from embarrassment.

SELECTIVE CHRONOLOGY OF
NINETEENTH-CENTURY EVENTS

1815	Defeat of Napoleon at Waterloo
	Congress of Vienna
	Formation of the United Kingdom of the Netherlands
1825	Decembrist uprising in Russia
1825–55	Reign of Nicholas I of Russia
1830	Revolution in France
	Belgian independence from United Kingdom of the Netherlands
1832	First suffrage reform act in Great Britain
1834	Constitutional monarchy in Portugal
1847	Parliamentary government in Belgium
1848	Revolutions in France, the Austrian empire, the German states, and the Italian states
1851	Coup d'état of Louis-Napoleon Bonaparte in France
1854–56	Crimean War
1859–61	Founding of the Kingdom of Italy
1861–64	Great Reforms in Russia
1867	Second suffrage reform act in Great Britain
1868	Parliamentary government in the Netherlands
1870	Rome incorporated into the Kingdom of Italy
	Fall of the Second Empire in France; beginning of the Third Republic

1871   Founding of the united German Reich with universal
                manhood suffrage at the national level
1876   Republican Party founded in Portugal
1878   Near universal manhood suffrage introduced in Portugal
1878–90   Anti-Socialist laws in Germany
1879   Founding of Calvinist Anti-Revolutionary Party in the
                Netherlands
1882   Suffrage extension in Italy
1884   Trade unions legalized in France
                Third suffrage reform act in Great Britain
                Newly formed Catholic Party wins electoral majority in
                Belgium
1886   Founding of the Pan-German League
1888   First Calvinist/Catholic coalition government in the
                Netherlands
1891   Legal recognition in Portugal of the right to associate
1892   Party of Italian Workers (later the PSI) founded
1892–1914   Giovanni Giolitti serves intermittent terms as prime minister
                of Italy
1893   General strike in Belgium, followed by introduction of
                universal manhood suffrage with plural voting
1898   General Pelloux imposed as prime minister of Italy by royal
                fiat
1901   Associations Law in France
1905   Revolution in Russia
1906   First meeting of State Duma (parliament) in Russia
1908   Imperial Associations Law in Germany
1910   Founding of First Republic in Portugal
1912   Universal manhood suffrage in Italy
1914   Austrian Reichstag prorogued by Emperor
                Franz-Joseph
                Outbreak of First World War
1917   Revolution in Russia
                Universal manhood suffrage in the Netherlands
1918–19   Revolution in Germany
1919   Universal manhood suffrage in Belgium
1926   Portuguese Republic overthrown and Salazar dictatorship
                established

INTRODUCTION

Philip Nord

Recent decades have witnessed a general, if perhaps no more than momentary, breakdown of authoritarian government in the Western world. The retreat began in the 1970s in Europe's southern tier and spread from there to Latin America before achieving a spectacular denouement in the "velvet revolutions" of the former East bloc. Dictatorships—military and civilian, right-wing and communist—found themselves displaced by new regimes brandishing promises of freedom and the good life. This wave of democratic transitions was heralded by many participants as a triumph of society over the state and prompted among social scientists a rash of inquiries into the possible connections between an activist citizenry and the democratic constitution of public life.

These inquiries came in a variety of colors, but two principal tints may be distinguished here. The first, neo-Tocquevillian, lays major stress on a vital associational life as freedom's bulwark against the inevitable intrusions of government. The marketplace in this school of thought is oftentimes celebrated as society's essential helpmate, furnishing it additional breathing room and resources needed to face down the state's depredations.[1] New Left survivors, however, are less inclined to cast government in the villain's part. The state from this perspective is still seen to have a vital, activist role to play as a guarantor of the public welfare. It is rather the market that is regarded with suspicion, its concealed workings posing a more serious threat to freedom than meddlesome bureaucrats. The problem from this angle is to renovate both the private and the public realms, and here is the point at which civil society enters, the spawning ground of new social movements committed to a general democratization of market and state alike.[2]

For all their differences, these two views share certain points in common. An autonomous civil society is judged the sine qua non of democratic government. It schools its residents in the habits of good citizenship; it acts as a check on the ambitions of the overmighty; and it occupies a place in-between. Publicness is its lifeblood, which sets it apart from family and property, domains of intimacy and private right. Yet, it has not the overt partisan coloration of political society or the policing pretensions of the state. It ends where government and public administration begin. The borders defining these various realms are neither fixed nor impermeable, but fluid as they are, they demarcate the terrain that is civil society's—an irregular topography dotted by institutions, associations, and movements that are never altogether freestanding but do together sculpt a space for self-activity.

Civil society, so conceived, is not coextensive with society as a whole but occupies a smaller swatch of territory. The family, the work place, nubs of informal sociability like the café or salon: these stand outside or at the frontiers of civil society, though civil society may draw on such institutions for sustenance and support (a point made in Jan Kubik's contribution). Nor does civil society encompass all forms of social activity. On this score the qualifier "civil" is meaningful, for it implies activity that is ordered, nonclandestine, and collective. The crowd, the underground cell, the criminal, all are social actors, but civil society is not the stage they have chosen to walk upon.

The present collection does not intend to upset the happy vision of civil society outlined above, just to refine it. Civil society was not, of course, the creation of nineteenth-century Europe, but there it experienced an unprecedented expansion that touched the continent as a whole. Ever densening networks of associational activity spread over small states as well as large, new nations as well as old. Even Russia, which seemed laggard in so many respects, harbored dreams of a freer life, dreams energized by the liberalizing reforms of 1861–64 and made flesh for a brief, exultant moment in the crucible of the 1905 revolution. Yet Europe before the Great War boasted just a handful of democratic states and none of them with pedigrees more than a few decades old. The point is all the more telling when the era's definition of democracy, less exacting than our own, is kept in mind: representative government elected on the basis of universal manhood suffrage plus at least qualified legal guarantees of the three fundamental freedoms of speech, press, and association. On these terms, France alone among the Great Powers might qualify, joined by an array of smaller states, among them Belgium, Denmark, Norway, the Netherlands, and Switzerland. Far more characteristic were liberal states with true representative institutions but restricted franchises, such as Great Britain, or semi-parliamentary states, like Germany, in which monarchs and militaries retained a critical measure of autonomy vis-à-vis representative institutions. In a word, burgeoning civil society translated into a democratization of public life in certain instances but by no means always.

To be sure, as the essays below demonstrate, states put up resistance, often staunch, to democratization. Everywhere, in nineteenth-century Europe, regimes hesitated to grant legal recognition to political association, and many were all too willing to deploy the army, police, and courts to constrict the public space available for the free expression of opinion. Yet, state behavior by itself does not account in full for the multiple failures of civic mobilization to engender democratic, even liberal forms of public activity.

Just as important in this connection are the constitution and character of civil society itself. The contours of associational life are not fixed. It is not just that the web of civic activism may thicken or thin depending on historical circumstance, but that the actual forms of associational life themselves may change: to become more or less inclusive in membership, perhaps, or more or less democratic in modes of self-governance. Not just that, the kinds of impulse driving men and women to civic action may evolve over time. Religious feeling, class affiliation, regional or national identity: the ebb and flow of such sentiments (and they do not exhaust the range of possibilities) pattern the unfolding of organizational life. The peculiar mix and balance of such sentiments at any given moment and the varied institutional forms that they may assume slant, in turn, the political potentialities of civic activism, either to enhance or blunt its democratic promise. There is good reason to link civic activism and democratic government, but it must be acknowledged at the same time that associational militancy may well take forms that are non- or even antidemocratic.

Why civil societies take such varying shapes is one of the principal themes of this book. The answer offered here comes in multiple parts. No doubt, the constraining influences of the state and public policy counted for much in molding patterns of civic behavior. Culture, economic conjuncture, and historical event, however, had a shaping impact just as important, if not more so. Civic activists inherited from the past a repertoire of resources to draw upon: institutional resources, for example, such as ingrained habits of municipal self-government, which were so powerful in the Netherlands and Italy; or symbolic resources, like the multivalent rhetorics of revolution, which cast such a long shadow over French public life in the nineteenth century. What was made of such resources depended in part on the opportunities available. Governments across the continent acted to constrain such opportunities, but the state's capacity to pattern society was not without limit. The rhythms of economic expansion generated ever new grievances and oftentimes the material means to express them; exogenous events—wars and revolutions—created unforeseen openings for action. The state might aspire to the regulation of society, but society itself time and again overflowed the bounds set upon it.

These preliminary remarks are meant to give both encouragement and pause to partisans of civil society. Civic activism may well be the bedrock of democratic life, but not all civil societies, however dense and vibrant, give birth to democratic polities (see Valerie Bunce's essay in this volume). States help to mold the process, but they are not always the most critical actors in determining the forms and objects of civic activism.

For the moment, though, these are but abstract claims. The essays that follow will put flesh on them. The range of cases studied is, to be sure, far from complete. Spain, Austria-Hungary, and the Scandinavian countries have not received coverage. On the other hand, all the major regions of the continent are represented: the East by Russia, the West by Great Britain and France, the North by Germany, the South by Italy. Small states, like Portugal, Belgium, and the Netherlands, are included in the discussion, alongside the usual array of the Great Powers. As for the issue of nationality, a broad spectrum of cases are subjected to detailed examination: from France and Portugal, the most venerable of Europe's supposed nation-states, through the new nations of Germany and Italy, to the Russian empire with its myriad constituent ethnicities. What then, in concrete terms, do these particular cases tell us about the changing shape and democratic potentialities of European civil society in the nineteenth century?

RHYTHMS OF CHANGE

The first and most striking observation is that civic activism seems to comes in bursts, and with each burst the mix of organizational forms mutates. Over the course of the nineteenth century, three moments of metamorphosis can be identified, the first post-1815, the second at midcentury, and the third in the fin de siècle.

In the repressive, postrevolutionary climate following on the Congress of Vienna, Europe's restoration states left little room indeed for autonomous organization of any kind. Urban males, however, gathered in circles and clubs, often exclusive in constitution, to enjoy the pleasures of sociability and cultural uplift. Membership in such assemblies was reserved for a choice few, whether aristocratic or bourgeois, who were selected on the basis of social or family connections. This was not, however, the only model of social organization available. Robert Morris's essay on nineteenth-century Great Britain traces the rise of a new form, the subscriber democracy, which opened its ranks to the respectable middle classes and governed itself according to principles of strict procedural democracy. Fraternity and good works were often the declared objects of such bodies but so too were a variety of quasi-political causes from free trade to temperance and the abolition of slavery. As Morris points out, such early nineteenth-century associations, whether closed or open, adopted an ambivalent stance toward the lower orders, alternating between reformist and disciplinarian modes. The latter found expression in the various voluntary militias and antivice brigades that proliferated in the troubled years after Waterloo.

The objects of such policing efforts, the lower classes, did not themselves slumber in passivity but pieced together neighborhood-based networks of self-help that were of particular appeal to artisan populations. For the more militant and, above all, when the climate of public life turned sour, there remained the option of clandestine action in underground conspiracies or semisecret societies such as Freemasonry. In Nicholas I's Russia, official tolerance of the voluntarist impulse was so low that even simple debating circles acquired willy-nilly a taint of conspiratorialism.[3]

The mix of these divers forms varied from state to state, England and Russia providing the extreme cases. In the former, the subscriber democracy had become the normative model by midcentury while in the latter, associational activity remained fitful and furtive. The year 1848 and its aftermath brought this first phase of civic mobilization to a dramatic and abrupt close. The explosion of associationism detonated by the revolutions of 1848 so terrified authorities that they shut down voluntary activity to the extent that circumstances permitted.

In the 1860s and 1870s, however, a second and yet more forceful eruption of civic activity unfolded. Contemporaries spoke of a mania for associations or Vereinseuphorie.[4] Professional organizations, education leagues, fraternal societies of every sort multiplied in number. The constituency was in large part middle class though labor too participated in the phenomenon, in part through a budding trade unionism as in Germany and England, but above all through the mutual aid and cooperative movements that made a mark almost everywhere on the continent.

The essays that follow suggest three observations apropos the Vereinseuphorie of midcentury. The exclusivist forms of earlier decades, which were the preferred mode of polite society (the notables in France, the Honoratioren in Germany) experienced ever more intense competition from the subscriber democracies so favored by the new middle classes. The thrust of associational activity tended to spill over into politics, fueling liberal and democratic movements, which in state after state gained or threatened to gain the upper hand. But whether or not such movements managed to leverage themselves into positions of authority, they forced a general opening up of public life. That opening up in turn diminished the attractions of clandestine militancy, which, nonetheless, never altogether disappeared from the repertoire of available organizational forms.

European civil societies metamorphosed yet once more in the closing decades of the century, and this transformation was in many ways the most portentous. Of primordial importance was the spreading mobilization of the countryside. In France, associations of a republican hue had first made inroads into rural areas in the era of the 1848 revolution, gains expanded and then consolidated in the 1860s and 1870s. In most other European states, however, apart from agricultural societies composed of wealthy landowners, the countryside had remained terra incognita to associational activism. Yet, in the waning decades of the century, peasants made a massive entrance into public life, and the Catholic Church—in Belgium, Germany, and Northern Italy—played the catalyst's part, drawing on its material resources and moral authority to gather rural folk into a thickening network of self-help, recreational, and devotional organizations. In Northern Italy, a socialist-sponsored rural syndicalism competed with the Church for peasant attention. And in the Netherlands, as Thomas Ertman's essay demonstrates, the fundamentalist wing of the Dutch Reformed Church erected its own associational bastions in the countryside that paralleled but did not overlap the Catholic Church's. Three additional points need to be made in this connection: first that such rural activism fed the expansion of ever more powerful confessional parties— the Catholic Party in Belgium for example or the German Center Party. In certain cases, nonconfessional parties profited as well: the Socialist Party in Italy and the newly founded peasant parties in the Scandinavian lands. But last of all, however massive the sweep of rural mobilization, much of the European countryside still remained untouched, locked into clientelistic relations of dependency, as in Portugal and Southern Italy, or insulated in semi-autonomous, hierarchical peasant communities as in much of Russia.

Rural activism in fin de siècle Europe, however, was matched, even surpassed, by an unprecedented upwelling of labor organization. Trade-union militancy shook the continent from end to end, no state escaping its impact. As with religious-based activism, the new labor militancy articulated itself in dense, associational webs, which, at the party political level, helped sustain a rebirth of socialism.

The "pillarization" of civil society, as the Dutch called it, confronted political society and the state with a novel and disturbing set of challenges. For liberals and middle-class democrats, the peasant and labor mobilizations of the fin de siècle threatened to be overwhelming. They found themselves in competition with burgeoning confessional and class-based parties, organized for national action but capable, via vast associational subcultures, of making an impact at the local level as well. The chummy clubs and enlightened fraternalism of bygone days did not seem up to the task of contesting with such powerful newcomers for public attention. Prospects looked no brighter from the perspective of state authorities interested in the preservation of good order. Civil society threatened to break apart into isolated networks, each sufficient unto itself. How powerful the thrust toward pillarization varied from case to case, so too how established parties and state authorities dealt with the challenge. But the particular character of the challenge and response was fateful in shaping the prospects for democracy in the century to come, as will be discussed below.

THE SOURCES OF CIVIC ACTIVISM

First, however, the forces powering the dynamo of nineteenth-century civic activism deserve a closer examination. What stands out at first glance is how small a part the state had in the process. Legal guarantees of the right to associate were often equivocal and slow in coming. England, which began to relax state controls on public meetings in the 1820s, appears to have been precocious in this respect. France, however, did not follow suit until 1881. The right to unionize was not recognized until three years later, and it was not until the Associations Law of 1901 that the legal status of party organizations was clarified. Even then, as Raymond Huard's essay demonstrates, religious congregations remained under strict state supervision.

The situation was no better in Germany. The North German Confederation in 1867 sanctioned local associational activity but prohibited nationwide federations of Vereine. That limitation was not rescinded until the Imperial Association Law of 1908, which permitted the linking up of voluntary bodies across localities. Even then Reich authorities insisted that associations, in the conduct of all public proceedings, confine themselves to communicating in German.[5] The French Republic feared Catholic associationism; the Germans feared the substantial Polish-speaking minority resident within Reich borders. As for tsarist Russia, it feared one and all. Civic organizations here never achieved legal recognition in the nineteenth century, surviving, in Laura Engelstein's telling phrase, "by the seat of their pants." For much of Europe for most of the century, civil society made its way outside the law, depending more on the state's begrudging toleration than on its official recognition.

This is not to say, of course, that state policy had no hand in configuring the expansion and forms of civic activism. Repressive conjunctures, as we have seen, strangled associational energies and gave a boost to clandestine modes of organizations. In Russia, the Great Reforms of midcentury created local representative assemblies, Zemstvos, which encouraged and fed on the organizational energies of liberal professionals. And in parliamentary states, the comprehensiveness of the franchise made a vast difference. A narrow suffrage worked to the advantage of notables and Honoratioren who entrenched themselves in enlightened but restrictive associational subcultures. The piecemeal widening of the franchise in England (it never achieved universality in the nineteenth century even for men) slowed and modulated the arrival of mass politics, making life easier for the liberal-minded. Their German counterparts were not so fortunate. The new Reich founded in 1871 permitted all sorts of extraordinary suffrage arrangements at the local level but at the national level extended the franchise to all adult males. Mass politics arrived with a vengeance here and the mass associations that were its complement, swamping liberals who maneuvered to hold on to certain mu-

nicipal strongholds but never succeeded in mounting a significant nationwide associational effort.

But this line of argument goes just so far. States grew more tolerant at midcentury at least in part under pressure from a mobilized public opinion. Representative institutions were not just the free gift of enlightened monarchs. The
first Prussian parliament was wrung as a concession during the revolution of
1848. It was military defeat in the Crimean War that prompted a hesitant tsar
to authorize the Zemstvo experiment. No doubt, in certain instances, statesmen
used suffrage policy to manipulate opinion. But just as often, the extension
of the franchise was the consequence of pressure from below. It took a series of
general strikes in Belgium to prod authorities into granting universal manhood
suffrage (tempered by plural voting) in 1893.

No, state policy did not operate in a vacuum but in tense dialogue with a
protean but organized opinion whose energies might be diverted or hemmed
in but never stanched. Whence came those energies?

From city life itself would come the first and simplest answer. The basic
lubricants of voluntary activity—cash, sites of contact, rudimentary levels of literacy—are to be found in greatest abundance in urban settings. The statement
is no more than a truism when applied to Europe's great metropolitan capitals,
London and Paris, with their well-developed merchant and artisanal economies;
but it has application as well to lesser centers of commercial and administrative
activity from Lisbon and Oporto in Portugal to the expanding industrial towns
of the English Midlands.

No doubt, as the saying goes, *Stadtluft macht frei*, but it might be added
that certain cities make freer than others—cities such as Paris, for example,
with its still fresh memories of revolutionary mobilization, or those with ancient traditions of municipal self-governance, like the port towns of the old
Hanseatic League or the former city-states of Tuscany and Lombardy. The
presence of a major university is liable to act as a further stimulant. The activity stirred might be no more exhilarating than the genteel gatherings of
learned folk but might just as well overflow into the rowdier forms of
student militancy. Not least of all, there is the civic potential of religious
institutions, of dissenting Protestant communities in particular with their
commitment to congregational self-governance, moral improvement, and
voluntarism. In the case of established Protestant Churches, that potential
might be moderated, but even church establishments can be shaken from
time to time by swells of evangelical enthusiasm that often splash into the
civic domain. It was from such wellsprings of dissenting and evangelical fervor that the urban cultures of early nineteenth-century England, from London to Leeds, drew so much of their vitality.

The material, symbolic, and institutional resources that urban cultures fed
on did not exhaust themselves over time. Quite the contrary. Europe in the
middle decades of the century was buoyed by an economic boom of un-

precedented scale, a boom that ignited the growth of cities and, with them, of the urban middle classes. A spasm of war-making seized the continent at the very same moment, culminating in the creation of two new states, Germany and Italy, and the constitutional overhaul of three of the older Great Powers: France, Austria-Hungary, and Russia. In all these instances of state-making and remaking, at issue were major institutions of public life—representative bodies, schools, armies—and how they were best constituted.

It was this combination of material prosperity and wide-ranging institutional redesign that motored the associational mania of midcentury. Economic organizations—chambers of commerce, employer associations, trade unions—grew apace, so too fraternal bodies and civic action groups. All that might be sought after were the pleasures of good company, but the new arrivals on the associational scene often came armed with a vocabulary of reform. Nation, science, liberty, progress, such were the watchwords of the day; these were powerful symbolic weapons with an immediate bearing on current institutional battles.

Take the issue of school reform as a case in point. The setting up of national systems of primary education had become a matter of public debate everywhere on the continent. But were the new systems to be secular in constitution or confessional, national in curriculum or multilingual? Officialdom to be sure had quite definite answers to these questions, but so too civil society, which mobilized, fractured, and exerted heavy and often effective pressure on authorities. In Belgium and France, well-organized and liberal- or democratic-minded education leagues lobbied for secularization and won, but secularization in turn provoked a Catholic backlash, so powerful in the Belgian case that the entire issue had to be revisited at century's end.

The Vereinseuphorie of the 1860s and 1870s proved but a warm-up to the paroxysm of associational activity that seized the continent as the century drew to a close. The Catholic subcultures, which had begun to take form at midcentury, blossomed in the fin de siècle. But the new Catholic associationism had to jostle for position in an ever more crowded associational universe, encountering competition from a proliferation of new arrivals: from a reawakened Protestantism (as in the Netherlands or Northern England); from fledgling nationalist movements; or, as was most often the case, from rival socialist subcultures.

The setting for this sea change in organizational life was the so-called Great Depression, a two-tiered phenomenon that remodeled both industry and agriculture. Against a general background of slowed economic growth, heavy industry (concentrated in regional enclaves) grew at a disproportionate pace; at the same time, the agricultural sector across Europe suffered a serious price deflation, prompting major property transfers (as rationalizing landlords snapped up smaller properties or cash-strapped landlords sold off) and a general hemorrhaging of marginal rural populations.

In Europe's growing factory towns and industrial areas gelled a new proletariat: numerous, cramped into tightly packed neighborhoods and communities, and more or less homogeneous social circumstances. A more complex set of developments unfolded in rural Europe. There was a general, although far from universal, erosion of clientelistic dependency vis-à-vis landlords, but the process could cut more than one way. Efficiency-minded estate-owners might gamble on turning a profit by boosting the scale of production, transforming the agricultural workforce along the way into a genuine rural proletariat. Or landlords might opt to beat a retreat, selling off lands and leaving peasant communities, ever more homogeneous in the wake of vast out-migrations cityward or abroad, to look after themselves.

Such transformations made working-class and rural communities more compact, at the same time leveling social distance within them. The groundwork for collective action based on new-formed social identities was laid in the process, but the form collective action took in the end varied from one end of the continent to the other. Socialist movements, which spoke the language of class often in apocalyptic accents, were well-placed to take advantage of the situation, but they were not alone. In Northern England, a chapel-based Protestantism, with its emphasis on self-reliance and moral redemption, left a lasting mark on the local labor movement. In Catholic Europe, lay and clerical currents inspired by sentiments of Christian compassion bent with a remarkable zeal to the good work of labor and peasant organizing. In certain instances, as in Ireland or Poland, where the gulf between landlord and peasant was overlain with ethnic as well as religious difference, the conversion of crystallizing social identities into associational activism came with a nationalist inflection. Nationalist movements here may have gotten started amongst angry townsmen in Dublin or Posen, but in the fin de siècle they began to penetrate the countryside as well.

How then is the associational climacteric of the late nineteenth century to be accounted for? The economic transformations of the 1880s and 1890s created openings for the crystallization of new social movements, but whether and how such movements emerged was structured by multiple determinants. The state and its repressive apparatus counted for much, of course, but so too religious institutions as well as city-born rhetorics whether of a socialist or nationalist tint.

There is no doubting the effervescence of civic activism in nineteenth-century Europe, and it was an activism that unfolded as often without state sanction as with it. Economic transformation and urban expansion pushed the process along, but civil society had resources of its own to feed off of: private wealth, institutional redoubts like churches and universities (even state-run universities might provide a modicum of institutional shelter to would-be civic activists), and a rich repertoire of historical symbols and memories that citizens in-the-making could tap into for inspiration and strength.

CIVIL SOCIETY AND DEMOCRACY

Such a conclusion is bound to hearten Tocquevillian romantics[6] who celebrate civil society as the seedbed of liberty. It is no doubt true that Europe on the eve of the Great War was far more liberal in constitution than it had been a century before. Representative institutions, however hamstrung, existed everywhere; associational life bustled; and it was possible, though still risky in many states, to voice a claim to liberty.

That said, democratic constitutions were a rarity. A handful of states had embraced universal manhood suffrage, but in almost all instances, women were excluded from the franchise, a situation just beginning to change on the war's eve in the Scandinavian states. Parliaments there were, but they often existed on sufferance as in Russia or operated under constitutional restraints as in Germany. It was not unusual for monarchs to run roughshod over parliamentary opinion as did Umberto I in Italy when he imposed General Luigi Pelloux as prime minister in 1898 without consultation or as did Franz-Joseph sixteen years later when he prorogued the Austrian Reichsrat altogether. The right of association did not fare much better. It had no legal sanction in Russia; it was recognized in Germany and France, but, as has been observed, Polish-speakers and religious congregations could not count on equal protection. As for Great Britain, its Irish counties for much of the fin de siècle were governed under special legislation, so-called coercion acts, which curtailed basic civil liberties.[7] And just because associational activity often flourished nonetheless, that did not mean that every association was devoted to liberal or democratic ends. Everywhere existed voluntary bodies committed to policing the morals of the deviant; everywhere, albeit to varying degrees, existed associations (like the League of Patriots in France or the Pan-German League in Germany) that pursued authoritarian or exclusionary agendas.[8]

In a word, civil society flourished, but democratic institutions much less so. The question then becomes, and it runs throughout this book, Why did democratic institutions take root in certain locales and not others? The essays below point to three crucial variables.

The first seems to have been the more or less stable integration of the countryside into the civil life of the nation.[9] Great Britain was an early urbanizer and did not experience the problem in acute form. The durability of France's Third Republic, consolidated in the 1880s, depended in no small part on the regime's success in rallying small-town and small-owning constituencies. Portugal, Russia, and Italy in contrast exemplify patterns of non- or violent integration. António Costa Pinto and Pedro Tavares de Almeida's essay makes clear that the associational dynamism of Portugal's two largest cities left the countryside unmoved. How rural folk, still bound by clientelistic ties, would conduct themselves under a democratic constitution remained an uncertainty, so much so that the republicans who came to power in 1910, although themselves professed democrats, balked at introducing universal manhood suffrage. The Russian peasantry represented a similar question mark, living as it did a life outside "society," insulated in hierarchical communities that ran separate court systems and undertook periodic redistributions of village land.

The Italian example presents a more complicated mix of possibilities. The enduring clientelism of the South calls to mind the Portuguese experience. In the Po Valley, on the other hand, a rural syndicalism took root and soon found itself locked in often violent confrontation with unyielding landlords. And in the waning decades of the century, yet a third pattern of rural activism began to emerge in the North Italian countryside. Catholic action groups set about organizing peasant society, and Northern Italy was far from unique in this respect. It was in large part under religious auspices, Catholic and Protestant, that German, Dutch, and Belgian peasants were delivered, in ever growing numbers, into the associational fold.

Civil society in nineteenth-century Europe originated as an epiphenomenon of urban life, but it did not take long before its capacity to absorb country folk was tested. The ways in which that process unfolded were critical to democratic prospects over the long term. The cases of France and England may be read as relative success stories in this respect. The failed assimilation of peasant populations set the stage for authoritarian or revolutionary movements in Portugal, Russia, and portions of Italy. Yet what of states in which rural integration was mediated by religion?

This question touches on a larger and more complicated issue. The essays below leave little doubt that religion constitutes a second, major variable shaping patterns of democratization, but how the variable played itself out in practice defies easy summary.

Associational movements of a confessional cast were widespread in nineteenth-century Europe. Did such confessional movements favor or inhibit the progress of democratic institutions? It is tempting to answer in Weberian accents: "favor" for Protestant subcultures, "inhibit" for their Catholic counterparts. The Calvinist connection in the Netherlands and Dissenting churches in England were breeding grounds for democratic sentiment. In Italy, France, and Portugal, on the other hand, the Catholic Church resisted the advance of liberal, let alone democratic, institutions. But, it might be asked, should the contrast come as a surprise, given the opposed ecclesiologies of the two religions, Protestantism emphasizing congregational autonomy and self-governance, Catholicism sacerdotal authority and the principle of hierarchy?

Such a conclusion contains an element of truth but is too one-sided. Two counterarguments come straightaway to mind. Even presuming a connection between Protestant religion and democratic impulse, it is an affinity much diluted when the Protestantism in question is connected to the state. The Anglican Church in England and Lutheran Church in Germany both sustained important associational networks, but neither appears to have charted a democratizing course of any moment. As for Catholicism's authoritarian biases, they were real enough in the nineteenth century, above all in the wake of the revolutions of 1848, but the case of Belgium presents an interesting exception.

Here as elsewhere in the decades of midcentury, Catholics riposted to the secularizing policies of a dominant liberalism, entrenching themselves in a formidable associational bulwark. The awakening of Catholic opinion took an immediate political turn, fueling formation of a Catholic Party that went on to win a landmark victory in the elections of 1884. The party did not quit office until after the war, acquiescing in the interim to the hedged suffrage bill of 1893, which conceded all adult males the right to vote but tempered the concession with provisions for plural voting. The Belgian case indicates no fundamental irreconcilability between Catholic associationism and democratic government (a point underscored by the record of Christian Democratic activism after the Second World War) and suggests as well the particular historical circumstances under which such an accommodation might be effected. Belgium achieved nationhood as a liberal parliamentary state by means of a revolutionary uprising against Dutch Protestant rule in 1830. Belgian Catholics identified themselves with the independence movement and, by implication, with the parliamentary regime it founded.

In most continental states in the fin de siècle, civil society pillarized. It might be thought that such fissuring would hinder democratization or at least the fashioning of stable, coherent citizenries, but such was not always the case. To the extent the "pillars" were themselves, in agenda and mode of self-organization, bearers of the democratic idea, their entree into public life gave democratic politics added impetus. The various mobilizations discussed above of Protestant minorities would seem to bear out such a conclusion. A similar claim can be made apropos the nascent labor movements that sprang up everywhere across Europe in the late nineteenth century. But what of Catholic subcultures? On this score the record is mixed. Over time, as such subcultures grew more complex, as they wrested a measure of autonomy vis-à-vis Church authorities and crystallized into independent political parties, they took on an ever more democratic, indeed, Christian Democratic cast. In the short term, however, with notable exceptions, the new Catholic associationism of the fin de siècle stood in ambiguous and often hostile relations to the democratizing trends of the period.

Such hostility, it might be added, was reciprocated in full measure by the era's liberals and democrats (once again with notable exceptions). This points to a third set of explanatory factors, touching not so much on problems of rural or confessional mobilization as on the varied reactions of established liberal and democratic subcultures to the associational climacteric of the fin de siècle. Mid-century liberals and democrats believed in science and material progress; they enjoyed primacy of place on the associational scene; and in certain instances—Belgium, England, France, the Netherlands—they had even managed to reshape national politics in their own image. Then came a host of newcomers—Catholics, Calvinists, socialists—who threatened to upset the proper order of things on all counts. How liberal and democratic associational cultures in the end negotiated the advent of mass politics was full of long-term consequence for the progress and stability of democratic institutions in the century to come.

It made a huge but not always decisive difference whether liberals and democrats bargained from a position of institutional strength. Had parliamentary institutions and party politics become more or less accepted features of public life by the 1880s? Was the franchise more or less inclusive? To the extent the answer to such questions was yes, the challenge of mass politics proved that much less difficult to assimilate.

The assimilation might be worked out at the level of party politics as was the case in Great Britain and France. The Liberal Party in England had long shown itself welcoming to organized Dissent, and the rebirth of Protestant activism in the fin de siècle actually served to re-energize the party. But was it in a similar position to absorb the new labor militancy? Historians have debated at length whether the failure of liberalism to block the emergence of an independent Labour Party was an inevitability or the consequence of conjunctural events. What can be said with certainty is that the boundaries between liberal and labor politics remained fluid. This fluidity made possible periodic liberal/labor alliances, which in turn worked to open the political system to labor participation. In France the Catholic reawakening at the end of the century was not of sufficient dimensions to disturb republican hegemony. More troublesome was working-class activism, which the Radical Party (formed in 1901) maneuvered to blunt with a dose of reform legislation. This failed to prevent the formation of a united socialist party. Yet, however tempted socialists were to hunker down in a revolutionary isolationism, they were at regular intervals enticed into coalitional arrangements with Radicals—cartels, blocs, and fronts—which tempered laborist separatism, without ever voiding it altogether.

In Belgium and the Netherlands, it was public policy, as much as coalitional politics, that played the central part in brokering the entree of class and confessional subcultures into the public domain. This is most evident in the area of educational policy. In both instances, substantial financial resources were poured into private confession-based school systems by governments more interested in religious reconciliation than secularist principle. In both instances, as well, out of pragmatism or of weakness, liberals agreed to go along.

But liberals, even when enjoying the institutional high ground, were not always prepared to bend to the winds of mass politics. Such at least the Italian case would seem to argue. To be sure, there was Giovanni Giolitti, the many times prime minister who in the decades before the Great War labored hard to lure Catholics and socialists into the deal-making of parliamentary politics through the legerdemain of *trasformismo*. But, in most histories of the prewar Italian state, Giolitti's project appears foredoomed. Foredoomed in part because of the unmasterable volatility of the forces with which Giolitti conjured, a Catholicism half-hearted in its acceptance of the new Italian state, a socialism sharpened in its revolutionary appetites by pitched battles with unrelenting bosses and estate-owners. But it was also foredoomed because of the limitations of liberal culture itself. This latter line of argument is elaborated below in separate essays by Alberto Banti and Adrian Lyttelton.

From this angle, what mattered most in framing liberal response to the fin de siècle political crisis was not so much the degree of parliamentarization in public affairs as the character of liberal associational life and its connectedness to parliamentary institutions. Banti and Lyttelton make the case that Italian liberal subculture was possessed of characteristics that hampered its capacity and will to chart a democratizing course for the nation. Vigorous associational networks flourished at the township level, but they never coalesced into a nationwide movement, leaving liberal associationism vulnerable to competition from new arrivals. A fraction of liberals at the same time harbored serious reservations about the competence of parliamentary and party institutions. Italian unification had been achieved, not by debate and politicking, but by war and diplomacy, and hence it was to the state that many liberals looked as the most effective instrument of national unity. When threatened (and given the weakness of liberal associational life liberals were in a real position of vulnerability), they were inclined to abandon parliamentary methods in favor of statist solutions. It is not difficult to see how this line of argument might be adapted to apply to the German experience, and Klaus Tenfelde's essay is suggestive in this respect. Liberal associational activity in the Wilhelmine Reich was intense at the municipal but less so at the national level, and local associations, prickly about maintaining a high-minded but specious apoliticism, nursed a certain disdain for the rough-and-tumble of party politics. Here, as in Italy, national unification had come late, the harvest of power politics rather than negotiation.

Still, the difficulties Wilhelmine Germany encountered negotiating the shoals of mass politics cannot be altogether laid at the door of liberals. Unlike Italy, which *was* a liberal state, the Reich was a pseudo-parliamentary regime topped by an unregenerate monarchical apparatus. More important than liberal frailties in constricting prospects for democracy were the militarist bluff and strut of traditional elites, which middle-class associations like the Pan-German League and Naval League were all too happy to emulate.

But the revolution of 1918 would sweep away the old order. Then at last Germany's liberal subculture would find itself center stage. Then too the weaknesses of liberal associational life would become salient—its fragmentation, its aloofness from party politics, its permeability to "idealistic" national appeals—all of which in the end sapped its capacity to resist the temptations of authoritarianism.[10]

In most instances, it might be concluded, the existence of a functioning and sovereign parliament afforded liberals the requisite confidence to come to terms with the democratizing pressures of the fin de siècle. But not so in belated nations like Italy and Germany. Here, liberals worried about the legitimacy and effectiveness of party politics; they worried too about associational newcomers better equipped than they to compete on the national scene. Stiffened by such worries, liberals hesitated to take the plunge into mass politics, abandoning the democratic cause to socialist and confessional movements that did not always have the strength or will to carry the day by themselves.

CONCLUSION

It is possible to approach the question of "civil society" in Weberian manner, treating the phenomenon as an ideal type with definite and uniform characteristics. Against this fixed standard, existing polities may be measured and their progress or lack of progress toward the ideal tracked.[11] The approach adopted in this volume is different. We start with actual civil societies, understood as complex formations that alter in dramatic ways over time. The question can then be posed: Under what circumstances do civil mobilizations generate more or less democratic outcomes? The answer comes in two parts, the first touching on the character of the civic mobilizations themselves, the second on the varied responses crafted by political society and the state.

Tocqueville identified the civic association as the basic building block of a democratic public life. It is an observation confirmed by the essays in this volume, although with certain modifications. How civic associations themselves are constituted matters. What is remarkable about nineteenth-century Europe is the rise of a new form of associationism, the "subscriber democracy," which translated the practices and rituals of democratic politics into everyday life. The form gained wide currency across the continent, and it spread, not so much one group at a time, but in associational bundles. Protestant religion, it would seem, was critical in this regard, fostering national and international networks of subscriber democracies. Yet, by century's end, lay Catholic movements had begun to adopt a similar strategy as well, laying the groundwork for this century's Christian Democratic subcultures.

Religion, it turns out, played a key part in nineteenth-century civic construction. The assimilation of rural constituencies into public life took on a new immediacy in the fin de siècle, and as often as not (Great Britain and France here stand as partial exceptions), it was via religion that associationism first breached the countryside. The confessional subcultures that coalesced in the process might in modus operandi and objective lend themselves to construction of a democratic public life, but they might not or might not altogether. It made a difference what the map of associational activity looked like at the moment such subcultures entered into the public domain. To the extent the terrain was already occupied by secular networks, national in reach and themselves inspired by a civic-mindedness laced with liberal or democratic purpose, then the new confessional activism posed less of a challenge. On the contrary, as in Belgium, it facilitated transformation of a liberal polity into a more democratic one.

This line of argument, of course, begs the question. Granted that established associational networks of liberal or democratic inclination mattered in negotiating the late-century coming of mass politics, where did such networks come from in the first place? At least in part from past inheritances. Legacies of urban or religious self-government, memories of revolutionary activism (1688, 1789, 1848), traditions of institutional autonomy: all afforded restive citizens resources for action and resources that colored action in more or less liberal/democratic hues. This was as true of the middle-class mobilizations of midcentury as of their working-class and artisanal Doppelgängers. And to the extent these mobilizations came to terms with democratic principle (a more serious impediment for middle-class activists than for labor), to that extent were the long-term prospects for democracy the brighter.

But state forms and policy too helped mold the political outcomes of the several waves of civic activism that rolled over the continent across the century. Such activism did not need legal sanction to survive, but it did require a minimum of official toleration. Otherwise, it was driven underground, and the stunted associational forms of clandestine activity proved poor soil for the sowing of democratic attitudes. Of no less importance was the constitutional character of the state. How representative was it? How wide the suffrage? How sovereign the parliament? The tsarist state came late and with the greatest reluctance to the parliamentary game; the constitution of the German Empire limited the Reichstag's authority in critical ways. These states confronted the associational climacteric of the fin de siècle without the ballast of a functioning or sovereign parliament. They weathered the storm, tsarism just by the skin of its teeth, Wilhelmine Germany in apparent good form. But subsequent mobilization for war necessitated a level of civilian and state cooperation that Imperial Russia could not muster and that in the end Imperial Germany could not sustain.[12] Both empires collapsed in defeat and revolution.

But even possession of a functioning and sovereign parliament in itself offers no sure guarantee of a successful democratization over the long term. Parliament itself must be able to connect with civil society, a connection mediated by party or policy (see Nancy Bermeo's discussion of this point in the concluding essay of this volume). Pluralist parties, adept at aggregating civic interests, maintained the French and British political systems on a democratic or democratizing course. Consociational policy did much the same for the Dutch and Belgians. Yet, in Giolittian Italy and Weimar Germany, the linkup between civil and political society proved difficult to keep up. The reasons were numerous. In the German case, hard times and festering memories of military defeat, a liberal subculture that sealed itself off from politics and the persistence from Wilhelmine times of a far-right subculture that reviled democracy, all combined to distance the *pays légal* from the *pays réel*. In the Italian case, the strains of the war revealed just how weak the political class's grip on public life was: on a countryside mired in clientelism or riven with class conflict, on a Catholic associational subculture just emerging from self-imposed isolation, on a liberal subculture that was fragmented and susceptible to statist solutions.

At issue, in this collection, is the democratic state and how it came to be. There is, of course, a substantial social science literature on this subject, and it is worth reflecting, by way of winding up, how our findings fit into that discussion.

Over thirty years ago, Barrington Moore proposed a society-centered model of democratic origins. Bourgeois revolutions overturned existing social relations in the nineteenth and twentieth centuries. Landed aristocracies came to terms with the new order or subverted it from above, peasants were herded along or exploded in opposition. In crudest summary, peasant explosion led to communism, landed resistance to fascism, aristocratic accommodation to democracy.[13]

As noted at the outset of this introduction, the debate on democratic origins has gotten a new lease on life in recent years, thanks to the intervention of civil society enthusiasts, both neo-Tocquevillian and New Left. No one has been a greater booster of the civil society concept than Robert Putnam, very much of the neo-Tocquevillian school. He begins with an observation: that democratic institutions in modern Italy have proven more effective in certain regions than in others. On closer inspection, such "democratic" regions turn out, centuries ago, to have enjoyed city-state government. In the city-state days of old, habits of self-activity were fostered, which have survived through the ages, providing fertile ground for modern democratic institutions. Putnam's conclusion is straightforward. A vital civil society is a precondition of effective democratic government,[14] and he believes the converse to be no less true. Let civic activism wane and democratic institutions will decay in proportion, hence Putnam's current anxiety about the fate of American democracy: bowling leagues are in decline, and it is to be feared the Republic will decline along with them.

There is a state-centered critique of Putnam's position, and Theda Skocpol is perhaps its best-known exponent. Skocpol worries first about the conservative political implications of neo-Tocquevillianism. In the late twentieth-century West, celebrations of society, of the self-reliance and creative potential of citizen activism, have time and again provided the rhetorical cover for assaults on the welfare state. And just how self-reliant and creative is civil society anyhow? Skocpol advances the claim that it is the state which first and foremost structures the terrain of associational life. Associational activity may be inspired from above in the interests of policy implementation. Even initiatives from below often have state-centered goals, aiming to influence policy or gain access to the goods government has to offer. States mold society or, in a more extreme formulation, it is democratic government that makes for a democratic citizenry.[15]

The interpretive line of the present collection lands closest to Putnam's, but with certain critical reservations. On Moore's account, democratic government is born of a bargain between thrusting bourgeois and prudent aristocrats, both under pressure from an aroused populace. The essays below will suggest various emendations to this scenario. Such deal-making, first of all, was not unique to states, like Great Britain or France, with more or less secure democratic futures but played itself out to mixed results across the continent as a whole. The consequence of such negotiations was not democratic government at all but liberal, quasi-liberal, or liberalizing regimes with varied constitutions and political cultures. How these regimes in turn negotiated the mass mobilizations of the late nineteenth century, such was the most crucial variable in determining whether democracy lay in the near future or not. On this account, the story of European democratization cannot be told without reference to civil society: to an emergent "public opinion" that shaped bourgeois/aristocratic deal-making in the first decades of the century; to the varieties of middle-class activism that underlay the liberal cultures of the 1860s and 1870s; to the eruption of peasant, labor, and confessional militancy, which did so much to reconstitute public life in the fin de siècle.

As for Skocpol, there is no denying the force of her arguments. Enlightened regimes may well see an advantage in putting up with civic activism or tapping into its energies to strengthen their own hand. Democratic governments do have an interest in educating democratic citizens. But where do democratic governments come from in the first place? The experience of nineteenth-century Europe suggests that pressures to expand public participation and democratize public life sprang almost always from civic sources. From time to time, states grasped that positive relations with an energetic citizenry might prove a stimulus to national strength, yet when they opened up the political process they most often got more than they bargained for. There is nothing in such reflections that should cause any partisan of the welfare state undue worry.

So, has Putnam got it right then? Among boosters of civil society, the temptation runs strong to equate civil society and democracy. A dense and active associational life, it is supposed, is bound sooner or later to engender democratic political forms. It is argued, here, however, that civil societies come in many shapes and that not all configurations, vibrant in constitution as they might be, are conducive to democratic government. The energies generated by civic activism do not of necessity feed into a politics of toleration and inclusion but may just as well be drawn on for repressive ends—to police the deviant or to advocate authoritarian goals—as the history of the twentieth century has demonstrated over and again.[16]

The problem is to figure out which turn, democratic or authoritarian, civic mobilization will take. The essays below have been grouped with this issue in mind. A first batch will look at civic configurations that failed to generate a democratic turn; a second will discuss more successful cases; a third and last will reflect on how the experience of nineteenth-century Europe may be brought to bear on the circumstances and democratic prospects of our own century.

NOTES

1. Ernest Gellner, *Conditions of Liberty: Civil Society and Its Rivals* (Harmondsworth: Penguin, 1994).

2. John Keane, ed., *Democracy and Civil Society* (London: Verso, 1988); Jean L. Cohen and Andrew Arato, *Civil Society and Political Theory* (Cambridge, Mass.: MIT Press, 1992).

3. Martin Malia, *Alexander Herzen and the Birth of Russian Socialism* (New York: Grosset and Dunlap, 1961). For a period after 1815, imperial authorities manifested a certain indulgence toward voluntary associations with charitable ends, but such toleration did not last long. See Adele Lindenmeyr, *Poverty Is Not a Vice: Charity, Society, and the State in Imperial Russia* (Princeton: Princeton University Press, 1996), ch. 5.

4. Klaus Tenfelde, "Die Entfaltung des Vereinswesens während der Industriellen Revolution in Deutschland (1850–1873)," in *Vereinswesen und bürgerliche Gesellschaft in Deutschland*, ed. Otto Dann (Munich: R. Oldenbourg, 1984), 63.

5. Eleanor L. Turk, "German Liberals and the Genesis of the Association Law of 1908," in *In Search of a Liberal Germany: Studies in the History of German Liberalism from 1789 to the Present*, ed. Konrad H. Jarausch and Larry Eugene Jones (New York: Berg, 1990), 255–56.

6. See Theda Skocpol's essay "Unraveling from Above," in *Ticking Time Bombs*, ed. Robert Kuttner (New York: New Press, 1996), 297.

7. The picture would be yet darker if Great Britain's policies in its imperial possessions overseas were included in the discussion.

8. See, for example, Geoff Eley, *Reshaping the German Right: Radical Nationalism and Political Change after Bismarck* (New Haven, Conn.: Yale University Press, 1980).

9. On this point, see also John D. Stephens, "Democratic Transition and Breakdown in Western Europe, 1870–1939: A Test of the Moore Thesis," *American Journal of Sociology* 94 (March 1989): 1066.

10. Michael John, "Associational Life and the Development of Liberalism in Hanover, 1848–66," in *In Search of a Liberal Germany*, ed. Jarausch and Jones, 161–85; David Blackbourn, "The German Bourgeoisie: An Introduction," and Celia Applegate, "Localism and the German Bourgeoisie: The 'Heimat' Movement in the Rhenish Palatinate before 1914," in *The German Bourgeoisie: Essays on the Social History of the German Middle Class from the Late Eighteenth to the Early Twentieth Century*, ed. David Blackbourn and Richard J. Evans (New York: Routledge, 1991), 22–25, 29, 248; Rudy Koshar, *Social Life, Local Politics, and Nazism: Marburg, 1880–1935* (Chapel Hill: University of North Carolina Press, 1986).

11. Jürgen Kocka, "The Difficult Rise of a Civil Society: Societal History of Modern Germany," in *German History since 1800*, ed. Mary Fulbrook (London: Arnold, 1997), 493–511.

12. On German mobilization, see John Horne, "Introduction: Mobilizing for 'Total War,' 1914–1918," and Wilhelm Deist, "The German Army, the Authoritarian Nation-State and Total War," in *State, Society and Mobilization in Europe during the First World War,* ed. John Horne (Cambridge: Cambridge University Press, 1997), 1–17, 160–72. I would like to express a special thanks to John Horne, who allowed me to read this volume while still in galleys.

13. Barrington Moore Jr., *Social Origins of Dictatorship and Democracy: Lord and Peasant in the Making of the Modern World* (Boston: Beacon, 1966).

14. Robert D. Putnam, *Making Democracy Work: Civic Traditions in Modern Italy* (Princeton: Princeton University Press, 1993).

15. Skocpol, "Unraveling from Above," 292–301; Krishan Kumar, "Civil Society: An Inquiry into the Usefulness of an Historical Term," *The British Journal of Sociology* 44 (September 1993): 375–95.

16. For an elaboration of this line of critique, see Eley, "Nations, Publics, and Political Cultures: Placing Habermas in the Nineteenth Century," in *Habermas and the Public Sphere,* ed. Craig Calhoun (Cambridge, Mass.: MIT Press, 1992), 318, 325; and Keith Tester, *Civil Society* (London: Routledge, 1992), 149.

I

PRELUDES TO FAILED DEMOCRACIES

1

ON LIBERALISM AND THE EMERGENCE OF CIVIL SOCIETY IN PORTUGAL

António Costa Pinto and Pedro Tavares de Almeida

A t the turn of the century, Portugal was a predominantly rural society with an oligarchic parliamentary system of government.[1] The contours of such a sociopolitical setting are highlighted when certain indicators are considered.

The first impressive indicator regards the occupational structure of the population. In 1900, a large majority of the labor force (62 percent) remained employed in the primary sector, with industry absorbing 22 percent and the service sector 16 percent. Although there were a few modern entrepreneurs, agrarian structures and activities were characterized by their marked backwardness and low productivity, and by the striking contrast between the extremely fragmented landholding patterns in the north and the *latifundia* (large estates) in the south. Owing to an unequal distribution of wealth and of access to vital resources, most peasants' means of livelihood were extremely precarious. Concomitantly, power relationships between the landed elite and the peasantry followed a rather stable patron–client model, which strongly undermined the development of horizontal solidarities and self-organization among the lower strata in the rural world. As for industrialization, when compared to western European standards, the prevailing pattern evinced a low level of technological innovation and capital investment and was also marked by an accentuated geographic concentration in the two major urban areas, Lisbon and Oporto. It should be stressed that, at the time, overall economic activities were not very specialized, thus precluding a clear differentiation of interests between landowners and industrialists.

Another significant feature closely connected with the limited scope of industrialization was the low level and uneven impact of urbanization. In spite of the growing pressure exerted by internal migration from the rural hinterland,[2] in 1900, the number of people living in towns represented only about 16 percent of the population, and only two cities had more than 100,000 inhabitants—Lisbon, the macrocephalic capital (350,000 inhabitants), and Oporto, a much smaller city to the north. Medium-sized urban centers were virtually nonexistent: only two cities, Braga and Setúbal (both lying in coastal areas), had between 20,000 and 25,000 inhabitants, and none had between 25,000 and 100,000.

Perhaps the most dramatic evidence of the country's sociocultural backwardness, however, lay in the very high illiteracy rate, which amounted to 78 percent of the population.[3] Moreover, this was in sharp contrast to the highly educated and rather cosmopolitan national governing elite, a large proportion of which was drawn from the University of Coimbra (the only university in Portugal at the time) and the Polytechnic and the Military Training Colleges in Lisbon.[4]

Finally, two significant traits of the political realm were the lack of genuine and widespread popular mobilization and the oligarchic tendency in the formation of the ruling elite. First, whereas civic and political activities were fairly lively in the major urban centers, most people in the rural areas and small provincial towns were alienated from public affairs. Their intermittent political participation, which occurred chiefly in electoral periods, was encouraged from above and strictly subject to hierarchical clientelistic bonds. Second, the limited base from which the political elite was recruited is witnessed inter alia by the important role that family ties played in the appointments of the latter and the small proportion of citizens who were eligible for parliamentary careers. Counterbalancing the relatively moderate franchise, eligibility for parliamentary functions was based on high property requirements, so only a meager 7 percent of the adult male population qualified, according to the official records available for the 1880s. The slow replacement of the ministerial, parliamentary, and prefectural personnel likewise confirms the closed nature of the ruling elite.[5]

Despite the structural and cultural constraints outlined above, Portugal was not a stagnant, change-resistant society, but rather a modernizing one that had been experiencing social change and political innovation since the mid-nineteenth century. In spite of its insufficiencies and discrepancies, the process of modernization induced significant transformations that should not be minimized or obscured. An understanding of the peculiar mode in which tradition and modernity were interwoven helps throw light on the specific configuration and dilemmas of the burgeoning civil society in Portugal under liberalism.

The initial impetus toward a radical reshaping of the traditional sociopolitical order dates back to 1834, when, following an earlier, frustrated attempt

(1820–23), the liberal parliamentary system was finally established in the aftermath of a civil war. Three basic changes, which are quite important for our further analysis, should be pointed out.

First, the military defeat of the legitimist forces entailed the collapse of the dominance of the old nobility (most of which formed the backbone of the absolutist cause) and the concomitant rise of the middle classes, which ended up holding hegemonic positions within the ruling elite. The precocious, irreversible waning of the aristocracy's influence seems to be a peculiar feature of the Portuguese historical experience when compared with the greater resistance and adaptation of most of its European counterparts to the changing sociopolitical processes of the nineteenth century.[6]

Second, a profound restructuring of the major symbols and institutions occurred, with the emergence of a new criterion of legitimacy based on the principles of citizenship and representative government and with the reformulation of the legal and organizational framework of collective action. In other words, it was then that the *ancien régime* was dismantled and the prerequisites for the development of a modern state bureaucracy, of liberal politics, and of civil society were set. In particular, the end of the compulsory guild system and the recognition of certain basic civic rights (freedom of speech, right to petition, right of assembly)[7] cleared the way for a pluralistic setting of voluntary associations[8] and the blossoming of "public opinion." Thus, as early as 1834, the first long-lasting private bodies for representing the merchants' interests (Associações do Comércio) formed in Lisbon and Oporto, and in the years that immediately followed, associational life and a free press (both supported by the urban middle classes) received their initial stimulus.

Third, the secular orientation and even the Masonic affiliations of the new ruling elite led to both a ban on religious congregations and the expropriation and further commercialization of the market for large ecclesiastical estates. This seriously damaged the material self-sufficiency of the Church and eroded its influence. Although the Church kept its symbolic pervasiveness in social life (namely by controlling the rituals connected to birth, marriage, and death), the clergy became subject to secular authority: They were largely supported by government stipends, and they were engaged in territorial administration, thus playing a cooperative, though subordinate, role in the building of the new liberal state apparatus. As a consequence, until the establishment of the Republican regime in 1910, the Church had neither an autonomous nor an adversarial role in the political arena, particularly concerning the promotion of Catholic, antiliberal organized groups.

Until the middle of the nineteenth century, times were turbulent and uncertain. Intense social agitation and political turmoil prevented the consolidation of the recently established constitutional order. There were violent, armed conflicts between the various liberal groups, which were divided by volatile factionalist antagonisms and ideological differences. Pacification of these groups only occurred after 1851, following a military coup that successfully enforced a fairly lasting consensus among the liberals. The former political factions and the dispersed, rather informal networks of local notables then tended to coalesce into the first two parties, which more or less regularly alternated in office usually on the basis of a mutual agreement, whether explicit or not. This new cycle of political consent and social appeasement[9] allowed the institutionalization of parliamentarianism and civil liberties and gave a new impetus to the modernization process.

Elections became routinized and, although they were perverted by governmental manipulation and clientelistic arrangements, they became a major arena for political struggle and negotiation.[10] The constitutional pact of 1852 (Acto Adicional) not only definitively set up a system of direct voting but also reduced the property requirements for the franchise. In the mid-1860s, about 10 percent of the population was entitled to vote, which indicates that the franchise was far more widespread than the rigid *régime censitaire* prevailing in most European countries at that time.[11] While the restrictive eligibility qualifications remained unchanged, the extent of suffrage varied throughout the nineteenth century. In 1878, both as a response to the growing claims for universal suffrage made by the radical liberals and the Democrats, and as a preventive measure to channel the emerging Republican opposition to the parliamentary arena, the conservative liberals extended the franchise to all men over the age of twenty-one who were literate or heads of household. As a result, the size of the electorate nearly doubled, and the number of persons entitled to vote grew to encompass 70 percent of the adult male population. Yet, in 1895, the conservative fear of the increasing urban electoral support for republicanism, as well as the attempt to curtail the inflationary costs of clientelist electioneering at a time of financial crisis, led to the reintroduction of a more restrictive franchise, which remained in force until the fall of the monarchic regime. During this last period, the electorate dropped to approximately 50 percent of the adult male population, and universal suffrage again became one of the Republican Party's major demands for democratization.

In the second half of the nineteenth century, a climate of political tolerance prevailed. Apart from a short period in the 1890s, in which repressive measures were implemented following a military republican upheaval in Oporto (1891), freedom of expression, of assembly, and of association were freely practiced. Only occasionally did even the most violent criticism against the king and his family lead to criminal prosecution, censorship, or the closing down of newspapers. In such a pluralistic context, a free press naturally flourished and played a decisive role in building a civic consciousness within the literate urban strata.

The effort to rationalize and modernize the normative and administrative framework of the state was in some ways a remarkable one. In the legal sphere, this endeavor translated into a far-reaching codification and incorporation of some of the most progressive laws adopted anywhere in Europe. In a few cases, even pioneering measures were introduced, as was the case in 1864 with the abolition of the death penalty. This was later complemented by the abolition of life sentences in 1884. The ongoing interest in legislative innovation in various domains of social life gave rise to contemporary criticism of the hasty importing of external models, which were said to be inadequate given the country's state of development, thus creating a gap between formal institutions and reality. It is likewise true, however, that some of these innovative measures eventually generated new collective attitudes and behavior patterns, though in a slow and unbalanced manner.

With regard to the state's capabilities and structure,[12] there was a continuous expansion of the means of coercion and administration, and the first decisive steps were taken toward a modern, rational bureaucratic organization. The growing territorial penetration of the administrative network was closely connected with, and stimulated by, the development, through public investment and financing, of modern transport and communication infrastructures (involving the paving of roads, building of railroads and harbors, installation of the telegraphic system), a process that also fostered the marketization of the domestic economy.[13] One of the consequences of the centralization of the state and the concomitant increase of its distributive and regulatory functions was the gradual undermining of the autonomy and bargaining power of the traditional local notables (the so-called *caciques*), who both by means of force and co-optation became more vulnerable to, and dependent on, governmental injunctions and commands. With the curtailment of the *caciques'* bargaining power, especially in the most peripheral regions, their main source of influence began to derive more and more from their ability to get access to or control over the distribution of public goods and services at the local level, thus causing a crucial change in the configuration of patronage. The premises of this were in a way "democratized" as private wealth (landowning) or high social status (noble lineage) ceased to be the major criterion for ascension to a local powerholding position, and many of the new emerging *caciques* were local and provincial government employees with a modest background.[14]

The expansion of the state apparatus and activities was also accompanied by a growing number of public jobs and a rising social demand for their constant increase. Within the context of restricted occupational choice, due to the late industrialization and slow expansion of independent professions, government employment was both a main channel for social mobility and a guarantee of material security. It should be emphasized, however, that the resultant economic dependence of the urban intermediate strata on the state— an undoubted sign of their fragility and lack of capacity to mobilize autonomous resources—hindered them from having a more effective role in the formation of an active civil society.

The two main manifestations of bureaucratization in the state structure were an increasing differentiation and internal specialization of administrative tasks and the introduction, as early as 1859, of a universalist recruitment criterion, involving competitive examinations, for middle-rank civil servants in the central administration.[15] Though the state administration still showed a low level of efficiency in some crucial areas (e.g., the exaction of direct taxation), caused primarily by the impact of particularistic interests and demands, a few relevant achievements were made, as witnessed by the great improvements in official statistics and territorial cartography. Also, the examination system (*concursos públicos*) allowed for a more accurate selection of applicants to some civil service categories and provided a means to restrain patronage.[16] It should be added that whereas in the peripheral administration there was regular replacement of personnel as the two major liberal parties rotated office, at the central level there was an increasing stability within officialdom.

Finally, regarding changes in the economic sphere, it should be noted that Portuguese agriculture failed to modernize. The growth of production derived mostly from increases in cultivated land (20 percent in 1867 and 35 percent in 1902). This failure remained a strong structural constraint. However, the new industrializing thrust from the 1870s onward,[17] although insufficient to compensate for the backwardness inheritance, had a social effect that should not be overlooked: the rise of a working class and the correlate labor movement, which was reflected in the vitalization of associational life and of new modes of protest (e.g., strikes).[18]

In sum, despite the extent and resilience of traditional elements and settings throughout the nineteenth century, Portugal experienced some crucial transformations; conflicting trends shaped the contours of liberal civil society and determined the potential and limits of its expansion.

THE DYNAMICS OF ASSOCIATIONAL LIFE

Our closer examination of the concrete manifestations of civil society in Portugal in the late nineteenth and early twentieth centuries focuses on the extent and composition of associational life. When, where, how, and how far did it disseminate? What was its social nature? How did it interact with the constellation of partisan political forces, and what was its impact on governmental decisions and outputs? Because of the lack of empirical evidence for many of these topics, only tentative answers can be offered here.

While the first steps toward the development of a free associational activism dated back to the 1830s and a new stimulus occurred in the 1850s, the late 1870s were the turning point for a fairly vigorous growth and an increasing diversification of the network of voluntary associations. In the first decade of this century there was a further impetus to this trend, amplified by the emergence of the Republican regime. Because the decisive moment in the expansion of associational life was closely connected with new dynamics in the industrialization and urbanization processes, as well as with the concomitant rise of a democratic movement, its urban character was reinforced, and Lisbon and Oporto stood as the major loci of dissemination. A suggestive example of this polarization lies in the mutual-aid associations (or friendly societies), which were the most widespread means of popular organization at the time.[19] Table 1.1 shows the quantitative evolution and contrasting spatial distribution of the number of societies and their membership.[20]

Table 1.1   Friendly Societies in Portugal, 1876–1915

Year	Lisbon* & Oporto*		Rest of the Country	
	Number	*Members*	*Number*	*Members*
1876	84	—	69	—
1889	303	118,650	89	20,220
1903	473	141,900	113	33,600
1909	502	324,000	125	42,309

*including their surrounding areas

Source: José Lobo de Avila Lima, *Socorros Mútuos e Seguros Sociais* (Coimbra: Imprensa da Universidade, 1909), 287–90.

In 1909, an official inquiry into trade-union activism presented a picture consistent with these figures: approximately 60 percent of unions were concentrated in Lisbon and Oporto.[21] The dominant role of the capital in the development of the labor movement was also evident. It is estimated that in 1894, when the first Portuguese union confederation was set up, 64 percent of its members were to be found in Lisbon and only 22 percent in Oporto.[22]

Unfortunately, empirical research on the diffusion of other types of voluntary associations is still very sparse. Nevertheless, it seems unquestionable that the energetic thrust of the late 1870s onward was closely connected with the rise of popular associativism and the labor movement; thus the urban lower middle classes and industrial workers played a key role in this process.

The changing social and political contents of associational life were connected to the concomitant growth of the strike movement. According to the most exhaustive survey on this topic,[23] from 1871 to 1886 there were 140 strikes, while in the period from 1887 to 1908, there were 1,428. These dynamics continued during the First Republic, since there were 2,046 strikes between 1910 and 1917. Whereas the overwhelming majority occurred in Lisbon and Oporto, by the turn of the century they extended to other urban centers, for example, the emerging industrial town of Setúbal. Industrial workers were indeed the main actors of the strike movement; however, an active role was also played by the lower middle classes, namely shopkeepers and salesclerks. As for motivation, research conducted on the 732 strikes held from 1871 to 1900 shows that low wages and long working hours were the main sources of protest, while some 12 percent of the strikes were solidarity-oriented.

The expansion of the urban network of voluntary associations, which was strongly stimulated by the actions of Republicans and Socialists, was also related to the growth of civic organizations and activities. Within a context where social cleavages and interest conflicts were still weakly politicized, nationalist and secularist (or anticlerical) symbols and claims became major sources of civic mobilization. In the last two decades of the nineteenth century, secularist associations and anticlerical demonstrations were mainly influenced by the Socialists; thereafter, the Republicans took the lead.[24] They also carried the banner of nationalism, which had a much wider scope. A decisive event in the flourishing of modern nationalism was the so-called British Ultimatum of January 1890, when Portugal was confronted by the European powers concerning her colonial domains in Africa. Tension with Great Britain had dramatically increased during the 1880s, culminating in an ultimatum that forced the Portuguese to abandon their aspirations to the territory of modern-day Zimbabwe, which would have united Angola and Mozambique. In reaction to this external imposition and to the lack of firmness of the liberal rulers, a mass civic movement permeated by strong anti-British sentiments erupted, including street demonstrations, rallies, congresses, and petitions.[25] Notwithstanding the early political and ideological heterogeneity of the movement, the Republicans were the main beneficiaries of this nationalist tide. Their capacity to exploit successfully the modern techniques of mass communication proved to be a key asset in this and other issues.

The growth of both associativism and civic movements was, in fact, connected with a remarkable expansion of the press, as the figures in table 1.2 suggest. This trend could even be labeled a genuine "communications explosion,"[26] a phrase that is perhaps somewhat exaggerated. But the truth is that the proliferation of the national and local political and associative press was a decisive instrument for the extension and gradual democratization of an urban public opinion, as evidenced by the fact that most of the press or-

Table 1.2   New Newspapers, 1850–1890

Period	Number
1850–59	39
1860–69	67
1870–79	90
1880–89	184

Source: José Manuel Tengarrinha, *História da Imprensa Periódica Portuguesa* (Lisbon: Portugália Editora, 1965), 176–77.

ganizations founded in the last decades of the nineteenth century had connections with the Republican Party and the labor associations.

The increasing vitality of associational life in the main urban centers
sharply contrasted with the relative lethargy in the small "agrarian towns" and
villages. By the turn of the century, rural associationism was, with few exceptions, very weak, and the little development it experienced was largely initiated
by the state. The prefects and other government officials regularly complained
about the difficulties they had in the promotion of agrarian organizations.[27]

One of the two most powerful interest groups in the rural world was that
connected with wine production and exportation, especially in the Douro area.
It was the oldest of its kind and had long-standing traditions. The interests of
this group were mainly expressed through the Oporto Commercial Association.[28] The second major interest group was the wheat producers' lobby in the
southern province of Alentejo, the area of *latifundia* and large-scale agriculture.
It was among the latter group that the associationism of rural landowners developed most rapidly, with the Central Association of Portuguese Agriculture
(ACAP), founded in 1860, primarily voicing their interests. Following the two
congresses held by the ACAP in 1888 and 1889 to defend special provisions for
cereal agriculture, the government gave its blessing to protectionist policies in
1889 (an initiative very much in tune with the general European trend), and extensive wheat cultivation came to dominate Alentejo throughout the twentieth
century.[29] In spite of the impact of the lobbying activities of the ACAP in the
late nineteenth century, its big associative leap and growing politicization did
not occur until the First Republic and was a result both of the radicalization of
social protest in Alentejo and of the emerging conflicts between the agrarian
and industrial interests in the cereals sector.[30]

The few mutualist associations of small or medium-sized independent
farmers tended to concentrate in the most developed regions of commercial
agriculture.[31] Until the Great War, this loose rural mutualism was rather atomized and also apolitical, despite the efforts of the small organized circles
of Catholics from the turn of the century. The *latifundia* area in the south,
where traditional clientelist bonds proved to be more precarious and vulnerable to social conflict, was the only part of the country where modern rural
syndicalism developed in the early twentieth century (see table 1.3). In 1912,
the Alentejo was affected by an unprecedented series of strikes—in part
stimulated by Anarchist militants—which were severely repressed. While
there was a rapid decline both of rural unionism and strikes in the Alentejo

Table 1.3   Rural Unions, 1905–1925

Year	1905	1910	1915	1920	1925
Number	1	4	168	37	67

Source: João Freire, *Anarquistas e Operários* (Oporto: Afrontamento, 1993), 123.

after the Great War, this region remained a major setting of social conflict and political radicalization in contemporary Portugal.[32]

THE ROLE OF PARTIES AND THE IMPACT OF INTEREST GROUPS' ACTIVITIES

The preceding overview already provides some information on the relationships between associational life and the spectrum of political forces in the late nineteenth and early twentieth centuries. The following survey of these forces will help to specify these links.

Let us start with the two main liberal, monarchic parties—the seemingly more conservative Regenerator Party (Partido Regenerador) and the Progressist Party. Basically, they were patronage parties, which vertically integrated loose networks of notables under the national leadership of the most active and influential members of the ruling elite. In spite of the more ideological nature of the Progressists, there was little fundamental difference in principle or policy distinguishing the two parties, a reflection of their rather undifferentiated social nature. Their leaders were drawn from the narrow yet growing bourgeois upper and middle strata and shared a similar educational and occupational background; moreover, their relations of "sociability" were strengthened by the fact that they regularly attended meetings in the same scientific, cultural, or leisure associations. These similarities do not mean, however, that conflicting corporate interests or claims did not permeate liberal party politics. Still, neither the Regenerators nor the Progressists voiced in a permanent or stable manner the aspirations and demands of specific organized interest groups, whether economic or professional. As Juan J. Linz has pointed out for a similar context in Spain, not only did "political alignments very often crosscut interest groups," but also "the political class could win elections without effectively assuming the representation of economic interests by using the state apparatus and the favors it could grant its clientelistic network."[33]

Although the ruling middle classes had a part in the development of different kinds of voluntary associations, such as economic interest organizations, professional associations, political clubs, literary and scientific societies, charity associations, and sports clubs, the direct role played by both liberal parties was very limited (although partisan rivalries did sometimes lead to the creation of distinct cultural or recreational associations in small towns). Beyond the efforts to maintain and extend their local committees, which were designed above all for electoral purposes (voter registration, canvassing), their greatest contribution was to the expansion of a provincial and local press, especially from the late 1870s onward.

By contrast, the rise of the pro-democratic and small revolutionary political groups was connected with the expansion of popular associationism.

In fact, the republican clubs, socialist cells, and later anarchist circles played a catalytic role in the development of education societies, secular and anticlerical associations, lower-middle-class professional associations (e.g., of shopkeepers and of salesclerks), cooperatives, mutual-aid associations, and trade unions. The Republicans sought to exploit this trend for political advantage more than anyone else.

Officially founded in 1876, but only with a unified leadership since 1883, the Republican Party became the main adversarial force in the political arena. Internally organized as a federation of political clubs, civic associations, and newspapers, it embodied the embryo of a modern mass party. While membership in liberal monarchic parties was based upon selective and elitist criteria, the Republicans tried to launch mass recruitment campaigns; thus, whereas their main leaders were drawn from the middle classes (intellectuals, civil servants, lawyers, and doctors), grassroots members were lower-rank officials, shopkeepers, salesclerks, craftsmen, and workers. At the same time, they experimented with new techniques of mass mobilization and propaganda (political rallies, civic demonstrations, poster campaigns, and the like). With the backing of a militant press and with vigorous efforts to create and disseminate a popular political literature, the Republicans worked hard to create an activist citizenry.

Ideologically, the Republican program articulated a demand for the democratization of the core values of the liberal credo, focusing both on the maximization of civil and political rights and on the "regime issue" and placing throughout a strong emphasis on nationalistic and secular anticlerical symbols. The Republican Party's best hope lay in capturing urban constituencies. To this end, they on occasion resorted to the expediency of clientelism but more often concentrated their efforts on the exploitation of expressive and symbolic resources, doing so in a rather flexible and effective manner.

Accordingly, and in spite of modest attempts to recruit in certain rural areas, the Republican Party's geographical scope remained essentially urban in character. In the late 1880s, over 60 percent of its clubs were to be found in Lisbon, with an additional 10 percent in Oporto. In 1907, though the distribution of clubs throughout the country had become less skewed, Lisbon was still home to 35 percent of all such organizations and Oporto to 21 percent. In 1883, the estimated number of members of these clubs in the capital was about three thousand.[34] Even if its first parliamentary seat was won in Oporto (1878), it was also in Lisbon that the Republican Party gained its most consistent and widest political support, soon becoming the dominant electoral force in the capital.[35] In rural or less urbanized constituencies, where popular associationism was almost nonexistent, the small groups of Republicans were powerless to damage the clientelist arrangements of the liberal parties; nevertheless, in 1908 they were able to win the municipal elections in a few southern villages and small towns, and in August 1910 they secured their first parliamentary seat in a rural multimember district in Alentejo. Once in power, the Republican Party and the new groups recently split from it were able to absorb and in part reconstitute the old clientelist networks of the liberal monarchic parties.

Notwithstanding the fact that the Republicans' electoral and parliamentary presence had overshadowed the Socialists' in the political arena, the latter played an active role in the development of a labor movement and in the diffusion of secularism among workers.[36] Founded in 1875 by a tiny group of intellectuals and skilled workers, the Socialist Party remained a very small but militant group. The growing influence of an *ouvriériste* or syndicalist ideology led to the enhancing of social reform at the expense of political issues and aims. By the turn of the century, however, the party's leading role in the workers' movement began to be challenged by the Anarchists, who were to become a fairly influential group on the eve of the Great War.[37]

At the opposite end of the political spectrum, attempts since the late 1890s to organize a Catholic movement had led to the creation of an incipient conservative associative network. Deprived of the active support of the Church for the reasons outlined above, both the Catholic party (founded in 1903 under the name of the Nationalist Party) and its organizational branches played a relatively minor role in both the political arena and associational life. The small parliamentary representation of the Nationalist Party was "tolerated" by both liberal parties, and in 1905 the Catholic Workers Circles had approximately twelve thousand members, a fairly small number when compared to the membership of associations related to Republicans and Socialists.[38] The most lasting influence of the Catholics was felt in the development of rural associationism, especially in a few areas in northern and central Portugal.[39] Moreover, the emergent Catholic circles of students and intellectuals were later to serve as an important focal point for the further conservative, pro-authoritarian politicization of a segment of the elite, in the aftermath of the Great War.[40]

A precise evaluation of the impact of organized interest groups on political decision making would require much further in-depth research. However, it seems undeniable that the pressures exerted by a rising urban and labor activism and by concomitant elites' efforts to defuse that activism's potential for social unrest through preemptive action led, in the 1890s, to a series of legislative reforms, regulating working conditions (e.g., the protection of female and child labor, the creation of a Labor Exchange) and the right of association itself. Even if these measures were weak and ineffective, they did "signal the institutional recognition of the working class as an actor in Portuguese life," as pointed out by Manuel Villaverde Cabral.[41] This trend is also visible in the development of official inquiries and academic studies on working conditions and the modes of labor organization and protest. As soon as the First Republic was established, the formal guarantees of labor's organizational rights were enlarged. The constitutional law of 1911 incorporated the right of association, and the decree enacted in December 1910 recognized for the first time the worker's right to strike, though under certain restrictive conditions.

All the main economic interest groups pursued lobbying activities on a continuous basis, both by publicizing their claims and acting behind the scenes, influencing the implementation of policy in several concrete instances. For a long period, the most active and powerful organizations were the two merchants' associations (Associações do Comércio) of Lisbon and Oporto, which on occasion gave voice to divergent viewpoints. In the last decades of the nineteenth century, the Portuguese Industrial Association (founded in Lisbon in 1860 under another name) and the above-mentioned ACAP also played increasingly prominent roles. They expressed sometimes conflicting demands, which led to moderate clashes, as was the case when issues of free trade versus protectionism came up. Overall, it should be emphasized that until the turn of the century, organized economic interests had only a modest direct intervention in the political arena. Following the "Republican revolution" in 1910 and the impact of the First World War, the panorama would change.

CIVIL SOCIETY, STATE, AND POLITICS

At this point, let us make a few final remarks. First of all, it should be emphasized that in spite of its relative economic and cultural backwardness in the western European context, Portugal experienced some precocious social changes and progressive political and legal innovations over the course of the nineteenth century, which contributed to the development of a pluralist and free associational life. A liberal, pro-democratic tradition was thus established.

But while it is clear that the institutionalization of liberalism and attempts to democratize its basic premises promoted the expansion of civil society, the scope of civil society and of the resources available to it still remained limited as the century drew to a close. In other words, civil society only comprised a restricted (though growing and fairly active) segment of the population. The largest groups and strata showed a low level of civic consciousness and organizational autonomy. These two characteristics were most evident in rural areas, where clientelism and resistance to associational activity remained pervasive. The weaknesses and incongruencies of the modernization process, which had been induced from above by a progressive but small liberal elite, certainly restrained the possibilities for civil society to grow more active and expand. The urban-centered "Republican revolution" of 1910, despite its professed intentions to promote the full-fledged modernization and democratization of Portuguese society and politics, failed to achieve either aim.

Moreover, the main actors in civil society had only limited resources with which to work. The urban middle class expanded slowly and depended heavily on the state, above all for job opportunities—a distinctive feature that would persist into the twentieth century. There was little room, indeed, for the free professions to expand. It is significant in this connection how many lawyers at the turn of the century had to supplement their private activities with state employment. And nearly all engineers and architects worked in some capacity for the Ministry of Public Works. At the same time, the number of workers in the modern industrial sector was not large, and their meager economic resources and lack of spare time did not always permit them an intense and continuous associational life. They were able to form organizations, but organizations whose activity was intermittent or short-lived.

The economic dependence of the middle classes on the state and the state's growing centralization no doubt inhibited the expansion of a liberal civil society. Still, it would be misleading to see the relations between state and civil society as altogether one-sided, the strength of the former causing the latter to weaken and wither. On the contrary, the development of public transport and communication infrastructures opened up new possibilities for the development of the press and the spread of associational life and civic activism. In addition, the government itself tried to promote rural associationism and, in major cities, certain forms of popular self-organization (e.g., friendly societies). The state welcomed and even encouraged such activism, at least early on before such associations became too politicized.

The sociopolitical profile of nineteenth-century Portugal—the early breakdown of traditionalist elites and symbolic structures, the subordination of the Church to the liberal state, the relatively low level of class conflict—accounts for the late development of antiliberal and antidemocratic civic groups. Although these grew to be more active in the late 1890s, it was only following the establishment of the First Republic, and mainly after the Great War, that they came to exercise a more pronounced ideological and political influence. Three major changes contributed to the growing activism and radicalism of the more conservative groups during the Republican regime.

First of all, the violent breakdown of the constitutional monarchy crystallized powerful political sentiments around the "regime issue." Intransigent monarchists, who made several attempts to overthrow the First Republic by force, were more and more drawn to an ideology of authoritarianism. In this context, a key role was played by the so-called Integralismo Lusitano—an organization of young monarchist intellectuals founded in 1914 on the model of the French Action Française. It would have a strong impact on the rightward trajectory of certain interest groups (namely, the agrarian ones) and of an important segment of the intelligentsia.

The Republic's anticlerical and radical secularizing policies, moreover, provoked a powerful Catholic backlash. The regime disestablished the Catholic Church: namely, it suppressed religious education in public schools; made compulsory the civil registration of births, marriages, and deaths; and enacted a divorce law that could be applied to Catholic marriages. These measures caused a serious confrontation between church and state and spurred the development of an organized Catholic activism with a growing authoritarian character. The new Catholic Center Party founded in 1917 (by Oliveira Salazar among others) is a case in point. Though it remained a small group it exercised a critical influence in certain intellectual and professional circles.

Latent social cleavages also became more overt, radicalizing organized interests with disruptive consequences for the overall stability of the regime. The Republic made efforts to legislate social and welfare reform, but such efforts were half-hearted at best. Its general failure in this area caused important segments of the labor movement to lose faith in the Republic, which was now more and more looked on as a "bourgeois regime." Trade unionism continued to expand, but the most important changes in labor organization were qualitative rather than quantitative: the incorporation of new social strata (rural laborers, civil servants, and tertiary sector workers in general) and the emergence of nationwide confederations. Also, the growing influence of Anarchosyndicalism within the Portuguese labor movement was a major factor contributing to the "antisystem" role played by the most militant trade unions during the Republican period.

Employers' groups too were prompted to reorganize. Upset by the general climate of social turmoil and angry over growing differences with Republican governments on matters of economic policy, business groups veered rightward. The existing associative network expanded in membership and geographical reach, and various and increasingly politicized efforts were made to unify the employers' movement, by the Confederation of Employers in 1920 and by the Union of Economic Interests in 1924. The latter in particular made no secret of its political ambitions, involving itself in the parliamentary elections of 1925 behind a clearly antidemocratic program. The existence of a dense and active civil society is often taken as an essential precondition to a democratic politics. But the First Republican period in Portuguese history points to a more complicated conclusion. Here, civic activism intensified and thickened, but it did so in a context of political polarization. Democratic institutions did not take root but weakened, as the subsequent rise of authoritarianism illustrates.[42] We do not mean by this that the breakdown of the democratizing Republican regime can be accounted for solely by the intensification of conflicts within civil society. The Portuguese experience, however, does suggest that the increasing demands and mobilization of civic groups may not always ensure the continued existence of democratic institutions.

NOTES

The authors would like to express their warmest thanks to Nancy Bermeo for her insightful comments on a draft version of this chapter and to Manuela Galhardo for her assistance in preparing the English version. Travel support from the Luso-American Development Foundation, Lisbon, for the two workshops in Princeton, is also gratefully acknowledged.

1. For an accurate definition of "oligarchic parliamentarism," see Nicos P. Mouzelis, *Politics in the Semi-Periphery: Early Parliamentarism and Late Industrialisation in the Balkans and Latin America* (London: Macmillan, 1986).

2. This flow of migration from rural areas was increasingly channeled abroad (almost exclusively to Brazil) in the last decades of the nineteenth century, thus reflecting the limited capacity of the urbanization process to absorb expansion. Emigration therefore became an important safety valve, averting massive unemployment and the danger of social unrest. On nineteenth-century emigration, see Miriam Halpern Pereira, *A Política Portuguesa de Emigração, 1850–1930* (Lisbon: A Regra do Jogo, 1982).

3. In comparison with the more rapid advances in the struggle against illiteracy in other southern European countries (especially Spain and Italy) with a similar socioeconomic and cultural profile, it has been recently suggested that the much slower and restricted dissemination of elementary public education in Portugal in the second half of the nineteenth century did not stem so much from the scarcity of state financial resources as from the lack of relevant pressures both from above and below, owing largely to the feeble intensity of social conflict and the absence of linguistic and cultural segmentation that might force the implementation of policies oriented toward national integration. See Jaime Reis, *O Atraso Económico Português em Perspectiva Histórica* (Lisbon: Imprensa Nacional, 1993), 227–53.

4. In nineteenth-century Portugal there was a significant proportion of army officers in the political and administrative elite, as the following figures illustrate: from 1851 to 1890 the officer corps constituted one-third of the ministers and nearly half of the top senior officials (*directores-gerais*) in the Ministry of Public Works. Four main reasons account for this: the role played by the army since the Napoleonic Wars as a major pathway up the social ladder; the genesis of the liberal regime itself, as the outcome of a civil war; the concern to engage army officers in the constitutional order as a means to prevent putschist temptations; and the military monopoly on certain forms of expertise (engineering, topography, mining) vital to building the infrastructures of a modern state. See, on this particular issue, Pedro Tavares de Almeida, "A Construção do Estado Liberal: Elite Política e Burocracia na Regeneração, 1851–1890," Ph.D. dissertation, Lisbon, Universidade Nova, 1995.

5. It should be noted that the oligarchical character of the political elite, which was apparent in the persistence of both formal and informal selective criteria of recruitment, the longevity of the careers of its members, and the extension of "endogamic" affiliations, was far from being a peculiarity of southern European polities in the late nineteenth and early twentieth centuries. See, for example, on England, the classic account by Sidney Low, *The Governance of England* (London: Unwin, 1904); and on the Netherlands, Mattei Dogan and Maria Scheffer van der Veen, "Le personnel ministériel hollandais (1848–1858)," *L'année sociologique* (1957–58): 95–125.

6. For an in-depth analysis of the historical causes of the precocious decline of the Portuguese aristocracy, see Nuno Gonçalo Monteiro, *O Crepúsculo dos Grandes* (Lisbon: Imprensa Nacional, 1998); for a comparative approach, see Arno J. Mayer, *The Persistence of the Old Regime—Europe to the Great War* (London: Pantheon, 1981).

7. As was the case elsewhere, the anti-associative prejudices of early liberal ideology impeded the prompt formal recognition of the freedom of association, although not its practice. The Civil Code of 1867 acknowledged the right to associate in general terms, but it was not until 1891 that corporate groups (whether of employers or of workers) were subjected to specific legal regulation for the first time. And even then, the formation of permanent political associations remained excluded.

8. For earlier, pre-liberal forms of organized "sociability," see Maria Alexandre Lousada, "Espaços de Sociabilidade em Lisboa, de finais do século XVIII a 1834," Ph.D. dissertation, Lisbon, Faculdade de Letras, 1996.

9. Except for a short period of disturbance in 1868–70—which was brought about by the combined effect of a domestic financial crisis and the resonance of political disruption in neighboring Spain—only in the 1890s did the first serious symptoms of social corrosion and political delegitimization of the liberal monarchic regime become visible, preparing the way for the victorious Republican insurrection of October 1910.

10. On this subject, see Pedro Tavares de Almeida, *Eleições e Caciquismo no Portugal Oitocentista, 1868–1890* (Lisbon: Difel, 1991).

11. See Stein Rokkan and Jean Meyriat, eds., *International Guide to Electoral Statistics* (The Hague-Paris: Mouton, 1969); and Thomas Mackie and Richard Rose, *The International Almanac of Electoral History* (London: Macmillan, 1991).

12. It should be remembered that in the first half of the nineteenth century, a dramatic sequence of convulsive events—the Napoleonic Wars and the subsequent flight of the king to Brazil, a series of revolutionary uprisings, civil war, and intense political instability—had disorganized the state and reduced its functions to a minimum.

13. The formation of a national economic market was achieved by the turn of the century: see David Justino, *A Formação do Espaço Económico Nacional: Portugal, 1810–1913* (Lisbon: Vega, 1988–89).

14. Significantly, whereas in 1861 about 46 percent of the members of the Chamber of Deputies were classified as landowners in official records, in 1890 this figure had dropped to 11 percent. Conversely, in those same years the combined proportion of civil servants and army officers who were members of parliament rose from 39 to 53 percent; and in 1901 it was already 63 percent. See Tavares de Almeida, *Eleições e Caciquismo*, 184–89, and José Manuel Sobral and Pedro Tavares de Almeida, "Caciquismo e Poder Político: Reflexões em torno das Eleições de 1901," *Análise Social* 18, nos. 72, 73, 74 (1982): 655.

15. One of the major inspirations for this reform was the Northcote–Trevelyan Report on the British Civil Service (1853). From 1859 onward, a new practice emerged in Portuguese administration, public examinations for existing vacant posts, with the final results being regularly published in the official journal of the state.

16. Though attempts at manipulation and cases of favoritism still affected the *concursos públicos*, in such instances it was possible to initiate an impartial official inquiry, which could lead to an annulment of falsified results.

17. Some estimates even record an industrial growth rate above the European average for the period from 1870 to 1913; see, for instance, Reis, *O Atraso Económico*, 160–68; and Pedro Lains, *A Economia Portuguesa no Século XIX* (Lisbon: Imprensa Nacional, 1995). For an account of the impediments to an early industrialization and an economic modernization, see Vitorino Magalhães Godinho, *Estrutura da Antiga Sociedade Portuguesa* (Lisbon: Arcadia, 1975); and Jorge Miguel Pedreira, "The Obstacles

to Early Industrialization in Portugal, 1800–1870: A Comparative Perspective," in *Between Development and Underdevelopment: The Precocious Attempts at Industrialization of the Periphery, 1800–1870,* ed. Jean Batou (Geneva: Librairie Droz, 1991), 347–79.

18. See, namely, Manuel Villaverde Cabral, *Portugal na Alvorada do Século XX* (Lisbon: A Regra do Jogo, 1979).

19. As Robert Putnam has noted regarding the nineteenth-century Italian mutual-aid societies and other forms of organized social solidarity, "although the manifest purposes of these organizations were nonpolitical, they served important latent political functions." See *Making Democracy Work: Civic Traditions in Modern Italy* (Princeton: Princeton University Press, 1993), 140.

20. Although the accuracy of these figures is questionable, as regards the estimated number of members of friendly societies, the general portrait still seems valid.

21. See Manuel Villaverde Cabral, *O Operariado nas Vésperas da República, 1909–1910* (Lisbon: Presença, 1977), 180–81.

22. See Carlos da Fonseca, *História do Movimento Operário e das Ideias Socialistas em Portugal* (Lisbon: Publicações Europa-América, n.d.), 192.

23. See José Manuel Tengarrinha, *Estudos de História Contemporânea em Portugal* (Lisbon: Editorial Caminho, 1983), 59–83.

24. See Fernando Catroga, "A Militância Laica e a Descristianização da Morte em Portugal, 1865–1911," Ph.D. dissertation, Coimbra, Faculdade de Letras, 1988.

25. See Nuno Severiano Teixeira, *O Ultimatum Inglês: Política Externa e Política Interna no Portugal de 1890* (Lisbon: Alfa, 1990); and Hermínio Martins, "Portugal," in *Contemporary Europe: Class, Status and Power,* ed. Margaret S. Archer and Salvador Giner (London: Wiedenfeld and Nicholson, 1971), 60–89.

26. See Hermínio Martins, "The Breakdown of the Portuguese Democratic Republic," paper presented at the Seventh World Congress of Sociology (Varna, 1970).

27. See, for instance, *Relatórios sobre o Estado da Administração Pública nos Distritos Administrativos do Continente do Reino e Ilhas Adjacentes* (Lisbon: Imprensa Nacional, 1857–1868) and *Boletim da Associação dos Estudantes de Agronomia e Periódico de Propaganda Agrícola* 6, no. 2 (January–February 1922): 33–34.

28. See Conceição Andrade Martins, *Memória do Vinho do Porto* (Lisbon: Instituto de Ciências Sociais, 1990).

29. See Reis, *O Atraso Económico,* 33–85.

30. See Kathleen C. Schwartzman, *The Social Origins of the Democratic Collapse: The First Portuguese Republic in the Global Economy* (Lawrence: University Press of Kansas, 1989).

31. See Pedro Ferreira dos Santos, *Guia Prático das Associações Agrícolas em Portugal* (Lisbon: RACAP, 1904), 35–38; and *Boletim da Previdência Social* 1, no. 3 (April–August 1917): 304–5.

32. See José Pacheco Pereira, *Conflitos Sociais nos Campos em Portugal* (Lisbon: Publicações Europa-América, 1982); and Nancy Bermeo, *The Revolution within the Revolution: Workers' Control in Rural Portugal* (Princeton: Princeton University Press, 1986).

33. See "A Century of Politics and Interests in Spain," in *Organizing Interests in Western Europe,* ed. Suzanne Berger (Cambridge: Cambridge University Press, 1981), 367, 375.

34. See Fernando Catroga, *O Republicanismo em Portugal: Da Formação ao 5 de Outubro de 1910* (Coimbra: Faculdade de Letras, 1991); and also, for the early twentieth century,

Vasco Pulido Valente, *O Poder e o Povo: a Revolução de 1910* (Lisbon: Publicações Dom Quixote, 1974).

35. See Pedro Tavares de Almeida, "Comportamentos Eleitorais em Lisboa (1878–1910)," *Análise Social* 21, no. 1 (1985): 111–53.

36 For instance, the Socialist Party organized civil processions in 1894 and held two anticlerical congresses in 1895 and 1900. See Maria Filomena Mónica, *O Movimento Socialista em Portugal, 1875–1934* (Lisbon: I.E.D., 1985).

37. See João Freire, *Anarquistas e Operários* (Oporto: Afrontamento, 1993).

38. See Marie-Christine Volovitch, "Le mouvement catholique au Portugal à la fin de la monarchie constitutionnelle, 1891–1913," Ph.D. dissertation, Paris, Sorbonne, 1983.

39. It should be stressed that in spite of the growing influence of Catholics on rural associativism throughout the First Republic, there never was in Portugal anything comparable to the powerful National Catholic Agrarian Confederation founded in 1917 in Spain. For an overview of the Catholic movements in early twentieth-century Europe, see Tom Buchanan and Martin Conway, eds., *Political Catholicism in Europe, 1918–1965* (Oxford: Oxford University Press, 1996); and Stathis N. Kalyvas, *The Rise of Christian Democracy in Europe* (Ithaca, N.Y.: Cornell University Press, 1996).

40. See Manuel Braga da Cruz, *As Origens da Democracia Cristã e o Salazarismo* (Lisbon: Presença, 1980).

41. See "The Demise of Liberalism and the Rise of Authoritarianism in Portugal, 1890–1930," lecture delivered at the King's College, London, 1993, 14.

42. See António Costa Pinto, *Salazar's Dictatorship and European Fascism: Problems of Interpretation* (New York: SSM-Columbia University Press, 1995), 85–146.

2

THE DREAM OF CIVIL SOCIETY
IN TSARIST RUSSIA:
LAW, STATE, AND RELIGION

Laura Engelstein

The search for "civil society" in historical context assumes a connection between forms of public association and expression and the political character of modern states. The connection is not easily found. The prototype of civil society is hard to define, and its local embodiments do not always match the ideal. Political regimes, furthermore, change over time: Germany has been authoritarian, fascist, and democratic, all in one century. But in one respect agreement reigns: western European and North American nations to some degree have generated an autonomous public life that helps sustain the democratic (or at least participatory) political impulse. On the margins of the European state system, sharing but not fully integrating the Western cultural heritage, Russia, it is said, has always lacked just these civic and political traits. Antonio Gramsci provides the classic statement of this contrast: "In Russia," he wrote in the 1920s, "the state was everything, civil society was primordial and gelatinous; in the West there was a proper relation between state and civil society, and when the state trembled a sturdy structure of civil society was at once revealed." When in 1917 the Russian autocracy not only trembled but tumbled to the ground, there was no "powerful system of fortresses and earthworks," in Gramsci's phrase, to prevent the Bolsheviks from erecting another absolutist regime in its place.[1]

The end of Communism has raised the issue yet again. Some commentators associate the failure of post-Soviet Russia to establish viable political institutions and an orderly public life with the state's ability to impair or extinguish civil society.[2] The fact that the Soviet system collapsed from within has convinced others, to the contrary, that social forces must have been at work in its demise. They conclude that elements of a civil society escaped the stranglehold of the allegedly "total" state and created the pressure for change.[3] In the same optimistic vein, some historians are finding evidence of a vital pre-1917 "middle sphere" that challenges the notion of Russian exceptionalism and offers present-day democrats a cultural precedent.[4]

These old and new arguments invite us to revisit the question of what relation the concept of civil society does in fact bear to the political life of imperial Russia. This essay argues that Gramsci was both right and wrong. The state was indeed powerful and strictly patrolled the social landscape, suspicious of any force outside its control. Yet the tsars could not rule entirely as they pleased, but contended with public opinion, if only on a limited scale. Society was not formless. Even the intolerant Nicholas I (r. 1825–55) accepted the existence of philanthropic associations, a type of civic participation, though often self-generated, that embodied the same values and devotion to hierarchy as the regime. Nor, try as he might, could he extinguish the discontent of intellectuals in the universities and drawing rooms of the capitals. Although most were loyal monarchists, they denounced the persistence of serfdom, chafed under the censorship of ideas, and thirsted for influence in public affairs.

When Alexander II (r. 1855–81) abolished serfdom and initiated the Great Reforms of 1861–64, he acted not only in response to Russia's defeat in the Crimean War, but also under pressure from intellectuals, forward-looking bureaucrats, and progressive members of the imperial family. He thus acknowledged that Russia's standing as an international power depended on its encouraging some of the features that sustained civil society in the West: the production and dispersion of science, technology, and other forms of knowledge; a professional elite; a market-driven labor force; a trained and literate army; and courts of law for the regulation of disputes.

In the absence of enabling political conditions, however, these changes generated an ambivalent and tension-ridden result: both the desire to perform the functions of an "actually existing civil society" and its chronic frustration. Yet the desire itself mitigated the contradiction: it is a case of wishful thinking embodying the wish. In struggling to produce what they thought of as the civil society they lacked, Russians de facto enacted its possibility at home, while at the same time experiencing the limits imposed by their own situation. Their efforts, which, I argue, constituted a partial exemplification of what they were striving for, took two forms: first, a critique of existing arrangements; and, second, projects of reform designed to overcome the restrictions under which they suffered and bring Russia into line with the imagined ideal. It should be said, however, that not all people who acted as though they were members of a recognizable civil society subscribed in principle to the goal of bringing it about. Some of the active participants in public debate over issues such as reform of the civil and criminal codes were ideological conservatives who defended patriarchal values and paternalistic government.[5] For liberals, however, the concept of civil society exercised a strong symbolic influence independent of its practical realization, while the process of articulating the goal brought it closer to home. Yet the dream did not come to pass, either before or after 1917. And this, as all parties to the conflict—would-be citizens, no less than autocrats and commissars—understood all too well, depended not so much on the contours of the social landscape as on its relation to the power of the state.

This understanding was embedded in the vocabulary of social description that Russians themselves devised. Nineteenth-century intellectuals were of course familiar with the notion of civil society as articulated in Western thought, but they also used terms adapted to the local configuration. They viewed their own history as the interaction of three forces: the state (*gosudarstvo*), the people (*narod*), and something called "society" or "the public" (*obshchestvo, obshchestvennost'*). The latter was a cultural category that largely overlapped with a sociological domain. Encompassing the educated residents of Russia's Westernized cities, the term "society" distinguished them, on the one hand, from bureaucrats (no less educated or urban, but servants of the regime) and from the common folk, on the other. Bureaucrats exercised power and established policy. They played a political role but only as instruments of the state. Members of "society" had political opinions, often, but not always, critical of the established order. Until the 1905 revolution induced the tsar to establish a national parliament and relax the censorship laws, freedom of expression was limited and society had few opportunities to play a constructive political role.[6]

Despite the three-part scheme, there was in fact no clean sociological divide in nineteenth-century Russia between state servitors and members of "society." Individual careers crossed the line; professions included public and private sectors; civic associations united officials and independent activists. Yet the contrast stood for an important principle: the possibility of public activity independent of the state—the dream in which "society" became "civil society," a matter not of persons or social categories but of structures. This vision took hold in the second half of the century, once the Great Reforms had inaugurated a new relationship between the autocracy and its subjects, educated and uneducated alike.[7] These reforms ended bonded labor and reconfigured the social map. They also created institutions of local self-administration (the *zemstvo*) and revamped the operation of the law. They did not, however, change the law's statutory content or modify the absolutist basis of autocratic rule.

The new dispensation allowed "society" to enter more actively into public affairs. But at the same time as the educated elite welcomed this chance, it spawned an offshoot that was opposed to any such participation: the so-called intelligentsia, dedicated to overturning the existing order and hostile to any constitutional reform. Though not responsible for the outbreak of revolution in 1905, radicals embraced the project of total transformation. The upheaval did not, however, destroy the old regime. To quell the wave of opposition engulfing the nation, Nicholas II (r. 1894–1917) authorized elections to a State Duma and the formation of recognized political parties. The tsar promised to endow the population with the "foundations of civic freedom based on the principles of real personal inviolability, freedom of conscience, speech, assembly, and union."

This concession to some extent represented a victory of social forces over the state. But it was also one of the final examples of the monarchy's long history of managing the society it ruled, hoping to encourage the national welfare while exercising maximum control. Beginning with the reign of Peter the Great, cultural standards as well as social standing were imposed by an active, interventionist regime. Noble status was a function of state service, not a mark of autonomy. Catherine the Great (r. 1762–96) aspired to create by fiat both a middling sort and a public opinion worthy of a European nation. Where Peter sponsored the publication of useful works that promoted technological advance, Catherine opened the door to private publishing and encouraged the airing of opinions in the press. Nicholas Novikov (1744–1818), at once publisher, author, and sponsor of educational and charitable ventures, exemplified the possibilities of independent cultural initiative. Freemasonry offered a context for civic activity, sustained a network of social ties, and promoted public responsibility.[8]

Eighteenth-century Russia had a lively public life. Private presses, a market in print, debating societies, literary salons, private theaters, public lectures, Masonic lodges—all linked inhabitants of the capitals and provincial centers in something of an empirewide conversation. Yet this world was limited in scope, audience, and resources and was fatally dependent on the autocrat's good will. Catherine, when it pleased her, cracked down on independent publishers. When Alexander Radishchev (1749–1802) printed, at his own expense, an attack on serfdom and absolute rule, she exiled him to Siberia. Novikov weathered the end of Catherine's reign in prison. Alexander I (r. 1801–25) outlawed the Freemasons in 1822.

More striking, perhaps, than the occasions when the sovereign intervened to quash the expression of ideas is the cozy relationship between ruler and opinion makers that prevailed under Catherine and Alexander I. Even Catherine's critics shared her professed Enlightenment views. Radishchev, who returned to the capital after the empress's death, served in various official roles. The court and high society of Alexander's time constituted a close-knit world, in which religious enthusiasm set the dominant tone. Reformers and conservatives may have differed in their ideas, but they were intimately connected and all close to the throne. Educated men and women of the period met in drawing rooms and private clubs, of which the literary societies frequented by writers such as Alexander Pushkin (1799–1837) are the most famous examples. By contrast, the men who staged the ill-fated protest in 1825 known as the Decembrist uprising had concocted their plans and articulated their ideas in the shelter of secret societies modeled on the Masonic lodges and nationalist associations of contemporary Europe. But even the Decembrists belonged to the world they opposed. The officials who investigated and tried the rebels were often their relatives and friends.[9]

The distinction between official circles and "the public" with opinions first achieved symbolic importance only in the reign of Nicholas I. In the 1840s, cultivated men gathered in each other's homes to discuss the taboo questions of the day through the respectable detour of philosophy and literature. These were still gentlemen of the aristocracy, intellectual amateurs who had honed their wits in the lecture halls of Moscow University, and then survived on personal incomes. Westernizers and Slavophiles amiably agreed to disagree with their partners in conversation, and all were hostile to Nicholas's oppressive rule. Publishing critical ideas was still a risky venture. Peter Chaadaev (1794–1856) was sent to a madhouse and his editor banished for printing the famous "Philosophical Letter" in which Chaadaev argued that Russia had been stranded on the margins of Western civilization. Alexander Herzen (1812–70) put his dangerous ideas to paper only when safely abroad.[10]

The joint product of imperial initiative, bureaucratic involvement, and public participation, the Great Reforms were the turning point. Enlightened principles and the spirit of professionalism had invaded the establishment, while the aristocracy was invited to help shape its own fate, although only its terms, not its direction, were open to discussion. Any contemplation of change sponsored by Alexander I or Nicholas I had been confined to secret committees. News circulated by rumor only, not press release. The key term connected with the Great Reforms, by contrast, was *glasnost'*—public accessibility, if only within limited bounds. It was a process open to outside participation and to the movement of ideas.[11]

Hoping to reinforce the basis of traditional autocratic rule by controlled application of its opposite principles, Alexander conceded some of the basic elements of modern Western society: a free labor supply; expanded educational access; institutions of public responsibility (the *zemstvo*s); and, most incompatible of all with the still intact framework of autocracy, an independent judiciary.[12] The result of all these changes was the generation of the component parts of what in the Western context can be called civil society: an expansion of publishing, periodicals in particular; the proliferation of professional organizations with a specialized press and claims to cultural authority; the opening of new venues of civic association; the extension of educational opportunity beyond the narrow service-oriented elite. And, indeed, the tenor of public discourse shifted. Doctors, lawyers, statisticians, and economists held opinions on social issues, and because their activities were so heavily monitored and constrained, they also developed opinions on directly political issues.[13]

The reforms had immediately generated a movement in some sections of the nobility for the extension of political rights: capping the *zemstvo* foundation with a constitutional roof was the demand.[14] At first, the elected noble deputies to the provincial *zemstvo* assemblies aimed at the establishment of a constitutional monarchy. Under the pressure of official intolerance and gathering social conflict, they moved ever farther to the Left, finding themselves eventually in alliance with radical forces in what became the revolution of 1905. Their efforts at responsible political activity must be considered part of the general tendency of post-Reform educated Russians to fashion a basis for civic life within the constraints of a relentlessly administrative regime. Yet this very regime had conceded the rudiments of an independent judicial system. If the *zemstvo* constitutionalists spoke as elected representatives of local elites, legal professionals spoke and acted in the name of the principles articulated by the Judicial Reforms of 1864, defending them against the same authority that had installed them. But professionalism in this period was a force that transcended the state–society divide.[15] The substance of the reform was the work of trained lawyers within the bureaucracy: here professionals worked in concert with the state to shape institutions that would considerably alter the state's relation to its subjects and enhance the lawyers' own public role. Independent legal practitioners then elaborated these principles in directions they had not been intended to go.

The Judicial Reforms created a sheltered arena, sanctioned by the state, in which information could be exchanged, opinions articulated, conflicting interests confronted and perhaps even reconciled. According to the new rules, the courts were to deliberate in public, respect due process, and submit all cases except crimes against the state to decision by jury. Professional standards were monitored by an independent bar, and judges could not be removed, in principle even by the monarch. Although the emperors in fact retained the privilege, as well as the right to supersede any provision of the law, they were surprisingly reluctant to violate this particular rule.[16] In the courtroom, before a public audience and in the presence of journalists free to publish their reports, defendants and their attorneys enjoyed the freedom of speech inaccessible to law-abiding subjects of the empire in their daily lives. Even during the honeymoon of reform, censorship persisted, public assemblies were monitored by the police, expressions of critical opinion were subject to criminal proceedings, and the activities of professional associations were kept within regulated bounds. The new courtrooms, by contrast, permitted the open expression of subversive ideas.

The freedom they granted led, of course, to the courts' undoing. As we have said, the social and legal changes introduced by the Reforms generated not only a new range of constructive civic engagement (on the part of physicians, lawyers, economists, and other professionals) but also a tendency to radical disaffection, embodied in the newly hatched intelligentsia. Young, angry, disappointed with the limited extent of reform, this cohort set itself in opposition not only to the absolutist regime but also to those still committed to institutional change. When they were arrested in the 1870s for preaching revolution in the villages, the activists used their trials as an occasion to articulate their ideas. They combined a vision of social justice with a contempt for precisely those institutions that threatened them with repression but also enabled them to address a wider public than they would have reached in any other way. And it was their performances before the bench, their impassioned speeches, their posture as martyrs to autocratic tyranny, that made them heroes of liberation in the eyes of an educated public that did not share their extreme views.[17] This sympathy emerged in response not only to court theatrics, but resulted also from a shared dissatisfaction with the tensions at the heart of the reforms. The refurbished envelope of due process still contained the outmoded statutes of the pre-Reform criminal code, which determined that subversive speech no less than active rebellion should put these young rebels within reach of Siberia or even the scaffold.

The simultaneous appearance of liberal and radical figures on the new public stage of post-Reform Russia was not, however, a function of its "backwardness." Even in western Europe, as Geoff Eley notes, the liberal public sphere never monopolized civic life, either in opposition to the old regime or as the kernel of an evolving bourgeois polity. It was from the start accompanied by a rival force: the plebeian or radical public, which used the same elements of open discussion and the circulation of opinion to challenge the social basis of bourgeois domination.[18] But if radicals in Europe pushed to democratize the political process, in Russia radicals denounced the political process itself as a tool of bourgeois oppression, no less nefarious (perhaps even more so) than the overt repression of the police–administrative regime. Such hostility to the law and to the respectable public's constitutional aspirations did not prevent the self-styled revolutionaries from invoking liberal values on their own behalf and from using the opportunity that liberal institutions provided. Thus Populist defendants insisted on their right to an audience, while denouncing the legal guarantees that gave them that right. They enlisted the services of liberal attorneys, while mocking their faith in due process. They mocked the idea of formal justice itself.

Having failed to secure a popular following by strategies of political propaganda—their failed mission to the countryside, where they preached to deaf ears—the Populists directed their eloquence at their peers. If they spoke in the interests of the excluded populace, however, they certainly did not represent it. They did not constitute a plebeian, as opposed to a liberal-bourgeois, public. Indeed, the only public they could address was that same "society" that marked itself off as much from the "people" as from the "state." And this distinction was sociologically more accurate in the first instance than in the second. In fact, the Populist orators on the judicial stage were not public figures in the civic sense, but rather emblems of exclusion. They did not speak for themselves but in the voice of self-denial, as ventriloquists, in the name of a social group whose interests conflicted, moreover, with those of the groups from which the spokesmen came. Seeking to minimize their personal roles, even as they claimed the stage for their own, their rhetoric was one of abnegation—welcoming harsh verdicts, courting exile, eager for the stigma of civil death.[19]

It has often been noted that women were active in the Populist movement, not only as terrorist accomplices but also as speakers in the famous trials. Their prominence does not mean that Russian popular movements were "feminist." The charismatic Populist women demonstrated in their very persons the excludedness of the movement for which they stood—its desire not to be part of an established public sphere, a civil society predicated on participation in community affairs, designed to enlarge and enhance the political capacity of the educated classes, and by extension, of the popular ones. They represented the renunciation of cultural as well as social privilege, a self-sacrifice and self-denial most strikingly embodied in the female sex. Some of these women abandoned their own children and husbands or lovers for the sake of the cause. But this apparent egoism rendered them no less iconic of feminine selflessness: in leaving their domestic roles behind they did not aspire to public recognition (as "emancipated women" might) but to a place beyond any social claims or public responsibilities. They aspired to sainthood, and this is how they were understood.

In using the courtroom as a stage, the Populists of the 1870s managed not only to engineer their own removal from the public world through sentencing and exile, but also to contribute to the destruction of the very boards on which they stood. The dramatic impact of the radicals' spectacle on the public opinion they despised prompted the regime to remove political trials from the new courts and to pursue the anti-Populist campaign by means of administrative repression: courts-martial, summary convictions, executions behind closed doors. The new courts were not themselves dismantled, but they ceased to provide a tribunal for political speech.

Lawyers and legal experts of the same liberal persuasion as those who had defended the radicals in the name of due process and the rule of law did not abandon their campaign for the affirmation and extension of these principles. While their efforts challenged the underlying principles of autocracy, they did not operate entirely outside of or in opposition to the state. Legal scholars praised the institutions of Western law in the pages of the journal of the Ministry of Justice. Indeed, the ministry was, for awhile, something of a snake in the bosom of the absolutist regime. Appointed to head it by Alexander II, Dmitrii Nabokov (1826–1904) retained his post long enough into the conservative 1880s to initiate reform of the pre-1864 civil and criminal codes. Commissions composed of state servitors and distinguished members of the legal profession met in closed session, but they widely canvassed the opinion of administrators and scholars in relation to the range of questions raised in both codes, and they published extensive commentaries on foreign laws. Neither their research nor their proceedings reached the wider public, but debates on the issues flooded the professional press and, in the case of marriage and inheritance law, provoked an outpouring of public opinion. These discussions evoked the "dream of a civil society" that haunted the Russian educated public, which, in debating, created that very "civil society" (if only in embryo), *iavochnym poriadkom*—without official permission, by the seat of their pants.[20]

The key distinction in the debates on the definition of private and public life and the relation between state, society, and the individual (the issues raised in civil and criminal code reform) concerned the nature of the state and the kind of law necessary to the fulfillment of that dream. The answer was obvious. What most of the Russian legal community wanted was the rule of law (the Rechtsstaat), not the vestigial eighteenth-century model of administrative rule and state tutelage over public life (the Polizeistaat) that had persisted into the modern age. It was only under the shelter of a legal edifice construed in this sense, constructed and empowered by the state as a matter of course, but keeping the state itself at a distance from its subjects, that public life could thrive.

An issue that was key to the relation of state and society concerned the laws governing religion. These were of particular importance in an empire whose populations embraced many different confessions. The official state religion was the Russian Orthodox Church, which occupied a privileged position in relation to the other faiths but was administratively subordinate to secular authority. In supporting government policy and discouraging movements for change, it fulfilled its official, conservative mission. Indeed, Church authorities resisted the proposed reforms of the civil code concerning divorce and family life and also opposed the revision of the laws governing religious worship. Insofar as these campaigns involved not only civil servants but also representatives of public opinion, the Church can be said in both cases to have contributed to civic debate, in the interests, however, of maintaining administrative control over public life and limiting the range of individual self-determination.

The Church thus participated in public debate only to restrict the scope of civil society. Yet the Church could not entirely escape the subversive encroachments of civic discourse: During the period of the Great Reforms, voices within the Church advocated changes in its own internal structures, and during the revolution of 1905, a movement for the reorganization of Church governance on a conciliar model echoed political themes articulated in the secular realm. Within the Orthodox fold significant differences of opinion made themselves heard even in peaceful times. A range of periodicals associated with various branches of the Church commented on secular as well as religious themes from differing points of view. Orthodoxy also influenced public life in another way. Providing a spiritual rationale and moral context for independent philanthropic activity, it strengthened the fabric of informal associations through which society governed its own affairs, sometimes in concert with government efforts, sometimes on its own.[21]

Although associated with traditional values of deference and hierarchy, the Church did not thus function as a simple impediment to the evolution of civic life. As the established religion, institutionally and politically tied to the state,

Orthodoxy could offer no independent platform for the expression of public opinion. Even its opposition to change was expressed "in house," as it were, as a function of its bureaucratic office. Yet, it should be remembered, on the one hand, that conservative, as well as liberal, ideas could animate public-spirited minds, and, on the other, that conservative institutions did not always stifle demands for change. Religious precepts inspired civic activism and political critiques (the case of the Slavophiles), while some clergymen managed to articulate dissenting positions without leaving the fold. In this sense, the situation of the Church mirrored the experience of society at large: forbidden from occupying neutral space, opinion makers used the structures designed to restrict their activity for precisely the purposes they were supposed to obstruct.

As for those who had abandoned Orthodoxy for heretical versions of the faith, they were for a long time unable to contribute anything to public discourse. The Old Believers who had confronted the monarch with pious resistance two hundred years before had by now made their peace with the state but continued to function in defiance of the law. Until late in the nineteenth century when policy began to change, the regime reinforced the community's doctrinal isolation with civil disabilities and restrictions on confessional life. After 1905, the Old Believers began publishing journals of their own, but other dissenters continued to suffer more aggressive forms of exclusion, pushing them literally off the social map.[22]

The juridical status of religion not only affected the development of public life and civic culture. It became an issue hotly debated as part of the process of strengthening the rudiments of civil society in the last years of tsarist rule. The Christian Orthodox Catholic Eastern Church was defined by law as the "preeminent and predominant religion" of the empire, subject to the administrative authority of the state. In view of the empire's cultural diversity, however, the law also promised adherents of other religions the freedom to worship "in the various languages and according to the laws and confessions of their ancestors," as well as the right to govern their own communities through institutions created by the state.[23] This "freedom of religion" (*svoboda very*) was, however, a peculiar grant. In the first place, the freedom to worship consisted of the right to persist in the faith of one's ancestors, that is, to continue to belong to the religious community into which one had been born. It did not endow individual believers with the right to change religious affiliation. In the second place, the price of recognition was subordination to administrative authority. And third, recognition did not mean equality.

The laws on religion established a hierarchy of belief, which positioned the various creeds according to their relationship to the dominant one. In addition to Orthodoxy, the state recognized four religions as legitimate faiths. The most respected were the non-Orthodox Christians (*inoslavnye*), also known as "Christians of foreign confessions" (*khristiane inostrannykh ispovedanii*): Protestants and Roman Catholics. Below them in rank were the non-Christians, or "alien believers" (*inovertsy*): Jews and Muslims. Pagan belief systems, though not institutionalized, were included in this second category, reflecting negatively on the status of the monotheistic traditions with which they were grouped. Confessions that derived from Orthodoxy, such as the Old Belief and its sectarian offshoots, were not considered religions at all. These heretics had no right to conduct worship, enact marriages, empower a clergy, or govern their own affairs. Membership in some of these groups qualified as a criminal offense. Under the principle of "religious toleration," understood as respect for the established Church, the law prohibited attempts to convert adherents of the recognized religions to any but the Orthodox faith, which alone had the right to proselytize. Indeed, the law made it virtually impossible to abandon the Church under any circumstances.[24]

Russians who thought of themselves either as inhabiting an existing civil society or helping to bring one to life criticized the disposition of religious affairs under imperial law and offered corresponding visions of how religion ought to be governed. Three such alternatives can serve to illustrate the range of opinion on this matter. The first, published in 1895, was formulated by the editorial commission charged with revising the criminal code.[25] The second, published in 1900 by a major legal journal, is the work of a liberal professor of jurisprudence.[26] The third consists of proposals and debates in the State Duma following the revolution of 1905. Each instance is a variation on the "dream" that is the subject of this chapter.

In relation to certain themes, the editorial commission offered fundamental challenges to the principles embodied in the existing criminal code, which dated from the reign of Nicholas I. Most of its members prided themselves on a progressive, secular view of the law. In the case of religion, however, their proposals were cautious. The active code positioned crimes against religion immediately after crimes against the state in order of political importance, on the grounds that "crimes against religion are in essence also rebellion against the secular authority." The commission agreed that the state must continue in the role of guardian of religious values, because "religion and the church are among the most important foundations of the political and social system." This was all the more so in Russia, "where the principles of the Christian faith and the Orthodox Church form the unifying link that holds together the numerous and varied elements of the population."[27] The reformers viewed religion as a social good in which the state had a protective interest, rather than an aspect of personal life subject only to private determination in which the state must not interfere. Questions of faith could not therefore be left entirely to the individual conscience.[28]

The current level of intrusion was nevertheless extreme, the commission felt. Precisely because "church and family are fundamental to the national political community [*gosudarstvennoe obshchezhitie*]," it argued somewhat obscurely, "attacks on religion and the church should be separated from attacks on the state and its institutions."[29] The draft code thus removed the section on crimes against religion from its privileged position immediately following crimes against the state and inserted it between threats to public welfare and crimes against the person. The repositioning was also a redefinition: religion bordered the public and the private, not the public and the political, in the commission's view. But even this modification departed too radically from tradition to find favor with the Ministry of Justice and the Holy Synod, which, in reviewing the draft, returned the statutes to their accustomed location.[30]

Repositioning aside, the statutes remained virtually unaltered. The reformers sustained the state's obligation to endorse certain values over others, defending the prohibition of socially harmful faiths (Mormons were among their examples) and retaining the state's authority over propaganda and conversion. Though mitigating the penalties imposed, the commission thus retained the hierarchy of protected and stigmatized creeds and continued to rank the harm alleged to result from conversion according to the status of the confessions involved. As their language and legal caution suggest, the reformers did not envision a civil society composed of rights-bearing individuals. They endorsed a national polity composed of collective bodies (families, confessions) sustaining an otherwise fragmented imperial conglomeration. In some areas of the law the reformers valued individual rights above respect for traditional hierarchies, but not in this case.[31]

One commentator explained the commission's muddle on the grounds that existing law on religion was so far removed from modern principles of jurisprudence that any reform in the modern spirit would have amounted to a complete and politically unacceptable challenge to the entire system.[32] Unconstrained by bureaucratic obligations, Professor Michael Reisner (1868–1928) of Tomsk University formulated a more radical critique of the laws on religion than his colleagues on the editorial commission. He was also more explicit in his vision of the civil society he hoped would emerge from changes in the legal edifice. Reisner criticized the monarchy for continuing to adhere to the model of the eighteenth-century administrative Polizeistaat, which allowed the state to supervise moral behavior by intervening in its subjects' private lives; tightly controlling the associations to which they belonged, including religious communities; penalizing deviation from officially sanctioned norms; and limiting the individual's ability to choose, even among legitimate options. In gaining legitimacy, the institutions thus lost spiritual authority, while their members lost the true benefits of faith. "Our law," Reisner complained, "does not observe the division between the state and the religious communities. It acknowledges neither their freedom, nor the freedom of personal belief and conscience." In endowing certain faiths with official status, the state was pursuing a political mission, using police enforcement and bureaucratic control. This mission was intended to secure the loyalty of the component peoples of the empire, while keeping them in their proper place. "Our law is interested in religion primarily as the basis of nationality [*natsional'nost'*]," Reisner critically observed, "as the spiritual nerve of the various tribes and peoples, not as one or another form of a person's relation to God."[33]

While professing devotion to spiritual values, the state in fact manifested an entirely instrumental conception of religion. "Our law supposes that religion is not practiced by individual persons but by national-spiritual entities—peoples, nations, tribes. But in fact religion will always be religion, and its true receptacle is not the nation but the individual human heart." The policy of dividing the spiritual field into official categories, prohibiting the formation of new confessions, and preventing believers from moving between them had produced a discrepancy between the formal structure and the essence of belief. "With the exception of a few members of 'harmful' sects," Reisner noted, "the entire population is listed under the recognized confessions. What it actually believes, how it worships, or if it believes anything at all—is another question." Only the abolition of religious censorship, guaranteed freedom of discussion and the press, and the universal right to promote one's faith would allow believers to make their own spiritual decisions and develop a culture of moral commitment to replace habits of obedience and deceit.[34]

The model Reisner contrasted to the repressive and punitive Polizeistaat was the "cultural rule-of-law state [*kul'turno-pravovoe gosudarstvo*]," a Rechtsstaat in which law made room for the creative operation of cultural influences. Instead of trying to impose morality by force, such a state recognizes "that the bearer of morality can only be the free, moral individual, that this individual cannot be created by magical powers but only through the strengthening of a series of social, legal, and political conditions, of which the most important is freedom guaranteed by law [*pravovaia svoboda*]." Far from harming religion, the rule-of-law state fosters the development of a free church, which "develops the enterprise and energy found neither in a church swallowed up by the state, nor, all the more so, in a theocracy." Only a legal structure that protected, rather than intruded, would permit the growth of self-governing religious associations that fostered the moral development of their members, allowing society to develop a moral sensibility of its own. By breaking the identification of secular with church authority, the rule-of-law state "provides each individual with freedom—that greatest of conditions for moral development—and in this way raises the moral level of its citizens."[35]

Reisner's attack on administrative rule and his endorsement of a modern law-abiding state protective of individual rights, including freedom of conscience, reflected the liberal values associated with the oppositional movement that emerged in the decades preceding 1905. In meetings called in private parlors without police approval (often dispersed by the police); in banquets dedicated to mobilizing educated opinion on the model of 1848; in newspapers published abroad; in associations like the one called "Conversation" (Beseda), joined by men who wanted freedoms but not constitutions; in congresses on public health and in *zemstvo* assemblies—the so-called Liberation Movement took form. The result of this process can be seen in fact as constituting a self-declared civil society, determined, *iavochnym poriadkom*, to wrest the Rechtsstaat from the hands of Polizei. Although revolution was not what these gentlemen (and the rare professional woman) had in mind, it was revolution—an act of violence, not discussion, fueled by popular anger, not well-articulated dissatisfaction, and animated by the slogans and symbols of the radical Left, so indifferent to legal scruple of any kind—that caused the regime to concede some of the constitutional demands the spokesmen of mobilized civil society put forth.[36]

The Manifesto of October 17, 1905, designed to subdue the revolutionary crisis, promised to guarantee basic civil liberties and opened the way to electoral politics and parliamentary debates. But even before this constitutional watershed, an imperial decree of April 17, 1905, "On strengthening the principles of religious toleration," guaranteed "to each of Our subjects freedom of belief and prayer according to the dictates of his conscience."[37] Its main contribution was to open the possibility of leaving Orthodoxy, but only in the direction of other Christian faiths. It also recognized Old Belief as a legitimate confession. The decree originated as a response to political disorders in the Baltic and Volga regions, where numerous Catholics, Protestants, and Muslims had been baptized into Orthodoxy. Loyal to their native beliefs, they were unable formally to leave the Orthodox Church without forfeiting their civil rights and risking confiscation of property and even their children. The April 17 decree made it possible for such converts legally to resume their original identities. That the decree was less a matter of principle than a strategic political concession confirmed Professor Reisner's view of tsarist law.[38]

Once the State Duma convened in 1906, it pressed for the extension of the principles outlined but unfulfilled by the decree. At first the movement for reform had the support of Minister of the Interior Peter Stolypin (1862–1911). In the face of opposition from the Synod and right-wing forces, Stolypin eventually changed his mind, and none of the Duma proposals ever became law. The proposals remained hypothetical, but the issues and arguments embodied in the reform campaign nevertheless demonstrate the conflict between "dream" and reality when it came to building the architecture of civil society, even in post-1905 Russia. In May 1906, for example, a group of Duma deputies presented a bill on "freedom of conscience" (*svoboda sovesti*). The choice of terms underscored their interest in strengthening the individual's right to define his own spiritual identity. By contrast, the term "religious toleration" (*veroterpimost'*) used in the title of the April 17 decree emphasized the state's relation to confessional authority. In substituting the phrase "according to the dictates of his conscience" for the current phrase "according to the laws and confessions of their ancestors," the text of the decree had departed from the existing framework designed to prevent adherents from making choices of their own. But though it allowed people to move among the Christian faiths, the decree maintained the Orthodox monopoly on propaganda, still penalized conversion from Christian to non-Christian creeds, and failed to recognize the possibility of refusing any religious affiliation. By contrast, the Duma bill, in addition to granting citizens the freedom to choose among the recognized faiths, form new ones, or remain outside organized religious life, declared all confessions of equal legal standing, able to seek converts outside the fold.[39]

In responding to the bill, the Ministry of Internal Affairs outlined the consequences for the regulation of civil life. First, the state would cease to interpose itself between individual believers and the institutions governing religious practice. The state would also cease to regulate the religious dimension of marriage and abdicate its power to influence the religious identity of children. In addition to limiting its own powers, the state would have to create new secular institutions: civil oaths, civil marriages, and nonconfessional burials. The Ministry raised four main objections to the bill. First, it argued that certain communities were national as well as religious in character. Even if, as the bill demanded, no civil disabilities were to attach to membership in any faith, the state would nevertheless be justified in limiting the rights of groups such as the Jews and the Poles, on political, not confessional, grounds. Second, it insisted that the Orthodox Church retain its close association with the state. Third, it was equally important that the state continue to regulate parents' rights to influence their children's religious identity. And finally, it denied that all religions deserved equal treatment. It goes without saying that the Holy Synod objected to any diminution of the Orthodox Church's central role in public affairs, including its monopoly on propaganda and its right to influence the conditions of interconfessional marriage.[40]

What can we conclude from these three views of the civil constitution of religious life, in terms of their content and their fate? First, it can be said that between 1895 and 1906 acceptable opinion on the matter had moved some distance along the continuum from traditional to progressive. The editorial commission appointed in the 1880s had been unwilling or unable seriously to challenge the bureaucratic construction of religion as an affair of state and a matter of regulated institutions, not personal or even communal autonomy. Its timid move toward attenuating the political implications of religion and associating it more closely with the operation of civic life met with official disapproval. The draft itself, even in amended form, never became law. By 1905, however, the tsar himself was ready to narrow the range of state intervention in religious life, beyond the extent the reformers had dared envision a decade before. But the decree of April 17 announced no new general principles, offering merely a series of specific provisions. Nor did its publication alter the behavior of the administrative authorities. Nor, when it came to completing the decree with legislative enactments, did the ministers endorse the Duma proposals. These proposals embodied the dream of a civil society, in which a public, composed of rights-bearing individuals, could shape its own moral and cultural universe, protected, rather than constrained, by the law. The proposals emanated, furthermore, from members of an active public, now constituted in relation to a national representative body.

So progress had been made, both in paradigm and in practice. Yet how much had actually changed? The old criminal statutes remained on the books. The Duma proposals went down to defeat. The Orthodox Church retained its monopoly on preaching to the unconverted, civil marriage did not exist, Jews still suffered state-sponsored discrimination—indeed state-sponsored persecution (the Beilis trial of 1911–13)—and the Duma itself was dissolved by imperial decree when its temper displeased the sovereign or his ministers. Ethnic and religious equality, along with universal—male and female—suffrage, were achieved only after February 1917. When the Bolsheviks came to power in October they endorsed the separation of church and state for their own reasons. Michael Reisner, now an official of the Commissariat of Justice, helped draft the new laws. This legislation granted freedom of conscience to the private person along the lines Reisner and other liberals had envisioned. At the same time, however, it destroyed the institutional basis of belief by depriving religious associations of juridical rights. Eventually, they were also forbidden to spread their beliefs. Atheism replaced Orthodoxy as the state-sponsored dogma.[41] Whatever Reisner's original motives in defending the moral power, hence civic value, of freely chosen faith, the new regime did not abolish state control in order to enhance the moral autonomy of citizens occupying public space. Its goal was rather to obliterate religion altogether, first as social practice and ultimately as private conviction. Law served the Soviet regime not to limit the role of the state but to enhance its power by rhetorical means and by the force of contradiction: mobilizing the illusion of legality in the service of administrative lawlessness.[42]

To return to Gramsci and the connection between public life and political institutions, one might conclude that civil society under the autocracy was indeed "primordial" in lacking a spine, an architecture sustained by the law, which would guarantee its independence. In the Soviet period, religious association succumbed to repression, along with other forms of public life. Yet both regimes collapsed in the end—not from the assault of civic forces, too weak in either case to attack from within, but from their own shortcomings. Their failure, in the name of security, to allow these forces to gather strength was perhaps as fatal to the existence of the states involved as it was to the political development they stunted.

NOTES

1. Antonio Gramsci, *Selections from the Prison Notebooks*, quoted in Geoff Eley, "Nations, Publics, and Political Cultures: Placing Habermas in the Nineteenth Century," in *Habermas and the Public Sphere*, ed. Craig Calhoun (Cambridge, Mass.: MIT Press,

1992), 325.

2. Martin Malia, *The Soviet Tragedy: A History of Socialism in Russia, 1917–1991* (New York: Free Press, 1994), says there was a civil society in tsarist Russia (67) but calls it "exceptionally weak" (70). Having asserted that its weakness left a "social void" that facilitated the Bolsheviks' coming to power (134–35), he then blames the Soviet regime for destroying "civil society," an event he dates variously: 1918 (120); 1920 (133); and 1930 (437), when, he says, it consisted of the "independent peasantry." He sees the return of civil society, if only in a "relatively unstructured form," as a product, not cause, of the system's eventual "implosion," but judges it too weak to sustain a postcommunist democratic structure (498).

3. Moshe Lewin, *The Gorbachev Phenomenon: A Historical Interpretation* (Berkeley: University of California Press, 1988), 80.

4. See Edith W. Clowes, Samuel D. Kassow, and James L. West, eds., *Between Tsar and People: Educated Society and the Quest for Public Identity in Late Imperial Russia* (Princeton: Princeton University Press, 1991), introduction, 6–7.

5. See William G. Wagner, "Ideology, Identity, and the Emergence of a Middle Class," in *Between Tsar and People*, 162–63.

6. See *Between Tsar and People*; Louise McReynolds, *The News under Russia's Old Regime: The Development of a Mass-Circulation Press* (Princeton: Princeton University Press, 1991); and Harley D. Balzer, ed., *Russia's Missing Middle Class: The Professions in Russian History* (Armonk, N.Y.: Sharpe, 1996).

7. See Ben Eklof, John Bushnell, and Larissa Zakharova, eds., *Russia's Great Reforms, 1855–1881* (Bloomington: Indiana University Press, 1994).

8. See Gary Marker, *Publishing, Printing, and the Origins of Intellectual Life in Russia, 1700–1800* (Princeton: Princeton University Press, 1985); Douglas Smith, *Working the Rough Stone: Freemasonry and Society in Eighteenth-Century Russia* (DeKalb: Northern Illinois University Press, 1999).

9. See Nicholas V. Riasanovsky, *A Parting of the Ways: Government and the Educated Public in Russia, 1801–1855* (Oxford: Clarendon, 1976), chap. 2; Alexander M. Martin, *Romantics, Reformers, Reactionaries: Russian Conservative Thought and Politics in the Reign of Alexander I* (DeKalb: Northern Illinois University Press, 1997); Iurii M. Lotman, "The Decembrist in Daily Life (Everyday Behavior as a Historical-Psychological Category)," in *The Semiotics of Russian Cultural History*, ed. Alexander D. Nakhimovsky and Alice Stone Nakhimovsky (Ithaca, N.Y.: Cornell University Press, 1985); William Mills Todd, *Fiction and Society in the Age of Pushkin: Ideology, Institutions, and Narrative* (Cambridge, Mass.: Harvard University Press, 1986); and Laura Engelstein, "Revolution and the Theater of Public Life in Imperial Russia," in *Revolution and the Meanings of Freedom in the Nineteenth Century*, ed. Isser Wolloch (Stanford: Stanford University Press, 1996).

10. Riasanovsky, *Parting of the Ways*, pt. 2.

11. See W. Bruce Lincoln, *In the Vanguard of Reform: Russia's Enlightened Bureaucrats 1825–1861* (DeKalb: Northern Illinois University Press, 1982).

12. See Richard S. Wortman, *The Development of a Russian Legal Consciousness* (Chicago: University of Chicago Press, 1976).

13. See, for example, Nancy Mandelker Frieden, *Russian Physicians in an Era of Reform and Revolution, 1856–1905* (Princeton: Princeton University Press, 1981); and John F. Hutchinson, *Politics and Public Health in Revolutionary Russia 1890–1918* (Baltimore:

Johns Hopkins University Press, 1990).

14. See Terence Emmons, *The Russian Landed Gentry and the Peasant Emancipation of 1861* (Cambridge: Cambridge University Press, 1968).

15. On the professional integrity of state prosecutors, see A. F. Koni, "Vospominaniia o dele Very Zasulich," in *Sobranie sochinenii*, 8 vols. (Moscow: Iuridicheskaia literatura, 1966), 2:81–84.

16. Jörg Baberowski, *Autokratie und Justiz: Zum Verhältnis von Rechtsstaatlichkeit und Rückständigkeit im ausgehenden Zaren reich 1864–1914* (Frankfurt am Main: Vittorio Klostermann, 1996); Eugene Huskey, *Russian Lawyers and the Soviet State: The Origins and Development of the Soviet Bar, 1917–1939* (Princeton: Princeton University Press, 1986), chap. 1; Jane Burbank, "Discipline and Punish in the Moscow Bar Association," *Russian Review* 54, no. 1 (1995): 44–64; Koni, "Vospominaniia," 203–9.

17. See Engelstein, "Revolution."

18. Eley, "Nations," 307.

19. See Engelstein, "Revolution."

20. On civil code reform, see William G. Wagner, *Marriage, Property, and Law in Late Imperial Russia* (Oxford: Clarendon, 1994); on criminal code reform, see Laura Engelstein, *The Keys to Happiness: Sex and the Search for Modernity in Fin-de-Siècle Russia* (Ithaca, N.Y.: Cornell University Press, 1992), chaps. 1–2.

21. See I. S. Beliustin, *Description of the Clergy in Rural Russia: The Memoir of a Nineteenth-Century Parish Priest*, ed. Gregory L. Freeze (Ithaca, N.Y.: Cornell University Press, 1985). Also Marc Szeftel, "Church and State in Imperial Russia"; John Meyendorff, "Russian Bishops and Church Reform in 1905"; and Paul R. Valliere, "The Idea of a Council in Russian Orthodoxy in 1905," in *Russian Orthodoxy under the Old Regime*, ed. Robert L. Nichols and Theofanis George Stavrou (Minneapolis: University of Minnesota Press, 1978); Adele Lindenmeyr, *Poverty Is Not a Vice: Charity, Society, and the State in Imperial Russia* (Princeton: Princeton University Press, 1996).

22. See Robert O. Crummey, *The Old Believers and the World of Anti-Christ: The Vyg Community and the Russian State, 1694–1855* (Madison: University of Wisconsin Press, 1970); Manfred Hildermeier, "Alter Glaube und neue Welt: Zur Sozialgeschichte des Raskol im 18. und 19. Jahrhundert," *Jahrbücher für Geschichte Osteuropas* 38 (1990): no. 3, 372–98; no. 4, 504–25; and Roy R. Robson, *Old Believers in Modern Russia* (DeKalb: Northern Illinois University Press, 1995).

23. Articles 40, 43, 45, 46, in *Svod zakonov rossiiskoi imperii*, ed. A. F. Volkov and Iu. D. Filipov, 4th ed., 16 vols. (St. Petersburg: Obshchestvennaia pol'za, 1904), 1:3–4.

24. Articles 70 and 77, in *Svod*, 14:75–76.

25. *Ugolovnoe ulozhenie: Proekt redaktsionnoi komissii i ob"iasneniia k nemu* [henceforth *UU*], 8 vols. (St. Petersburg: Pravitel'stvuiushchii senat, 1895), 4:3–147.

26. M. A. Reisner, "Moral', pravo i religiia po deistvuiushchemu russkomu zakonu," pts. 1–4, *Vestnik prava* (1900): no. 3, 1–18; no. 4–5, 1–49; no. 8, 1–34; no. 10, 1–46.

27. *UU*, 4:48, 50.

28. *UU*, 4:105.

29. *UU*, 4:51.

30. Ardalion Popov, *Sud i nakazaniia za prestupleniia protiv very i nravstvennosti po russkomu pravu* (Kazan: Imperatorskii universitet, 1904), 497.

31. *UU*, 4:104–5, 116; Popov, *Sud*, 479–82; also Wagner, *Marriage*; and Engelstein, *Keys*.

32. Popov, *Sud*, 471–72, 486–87.

33. Reisner, "Moral'," pt. 2, pp. 6, 47. For other Russian jurists of the period who shared many of Reisner's opinions, see Popov, *Sud*, 452–64.

34. Reisner, "Moral'," pt. 3, pp. 8–10; pt. 4, 18–38.

35. Reisner, "Moral'," pt. 3, p. 3; pt. 4, 1–3.

36. See Shmuel Galai, *The Liberation Movement in Russia, 1900–1905* (Cambridge: Cambridge University Press, 1973); Abraham Ascher, *The Revolution of 1905: Russia in Disarray* (Stanford: Stanford University Press, 1988).

37. "Imennoi Vysochaishii ukaz, dannyi Senatu: Ob ukreplenii nachal veroterpimosti" (no. 26125), *Polnoe sobranie zakonov rossiiskoi imperii*, ser. 3, 33 vols. (St. Petersburg: Gosudarstvennaia tipografiia, 1905), 25:257–58.

38. See M. A. Reisner, "Svoboda sovesti i zakon 17 aprelia 1905 g.," *Gosudarstvo i veruiushchaia lichnost': Sbornik statei* (St. Petersburg: Obshchestvennaia pol'za, 1905), 390–92, 417–18.

39. "Materialy po voprosu o svobode sovesti," Archives of the Russian Academy of Sciences [ARAN], collection [f.] 192, inventory [op.] 3, file [d.] 17, sheets [ll.] 15–18: "Osnovnye polozheniia zakonoproekta o svobode sovesti." See also Peter Waldron, "Religious Toleration in Late Imperial Russia," in *Civil Rights in Imperial Russia*, ed. Olga Crisp and Linda Edmondson (Oxford: Oxford University Press, 1989), 112–13, 117.

40. "Materialy po voprosu o svobode sovesti," ARAN, f. 192, op. 3, d. 17, ll. 19–24 (Ministerstvo vnutrennikh del, departament dukhovnykh del inostrannykh ispovedanii, June 16, 1906, no. 3432, "Po proektu osnovnykh polozhenii o svobode sovesti"); ll. 27–48 (*Spravka o svobode sovesti* [St. Petersburg: Ministerstvo vnutrennikh del, 1906]).

41. See Joshua Rothenberg, "The Legal Status of Religion in the Soviet Union," in *Aspects of Religion in the Soviet Union, 1917–1967*, ed. Richard H. Marshall Jr. (Chicago: University of Chicago Press, 1971), 63–64, 82; John Shelton Curtiss, *The Russian Church and the Soviet State, 1917–1950* (Boston: Little Brown, 1953), 230. For texts, see "K istorii otdeleniia tserkvi ot gosudarstva i shkoly ot tserkvi v SSSR: Dokumenty i materialy," *Voprosy istorii religii i ateizma: Sbornik statei*, 5 (Moscow: Akademiia nauk, 1958), 19–22.

42. See William B. Husband, *"Godless Communists": Atheism and Society in Soviet Russia, 1917–1932* (DeKalb: Northern Illinois University Press, 2000).

3

PUBLIC OPINION
AND ASSOCIATIONS IN
NINETEENTH-CENTURY ITALY

Alberto Mario Banti

This chapter examines the structure of associations of civil society in nine-teenth-century Italy and its effects on the evolution of political trends. Al-though emphasis is placed on the morphology of associational networks, the main ideological messages of the various associations are also described and an-alyzed. Also highlighted are some general considerations about their particular character and the applicability of terms such as "liberal," "democratic," or "con-servative" to nineteenth-century Italian reality. I say "applicability" because only with caution can we describe the different areas of Italian public opinion using these terms. This caution is dictated by a number of considerations.

First, a diversified pro-liberal current, which was formed at the end of the eighteenth century and powerfully strengthened during the nineteenth century, certainly existed. Nevertheless, historians who have studied Italian liberal thought have pointed out some distinctive characteristics. Like their counter-parts elsewhere, Italian liberals had a strong elitist notion of representation; for example, only the so-called best, that is, the rich and educated, had the right to vote. As opposed to Anglo-Saxon liberalism, Italian liberalism was not charac-terized by any theory or constitutional practice of checks and balances. Rather, Italian liberals cultivated the idea of a strong government that was able to mod-ernize quickly an economically and socially backward country. Over time this preference persuaded many Italian liberals to take a stance of open mistrust vis-à-vis parliament and its functions. Thus, paradoxically, Italian antiparliamen-tarianism, fed by thinkers of acknowledged intellectual stature such as Gaetano

Mosca and Vilfredo Pareto, was not created within conservative or antiliberal circles but was supported by powerful intellectual and political figures who declared themselves liberals.[1]

Second, alongside this current of opinion, another was formed, that of the so-called intransigent Catholics. This section of public opinion was made up of Catholics who followed Pope Pius IX in his dispute with the new Kingdom of Italy, which had been formed in 1859–60. It is not easy to put the Italian Catholic movement into a clear-cut ideological category. On the one hand, it was against the institutions of the Italian liberal state and even against liberalism as an ideology; on the other hand, it also included important schools of thought that emphasized the gospel message and aspired to greater social justice. The least one can say, then, is that this movement had a composite character. Real reactionaries, who dreamed of the return to a papal theocracy, could be found in Catholic ranks, as well as courageous trade-unionist peasants, who fought against landowners in the name of the gospel and the pope's teachings. And between these two extremes, a number of intermediate positions were held.[2]

Third, there was a current that could almost certainly be identified as democratic, but with some qualifications. Originally the main tendency of Italian democratic opinion was republican, inspired by the ideas of Giuseppe Mazzini. For this sector of public opinion, the main goal was the establishment of a democratic republic, equipped with representative institutions based on universal suffrage.[3] During the second half of the century, groups of socialists began to operate alongside the republicans, and in 1892 they founded their own party. The tactics of the Italian Socialist Party (PSI) called for participation in political and administrative elections. Its strategic aim, however, was not to establish a democratic republic but to build something new and completely different from the projects of the other "political families," namely, a socialist society.[4] In the end, the term "democratic" took on a very different meaning when applied to republicans as opposed to socialists.

The dealings between political families, who spoke languages that were mutually exclusive, were marked by conflict. Liberals, Catholics, republicans, and socialists were animated by irreconcilable visions of state and society. The political struggle was thought of as a zero-sum struggle; whoever won, won all.

But what were the associational forms that were used to spread these ideological positions? In what way did the forms of the associational life shape the character of civil society?

CLUBS AND ASSOCIATIONS
IN PREUNIFICATION ITALY (1796–1860)

In Italy, it was at the end of the premodern era, when the organizational forms associated with the system of estates was abolished, that the first networks of formal associations got started. We can date the origins of this transition sometime between the end of the eighteenth century and the beginning of the nineteenth. At that time, with the arrival of Napoleon I's forces and the creation of states that were more or less directly dependent on France, new civil and constitutional laws were introduced. Those laws were based on the central idea of a society composed of citizens who were equals in the eyes of the law, even though they did not have the same political rights.[5] The building of this new institutional framework was of great importance and had traumatic effects for several reasons. The destruction of estate jurisdiction had the greatest impact. Privileges previously held by citizens' corps, guilds, and aristocratic groups were abolished. Above all, the new laws totally eliminated feudal jurisdictions, which, particularly in the ancient Kingdom of Naples, had been fundamental privileges of the nobility and which both on the mainland and in Sicily had been crucial administrative subdivisions of the state.

The elimination of estates and their privileges posed an enormous problem of legitimization and self-definition for the old noble or estate elites, as well as for individuals and groups who, in the context of the institutions of the new Napoleonic states, sought to rise socially. One of the most innovative forms in Italy, through which people tried to redefine the map of social boundaries, was the establishment of voluntary associations. Almost everywhere in Italy during the early years of the nineteenth century, there was considerable growth in the creation of reading rooms, scientific associations, associations for the improvement of arts and industry, aristocratic clubhouses, and recreation clubs, all with diverse social aims and characteristics.

Most of these associations had an important implicit social goal: to provide the means for creating new languages of social identification. From this point of view (and necessarily simplifying the picture), there are primarily two organizational models to consider.

The first is a selective associational model, whose structure was that of a club that imposed rigorous restrictions on new membership. There were two types of restrictions: economic (prospective members had to pay high fees to join) and relational (they were allowed to join only through sponsorship of existing members and with the approval of the assembled members of the association). No matter what their aims (scientific, cultural, recreational, or other), the associations that were thus organized implemented strategies that redefined the social geography and reconstructed the spaces of elite life. It is not surprising that the members of these associations were mostly aristocrats, landowners, professionals, officials, and well-to-do merchants, that is, members of the rich, prestigious, and educated upper classes. Moreover, the ways in which these organizations thought about themselves worked to the exclusion of women. These were public bodies, and women, as creatures of the private sphere, were ineligible for membership "by nature."

The second associational form was more inclusive. The era's Jacobin clubs (understood to encompass both Jacobin political societies and cultural associations with a more indirect Jacobin orientation) provided the model. The structure of these associations was the opposite of the selective clubs. Membership dues were low, and entrance was normally free. Prospective members had to decide that they wanted to belong and to follow certain enrollment procedures. These associations seemed less rigidly defined and more oriented toward forms of democratic assembly. Even the social composition of these associations was more open. There was room for craftsmen, merchants, and lower-level clerks alongside landowners and professionals, some of whom were even of aristocratic origins. Because of both their declared political aims and distinctive internal setup, these inclusive associations played a meaningful role in the spread of democratic political conceptions.

During the Napoleonic era, the inclusive clubs were subject to inspections by the governments and later were banned outright. Because of their democratic character, the Jacobin clubs appeared as a threat to the sociopolitical order of the Napoleonic states (the Kingdom of Italy in the north, the Kingdom of Naples in the south). The selective clubs, however, although they were also subject to close government inspections, continued to prosper, ready to promote scientific-cultural initiatives but inclined to restrain any straying onto more openly political terrain.[6]

The picture did not change much in the fifty years preceding the unification of Italy. The states that were reestablished after the fall of Napoleon accepted the regulations on associations that the previous Napoleonic states had set up. They tolerated associations that provided the requisite political and social guarantees, that is, associations that did not include either democrats or social outsiders. Further, these were selective clubs, associations of elites, which, whatever their professed aims, eschewed by charter rule any discussion of political matters. Of course, such political silence was a necessary requirement without which the authorities would not allow the clubs to exist. An extreme example is the case of the Kingdom of Two Sicilies, which admitted only associations set up and sponsored by the government.[7]

These associations, for the most part, functioned as circles where strategies of social distinction were carried out. The social structures of clubs differed from place to place. For example, the elite associations established in Turin had a clear-cut hierarchy: nobles patronized the Whist Club, to which very few bourgeois were admitted, and the most important members of the bourgeoisie joined the Philharmonic Club. Elsewhere (Milan, Piacenza, Florence, and Naples), the clubs had a mixed aristocrat–bourgeois character.[8] To explain the local variations would require a microanalysis that is not possible here. Nevertheless, for all the variety there were uniform elements shared by all such associations. They were urban organizations that recruited on a selective basis and pursued on the whole cultural or recreational purposes (newspapers or books, scientific and literary debate, the sponsorship of balls or conferences, card-playing). They also were rather numerous, with each city supporting several associations that had different aims. Clubs were often in competition with each other and had differentiated memberships (a person who belonged to one club normally did not belong to another).

Even if, in themselves, these associations could not deal explicitly with subjects of a political nature, they did provide meeting places for individuals who often belonged to informal or secret societies with a liberal slant. And political feelings did on occasion bubble to the surface in club activities, above all when issues of national identity came up for discussion. Conferences on the Italian language, on the history of Italian civilization and geography, on scientific and technological innovations originating in Italy provided elites the opportunity to stake out positions of a political nature. But the debate had to be indirect.

Only after 1848 was there even one state in Italy, the Kingdom of Sardinia, which was liberal and parliamentary in constitution, providing legal guarantees for associational activity: the Kingdom's founding charter recognized in general terms the right of association, a recognition whose practical meaning was spelled out in the government ordinance of September 26, 1848.[9]

NATIONAL IDENTITY AND POLITICAL LANGUAGES

Associations, therefore, defined a new geography of social distinction in the wake of the abolition of estate privilege. They served as an instrument for the self-definition of emergent post-revolutionary elites. But new elites needed more than social space in which to develop. They needed as well a new language of self-legitimization.

The language of national identity was of critical importance in nineteenth-century Italy. It was taken for granted by many that an Italian nation existed, although that was in fact a questionable claim from many points of view. Still, the argument was made that Italy was a unified entity, unified on the basis of a common ethnic heritage as well as a shared language, historical traditions, religion, and culture. What was lacking was a unified institutional framework that would give expression to an as yet inchoate national will. The reorganization of the Italian state system at the Restoration (the number of states on the peninsula was reduced from nine to seven) added fresh impetus to the growing debate about what direction institutional reform should take. Postrevolutionary elites positioned themselves to set the terms of the argument. In this way, a variety of different questions became joined together: the problem of national unification, the issue of institutional renovation, and the extent and character of elite authority.

The problem of national unification, however, stirred deep political divisions. Four different schools of thought emerged on the subject, and around each crystallized a powerful associational subculture. Understanding how these various discourses came to be framed will help us to understand the fissured associational topography that emerged in Italy in the era of national unification.

The least influential discourse or language was reactionary—anti-unitary. A number of thinkers expressed conservative opposition both to unification and to the introduction of representative institutions. Such opinions were voiced in newspapers and magazines, which often enjoyed a fairly wide circulation thanks to financial support from governments that felt threatened by nationalist trends. Once unity was achieved, however, such support dried up, and the anti-unity current with it. The new Kingdom of Italy was proclaimed in March 1861. Afterwards, there were a few who remained nostalgic for the states and kingdoms of bygone days, but they carried little political weight.

The first half of the century, however, also produced two schools of thought that favored creation of an Italian national state. What distinguished these was not the structural character of the state to come (whether it would be a centralized regime or a confederation of autonomous states). There were in fact centralists and federalists in both camps. Rather, the cleavage, which was quite typical in nineteenth-century Europe, pitted liberals against democrats. Even though the differences between liberal and democratic ideas in Italy concerned specific policies to be followed in economic and social fields, or the nature and limits of representation, the main argument turned on constitutional patterns. After 1848–49, liberal leaders maintained that the new Italian state had to be established at the initiative of the king of Sardinia; had to have a monarchical-constitutional structure, such as that in force in the Kingdom of Sardinia; and had to establish itself in absolute continuity with the institutions of the Sardinian state. In contrast, democratic leaders pushed for a constituent assembly, to be elected on the basis of universal manhood suffrage. Moreover, they wanted to introduce democratic institutions and abolish the monarchy.

The liberal position was strengthened by at least three factors. First, after the defeats of 1848–49, Vittorio Emanuele II, king of Sardinia, was the only Italian king who agreed to maintain a liberal constitution (granted in March 1848, by his father Carlo Alberto). In this way he became a practical and symbolic point of reference for all Italian liberals. Second, in 1859 Vittorio Emanuele, with decisive military support from Napoleon III's France, emerged victorious in a war against Austria for the liberation of Lombardy. The aim of the conflict was the expansion of Sardinia's constitutional kingdom in northern Italy. Nevertheless, the war itself triggered a chain reaction of insurrections across the peninsula—in Emilia and Romagna, the Papal States, the Duchies of Parma and Modena, and the Grand Duchy of Tuscany—so that all these territories were soon absorbed into a larger and stronger Sardinian state. The third factor was the fallout from Giuseppe Garibaldi's so-called Sicilian expedition.

In the spring of 1860, Garibaldi, at the head of an irregular volunteer force, had landed in Sicily, dealing an overwhelming defeat to the armies of the Bourbon Kingdom of the Two Sicilies. In September, Garibaldi had begun contemplating a move northward from Naples to Rome. Vittorio Emanuele, however, acted to block Garibaldi's advance, dispatching a Sardinian army down through Umbria into the former Papal States. The king, urged on by Prime Minister Camillo Cavour, had undertaken this course because he was worried about Garibaldi's democratizing ambitions. As of October, a split threatened to cut the peninsula in two, between a democratic South and a liberal monarchical North. The confrontation dissipated, however, when Garibaldi backed down, agreeing to cede the newly emancipated southern lands to King Vittorio Emanuele II in the name of Italian unity.[10]

This decision, much applauded in patriotic rhetoric, did not resolve the conflict between democratic-republican and liberal-monarchic opinions. After the 1859–60 wars, democratic opinion, inspired by the authoritative leadership of Giuseppe Mazzini, was still pressuring for the election of a constituent assembly, which would discuss the features of the new state and possibly put the abolition of the monarchy and the establishment of a republic on its agenda. Another point of contention was the liberation of the "unredeemed" lands: Rome and Latium (still under the dominion of the pope) and Venice and the Veneto (still under Austrian control). While liberals looked to the diplomatic action of the government and, if necessary, to the army of the new Kingdom of Italy for a solution, the democrats advocated the military action of a revolutionary force. In the years after unification, democrats continued to believe in the myth of Garibaldi's Sicilian exploits. They set about organizing paramilitary groups with the aim of completing the unification of Italy by force and in fact mounted several unsuccessful illegal efforts to that end, to capture Rome in particular.

To conclude, while liberals and democratic-republicans may both have spoken the same language of national unification, they espoused mutually incompatible constitutional visions. The republicans did not believe in the legitimacy of the new state. The liberals on the other hand, who enjoyed the upper hand after winning the elections of January–February 1861, declared the republican opposition unconstitutional, subversive, and inimical to the institutions of a unified Italy.

After 1861 an important segment of the left-wing political leadership split from the democratic-republican camp. They declared loyalty to the crown and the constitution, establishing the so-called constitutional Left. A rather important part of the democratic-republicans, however, remained hostile to liberals and to official institutions. In the long run, this latter group appeared to be made up of two branches, the one republican and the other, later on, socialist. Both were animated by the same opposition to the liberal state, but they had very different ultimate goals: The republicans sought a bourgeois democratic republic, and the socialists, a socialist society.[11] Even though these two political groups sprang originally from the same political ground, a divergence of goals in the end separated them into two distinct political currents.

The fourth political language was that of the so-called "Catholic intransigence." The establishment of the unity of Italy involved the occupation and progressive dismembering of the Papal States, a territory covering central Italy, governed by the pope. Pope Pius IX reacted furiously to the process. He systematically refused to acknowledge the legitimacy of the Kingdom of Italy, a state of "bandits without law or God," which had, in his view, been founded through a despicable act of theft. The Kingdom of Italy on the other hand did acknowledge the pope as the spiritual father of Catholicism and recognized him as the head of an independent state (reduced in size after September 20, 1870, to the tiny dimensions of the Vatican). The pope, however, insisted on a restoration of his temporal power, which he believed essential to the successful carrying out of his spiritual teachings. He blamed the new constitutional kingdom for his humiliation. Indeed, his opposition to unification was so strong that it spilled over into a general condemnation of the institutional and philosophical foundations of liberalism itself.

And the pope spoke as the head of the Catholic Church, not just as an old deposed sovereign. He may have protested for political reasons, but his protests implicated the flock of the faithful as well. It was therefore hardly surprising that the pope's position had important consequences for the political culture of a now united Italy. Catholic opinion divided in two: Liberal Catholics were willing to concede that the Church, whose mission after all was spiritual, had no special claims on the territorial integrity of the new state; intransigent Catholics on the other hand toed the papal line, refusing either to recognize the legitimacy of the new constitutional order or even to participate in the electoral process.[12] As a result, a shared religious faith, which could have been a source of great national cohesion, instead became a cause of deep divisions among Italians.

THE ASSOCIATIONS OF THE LIBERAL ELITES

After the establishment of the Kingdom of Italy, associational life grew richer and more complex. A new generation of associations sprang up alongside the old social clubs. The associational map was redrawn in ways that were intimately connected to the ideological map sketched above.

The various recreation clubs, reading rooms, and scientific societies, which had served as gathering places for local notables, now became the basic building blocks of liberal political culture. In the rooms of such associations, candidates for political and administrative office were chosen, electoral committees were formed to organize the registration of voters and canvas votes, and banquets or dances were convened to honor one candidate or another. Next to these more traditional forms of elite association, a new type of liberal association, the mutual aid, or workers society, was created, first in constitutional Piedmont, and then in other regions. These societies were often founded in the hope of broadening the social bases of liberalism. After 1861, all these associational forms were replicated in southern Italy, where numerous elite associations were created.[13]

The organizational structures of liberal associational life had several common features. For the entire period from unification to World War I, liberal clubs and associations did not have a national organization. Their wealth and fields of action were exclusively local or, better yet, urban. The peculiar constitution of local politics reinforced the provincial character of associational life. The suffrage laws of 1860 and 1882 defined a small electorate restricted by age, gender, property qualification, and literacy.[14] Under these circumstances, the task of representation took on a localistic-clientelistic character. The elected deputy acted as a broker for the interests of his constituency or even for single voters through a system of personal recommendations. In exchange for favors received on behalf of his constituency or friends, the deputy in turn gave his backing to a minister or prime minister.[15]

This system suited perfectly the subjective experience of Italian elites. The bourgeois world in this period was an extraordinarily fragmented mosaic of groups for whom inclusion in the local sociopolitical milieu was the primary goal. Normally, little linked a landowner in Pavia to an owner of large landed estates and citrus groves in eastern Sicily, a lawyer in Milan to one from Naples, or even a rich, successful lawyer to one of the numerous second-rank lawyers eking out a living in the same city; and an entrepreneur involved in the production of cotton fabric in Brianza had little in common with a stockholder or manager of an iron business in Liguria.

The examples could be multiplied, so fragmented was the character of bourgeois life, divided as it was by real communication gaps. In such a setting, the range of influence exerted by associations did not extend much beyond the local. Newspapers remained local in circulation and marriages and friendships deeply rooted in the local environment. This provincial-mindedness fed a localistic outlook that in turn had a shaping impact on how economic interests and professional groups thought about themselves and behaved. A provincialism based on personal relationships strengthened the particularism of interests, reversing ethical priorities away from the "far-away/national" in favor of the "close-by/local."[16]

Given the peculiar character of upper middle-class life in the new united Italy, it is not hard to understand the persistent localist implosion of liberal politics. Not all systems of notable governance are subject to localistic collapse, but such was the case in Italy. This collapse was fed by the localist and particularist social practices of bourgeois life. A notable-based political culture—which personalized the links between parliament, deputy, and constituency—exacerbated the situation. To many urban, provincial bourgeois, this scheme of political representation seemed far more congenial than any form of permanent party organization whose discipline and internal restrictions they feared, and not by chance. When liberals spoke up on behalf of the ideal parliamentary representative—an individual free of all ties and free most of all from the ties of a party organization—it was in reality the priority and independence of particularist interests and local needs that they were defending.

SOUTHERN PECULIARITIES

The organizational forms of liberal opinion in northern and central Italy differed significantly from those in southern Italy. A general discussion of associational structures tends to gloss over regional variants, so it is important to take a moment to highlight a rather important, region-based difference in the associational networks of Italy's liberal elite. Even if, in certain formal respects, the characteristics of elite associational life were the same across the country, this was not the case when it came to how these networks actually functioned, or to the power they exercised over the lives of the individuals involved.

The first difference may be found in the differing nature of clientelistic networks. To what extent did liberal networks succeed in integrating the lower orders? In northern and central Italy, as in the south, the center of associational and political action was the city. The spread of associations to rural areas proved to be difficult and episodic. In the north and center, cities exercised an economic dominion over surrounding rural areas where most peasants lived and worked. Many city-based notables owned land in the countryside, which brought them into contact with the local peasantry, but otherwise townsmen had little personal contact with country folk, above all with day laborers who moved from farm to farm working at temporary jobs and who in the Po Valley made up the most numerous, worst paid, and most conflictual group in the rural labor force.[17]

By contrast, in southern Italy the settlement structure consisted of big rural towns (called "agro-towns" by anthropologists), where both landowners and peasants were concentrated, surrounded by vast rural areas often without any stable settlement. In these agro-towns the relations between local notables and the farming classes were more frequent and direct than in the rest of the country.[18] The clientelistic brokerage and the associational network had, so to speak, a wider and more structured social inclusiveness than in central and northern Italy.

A second distinction, which further supports the notion that networks of southern notables were more inclusive, is to be found in the varying patterns of factionalism within liberal associational life. Division and conflict within elites was characteristic of political life in the cities of southern Italy as in those of the north and center. The most recent historiography, however, suggests that in southern regions the divisions were particularly long-lived, tended to divide communities into rigid vertical hierarchies, and were of such intensity as to drive elite factions to maximize the internal cohesion of their particular groups. The origins of these factional disputes can be traced back to the era when feudal institutions were abolished (1806–12). Indeed, it seems sometimes that such disputes were but transpositions, in a nonfeudal context, of older feudal divisions abetted by the weakness and decentralized character of the old Bourbon administrative structure, a circumstance that allowed old patterns of division to survive and fester.[19]

The third difference is the presence of permanent criminal organizations in various areas of the former Kingdom of the Two Sicilies, the most important of which was, without any doubt, the *mafia*. In a classical hypothesis, recently revived by a number of historians, the presence of armed groups that practiced extortion, promised protection, or took on dirty jobs was, to a certain extent, an effect of the deadly combination of a delayed abolition of the feudal system and a weak organization of the administrative apparatus of the state in the south. The old feudal constabulary, once feudal institutions were dissolved and its professional relations with the aristocracy interrupted, went "freelance," operating as autonomous armed bands. These criminal groups, which were based of course on an intensive and illegal use of violence, managed to survive because they did not just limit themselves to intimidation and brutal aggression. As Diego Gambetta has pointed out, "they sold protection," a particularly desirable commodity in the conflictual setting of southern Italy, where strong institutional structures were lacking. In addition, southern elites seemed to stand by the traditional belief that the private use of violence was not after all so illegal as all that, a belief that inclined them to employ without many qualms the services of organized criminals. Even if the phenomenon in its nineteenth-century manifestation was not universal to the whole of Sicily or southern Italy, it was still widespread and had a frequent connection with the associational world of the southern notables.[20]

CATHOLIC, REPUBLICAN, AND SOCIALIST ASSOCIATIONS

Thus, the civil society of southern Italy did not seem all that civil. Nevertheless, the southern liberal notables were better able to exercise a more solid hegemony than liberal elites in many areas of central and northern Italy. This peculiarity could be a result of the effectiveness of the patronage networks that surrounded the notables in the southern agro-towns. Those networks were able to include peasants and day laborers and to meet (in some way) their need to relate to the state and the market. This mediational function made the propaganda of Catholics, republicans, or socialists less attractive, even if it did not completely hinder periodic and brutal peasant riots. In contrast, in the northern countryside, landowners had no direct or continuous relationship with the day laborers, who were excluded from the notables' social networks. Thus, Catholics, republicans, and socialists in the north found a rural population that, secluded as it was from the world of the liberal elites, was willing to listen to harsh criticism against the notables and the institutions of the liberal state. But what associative forms did the anticonstitutional groups use to spread their propaganda?

The organizational forms of the Catholic world were to a degree typical of a pre-nineteenth-century social context.[21] Nevertheless, the true spread of intransigent Catholic associationism did not begin until 1875 with the founding of the Opera dei Congressi, a national organization that was divided into diocesan and parochial committees, thus following in form the structure of the ecclesiastical administration. The organization's main aims were the defense of the pope's rights, the fight for freedom in teaching and against compulsory public education, and the support of guild-like solutions in social relations. From an organizational point of view, the creation of specific associations for young people, women, and laborers was proposed, and these were established in the following decade. In 1897, for example, the Opera boasted 708 youth sections, 17 university groups, 554 rural funds, 688 worker associations, 116 Catholic Youth Organization groups, 24 newspapers, and 155 magazines. In terms of national distribution, the Opera had solid implantation in central and northern Italy. Of the approximately four thousand diocesan committees active in 1897, 2,092 were in the north, 1,536 in the center, 206 in the south, and 144 in the Islands.[22]

As for the democrats, it was Mazzinian associational networks that were the most important at the outset. In line with a tradition dating back to the final years of Napoleon I's regime and later revived in 1831 with the establishment of Mazzini's Giovine Italia, the republican associational network maintained its secret insurrectionary character even after unification. But alongside these secret societies emerged more public groups that upheld republican ideals and provided the republican movement an organizational foothold among the working class, in particular via working-class clubs. At the beginning of the 1870s, after the capture of Rome (one of the main aims of the movement) and after the death of Mazzini in 1872, there was an extremely important change in the movement: public political organizations, coordinated by a central body, were created as its mainstay. The republican public associations had various organizational forms: working-class libraries, youth clubs, women's groups, working-class clubs, and target-shooting clubs. As far as more strictly political organizations were concerned, between 1874 and 1889, the societies that were members of the Patto di Fratellanza, the main coordinating organization, multiplied in number from 300 to 450. The distribution of member societies in Italy ran as follows: Emilia Romagna had approximately two hundred societies; Liguria, one hundred; Lombardy, seventy; Tuscany, the Marches, and Umbria, fifty each. The number of members totaled around four hundred thousand.[23]

Similar structures also were built by socialist organizations, and in particular the Party of Italian Workers (later the PSI) founded in Genoa in 1892. Working-class groups, sporting clubs, theatrical societies, and socialist *case del popolo* (socialist clubhouses) were the main associational forms of socialist organization. A powerful political message and deep involvement in trade-union organization (in this case, city-based trade unions and, above all, peasant leagues in the countryside) strongly contributed to the enormous success of the PSI. According to figures from 1897, the territorial distribution of party affiliates showed that central and northern Italy again predominated in militancy (69.24 percent of a total of 26,857 members were in the north; 19.82 percent in the center; and 10.86 percent in the south). Central and northern predominance was even more pronounced in 1914 (70.76 percent of a total of 57,274 members were in the north, 21.66 percent in the center, and 7.49 percent in the south).[24] This associational bulwark became the base for a political project that maintained a radical social and political opposition to the institutions of the liberal state and bourgeois society.[25]

Opposition associational networks were thus concentrated primarily in the provincial towns and countryside of northern and central Italy. The spread of such associations in southern Italy was less significant.[26] The greatest area of strength for Catholic associations and, above all, for the socialist movement was the countryside of the Po Valley, an area barely touched by the associational networks of liberal notables. The northern Italian rural world was thus home ground for the opposition.

A final and fundamental difference distinguished the nonliberal from the liberal associational environment. Liberal associational forms remained strongly anchored in a local context. They were structured around a single notable, or a family or larger group of notables. For the above-mentioned reasons, the clientelistic political intermediation between local constituencies and the national parliament remained the fundamental outlet for the expression of the liberal public opinion. The organizational forms of Catholics, republicans, or socialists, however, even if sustained by strong local identities, were embedded in larger, more centralized, national organizational structures. They also had an explicit inclusive intent; that is, they actively sought the support of the working classes, which were excluded from political citizenship. Finally, they were based on a political mythology characterized by a profound diffidence, if not open hostility, toward the institutions of the liberal state.

In this situation there is a striking paradox. The groups created around political languages that denied legitimacy to the liberal state were the very same ones most successful at building national organizational networks, a feat that the liberals themselves were never able to reproduce.

CONCLUSION

The Italian case cannot easily be described in terms of a linear progression that rid Italian society of authoritarian institutions and led it toward democratic ones. A dense associational life existed on the peninsula, no doubt, but it is hard to see the relevance of such a bare assertion.

Rather, what the Italian case demonstrates is how a rapid and effective state-building process managed by liberal-oriented elites can go hand in hand with the development of multiple political communities that were parallel and often mutually exclusive. There was not *one* nationalization of the masses, *one* civil society, *one* way of imagining "modernity," "liberty," "democracy," or "constitution." Instead, there emerged many "imagined communities," different conceptions of belonging based on distinct networks of different mythological models. In Italy, the heritage of the past, divergent forms of identity creation, and the peculiar structuring of associational life played determining roles in shaping a civil society that was divided by profound ideological, social, and territorial differences.

These differences have continued to manifest themselves in varying forms well into the twentieth century, beyond fascism and beyond the experience of the first fifty years of the Republic. Present-day political differences seem to be rooted in different understandings of constitutional structure and in different ways of thinking about the organization of the national community. The ongoing disagreement over how the fundamental rules governing collective action should be constituted, a major source of the intense debate that has rocked the Italian political scene in recent years, is a reminder that the nation-building process has never really been completed. It is a predicament whose roots, I believe, are in large part buried in nineteenth-century Italian history.

NOTES

1. G. De Ruggiero, *The History of European Liberalism* (Oxford: Oxford University Press, 1927); A. Asor Rosa, "La cultura," in *Storia d'Italia*. Vol. 4, Part 2: Dall'Unità a oggi (Turin: Einaudi, 1975); E. Ragionieri, "La storia politica e sociale," in *Storia d'Italia*. Vol. 4, Part 3: Dall'Unità a oggi (Turin: Einaudi, 1976); R. Romanelli, *L'Italia liberale (1861–1900)* (Bologna: Il Mulino, 1990); M. Fioravanti, "Costituzione, amministrazione e trasformazione dello Stato," in *Cultura giuridica in Italia dall'Unità alla Repubblica*, ed. A. Schiavone (Rome-Bari: Laterza, 1990); A. M. Banti, "Retoriche e idiomi: L'antiparlamentarismo nell'Italia di fine Ottocento," Storica 3 (1995).

2. G. Candeloro, *Il movimento cattolico in Italia* (Rome: Editori Riuniti, 1953); A. C. Jemolo, *Chiesa e stato in Italia dalla unificazione ai giorni nostri* (Turin: Einaudi, 1955); G. De Rosa, *Il movimento cattolico in Italia: Dalla restaurazione all'età giolittiana* (Bari: Laterza, 1970); M. G. Rossi, "Il movimento cattolico tra Chiesa e Stato," in *Storia d'Italia. Vol. 3: Liberalismo e democrazia*, 1887–1914, ed. G. Sabbatucci and V. Vidotto (Rome-Bari: Laterza, 1995).

3. F. Della Peruta, *I democratici e la rivoluzione italiana: Dibattiti e contrasti politici all'indomani del 1848* (Milan: Feltrinelli, 1958); F. Della Peruta, *Mazzini e i rivoluzionari italiani: Il "partito d'azione."* 1830–1845 (Milan: Feltrinelli, 1974); C. Lovett, *The Democratic Movement in Italy* 1830–1876 (Cambridge, Mass.: Harvard University Press, 1982).

4. R. Vivarelli, *Storia delle origini del fascismo. Vol. 2: L'Italia dalla grande guerra alla marcia su Roma* (Bologna: Il Mulino, 1991), 211–428.

5. The term "political rights" refers to the possibility of participating in the production of laws (legislative function) or in the execution of laws (executive function). For the theoretical and historical distinction between civil, political, and social citizenship, see T. H. Marshall, *Citizenship and Social Class* (Cambridge: Cambridge University Press, 1950).

6. "Élites e associazioni nell'Italia dell'Ottocento," *Quaderni storici* 77 (1991); M. Meriggi, *Milano borghese: Circoli ed élites nell'Ottocento* (Venice: Marsilio, 1992).

7. D. L. Caglioti, *Associazionismo e sociabilità d'élite a Napoli nel XIX secolo* (Naples: Liguori, 1996); and "Circoli, società e accademie nella Napoli postunitaria," *Meridiana: Rivista di storia e scienze sociali* 22–23 (1995).

8. A. Cardoza, "Tra casta e classe: Clubs maschili dell'élite torinese, 1840–1914," *Quaderni storici* 77 (1991); Meriggi, *Milano borghese*; A. M. Banti, *Terra e denaro: Una borghesia padana dell'Ottocento* (Venice: Marsilio, 1989); R. Romanelli, "Il casino, l'accademia e il circolo: Forme e tendenze dell'associazionismo d'élite nella Firenze dell'Ottocento," in *Fra storia e storiografia: Scritti in onore di Pasquale Villani*, ed. P. Macry and A. Massafra (Bologna: Il Mulino, 1994); and Caglioti, *Associazionismo e sociabilità d'élite a Napoli.*

9. Already in the 1840s, however, club halls like the Associazione Agraria Subalpina of Turin had become theaters of open and heated quasi-political debate. R. Romeo, *Vita di Cavour* (Rome-Bari: Laterza, 1984), 102–9; A. L. Cardoza, "L'Associazione Agraria Subalpina ed i rapporti tra nobiltà e borghesia nel Piemonte preunitario," in *Fra studio, politica ed economia: La Società Agraria dalle origini all'età giolittiana*, ed. R. Finzi (Bologna: Istituto per la Storia di Bologna, 1992). The Kingdom of Sardinia included Piedmont, Liguria, Sardinia, and Savoy; after 1849 the king was Vittorio Emanuele II of the royal family of Savoy.

10. D. Mack Smith, *Cavour and Garibaldi, 1860: A Study in Political Conflict* (Cambridge: Cambridge University Press, 1985); G. Candeloro, *Storia dell'Italia moderna. Vol. 4: Dalla rivoluzione nazionale all'Unità*, 1849–1860 (Milan: Feltrinelli, 1964).

11. Romanelli, *L'Italia liberale*; A. Scirocco, *I democratici italiani da Sapri a Porta Pia* (Naples: Esi, 1969); A. Comba, "Movimento repubblicano," in *Storia d'Italia. Vol. 2: Il mondo contemporaneo*, ed. F. Levi, U. Levra, and N. Tranfaglia (Florence: La Nuova Italia 1978); M. Ridolfi, *Il partito della Repubblica: I repubblicani in Romagna e le origini del PRI nell'Italia liberale (1872–1895)* (Milan: Franco Angeli, 1989); R. Zangheri, *Storia del socialismo italiano. Vol. 1: Dalla rivoluzione francese a Andrea Costa* (Turin: Einaudi, 1993).

12. Candeloro, *Il movimento cattolico in Italia*; Jemolo, *Chiesa e stato in Italia*; De Rosa, *Il movimento cattolico in Italia*; Rossi, "Il movimento cattolico tra Chiesa e Stato."

13. Élites e associazioni"; Caglioti, *Associazionismo e sociabilità d'élite a Napoli*; M. Ridolfi, *Il circolo virtuoso: Sociabilità democratica, associazionismo e rappresentanza politica nell'Ottocento* (Florence: Centro Editoriale Toscano, 1990).

14. After the reform of 1882, the property requirement was dropped. The number of enfranchised voters represented about 2 percent of the total population between 1861 and 1882 and approximately 7–8 percent between 1882 and 1912.

15. F. Cammarano, "La costruzione dello Stato e la classe dirigente," in *Storia d'Italia. Vol. 2: Il nuovo stato e la società civile: 1861–1887*, ed. G. Sabbatucci and V. Vidotto (Rome-Bari: Laterza, 1995).

16. A. M. Banti, *Storia della borghesia italiana: L'età liberale* (Rome: Donzelli, 1996).

17. P. Bevilacqua, ed., *Storia dell'agricoltura italiana*, 3 vols. (Venice: Marsilio, 1989–91).

18. A. Blok, "South Italian Agro-Towns," *Comparative Studies in Society and History* 11 (1969).

19. G. Civile, *Il comune rustico: Storia sociale di un paese del Mezzogiorno* (Bologna: Il Mulino, 1990); P. Pezzino, *Il paradiso abitato da diavoli: Società, élites, istituzioni nel Mezzogiorno contemporaneo* (Milan: Franco Angeli, 1992); L. Riall, *The Italian Risorgimento: State, Society and National Unification* (London: Routledge, 1994).

20. G. Fiume, "Bandits, Violence and the Organization of Power in Sicily in the Early Nineteenth Century," in *Society and Politics in the Age of the Risorgimento*, ed. J. Davis and P. Ginsborg (Cambridge: Cambridge University Press, 1991); D. Gambetta, *La mafia siciliana: Un'industria della protezione privata* (Turin: Einaudi, 1992); P. Pezzino, *Una certa reciprocità di favori: Mafia e modernizzazione violenta nella Sicilia postunitaria* (Milan: Franco Angeli, 1990).

21. There were, for example, confraternities, or confessional organizations, dedicated to various social and ritual tasks (religious celebrations, processions, funerals, etc.), which were widespread throughout Italy.

22. Candeloro, *Il movimento cattolico in Italia*; De Rosa, *Il movimento cattolico in Italia*; Rossi, "Il movimento cattolico tra Chiesa e Stato"; L. Ferrari, "Il laicato cattolico fra Otto e Novecento: Dalle associazioni devozionali alle organizzazioni militanti di massa," *Storia d'Italia: Annali*. Vol. 9: La Chiesa e il potere politico dal Medioevo all'età contemporanea, ed. G. Chittolini and G. Miccoli (Turin: Einaudi, 1987).

23. Ridolfi, *Il partito della Repubblica*; Comba, "Movimento repubblicano."

24. M. Ridolfi, *Il PSI e la nascita del partito di massa: 1892–1922* (Rome: Laterza, 1992).

25. Here I will give only three examples: the bylaws of the PSI at the time it was founded (1892) states in its preamble the party's fundamental aim: "the socialization of means of production," adding that this goal could be reached only through "a greater fight to capture government powers (national government, municipalities, public administrations, etc.) in order to transform them from instruments that today oppress and exploit, into an instrument for the political and economic expropriation of the dominant class." In 1904, the Party Congress approved an agenda declaring that "the method of class struggle does not permit the support of any government policy, nor the participation of the socialists in the government." The 1919 Party Congress approved a proposal that the PSI join the Third International. It was further decided that the party should participate in elections "within the existing bourgeois order to better propagandize on behalf of the communist principles and to aid in the destruction of bourgeois institutions." The proposal went on, "The Congress is convinced that the proletariat must resort to the use of violence to defend against bourgeois violence, to seize power, and to consolidate the conquests of the revolution." F. Pedone, *Novant'anni di pensiero e azione socialista attraverso i congressi del PSI*, vols. 1 and 2 (Palermo: Marsilio, 1983).

26. Looking at these distinctions, Robert Putnam has recently argued that the past and present associative system of northern Italy has been deeply characterized by a sense of civicness, a cultural quality that is almost impossible to find in southern Italy;

moreover, he has claimed that such quality is a prerequisite for a good working of democratic institutions (R. D. Putnam, *Making Democracy Work: Civic Traditions in Modern Italy* [Princeton: Princeton University Press, 1993]). Unfortunately, Putnam's analysis does not help to clarify the relation between northern Italian civicness and various phenomena profoundly rooted in the history of that area, such as fascist action squads, political corruption (pointed out by the so-called Clean Hands judicial inquiry), or the regional separatism of the Lega Nord movement. In my opinion this is a gap that weakens Putnam's general interpretation; on the other hand, my reconstruction reaches results that are very distant from the fundamental idea of Putnam's book, according to which the stronger the associative activism of a society, the broader the diffusion of democratic ideas. For an accurate overview of the historiographic shortcomings in Putnam's book see S. Lupo, "Usi e abusi del passato: Le radici dell'Italia di Putnam," *Meridiana: Rivista di storia e scienze sociali* 18 (1993).

4

LIBERALISM AND CIVIL SOCIETY IN ITALY: FROM HEGEMONY TO MEDIATION

Adrian Lyttelton

When overtly political representation is denied, or limited to channels carefully controlled by government, the construction of "civil society," together with its correlates "public opinion" and "public space," can be seen as the most important task for collective action. The only alternative is revolution, and in early nineteenth-century Italy the failure of revolutionary conspiracies to achieve lasting results helped to give growing prestige to the rival strategy. It was known, in fact, under the revealing title of "conspiracy in the light of day." However, it would miss the point entirely to imagine that the development of civil society was simply a way of conducting politics under another name. It involved both the creation of new associations to meet new social needs (e.g., lay primary education or the diffusion of scientific information) and the exploitation of existing patterns of sociability. The relationship of civil society to the state after the achievement of independence and representative government becomes much more problematic. Associations could be seen both by individualist liberals and by centralizing democrats as irrelevancies or even obstacles to the legitimate expression of interests or the popular will. More important, a political class that relied on elite associations and personal networks proved largely unable or unwilling to co-opt the new universe of popular associations that developed after 1861. This entailed the abandonment of a strategy of hegemony through civil society for the alternatives of repression or mediation. The state administration was a decisive actor in both of the latter strategies; however, in the strategy of mediation the liberal political class continued to control many of the decisive linkages between state and civil society. It would be wrong to believe that the strategy of mediation was, as it has sometimes been depicted, confined to the exercise of the traditional patron–client relationship. It was raised to a higher plane by the Piedmontese statesman Giovanni Giolitti, who saw his task as mediating between the monarchic state and the new, emerging political and social forces. But, as the organizations of civil society acquired greater density, the pressures for a more direct representation of social demands mounted. Intellectual opinion became increasingly sceptical about the ability of the parliamentary class to control social conflicts or to guide the processes of modernization.

LIBERALISM AND CIVIL SOCIETY IN THE RISORGIMENTO

The expansion of liberalism in Italy in the decade before the revolutions of 1848 coincided with a "mania for associations."[1] The "spirit of association," in fact, can be considered as "a metaphor for liberalism," defined as the self-organization of a carefully delimited civil society.[2] This identification was particularly well developed in northern Italian cities such as Milan and Turin. Elite social clubs, founded and directed by nobles, opened their membership to select groups of bourgeois in banking, commerce, and the professions. The bourgeoisie also had their own clubs, in which nobles were a minority. These clubs, in spite of their original character as leisure associations, largely defined the social universe from which the political leaders of moderate liberalism were drawn. For progressive and market-oriented noble landowners, liberalism and the development of free associations were both a way of compensating for the reduction of the collective power of the nobility by bureaucratic centralization and of adaptation to a more individualistic and commercial society. Foreign–French and English–models and examples were all-important in determining expectations.

Jan Kubik's hypothesis that under an authoritarian regime the mobilization of civil society requires the support of "familial, domestic, and kinship networks" is applicable to the situation of nineteenth-century Italy. But it must be remembered that the premises of nineteenth-century monarchies were very different from those of twentieth-century authoritarian or totalitarian regimes. The consensus of traditional social elites was regarded as essential for the stability of the system. The case of Bologna shows how in the period leading up to 1848 even the local representatives of the reactionary papal government tried to avoid a head-on conflict with social elites and were consequently unable to check the growth of liberalism. In spite of the surveillance exercized by the papal authorities, in 1838 the elite club, the Società del Casino, made the future liberal politician Marco Minghetti director of its *gabinetto di lettura* (reading room), which served as a center for the diffusion of political information. The tolerance of the papal authorities was remarkable, since more than half of its members were suspect of involvement in the 1831 revolution in the city. The aristocratic character of the club had been modified by an influx of new members in 1830. Nonetheless, the representative of papal authority, the cardinal legate, resisted pressures from Rome to support the attempt by a group of reactionary nobles to regain control. In 1846–48 the club participated with enthusiasm in the explosion of liberal and national fervor that followed the election of Pius IX as pope, organizing banquets for the Civic Guard and opening a room for military and gymnastic training. The club was closed by the commander of the Austrian occupying force in 1850 because it had refused to admit the officers of his garrison.[3]

One important issue that has been too little investigated is that of the relationship between formal and informal associations, whether elite or popular. At the elite level, the *salon,* almost always headed by an aristocratic lady, brought together the more intelligent nobles, bourgeois opinion-leaders, and intellectuals. Businessmen, however, seem to have participated more rarely. The *salon* allowed women a leading role, which was challenged by the masculine world of clubs and associations. In Milan during the Risorgimento the salon of the Countess Maffei acquired particular fame as a center for liberal opinion. Writer Carlo Tenca and Giuseppe Verdi were among its habitués. Opinions could be expressed with greater freedom in a private setting than in the context of a formal association. It was harder for bourgeois women than for bourgeois men to challenge noble leadership. They lacked not only social prestige but traditions of independence.[4]

More directly, civic associations involved a wider membership and allowed greater scope for bourgeois leadership, especially by the professional classes. Societies for the encouragement of science or arts and crafts, Economic Societies, Agrarian Societies, Societies for Popular Education: these were the arenas in which civil society showed itself capable of self-organization and which laid the foundations for the creation of a "national opinion." Some of these associations had a close tie with particular journals. In considering civil society in this period—and indeed until approximately 1890—it would be artificial to separate associations from journals or newspapers, especially since the offices of the latter were often centers for discussion.

The same kind of people who staffed the associations—a mix of progressive aristocrats, administrators, and experts—attended the National Scientific Congresses (associations took part directly, as such, in the congresses). The fact that, after initial hostility, both the Austrian government of the Lombardo-Veneto and the Bourbon Kingdom of the Two Sicilies gave permission for congresses to be held on their territory was in itself a proof of the new contractual power of civil society vis-à-vis the absolutist state. The stricter censorship imposed by the Bourbon Kingdom, together with control over the book trade, imposed barriers to the circulation of ideas between northern and southern Italy, but in spite of this links between the southern intelligentsia and northern liberals multiplied.

Agrarian and Economic Societies had a particular importance. Since industrialization was restricted to a very few areas, only associations that represented landed property and pursued agricultural improvement could claim to stand for the general interests of society. An elite of modernizing proprietors with an interest in commercial agriculture and the removal of obstacles to free trade formed the core group of Risorgimento liberalism: Camillo Cavour in Piedmont, Bettino Ricasoli in Tuscany, and Minghetti in Bologna were all improving landlords. In Piedmont, the Agrarian Association became a forum for political discussion in the years preceding the formal grant of the constitution in 1848. Aristocratic leadership was contested by democrats from the professional classes. Elsewhere, the absolutist monarchies were successful in preventing politicization and in confining the societies to local and technical functions. Even so, they favored the aggregation of the leaders of civil society in the provinces and allowed the "improvers" to play a hegemonic role. Economic improvement societies often owed their origin to the action of the state, as in Milan under the Habsburgs in the late eighteenth century and in Naples both under the brief reign of Joachim Murat (1808–15) and later under the Bourbons. If one considers also education and the expansion of the professions, one must recognize that the search by reforming governments to open up channels of communication with society alternative to those of the old society of orders and to train competent administrators laid the foundations, somewhat ironically, for later liberal achievement. How far the institutions of civil society achieved a real autonomy from the state is an open question that requires more detailed case-by-case investigation. The large landowners of Lombardy and Tuscany had economic and cultural resources that allowed them to claim more autonomy than their counterparts in Naples, who were more dependent on both financial assistance and expert advice. However, even in the south, self-financing became increasingly important. The economic associations of Naples succeeded in mobilizing a broad constituency of middling proprietors and professional men.[5] This reflected the unstable situation produced by the end of feudalism, in which the hegemony of the old aristocracy had been shaken. As in the north, the economic associations were responsible for creating a new independent public sphere in which opinion could be formed. The strict control over the University of Naples exercised by the Bourbon monarchy was successfully circumvented by the proliferation of private universities; the best of these were loosely structured associations of friends and pupils grouped around a leading intellectual.

Why did this nascent civil society in the south fail to survive 1848? Its social, economic, and cultural underpinnings were undoubtedly weaker than those in the north. Massive illiteracy was an obstacle to the downward diffusion of liberal or democratic ideas. The low legitimacy enjoyed by private landed property in the aftermath of feudalism, with the concomitant ferocity of struggles over the ownership and occupation of *public* property (demesne and Church lands), prevented the emergence of a secure form of proprietorial hegemony. The fear of peasant rebellion and brigandage undermined the confidence of the "civil estate" (*ceto civile*); this insecurity favored both radicalism and reaction. The importance of public resources in a situation of general scarcity also fueled local factional conflict among the notables, both before and after unification. The isolation of communities, as well as their internal conflicts, made it difficult for elites to exercise a unifying function even at the provincial level.[6] However, a recent interpretation has argued that the defeat of the liberal movement in 1848 was critical in destroying the confidence of civil society's representatives.[7] The divisions between moderate liberals and democrats, and between representatives of Naples and the provinces, were particularly damaging, and the Bourbons, as an indigenous monarchy, were better placed than the foreign Habsburgs to exploit these divisions. It was this political situation that blocked "the legal way to democratization."[8] Fear of peasant agitation and "anarchy" led the new landowning classes to dissociate themselves from the democrats and finally to accept the restoration of Bourbon absolutism as the lesser evil, while the leaders of moderate liberalism turned to the Piedmontese monarchy as the only force capable of preventing the dissolution of society. They were to be among the strongest advocates of centralization in 1860–61. Repression was more severe and more long-lasting than in northern Italy; the Bourbons were not restrained by fear of European opinion, as the Habsburgs to some degree were. So the weakness of southern civil society in 1860 was not uniquely the result of backwardness and still less of an incapacity to form associations.

Throughout Italy, the ultimate failure of the 1848 revolutions proved that the project of organizing a "public sphere" of national dimensions was premature. The various centers of revolution proved incapable of formulating a common project or strategy. Municipal rivalries—between Venice and the mainland cities of the Veneto, between Genoa and Piedmont, Livorno and Florence, Palermo and Naples—had a paralyzing effect. Milan, probably the city where civil society was most highly developed, proved incapable of developing an autonomous political initiative, in spite of the heroic insurgency of the Five Days, which succeeded in expelling the Austrian army from the city. Even the improvised leaders of the revolution, middle-class democrats like Carlo Cattaneo and Enrico Cernuschi, were not prepared to challenge the traditional dominance of Milan's patrician families, and as a result their protests against Piedmontese annexation were ineffective. In the aftermath of 1848, repression became more severe in the old states, and the space for civil society was correspondingly restricted. But the continuity of the development of civil society was preserved in Piedmont, which kept its liberal constitution. Exiles from other states played an important role in Piedmontese political and social life.

The "heroic age" of civil society—in Risorgimento Italy as well as contemporary Europe—coincides with the struggle for effective representation. "Civil society" and "opinion" are not just realities, but normative ideals to be realized. Afterwards, the very success in winning freedom allows the more aggressive affirmation of particular interests and thereby leads to disillusionment about the decline of civic idealism. Many leaders of "civil society" were co-opted by the political system and even the administration, and their talents were not always replaceable. These "post-Risorgimento phenomena" have parallels in many other situations in which a national movement claiming to represent civil society takes power.

ASSOCIATIONS IN THE LIBERAL STATE

State and Society in Liberal Italy

The hypothesis that the development of a liberal form of democracy (as opposed to Jacobin, populist, or plebiscitarian variants) depends on the vitality of civil society may be described as Tocquevillian. But in looking at the problem of liberalism from a Tocquevillian perspective, it must be remembered that Alexis de Tocqueville himself was not optimistic about the role of associations in the continental Europe of his day. Where the organization of parties and formal equality of social conditions preceded or accompanied rather than followed the exercise of political liberty, as he held to be the case in France, the chances that rival political associations would accept the kind of self-limitation that was necessary if liberty were to be preserved appeared slight. From the point of view of the Tocquevillian model, Italy had additional unfavorable features. In the great debate on the freedom of association that took place in 1878–79, the prime minister of the day, Agostino Depretis, contrasted American and Italian conditions in Tocquevillian terms in order to justify preventive action against subversion and the dissolution of republican associations.[9]

The "passive revolutions" of the years 1796–99, in which French bayonets installed short-lived republican governments, and the later domination of Napoleon had imposed legal equality from above, in conjunction with a harsh military occupation that alienated popular sentiment from the governing elites. The destruction of the "society of orders" was not initially achieved by a strong indigenous movement, but had to rely almost exclusively on the force of the state administration. This favored the persistence of an absolutist model of the relationship between the citizen and the administration.

For most democrats the goal of national unification in practice if not in theory conflicted with the goal of democratizing state structures. Most members of the "historic Left" conceived of the centralized state as a necessary corrective to the local dominance of old social elites and the threat of "municipalism," or the primacy of communal and regional–state loyalties. The result was that the Napoleonic prefectoral system, with its powerful capacity for the interdiction of local initiatives, remained intact.

The uncompromising denial of the legitimacy of the new nation-state by the papacy made it difficult and dangerous for either liberals or democrats to put their trust in the spontaneous forces of civil society. In a negative sense, the difficulty of relying on religion as a force for social control weakened the confidence of liberal governing elites and encouraged a "siege mentality."

The discovery of the south by northern politicians and administrators was traumatic. Marco Minghetti expressed with clarity (and relative moderation) the common conviction of the moderate liberals of Cavour's governing party, the "historic Right," that southern civil society lacked autonomy or stability and must be "sometimes stimulated, sometimes restrained, and always accompanied" by the action of the state. And Minghetti was the most "Tocquevillian" of all the leaders of the Right in his insistence that the state could not substitute for civil society.[10]

The problem of the south and the problem of the Church indicated a similar conclusion. In many parts of Italy, the conditions for the growth of a true civil society did not exist and had to be created by deliberate state action. Legality, freedom of opinion, and the impulse toward association were hothouse plants. Kinship and devotion were still the primary instruments of social aggregation.[11] The great literary historian and Italy's first minister of education, Francesco de Sanctis, a native of the Mezzogiorno, took a much more forthright statist view than Minghetti. The state was "the undivided force of Italian intelligence," with "the mission to give the impulse to all the lower social strata, to organize them, to accelerate the movement of society."[12] In welfare and in education, the concern to check and control Church influence helped to ensure the victory of a bureaucratic model that did not leave much scope for autonomous social initiative. But local political management was certainly not the answer. The depredation of the Opere Pie (charities) by rapacious communal administrators, particularly in the south, was one of the major scandals of the period 1860–90.

This situation gave rise to what the historian Raffaele Romanelli has called the dilemma of the "impossible command."[13] It was a new version of the dilemma of forcing men to be free. The liberal state had to intervene to create the conditions for the exercise of freedom, and yet by so doing it restricted the sphere of autonomy of civil society, which the governing class, as liberals, were bound to protect. Hence the hesitations and absence of coherence in the liberal Right's project of "revolution from above." If the absence of civic development justified the intervention of the state as a surrogate at the time of unification, it may be suggested that with time the relationship changed. The thesis that civil society was corrupt and in need of guidance from above could become self-confirming: associations that arose outside the orbit of the state might be treated as automatically suspect.

In fact, the freedom of association was poorly protected. As so often happens, emergency measures crystallized into permanent institutional practice. The almost unlimited discretionary power of the prefects to act in defense of public order was the critical point, together with the lack of autonomy of the judiciary from the executive. The control of public prosecutors by the Ministry of Justice had a direct impact on the freedom of associations, particularly of the working class and peasants.

Nevertheless, associative life flourished in spite of the restrictions imposed by the state. How was this possible? In general terms, I believe that Giovanna Zincone's concept of a *weak* state-centered model of development provides a useful framework.[14] Zincone makes two points that are worth emphasizing here. First, the state had an urgent need to expand the base of its support, but its limited fiscal resources imposed severe limits on its ability to do so. Hence the adoption of a strategy of the discretional grant of favors, mediated by the political class. Second, Italian liberalism passed from a "society-centered" model to a "state-centered" model as a result of the stresses of unification and the difficulty of controlling the south. But this "induced statism" was at first weak in its cultural foundations as well as its material and institutional resources.[15] If the freedom of action of the administrative state acknowledged few limits de jure, the parliamentary regime made possible the successful negotiation de facto of areas of liberty in which associations could function freely. While there was no effective legal recourse against the dissolution of associations by the prefects, or the prohibition of meeings by the police, the authorities were anxious not to alienate the support of parliamentary deputies, who could and did protest on behalf of their constituents.[16] The attempts at decisive repression carried out in the 1890s entailed the attempt to bypass or reduce parliamentary power, and, for that reason, they divided the political class. Moreover, the lesson of Germany suggested the ineffectiveness of a repressive policy toward socialism. Catholic associations, in spite of their hostility to the state, were generally law-abiding, and the government of Antonio Di Rudini's action against them in 1898 alienated many of his own supporters in the liberal Right, who were often allies of the Catholics in local politics. So the attempt to close off the access of new, mass-based associations to public space was in the main unsuccessful, although it must be emphasized that it had been decisive in consolidating their distrust of the state. But the limits of public space were *negotiated* rather than unequivocally protected by law. In the long term, this situation posed a very serious and indeed fatal problem for the liberal state.

Democratization and the Development of Popular Associations (1860–1900)

After unification, in northern and central Italy the old associations or clubs of the aristocracy and the bourgeoisie validated their role as instruments for the selection and formation of a new civic elite. They served as the meeting-place for the governing elite of the city, in which politicians, municipal administrators, and leading businessmen could discuss their common affairs. In Milan in 1890, 40 percent of the *consiglieri comunali* belonged to one of the three most important social *circoli*.[17] Down to 1882, the highly restricted suffrage made for a cosy relationship between urban social elites and the political sphere. But in the meantime, the "spirit of association" was spreading rapidly among the middle and the working classes. In Milan by 1881 there were about one hundred workers' associations with twelve thousand members; seven thousand were grouped in one confederation, under radical democratic leadership. The smoothness of the "fit" between the old civic associations and the structures of economic and political power may have contributed to the sense of shock with which the civic elites reacted to the rise of popular associations and their entry into the political sphere. The occupation of public space—the piazza—by these new groups intensified alarm.

Initially the moderate liberals had been concerned to promote and control some forms of popular association. In the first years after unification, they helped to promote a very rapid growth in the formation of mutual aid societies among workers. They saw the mutual aid societies as a way of rendering workers capable of becoming self-sufficient citizens and exercising free rational choice (even if this was supposed to imply a recognition of the need for deference to their employers). The moral function of the associations in promoting thrift and cooperation was emphasized. The moderates were particularly successful in Piedmont, where there was considerable continuity between the workers' societies and the older traditions of corporations and religious confraternities and where there was a fund of popular loyalty to the monarchy to draw upon. But in other regions they were not successful in maintaining control. Their attempt to limit the activity of the workers' societies to strictly economic questions and to exclude politics was successfully challenged by the Republicans. Robert Putnam, concerned to emphasize the importance of a generalized civic sociability, underrates the strong political inspiration behind much of the surge in popular associations during the period from 1876 to 1894.[18]

The Artisan Brotherhoods, inspired by Mazzini, were the first broadly diffused form of popular association with a clear political program. In the small towns of the Romagna, Tuscany, and some other parts of central Italy popular republicanism could draw on memories of the short-lived democratic regimes of 1849, when political circles and clubs and civic banquets had flourished briefly. Nor should one ignore popular participation in the patriotic mobilization of 1859–60. This was more ambiguous politically. Artisans in the industrial center of Prato joined processions led by *capi-maestri* (master artisans) or industrialists celebrating the virtues of patriotic concord. This was at a time when King Victor Emanuel had succeeded in co-opting the immense popularity of Giuseppe Garibaldi. Prato had five thousand subscribers to the Million Rifles Fund, designed to provide arms for Garibaldi.[19] Bergamo, the center of an important "proto-industrial" district, provided the largest number of volunteers for Garibaldi's expedition to Sicily. But after 1861 the Garibaldian tradition, organized in veterans' societies, was once again linked to the democratic opposition. In the 1870s mutual aid societies and republican *fratellanze* became widely diffused in rural areas, although their social base may have been among artisans rather than peasants. Democratic popular associations in general advanced rapidly during the years 1876–80, in the more favorable climate created by the electoral victory of the Left. They played an important role in the agitation for suffrage reform. Altogether, we can see the period 1876–82 as a critical turning point. In spite of the expansion of suffrage, the tendencies toward a broader democratization of politics were checked, and after that date the divergence between civil society and the political realm tended to increase. Why?

First, in 1882, the moderate Left allied with the moderate Right to form the government majority, thus inaugurating the system known as *trasformismo*. Rather than encouraging democratic associations to participate in broader political coalitions, *trasformismo* pushed them to the margins of politics. The Left's access to central state power encouraged the integration of local political elites through clientelism.

Second, ideological differences between republicans and socialists weakened the democratic coalition. Among the republicans, abstention from electoral politics was still a powerful tendency that helped to prevent the formation of an organized party until the 1890s.

In addition, the advance of industry and a more widespread tendency toward greater class differentiation weakened the basis for a broad, popular, democratic consensus. From about 1880 to 1892 many workers' societies expanded their aims from mutual aid to "resistance," or class conflict. In Milan and Genoa, the suffrage reform initially gave a boost to republican organizations. But by the end of the decade disillusionment had set in, and workers turned in increasing numbers to trade unions, whose inspiration was generically socialist. In Genoa, the republican organizations had included independent artisans, shopkeepers, and even professionals: the new trend was to insist on a narrower definition of the working class. In and around Milan, a growing influence was exercised by the Partito Operaio (1882), which insisted on the primacy of economic over political action and actively promoted the formation of trade unions among rural as well as urban workers. The foundation of the Socialist Party (1892–93) marked a partial turn back toward "politics"; however, in contrast to the Republican and Radical Parties, the majority of constituent associations were trade unions and workers' societies, not political associations. Subsequently, the Socialist Party adopted a system of individual membership, and trade unions and cooperatives became formally independent of the party.

Concentration on areas of industrialization or high class conflict may distort the overall picture. Mutual aid societies remained the most widely diffused form of popular organization at the turn of the century, with 936,000 members, compared to about 500,000 members of cooperatives, and about 250,000 in socialist-inspired trade unions, while the Socialist Party never exceeded 50,000 members before World War I. In 1862, the south had only twenty-eight out of a total of 443 mutual aid societies in the nation. But their diffusion in the Mezzogiorno was rapid during the next twenty years, particularly between 1873 and 1885: in the latter year they had a membership of 194,000. This rapid rate of growth, however, was not maintained; in the next twenty years numbers declined to 117,000. The impact of the agrarian crisis and of the decline of many traditional handicrafts probably weakened the social base of the societies. In some regions, their decline was clearly linked to the onset of mass emigration. The previous period of growth, however, is important in demonstrating the "diffusion effect" whereby models of organization spread from the more advanced regions. The professional classes, particularly lawyers and doctors, were often pioneers in the diffusion of information and techniques of organization. It is true, however, that both workers' societies and cooperatives tended to play a different role in the south. Whereas in the north they formed part of an integrated "horizontal" structure of popular associations, in the south they were typically absorbed into the clientele networks of deputies. Political activity absorbed a large part of their meager funds. In the Sicilian city of Syracuse, for example, working-class and artisan associations, veterans' associations, rifle and sporting clubs, and the local branch of the Dante Alighieri association for the promotion of the Italian language and culture were all drawn into the patronage networks formed by rival factions of notables drawn from the professional classes. Personal rather than party ties linked these notables to national political leaders and directly to the state administration.[20] But it should be emphasized that the growth of associations meant that the clientele system did not in fact remain static; it underwent a kind of democratic deepening, in which patrons and mediators had to devote some attention to collective interests, instead of merely individual notables or *grandi elettori*. This has been one of the secrets of its longevity.

From the point of view of liberals in northern and central Italy, however, the attempt to secure hegemony over the urban working classes through their associations could be seen to be a failure by the 1890s. A second attempt to expand their popular base had peasant proprietors and tenants as its main target. Luigi Luzzatti and Leone Wollemborg, liberals from the Veneto, where the tradition of paternalism was particularly strong, promoted the movement to organize cooperative savings banks to provide credit to peasant farmers and artisans.

But the political benefit was reaped by the Catholics, who appropriated the idea and carried it out far more successfully. When it came to organizing peasants, the active involvement of the clergy was an asset that could not be matched. The vigilant eye of the priest rather than the puritan conscience guaranteed thrift, and the liberal ideal of the responsible, independent small proprietor was realized under the Catholic aegis. After World War I, the areas where the rate of formation of new peasant property was highest were those in which the network of Catholic credit institutions and cooperatives was particularly strong.

The Church could invest its dependent lay associations with the symbolic resources of traditional devotion, even when these associations performed new, secular functions. However, there were limits within which this identification could operate. After much hesitation, the Church ended by sanctioning the formation of Christian trade unions, but their activities had to be reconciled with the goals of social harmony and the union of the Christian community. The Church's patronage of unions and, later, of party political associations, was exercized at arm's length, so to speak; it was conditional and revocable. The dependence of Catholic lay associations on the symbolic resources of the Church therefore limited their autonomy and freedom of action.

It must be remembered that the relationship between Church and state in Italy was unique. The Church officially prohibited Catholics from taking part in national elections. But they were free to organize in local politics and did so to considerable effect, forming "clerico-moderate" alliances with conservative liberals. These were countered by democratic blocs including radicals, and sometimes even republicans and socialists. Mass participation, in consequence, was more extensive and presented more clearly structured alternatives at the municipal than at the national level.

Another weakness of the Catholic movement was its isolation from the most influential channels of elite communication, through the press and the universities. Locally, the Catholics were very successful in building up their own popular press and in utilizing other methods of communication, such as parish theaters, but their relative scarcity of access to the national media condemned them to cultural and political provincialism.

An important result of this asymmetry between local and national politics is that it confirmed the tendency to criticize parliament as poorly representative of civil society. For socialists too there was a disparity between the local and the national dimension, though this affected *government* not representation. While participation in national government was still officially ruled out, local power could be exercised without offense to orthodoxy. The greatest achievements of the moderate reformists of the Socialist Party were in "municipal socialism." So here too the idea that the commune had organic links with civil society, while the national parliament and state did not, was a natural conclusion.

More serious still than the liberal failure to develop a popular associative base was their reaction to this failure. During the 1890s the majority of the administration and the political class repudiated the "spirit of association" and, with it, the substance of liberalism itself. The illiberal potential of the restrictions on free association in the name of public order was freely exploited. The former Garibaldian democrat Francesco Crispi and the aristocratic leader of the Right, Di Rudini, showed little difference in this respect.

THE EXPANSION OF CIVIL SOCIETY
AND THE CRISIS OF LIBERALISM (1900–1914)

Giolitti's Project and Civil Society

The "civil society" perspective is very useful in assessing the revived liberalism of Giolitti after 1901. Substantially, Giolitti and the democratic wing of the liberals drew the conclusion from the failures of the previous decade that the defense of the liberal state would be a self-contradictory aim without a new opening to civil society. The true mission of liberalism was to provide the institutional framework for a gradual and orderly transition to democracy. Any other policy would alienate both the "most numerous classes" and "men of culture," the decisive forces in a modern society. "The Italian monarchy must find its basis not in the interests of narrow privileged classes, but in the affection of the immense majority of the nation." Economic and social progress would eventually create the conditions for an expansion of formal political participation.[21] The economic expansion of the period favored this approach by strengthening the contractual power and financial viability of trade unions and other associations, although in these respects Italy still lagged behind the most advanced European states. The development of a national market and the commercialization of agriculture were intrinsically favorable to the development of civil society.

Giolitti's wager was that the inherently democratic development of civil society would overcome the antidemocratic tendencies present in the ideology of both socialists and Catholics. Both revolutionary extremism and the intransigent defense of traditional values would be eroded through democratic participation. The growth of socialist and Catholic associations should therefore not be repressed but actively encouraged. Giolitti said that he feared "inorganic," disorganized movements (anarchism, southern rural protest) far more than "organic" ones. Through participation in civil society, workers and peasants would learn that they had a stake in liberal democracy and that the state could be a friend as well as an enemy.

What were the weaknesses of this progressive policy, and why did it eventually break down?

First, Giolitti's style of government has been described variously as a "parliamentary dictatorship" and as a "bureaucratic project." These descriptions are contradictory and incomplete. But they do point to a deficiency. Giolitti's strategy could not secure the hegemony of liberalism as a political force. It did not restore liberal self-confidence and esteem. Rather than becoming an active agent in the process of democratization, the liberal political elite seemed to be reduced to the function of mediating between extraneous and potentially destructive forces. Giolitti's project threatened to become a liberalism without liberals. The rise of socialism and the erosion of rural deference led to a slow but continuous decline in liberal representation in northern Italy. The deficiency in modern methods of party organization was an obstacle to the mobilization even of those professional and middle classes on whom the liberals could still count. Electorally, the liberals became increasingly dependent on the south, where clientelistic politics and heavy government interference with elections gave them very dubious legitimacy. The failure to found a true national Liberal Party was part consequence and part cause of this situation.

Second, Giolitti's policy entailed concessions to antiliberal forces. The ideal of free enterprise could not be upheld with intransigence without the risk of provoking a new cycle of rebellion and repression. This points to a dilemma at the heart of liberalism (not only in Italy), the contradiction between economic individualism and political associationism. This was not formally contradictory insofar as associations were supposed to be formed by free individual choice. But a number of awkward problems arose as associations broadened their scope and membership. What rights did they have to compel their members to obey the rules and meet their obligations? Did the state, on the contrary, have the duty to protect individuals against the economic and social coercion exercised by trade unions? Should the state formally recognize the existence of voluntary associations? Can they formally participate in political and economic decision making, and, if so, how? The assumption that, given their freedom, working-class associations would cooperate in maintaining law and order proved only very partially true. If anarchist terrorism declined, revolutionary syndicalism posed a new kind of threat. Public order remained a highly contentious issue, and the proclaimed "neutrality of the state" in labor disputes was hard to define in practice. In these circumstances, Giolitti's wager on the positive results of democratic participation failed to convince many liberals. In the view of his opponents, Giolitti's policy of conciliation and accommodation only had the effect of weakening respect for the law and the state, and thereby imperiled the very existence of the liberal bourgeoisie.

Third, Within the Left, on the other hand, overtures to the Catholic movement aroused intense suspicion, although it would be difficult to prove that Giolitti seriously compromised the ideals of the lay state. The papal ban on participation in national politics was relaxed, though not revoked, from 1904 on, and this produced an increasing polarization between proclericals and anticlericals, which weakened the liberal center.

Bourgeois Interest Groups

Here the most menacing development was the adoption by modernizing groups in both agriculture and industry of the nationalist version of syndicalist rhetoric. What nationalists and syndicalists had in common was antipathy to parliamentary government and the mediation of social conflict by politicians. The most modern wing of the agrarians, the active entrepreneurs of the Po Valley, rejected both parliamentary and government mediation and put their trust in a form of employers' syndicalism. The industrialists were less aggressive. But fundamentally the message that came from the most modern sectors—especially the engineering industries of Turin—was the same. The industrialists must trust their own strength and organize outside parliament. There was an explicit rejection of parliamentary mediation. Not only was it too favorable to labor (out of weakness, rather than conviction), it was also based on a backward preindustrial culture. While agreed in their diagnosis that the intervention of the bureaucracy and the political class disturbed the natural balance of social forces, industrialists and agrarians each believed the other to enjoy illegitimate influence. For the industrialists, the composition of the political class failed to register economic modernization and the growth of industry; for the agrarians, business lobbies, working in secret, had a disproportionate influence on government.

One should not exaggerate the extent to which the syndicalist option was dominant or irreversible in prewar Italy. In reality, both among agrarians and industrialists, the voices favoring compromise, conciliation, and parliamentary channels were not silenced. The movement of the agricultural consortia (Federconsorzi) interested in economic modernization rather than labor relations was not hostile to the Giolittian approach: one of its founders, Giovanni Ranieri, became minister of agriculture. But the idea that economic modernization was incompatible with liberal individualism, or democratic vote-counting, had gained an influential audience. Rather than memories, these groups exploited a vision of the future that contradicted the democratic-evolutionary model. Not only the growth of class conflict in the years 1912–14 but the menacing international situation contributed to the discredit of the model, even before the actual outbreak of war. In spite of severe problems of coordination, the success of industry and agriculture in creating national summit organizations (National Agrarian Confederation, 1909; Confederation of Industry, 1910) contrasted with the political fragmentation of the liberal groups in parliament.

The Organizations of the Middle Classes

The impression that the middle classes were "disorganized" needs to be revised or at least more carefully defined. In reality, there existed a broad spectrum of professional orders, voluntary professional associations, and cultural and patriotic groups. The representation of white-collar workers in the public sector by trade unions and cooperatives was proportionately greater than that of many working-class groups. Teachers, state employees, and shopkeepers were organized and vocal. In general, the self-consciousness of these civic groups was still orientated in a progressive direction. But no party expressed their demands. Local orientations and regional diversity were still a serious obstacle. Giolitti's strategy of mediation depended on flexibility and was incompatible with the existence of a strong Liberal Party structure. Only his conservative opponents pressed for the creation of an organized party, and without success. The Radical Party tried to take on the role of the defender of the middle classes and petty bourgeoisie, but it failed to maintain a clear image or devise a consistent strategy.

Perhaps, as Gramsci suggested, the nearest to a unitary organization that the middle classes possessed was Freemasonry. During the Giolittian period the Freemasons expanded their social and political base under the skillful leadership of Ernesto Nathan, the only anticlerical to succeed in becoming mayor of Rome. Freemasons were undoubtedly active in promoting democratic and lay associations. But Freemasonry itself, with its secrecy and ritual, cannot be held to meet the requirements for a constituent element of civil society. Indeed, the persistence of the secret society model was unfavorable to political transparency and increased the importance of cross-cutting linkages between notables of different parties and members of the public administration.[22]

In any case, the Catholic/anticlerical cleavage ran through the middle classes and divided them. So did the issue of socialism. In general, the associations of the public sector were sympathetic to reformist socialism, while those of small enterprise were strongly opposed. The middle classes identified more strongly with the state than other groups, but patriotism rather than democracy was the unifying ideological force. Patriotic associations (e.g., the Dante Alighieri society, which officially existed to promote the Italian language, and unofficially supported irredentism in the Italian borderlands) were able to create a consensus that united different political tendencies. The result was a growing ambiguity between democratic and nationalist or imperialist aims. The conflict between "interventionists" and "neutralists" in 1914–15 demonstrated that the "patriots" were a minority in the nation, but that, nonetheless, if they mobilized effectively they could win. This double realization was the premise for a rejection of majority rule in the superior interests of the nation, while the scattered archipelago of middle-class associations lacked any firm political or ideological grounding to protect them against antidemocratic appeals. In the postwar period, both their material and strategic resources came to seem inadequate in the face of mass politics. Only symbolic resources (the nation, the flag, victory, the completion of the Risorgimento) could be invoked to redress the balance.

The Industrial Working Class, Agricultural Laborers, and Peasants

Italian workers were distinguished by high militancy and low permanent membership in trade unions. Generally low wages, by European standards, made for difficulty in maintaining continuous organization. This was particularly true of women workers, predominant in the textile industries. In the great strike wave of 1901 only 4 percent of strikes in the textile industries were led by unions. There was a temptation to use violence and the disruption of public order as substitutes for inadequate material resources. When moderate trade unionists accused the extremists of adopting suicidal tactics of confrontation, the latter could reply that without the threat of violence and disorder, the moderates would have a hard time extracting concessions from employers. The failures of conventional trade-union action encouraged the alternative of revolutionary syndicalism.

The most successful forms of working-class organization, the Camere del Lavoro, were structured by territory, not occupation. This territory or community-based model of organization appeared to bourgeois opinion as a menacing "counter-power" threatening state institutions. The local general strike and other forms of highly visible mobilization were effective in creating solidarity and in exerting pressure on behalf of lower-paid workers whose contractual position was weak. On the other hand, under reformist leadership socialist municipalities and cooperatives enjoyed good relations with the state. The producers' cooperative movement, indeed, was dependent on the government for cheap credit and preference in public works contracts.

The socialist movement was a major agent of democratic socialization. Party branches; unions; cooperatives; mutual aid societies; educational, cultural, and recreational associations formed a tightly interlocking web. The Casa del Popolo was the symbolic center. But local success accentuated the tendency of working-class associations to form a closed universe, with "the illusion of self-sufficiency."[23] This was especially true in rural areas, where Italian socialism enjoyed its most surprising successes. The great tour de force of Italian socialism was the organization of the agricultural laborers of the Po Valley (and some sharecroppers and tenants) in trade unions (known as *leghe*, leagues) united after 1901 in a single Federation (Federterra). The frequency of agricultural strikes was out of proportion with that of any other west European nation.[24] The cultural gap between town and country was bridged by socialist "evangelists," who deliberately made use of religious language and dialect in their propaganda. The motif of "Jesus the first socialist" was very popular. Socialist egalitarianism was grafted onto traditional community solidarity. As a pathbreaking achievement in the political socialization of the rural population, the agrarian socialism of the Po Valley made a long-term contribution to the democratization of Italian society. But in the short term it posed grave difficulties for the liberal state. Both structural conditions and ideology were more favorable to the creation of a millennialist collectivism than to the development of a pluralist civil society. The difficulties of enforcing discipline and combating the use of blackleg labor in areas of high structural unemployment dictated an ever more ambitious strategy aimed to secure a monopoly control over the labor market and to impose fixed labor quotas on employers. It was much harder to maintain a democratic framework of negotiation than in the industrial field. The Giolittian compromise could only work so long as socialist deputies were willing to negotiate with prefects and liberal representatives to mediate and anticipate conflict. The victory of the intransigents in the Socialist Party in 1912 signified the rejection, in principle, of mediation, although in practice the party did not succeed in imposing discipline on individual parliamentarians until 1919.

Socialist organization of small peasant proprietors and tenants (which had success in some areas, e.g., the province of Alessandria in Piedmont) was at first hampered by doctrinal rigidity. Against the evidence, it was affirmed that small property was destined to disappear, and at the first Congress of Federterra the acceptance of collectivization was made obligatory for all members. After 1906, however, in practice the organization became less intransigent in its outlook, although the option for collectivization was never reversed. Although Tuscany remained a bastion of landlord hegemony, in some areas the socialists succeeded in organizing the traditionally deferential sharecroppers. Instead, the Catholic network of credit institutions and cooperatives was effective in providing support to existing and aspiring peasant proprietors. Class conflict was complicated and exacerbated by political conflict as socialist, Catholic, republican, and landlord-sponsored peasant organizations competed for control over sharecroppers, tenant farmers, and other "intermediate groups" in the countryside. The capacity of socialists to mobilize these groups against the employers in large areas of the Po Valley and the imposing strength of the Federterra obscured the ultimate incongruity of their interests with the socialist program.

CONCLUSION

Parties, interest groups, and professional associations seem to have gained in importance in relation to other forms of civic groups during the period from 1890 to 1914. Single-issue associations (e.g., those for electoral reform, including women's suffrage) were not very active or successful. Civic cultures, whether elite or popular, remained strongly local in orientation. The Socialist Party did succeed in nationalizing politics to a certain extent. Northern workers were willing to engage in general strikes in protest against government violence in the south. But the Chambers of Labor (see above) were a powerful force for provincial autonomy in the labor movement, and they were not subject to direction by the Socialist Party. Robert Putnam's discussion of "civic community" in Italy, since it originates from a comparison of the effectiveness of regional governments, does not really examine the relationship of the civic ideal to the national state.[25] At the beginning of the 1880s, with the movement for the extension of the suffrage, and at the end of the 1890s, when socialists, republicans, radicals, and finally progressive liberals united in protest against the dissolution of popular associations and measures limiting the freedom of the press, a broadly based movement for democratization had made a brief but decisive impact. But class, regional, and ideological divisions (and the international conjuncture) all prevented the emergence of any similar consensus in the decisive years 1910–14, when universal suffrage was introduced.

The preceding leads to four final conclusions:

1. In looking at the impact of civic groups on democratization we need not only to look at their intrinsically "progressive" and democratic or antidemocratic character, but at their ability to form effective alliances. These alliances do not have to be permanent, but they do have to have the capability to influence the outcome of decisive transitions in the progress toward democracy, or crises in which it is put in doubt.

2. Alberto Banti's analysis of the competing political languages employed in liberal Italy is valuable. I would add that more systematic attention should be paid to the languages—political, juridical, economic—used to formulate concepts of society and its relationship to the state. At the time of unification the weakness, or absence, of civil society was seen as the major problem. I have the impression, instead, that the term "civil society" loses its positive connotations and passes out of fashion. The proliferation of associations was not matched by a reinforcement of the *values* of civil society. In the years before the war, the growth of what we call "civil society" (the expansion of the public sphere, means of communication, and associations) was perceived by many liberals as a process of fragmentation. Discourse about the nation and discourse about society therefore tend to diverge: the nation unites; "interests" divide. Theoretical closure combined with practical tolerance means that the growth of civil society can be seen as a threat to the state. In addition, the rhetoric of "science" and "progress," which served as a bridge between the languages of socialism and democracy, was losing its force by the period 1911–14.

3. A consensus on the need to expand social rights will not usually be enough to overcome ideological differences about ultimate objectives, while movements to expand suffrage or defend civil liberties would seem to have greater unifying potential.

4. Local democratization need not favor and may even impede the emergence of effective national democratic structures. The degree to which material (geographical or economic), social, or ideological conditions favor "the illusion of self-sufficiency" (see above) would seem to be crucial.

NOTES

1. M. Meriggi, *Milano borghese: Circoli ed elites nell' Ottocento* (Venice: Marsilio, 1992), 92–94.

2. It should be noted that in the vocabulary of the time the "spirit of association" embraced not only civic but also purely economic associations, for example, joint stock companies.

3. P. Morabito, "Divertimento e elites sociali a Bologna nella prima metà dell'Ottocento: La Società del Casino," *Cheiron* (1988): 182–90.

4. See M. I. Palazzolo, *Salotti di cultura nell'Italia dell'Ottocento* (Milan: Franco Angeli, 1985); one of the few weaknesses of Meriggi's excellent study of Milan (see note 1 above) is his refusal to examine the interpenetration of the "private" world of the *salon* and the "public" world of the association and the role of the former in the selection of the elite.

5. M. Petrusewicz, "Agromania: Inventori agrari nelle periferie europee dell'Ottocento," in *Storia dell'agricoltura italiana in età contemporanea. Vol. 3: Mercati e istituzioni,* ed. P. Bevilacqua (Venice: Marsilio, 1991), 339–40.

6. For an example, see G. Civile, *Il comune rustico* (Bologna: Il Mulino, 1990), 55–74.

7. E. Di Ciommo, *La nazione possibile: Mezzogiorno e questione nazionale nel 1848* (Milan: Franco Angeli, 1993), 209–360.

8. Di Ciommo, *La nazione possibile,* 292.

9. Depretis stated,

Can we take the regulations of the great American republic and transplant them exactly as they are to our country? Over there the political revolution was accompanied by a religious revolution. There the individual does not concern himself with the government and aims to be self-sufficient, and as he cannot do everything himself, he looks for strength in association. . . . Now consider the conditions in our country, where so much is expected from the government, and tell me if it is possible to import here the institutions of the American republic (A. Depretis, *Discorsi parlamentari* [Rome, 1891], 7: 93–94: speech of December 11, 1878).

Depretis's argument in a later speech (April 1879) that administrative action to dissolve associations was justifiable if there was evidence of "*preparation* to commit a crime" (my emphasis), was described by the eminent politician and jurist of the Right, Silvio Spaventa, as "a monstrous, disguised and arbitrary abuse, elevated to the dignity of a law." E. Cheli, "Libertà di associazione e poteri di polizia: Profili storici," in *Atti del Congresso Celebrativo del Centenario delle leggi amministrative di unificazione. Part 4: La tutela del cittadino; Vol. 2: La pubblica sicurezza,* ed. P. Barile (Vicenza: Neri Pozza, 1967), 286.

10. "The functions of benevolence and improvement belong to the family, to voluntary associations and to churches . . . only in their absence can the government assume partial responsibility for them" (U. Allegretti, *Profilo di storia costituzionale italiana: Individualismo e assolutismo nell'Italia liberale* [Bologna: Il Mulino, 1989], 179–80).

11. Gellner's insistence that civil society has to struggle not only against state power but against the undifferentiated loyalties of "cousin-ridden and ritual-ridden" communities is particularly applicable to southern Italy. (E. Gellner, *Conditions of Liberty: Civil Society and Its Rivals* [London: Penguin, 1996], 12.)

12. F. de Sanctis, *Il Mezzogiorno e lo stato unitario,* ed. F. Ferri (Turin: Einaudi, 1960), 209.

13. See R. Romanelli, *Il comando impossibile: Stato e società nell'Italia liberale* (Bologna: Il Mulino, 1988).

14. See G. Zincone, *Da sudditi a cittadini: Le vie dello stato e le vie della società civile* (Bologna: Il Mulino, 1992).

15. It is significant that at a later date (1890s–1900s) southern intellectuals—Vittorio Emanuele Orlando in law, Benedetto Croce and Giovanni Gentile in philosophy—were foremost in the construction of doctrines that legitimized the primacy of the state.

16. See C. M. Lovett, *The Democratic Movement, 1848–1876* (Cambridge, Mass.: Harvard University Press, 1982), 235. In Potenza (Basilicata), the local leaders of the parliamentary Left "conferred an aura of patriotism and respectability upon . . . organizations that were otherwise easily branded as subversive of the social order." See also Cheli, "Libertà di associazione e poteri di polizia," 295. The liberal regime preserved the primacy of politics by avoiding the consolidation of precise legal norms or structures to regulate the right of freedom of association.

17. Meriggi, *Milano borghese*, 185.

18. R. Putnam, *Making Democracy Work: Civic Traditions in Modern Italy* (Princeton: Princeton University Press, 1993), 140–41. Even before unification, the radical and republican Left were committed to a conscious strategy of expanding associative life. There was a significant difference, however, between Mazzini, who favored a unified and strongly politicized model of organization, and Carlo Cattaneo, who insisted that the "multiplication" of associations of *all* kinds was the way to develop democracy: "*tutto fa brodo*" (anything goes). (A. Galante Garrone, *I radicali in Italia, 1843–1925* [Milan, 1973], 64–65.) The Mazzinian model was more influential.

19. S. Soldani, "Vita quotidiana e vita di societa in un centro industriosa," in *Prato: Storia di una citta. Vol. 3, Part 2: Il tempo dell' industria (1815–1943)*, ed. G. Mori, 717–18.

20. S. Adorno, "Professionisti in una periferia: Siracusa 1860–1930," *Storia d'Italia, Annali. Vol. 10: I professionisti*, ed. M. Malatesta (Turin: Einaudi, 1996), 629, 633–36. Putnam, *Making Democracy Work*, 144–45, ignores the evidence for the growth of associations in the south after 1860.

21. S. Romano, *Giolitti: Lo stile del potere* (Milan: Bompiani, 1989), 116.

22. See above, 16.

23. G. Crainz and G. Nenci, *Il movimento contadino*, in *Storia dell'agricoltura*, 615.

24. Crainz and Nenci, *Il movimento contadino*, table 1, 606.

25. For his definition of the "civic community," see *Making Democracy Work*, 87–91.

5

CIVIL SOCIETY AND THE MIDDLE CLASSES IN NINETEENTH-CENTURY GERMANY

Klaus Tenfelde

A GERMAN VILLAGE CASE

In Eschau, which today is a village of some one thousand inhabitants in Hesse, not far from Frankfurt, two competitive choral organizations were formed in the 1880s. Apparently, a single village choral society had existed for decades, but no firm information about it has been found in archival sources. The members of the associations today remember the division in the 1880s only as a point of departure. Tentatively, the organizations were then called Frohsinn (joy, loosely translated) and Harmonie (harmony),[1] both typical names of German choral associations.

The reasons for the division in the 1880s are not clear. During the decade of antisocialist law (1878–90) and thereafter, many associations divided along lines of class difference or political antagonism. Within Eschau, however, it seems that the alignment of the choral societies with one or the other of two pubs in town played a decisive role. Various family connections, above all, how the societies positioned themselves vis-à-vis the politically influential family of the mayor, also played a decisive role. The region itself was rather poor, characterized by Arbeiterbauern or worker-farmers, who clung tenaciously to their small holdings,[2] taking skilled jobs elsewhere to supplement family income and secure the small plots they enjoyed within village boundaries. They built a special type of village existence at the borderline between the lower class and the lower middle class, quite typical in Germany at the end of the nineteenth century, though usually overlooked within labor history.

From the beginning, both associations competed to organize public life in the village. A voluntary fire brigade as well as a sports club was formed, which served to a degree to mediate the tensions that resulted from the bipolarity of the choral associations. Also, the priest of the local parish more or less successfully served as a mediator (Catholicism strongly dominated the area throughout the century), but in general, these two principal clubs have dominated the organization of village life in Eschau until today. Of course they established the settlement's fame as a singers' village, but it is of greater interest to explore the more or less hidden functions they exerted in shaping the public life of the village. Both clubs unexpectedly managed to survive even the emergence of National Socialism. Recognizing the deep roots they had in the village, Nazi party officials hesitated to bring the groups into line, and so they contrived to exist throughout the life of the dictatorship.

Today, both clubs maintain a clear affiliation with one or the other of the major political organizations in Germany—one club is associated with Social Democracy, the other with Christian Democracy—however, this seems to be a fairly recent development. At a fundamental level, it is the clan structure of the village that has decisively shaped local club competition. Families tended to associate themselves strongly with one of the two clubs across generations. It was crucial which club outsiders settling in the village made up their minds to join. Such a decision would bring the process of settlement to a close, shaping all future activity within village boundaries. Not too long ago, club members patronized only the butchers, bakers, retailers, and even hairdressers associated with their particular choral group—a bipolarity that ceased only because of the most recent commercialization of small enterprise and business. The respective pubs still form the local centers of club activity. Club activity has competitively organized the public sphere until today. Apart from what is usual within associational life—that is, regular rehearsals, regional competitions, and other events open only to the membership of each club—public celebrations of the village as a whole are organized competitively, serving to satisfy the needs of the village population. It is important to realize that club membership is not completely defined by either social or political alignment. Rather, people want to belong to one or the other half of the population, and they define their social existence by a certain degree of exclusivity in relation to the respective others and to outsiders in general. Apparently, the clubs worked to meet basic anthropological needs.

Seen against the background of the history of associationism in Germany, Eschau serves as a nice example to illustrate, first, the important role that associational life in its manifold variations played within German society. It is not possible to count precisely the number of clubs in existence or the millions of members. As opposed to earlier times, associations today may or may not be officially registered. They may or may not be members of larger networks dedicated to a particular purpose, and they may or may not be organized regionally and nationally. They may be steeped in tradition or be more contemporary in their organization. Quite frequently, they exist only for months and never come to public (and archival) attention.

In the early 1990s, a survey taken in the territory of the old Federal Republic estimated that 220,000 clubs, not including those of a rather informal and solely social character, existed in that part of the country.[3] There is a question as to whether club membership has risen or fallen recently. It is clear, however, that membership in the most important club network, that is, the Deutscher Sportbund (German Sports Federation), has doubled since the 1970s to twenty-three million in the early 1990s, and membership in the Allgemeiner Deutscher Automobilclub (General German Automobile Association) may have grown even more. I doubt that, at least in the western part of the country, there would be many Germans beyond the age of, say, twenty, who are not members of a club in one way or another, actively or passively, secretly or openly, consciously or unconsciously. Many people do not know that they formally participate in an association when they join the Red Cross, work with Greenpeace, or have their children enrolled in a private school. Within public consciousness, trade-union membership, for instance, has separated from associational life, as well as membership in political parties or possession of shares in one of the many shareholder companies.

Secondly, the Eschau case serves to illustrate the fact that associational life made its way into the countryside somewhat late in the game. Throughout the twentieth century, however, it has displayed a strong presence at the village level, and today may be more important there than in the cities, where a certain degree of individualization and commercialization of life has set in. It was in the middle-sized German town of some five thousand to twenty thousand inhabitants that associational life sprang up in the late eighteenth century and blossomed during the second half of the nineteenth century, and this is the empirical background with which I shall be dealing throughout this chapter.

Thirdly, the example of Eschau shows that the history of associations does not easily connect to any notion of civil society, to democracy in general, or a certain type of democracy in particular. I shall come back to this point in the last section of this chapter.

THE EMERGENCE OF ASSOCIATIONISM:
A SOCIAL HISTORICAL EXPLANATION

Among the many developments European societies shared in common during the nineteenth century was one that time and again provoked the astonishment of contemporary observers—the social process of organization. In his "Remarks on Associations"(1829), William E. Channing offered that, "in truth, one of the most remarkable circumstances or features of our age is the energy with which the principle of combination, or of action by joint forces, by associated numbers, is manifesting itself." Moreover, he went on, "everything is done now by societies."[4] Even in France, where legal restrictions strongly hampered the process, Alphonse de Lamartine recognized the power of associations, "a most irresistible power of our times."[5] It is not an accident that a French nobleman of the time, Alexis de Tocqueville, was moved to remark on the abundance of associations in American civil life in 1831–32, elevating the observation into a cornerstone of his theory of democratic society.[6] Germany, in fact, was no exception in this respect. Quite the contrary, at about the same time that Channing and Lamartine published their observations, Karl Immermann, for example, mentioned in one of his letters that in those days everybody belonged to some association, "be it an art society, an association to improve prisoners (Gefängnisgesellschaft), a shareholders' company or something else."[7] Georg von Viebahn, a well-known statistician and social critic in the mid-nineteenth century, considered associations of all kinds to be the only "moving and powerful principle of our times."[8] Numerous other personalities could be quoted.

German associationism took on many different forms across the centuries. Its roots can be traced back easily to the late Middle Ages.[9] Early German liberal thought, moreover, made a clear connection between a free associationism designed to meet citizens' needs and political aspirations and the achievement of a republican utopia. In contrast to English experience, however, legal provisions recognizing the right to meet and organize on a voluntary basis were a rarity on the continent, above all in the German territories. Constitutionalist movements did include the right to associate in their lists of demands, but such demands went unmet through the post-Napoleonic years, the era of Metternich, who was at the time the notorious arch-chancellor of the German Federation. In Prussia, the freedom of association did not receive a constitutional guarantee until 1849, and even then it remained subject to all sorts of limitations until the end of the Kaiserreich. Such limitations were applied with particular rigor to organizations with expressly political aims. A special set of rules, moreover, was introduced, governing the activities of share companies, mutual aid societies, and cooperatives. The right to form coalitions to intervene in industrial disputes—a right fundamental to trade-union organization—may be cited as an example in this connection. Saxony and the North German Confederation did not acknowledge the right until the 1860s. It remained a subject of intense debate in the decades to come, even as the labor movement grew in size, and did not become a sure thing until after the revolution of 1918–19, when it was codified in the new Weimar constitution.

In general, associational activity in Germany remained severely hampered well into the nineteenth century by a lack of legal recognition and by the repressive attitude of governments. Even after that, worried authorities continued to subject organizations to a high degree of legal scrutiny. The right to organize for political purposes was still restricted, confined to males of a certain m imum age who had to give authorities notice of their activities and subj themselves to police control. Supralocal organizations were banned altoget until late in the century.

Up to the revolutions of 1848–49, which swept away the Metternichian political system, the repressive posture of German governments extended to organizations of all kinds, whether economic, political, or social (i.e., limited to recreational, mutual aid, or cultural activities). Concerning the latter, government officials and the police would at a minimum strive to determine what the intentions of the organizations were and would send out spies to collect information for that purpose. Archival sources reveal abundant information on such procedures. The free press was forbidden. Even in the domain of economic activity, governments by and large insisted on their prerogative to grant or withhold their consent to the formation of businesses. To an extent, this repressive climate worked to stifle associational initiatives in the first half of the century. But not completely, for certain structural conditions were at work (and had been since the late eighteenth century), which favored the emergence of a precocious middle-class associationism.[10]

Concerning the latter development, another German peculiarity must be mentioned. At the end of the eighteenth century, and at least in comparison to England, the degree of urbanization in Germany was extremely low. Nowhere in the German territories (except, of course, those few large cities that, representing sovereign territories, survived the end of the Holy Roman Empire) did the proportion of those living in settlements of more than two thousand inhabitants exceed 10 percent. The largest and most influential states in fact displayed a rather low level of urbanization. Nonetheless, as much recent research has established, towns played an important role in German history. Here were centers of commercial activity and education, which thanks to certain legal circumstances enjoyed a measure of self-government. Such conditions permitted the crystallization of a way of life different in fundamental ways from the feudal order that prevailed in the surrounding countryside.[11] As mentioned before and as many authors have acknowledged, associationism first developed in the towns.[12] Indeed, everywhere in the eighteenth century, the town had become a focus of voluntary organization, and in this domain the educated middle class undeniably took the lead.

Thus, in general, the city provided the essential framework for the rise of associationism in late eighteenth-century Germany. The process fed off of a variety of nonfamily, nongovernmental organizations already in place—churches, foundations, charity clubs, and guilds—but eighteenth-century developments, both social and political, supplied further initiatives to organize. The process, however, played itself out in different ways in different places, depending on the respective degree and phase of urbanization. The urban setting brought together and concentrated a variety of influences that set the stage for the development of organization above the family level. Not all of these influences can be discussed in detail here. In an attempt to comprehend roughly the major driving forces behind associationism, we must consider four points.

First, government retreated from economic and social regulation, and feudal ties in the countryside were abolished. Both processes peaked during the Prussian reform period at the end of the Napoleonic Wars, but they had been introduced earlier, in different territories, and the abolition of the guild system outside Prussia was not completed until the 1860s. In the countryside and especially in eastern Prussia, semifeudal dependencies of work and life even outlasted the Kaiserreich to a degree. As such legal changes proceeded, more and more people felt the need to organize on a voluntary basis in order to protect their professional interests. Merchants and entrepreneurs were among the first to ask for collective representation, and thus chambers of commerce came into being. Among journeymen, mutual aid associations, which in many places had been in existence for centuries, now came to fill an important gap left partly by the retreat of the guilds. Such associations helped to secure journeymen against at least some of the risks of life. These journeymen were among the first to organize secretly during the Metternich era. They were, however, prosecuted for such efforts, which earned them a certain celebrity abroad in Paris, Brussels, and elsewhere as founding cells of the labor movement.[13] Thus, to a degree, the disappearance or abolition of legally imposed ties regulating economic relations sharpened the need for voluntary alternatives. In this sense, the decline of corporate institutions created a vacuum that came to be filled by self-organization.

Second, the rapid growth of markets—capital, consumer, and labor—most notably since the 1840s, provided incentives to organize, especially on the basis of self-interest. Free enterprise by itself demanded new types of capital and labor-market organization, which, thanks to liberalized economic policies, were made increasingly possible during the postrevolutionary decade. One of the most important examples is the Prussian mining industry, which in the past had been run by government officials. It took more than forty years of legislative wrangling before the mining industry was at last overhauled, allowing entrepreneurs for the first time in German history full command of the capital they had invested. The Prussian General Mining Law of 1865 served as a model for similar laws in other German territories. Thus by the 1870s, ore, salt, and coal could be produced freely according to supply and demand, while labor became less corporate in organization and subject to market regulation and entrepreneurial authority. Over the course of the legislative debate, mining employers formed a powerful interest-group association, encountering no opposition from the government, in stark contrast to the experience of mineworkers. It took miners another three decades to get a stable trade-union movement off the ground, hampered as they were by the combined antisocialist efforts of both employers and governments. It is not hard to understand why the case of the mining industry was of such critical importance. These were the years of Germany's economic take-off (c. 1850–73), and the coal and steel industries emerged as leading sectors, employing a substantial portion of the labor force. The rise of organized capitalism from the 1890s would seem to provide additional evidence, supporting the notion that associational growth is driven by market forces.

Third, a sort of urban theory of growth of associations should be considered. Under a feudal regime, and notwithstanding the many variations the system had seen during a thousand years of European history, a type of personalized authoritarian dependency undoubtedly prevailed in the countryside. The family was at the core of village life, either within a relatively free farmers' society and its corresponding clan structures or within the bonds of feudal dependencies, which transferred privileges and obligations from one generation to another. Rural and village societies were self-regulated within a proprietary order, which clearly embodied authority in the person of the local noble lord. Ideally, the rural market was rather closed, rendering surplus production to the feudal authorities and providing for self-sufficiency within a well-established framework of deliveries. In contrast, urban existence undermined the family's role as a productive and reproductive unit, confining it more and more to the latter function. At the same time, the numerous mutual dependencies of urban life, a consequence of an increasingly sophisticated division of labor, eventually gave rise to different types of organization above the level of the family and for many different purposes. The exigencies of self-government and political participation, moreover, necessitated a recourse to suprafamilial forms of organization. Similar pressures were at work in the domains of education, charity, and mutual aid. For many liberals, the experience of self-government at the town level showed just how much could be achieved through collective effort and association in common.

Fourth, the emergence of the German middle class must be taken into account.[14] Throughout the eighteenth century, the educated class had grown and achieved respectable status at a time of "enlightened absolutism" when state bureaucracies were just coming into being. From this, a distinctive middle-class culture evolved. In addition, urban merchants, wealthy artisans, and proto-industrial entrepreneurs formed a self-conscious, resident, upper middle class, which found ways to perpetuate its influence, especially during the reform of urban self-government. Thus, within the towns and cities during the transition to a more urbane way of life, a sort of multifunctional type of middle-class organization became fashionable almost everywhere—the local middle- and upper-class club, frequently named "Harmonie" (harmony), "Ressource" (resource), or "Geselligkeitsverein" (social life organization).[15] In contrast to the many middle-class attempts to organize according to professional and regional or economic and national interests, such multifunctional clubs remained basically local in scope, but their approach increasingly turned political. Local franchise systems to one degree or another worked to the political advantage of the middle and upper classes. The clubs where such people congregated, without ever becoming genuine political parties, had an important representative role to play, concentrating middle-class interests and expressing them to town administrations and governing bodies. Throughout the nineteenth century, especially in midsized towns, the middle class stood in need of networks of communication: to make the "marriage market" work, to aggregate political and economic interests (often by secret means), and to coordinate educational and cultural activities. The clubs served all such purposes, yet they might divide on religious or political ground. Protestants and liberal professionals, for example, might gather in one club while businessmen and civil servants gathered in another. Things differed widely according to local traditions, structural conditions, personal influence, and other peculiarities. In any case, clubs met a variety of needs—educational, economic, and cultural—that arose from urban experience. Such needs may have been met in the past by churches and various family networks, but these institutions were now in decline, creating openings for a new type of organization.

Finally, a political theory of associational growth should be considered. In general, middle-class organization was needed to battle late absolutism, and such struggles took many different forms. As already mentioned, entrepreneurs had begun to organize in order to defend their economic interests. What they most wanted from government authorities in the first place was simple recognition of their right to engage in such activities. Liberal currents were also at work on the associational front. Since the Wars of Liberation and the return to the old order at Vienna in 1815, they had been pushing territorial governments to accept constitutional institutions and embrace the cause of national unity, an old but now revived aspiration of central European history. To be sure liberalism as a political movement may well have miscarried at the national level, a victim of the failed revolutions of 1848–49 and the imposition of unification from above by conservative forces in 1871. Yet, liberalism as an urban movement had achieved a complete victory by the end of the nineteenth century.[16] At the time of the 1848–49 revolutions, a system of political parties evolved in a matter of months.[17] Legislation in subsequent years worked to hamper and limit party formation. Nonetheless, genuine party structures began to take shape in the 1860s and over the course of the first decades of the new Bismarckian empire. This was no mean feat and a phenomenon full of consequence in a society where the right to organize had still to be fought for, where new types of social relations were creating ever more pressing needs for self-expression and self-organization.

It is possible to distinguish a variety of factors promoting the transition to a society based on the principle of self-organization. It should be recognized at the same time, however, that in practice these forces were not parallel but interrelated phenomena. Early industrialization, for example, strengthened employers in the textile sector, and later in heavy industry. It accelerated urban growth, which in turn loosened family ties and fostered demands for mediating organizations of a new kind. As a result, we can clearly identify "waves" of new associations connected with the phases of urban growth, which in turn represented, to a degree, phases of economic growth. The evolution of the political system also had a shaping effect on rates of associational activism as even the most cursory review of events at the local level would attest. The general health of the economy had the same effect. More associations were formed, and membership rates were higher in periods of economic growth than in periods of recession.[18]

At this point, it may be useful to define what I mean by "associations." Associations (Vereine) are groups of unrelated individuals (almost exclusively men in nineteenth-century Germany) who voluntarily convene to pursue a common aim (or several aims) and formulate statutes and articles by which formal procedures are established to delegate authority to a body of club officials. A managing committee is installed, which acts for the membership and supervises financial affairs, which, it is important to note, must be paid for by the membership itself.

By design, this definition is very broad.[19] As a result, an association may be any organizational body not associated with government and bureaucracy but above the level of families and family networks, constituted on a voluntary basis and financed through membership contributions. This may be questionable in the case of the churches, but it is not by accident that many of the Protestant churches at least temporarily took the shape of associations. The empirical evidence shows that in the process of self-organization, Protestant territories clearly took the lead, which may be due, to a degree, to the nature of Protestant beliefs and to differences in the way Protestant and Catholic churches were organized. Official German Catholicism did not actively promote lay organization until the mid- to late 1860s. Yet the problem is rather intricate. Protestants also tended to be better educated, were urban in residence, and better disposed to free enterprise, while Catholics remained bound to the old agrarian and artisan middle classes. The chain of causality is tangled here.

Given the notion of associationism presented here, a rather wide range of organizations—some of which took the form of free associations only for a short period—qualifies for discussion. Within the German territories from about 1830 until the end of the nineteenth century, these might include shareholder companies as well as saving banks; chambers of commerce as well as political parties, charity clubs, funeral societies or clubs for the abolition of luxury clothing, mutual aid organizations, leisure-time organizations such as choral societies and gymnastic clubs, clubs for the advancement of smoking, fire brigades, chambers of lawyers and physicians, and societies for the advancement of theater or music or the sciences. Most such associations started out as local bodies that varied in form depending on the objects they pursued and local legal provisions. They might develop into umbrella organizations. And more and more in the 1860s, they began to organize on a regional and even national basis. National organizations of this sort sometimes preceded unification and sometimes, as with German-Austrian societies, exerted a geographical reach that exceeded the boundaries of the new German Reich.

ASSOCIATIONISM AND MILIEU ORGANIZATION

As indicated above, the formative period of associationism came with the Enlightenment; the growth of cities; the improvement of supralocal communication systems; and, especially in the late eighteenth century, proto-industrialization.[20] Reading clubs, literary societies, and scientific academies sprang up in university communities or were made possible by the development of the press and the publishing trade. Interestingly, agrarian academies were among the first to be formed, usually by large landowners in east Prussia. Especially during the eighteenth century, the educated middle classes and parts of the nobility joined in secret societies such as the Freemasons or the so-called Illuminati (Illuminaten).[21]

The late Enlightenment accorded a special status to persons of education (Bildung) who felt a particular incentive to organize.[22] As a peculiar invention of their own, the educated classes during the last quarter of the eighteenth century formed reading circles (Lesegesellschaften), which also played a role in France, Switzerland, and other European countries.[23] Such societies frequently accrued additional purposes such as charity, mutual assistance, and leisure-time organization, so that they silently but effectively evolved into influential power centers within their respective communities. As mentioned before, a club system of that kind existed in many midsized German communities at the turn of the century. Also, for a very short period in the 1790s and as a response to the French Revolution, political clubs came into being, especially in the Rhinelands.[24]

Within the political system created by the Congress of Vienna in 1815 and consequent upon the shared repressive objectives of the leading powers (Prussia and Habsburgian Austria), organizations with a clear-cut political agenda were prohibited. Following certain political events such as the assassination of August von Kotzebue in 1819 and especially the 1830 revolution in France, decrees were issued that made it yet more difficult to engage in organized political activity or to publish periodical and pamphlet literature in favor of republicanism, democracy, and national unity. Student agitation in favor of democracy and national unity, concentrated in the famous fraternities (Burschenschaften[25]), was subject to energetic persecution. Thus, centers of liberal and democratic effort had to be formed abroad, such as Young Germany (Junges Deutschland) in France and Switzerland. The early history of socialism began with the League of the Ostracized (Bund der Geächteten) in Paris in the 1830s, which later became the League of Communists led by Karl Marx.[26]

Such examples suffice to show that under the rule of the secret Metternichian police, new free associations could not develop unless they were introduced by governments themselves, such as the important Central Association for the Welfare of the Working Classes (Centralverein für das Wohl der arbeitenden Klassen). That association originated in 1844 as a response to pauperism and was conceived by government officials in Prussia as an instrument of social reform.[27] During a time when parliaments rarely existed, liberals and democrats were persecuted, and economic policy was directed to a large extent by governments, the forming of associations was severely suppressed or did not evolve at all. Thus, as a response to the need to associate above the family level, which was felt so widely among the middle classes, the forming of associations became a private affair. The salon was one of the private forms of association where well-educated people joined informally to pursue cultural interests—again, a European phenomenon.[28]

In the spring of 1848, the situation changed dramatically. The right to associate figured prominently among the famous March Demands of 1848, and subsequently, several networks of political organization flooded German cities. Due to the faction-building process in the Frankfurt parliament and the national assemblies of the German states, a diversity of political tendencies sorted themselves out, ranging from moderate conservatives, monarchists, and Catholics to radical democrats; moderate liberals; national liberals; and, from the summer of 1848, working-class socialists. The era of an untrammeled political associationism lasted for a year or so and then faded away with the revival of the old political powers in 1849. Yet as a result of the revolution, most legal restrictions on nonpolitical associationism had been removed permanently. In fact, the two decades between the revolution and the foundation of the Kaiserreich proved to be the truly formative period of associationism in Germany.[29] Evidence for this claim can be found in a variety of local studies that make two points clear. New associations were being formed at an unprecedented pace, and all associations, whether old or new, were expanding in membership and geographical reach.[30]

There were many incentives to form associations during these decades. In business, capital was needed urgently. New share companies came into being in consequence, and the banking system expanded rapidly. In general, wealth increased and was more and more concentrated in the hands of the middle class, who began to set up foundations of various kinds.[31] Entrepreneurs, in addition to existing chambers of commerce, formed business associations and, for the first time, organizations that aimed at market control. In the sciences, regional and national organizations of all kinds sprang up. Not all of them were of a purely scientific character. For lawyers and physicians, associations provided the means to pursue professional interests. The cooperative movement[32] spread, as did mutual help organizations or the traditional gymnastics clubs. Among the workers' educational clubs, the middle class still exerted a major influence, while political organizations above the local level and trade unions, as mentioned above, remained legally prohibited.

The political climate relaxed somewhat in 1861, when William I succeeded his brother Frederick William IV to the Prussian throne. Earlier, in 1859, the German National Association (Deutscher Nationalverein[33]) had been founded in Frankfurt. Moderate liberals had joined together to pursue the aim of German unity on the grounds of the constitution that had been drafted by the National Convention of 1848–49. The organization of liberalism in general was shaped by electoral committees (Wahlvereine), which were formed at election time but often, especially in Prussia, continued to function beyond the electoral period. After the foundation of the German Progressive Party (Deutsche Fortschrittspartei) in 1861, which also profited from the thaw of the 1860s, liberalism gained a majority that was soon threatened when Bismarck became the prime minister of Prussia in 1862.

Thus, during the 1860s, the modern party system in Germany was established. Its reach extended to embrace the labor movement as well, which was organized as a political party by Ferdinand Lassalle in 1863.[34] It has sometimes been thought that the early emergence of social democracy in Germany, prior to the consolidation of a significant trade-union movement, is indicative of the primary importance of "the political" in shaping the labor Left. Yet certain forerunners of the modern trade-union movement had developed as early as 1848–49, and strike movements had increased during the 1850s, despite the fact that the right of association was still denied. The Lassallean movement, in accordance with the theoretical assumptions of its leader, disapproved of trade unions, though the battle for political emancipation had not yet been distinguished clearly from the battle for economic interest.

The true meaning of the organizational movement can best be seen on the local level.[35] It is here that associationism came to reshape community life to a large degree. The more German cities grew beyond the scope of, say, ten thousand inhabitants, the more the need was felt to organize above the level of families and outside the institutional structures made available by the churches. The movement became increasingly unpolitical. Many leisure-time associations such as carnival clubs or societies for the rescue of house servants from prostitution came into being. The two most important currents of club life that had developed well before 1848, that is, the gymnastics clubs and the choral societies, experienced tremendous growth from the 1850s, which diluted their sometimes oppositional character. As of 1871 many of them had turned patriotic if not nationalist. Student fraternities followed suit. Increasingly almost all aspects of culture, sports, and leisure were organized in associations.

No doubt, clubs should be considered among the most flexible of social organizations. In general, associationism since the 1860s rapidly spread from the middle to the lower classes and from the city to the country. Were there any structural processes that might explain the different, and to a large degree, conflicting, paths that were followed by certain groups and types of associations, according to purpose, political alliance, and social composition? How was the process of class-building, for example, reflected in patterns of associational activity?

We can confidently maintain that a modern working class did not come into being in Germany until 1850. The modern worker, by definition, is someone dependent on wages and employed in a centralized industrial unit. The number of such people at the time of the revolutions of 1848–49 has been estimated at five hundred thousand. By 1873, however, the number of workers employed in industry and mining had shot up to 1.8 million. During the same time period, employment in all manufacturing professions (including home industries and artisan trades) increased to 5.4 million.[36] Though the urban middle class during the 1870s was still the backbone of associationism, workers increasingly formed trade unions that achieved their first peak of popularity during the late 1860s or flocked to urban choral societies and sports, leisure, or mutual aid organizations.

Initially, especially in small and midsized towns, such organizational processes did not necessarily divide according to class lines. The "division of middle-class and proletarian democracy"[37] first occurred in the big industrialized cities, whereas in villages and small towns (especially in the south), associations never experienced such a division. Even so, the division gained decisive impetus after the foundation of the Reich, when the persecution of working-class organizations became a major concern of governments and police officials, especially in Prussia and Saxony. The antisocialist law enacted in 1878 and which lasted until 1890 highlighted a policy that aimed at integration by order and discipline instead of participation and consensus. With few exceptions, socialist and trade-union organizations as well as the socialist press were prohibited, and many leading socialists and trade unionists were driven into exile. The movement, however, survived because its Reichstag faction was allowed to continue work and because of secret meetings and the disguised activities of "non-political" associations such as mutual aid societies and choral clubs. Gradually, the trade-union movement too began to recover. In 1889–90, it helped bring an end to the era of persecution and contributed to the fall of Chancellor Bismarck.

The end of general persecution did not put an end to the politics of stigmatization and social isolation. On the whole, such policies, and especially the heroic experience of survival during the antisocialist law, worked to knit the social-democratic working-class organizations more closely together. Social democrats and trade unionists were cemented shoulder to shoulder, as were members of the cooperative movement that began to revive in the 1890s. In addition, social democrats and trade unionists now started to establish a far-reaching organizational network that in today's research has come to be called Arbeiterbewegungskultur or labor movement culture.[38] More or less closely related to the labor movement, numerous societies and associational networks, especially in sports and culture, were formed to serve the needs of workers. Among them, workers' choral societies and sports clubs figured prominently, supplemented by a wide variety of associations: to promote bi-cycle riding, theater-going, respect for nature, and education; to support working-class youth; and to serve the needs of women, pregnant women and new mothers in particular. After the turn of the century, the membership in such organizations took off, clearly outstripping party membership, and in later years, especially during the Weimar Republic, certain of these organiza-tional networks became genuine mass phenomena.[39]

A peculiar set of legal, political, and social conditions contributed to the creation of a deeply rooted labor culture in Germany, a culture that prospered for at least two generations and which was very much implicated in the process of class building. Thus, working-class networks associated with social democ-racy and the socialist trade unions formed one of the two large historical mi-lieus created by industrialization and urbanization under "German conditions." Milieus may be understood to represent "social entities formed through the co-incidence of several structural influences such as religion, regional tradition, economic condition, cultural orientation, or class structure."[40] As sociocultural entities, such milieus tend to shape the living conditions and lifestyles of those who become involved by birth and socialization. In the case of the labor move-ment, the milieu was structured largely by class affiliation, the experience of po-litical repression, and the economic conditions of working-class life.

By contrast, the other large historical milieu of German social history, that is, Catholicism, derived its main constitutive elements from tradition and be-lief.[41] Catholic bishops and priests would turn only reluctantly to lay Catholi-cism to be organized by associations. The Church hierarchy was hesitant to en-courage the organizational efforts of lay Catholics. In the late 1860s, however, bishops and priests began to change their minds, persuaded by the success of Adolf Kolping's Catholic journeymen's movement and by the efforts of the so-called red chaplains to attract working-class support in west Prussia. The hier-archy sanctioned lay associationism on both the regional and national levels. Such organizational efforts were furthered by the stigmatization of Catholicism as a minority religion. Such stigmatization was powerful in Prussia where anti-Catholic prejudice reached back to the early years of the nineteenth century, but prejudice made itself felt not just in Protestant regions of Germany. In Catholic Bavaria, a liberal anticlericalism had long battled against confessional schools, well before Bismarck launched the Kulturkampf (cultural struggle) in the early years of the new Reich. The attempts at stigmatizing the Catholic mi-nority by law compare, in fact, with the attempts to outlaw social democracy, at least as far as functional consequences are concerned. It gave lay Catholics a strong incentive to organize. The construction of associational networks began at the parish level but spread outward and upward from there. The persecution of the socialists gave added impetus to the Catholic organizational drive. An attempt was made to exploit momentary socialist weakness, as workers became the target of Catholic recruiting efforts. The creation of Christian trade unions in the 1890s was a major consequence of this circumstance.

Further developments within the framework of Catholic associations are not of interest here. Suffice it to say that in many respects both large historical milieus are comparable: Associationism served as the backbone of milieu organization, and the milieu became hereditary. They worked as socializing agents for their respective memberships.[42] The fact that both major historical milieus competed to attract support among workers added to the respective strength of each but at the same time impaired class unity, pitting partisans of a confessionally based class identity against partisans of a social democratic vision of class interest. The competition also exacerbated ideological tensions among workers. Which side a worker took was no idle matter but involved a commitment to an encompassing system of "right" belief and conviction. Recent research shows the degree to which such tensions penetrated to the very core of working-class family life, shaping marriage patterns, social networks, and practices of socialization.[43]

STRUCTURAL DIFFERENTIATION

It might be thought that the fissured character of German associationism (which grew more and more pronounced up to 1914 and invites comparison with the experience of other confessionally divided European countries)[44] was on the whole a lower-class phenomenon. Yet in fact, all levels of German society were divided by religious and class difference. Lay Catholics aspired to be an above-class movement, but such aspirations were hard to realize. Catholic working-class associations were almost 100 percent proletarian in composition, ornamented only by the occasional honorary middle-class member. At the borderline between the working class and petty bourgeoisie, the decision to join one association or another was a weighty one, involving fundamental issues of self-esteem and status expectation. Labor was a stigmatized group and remained so, solidifying the gap between lower- and middle-class–based associational networks. Exclusive practices were no less the rule at the other end of the social scale, among the urban upper-middle classes. A newcomer or first generation social climber had no chance to join one of the few leading urban clubs, which frequently enjoyed a tradition of a century or more. Such people tended to form their own clubs. How bourgeois clubs dealt with the local nobility and high-ranking military personnel provides a particularly interesting case. Leading burghers, dazzled by the glamour of a uniform, might be tempted to invite the participation of senior officers. On the other hand, conscious of themselves as bourgeois, they might hesitate to court officers who were often noble in origin. As for the nobility itself, almost everywhere titled people preferred to socialize among themselves. The best clubs, as a matter of course, excluded all members of the "regular" middle class—small and middling shopkeepers and businessmen; white-collar employees and civil servants; indeed, everyone who actually had to work for a living. Even professional academics had a hard time gaining access.

Unlike the mass organizations discussed above, some exclusive clubs did not pursue an explicit political agenda. They claimed not to be interested in class or confessional issues. In fact, however, they had hidden agendas of all kinds. Led and even to a degree manipulated by powerful economic and political interests, these organizations fostered the fears and wishes of many Germans, from patriotism to extreme nationalism, from rigid antisocialism to the most dreadful anti-Semitism.

Apart from considerations of confession and class, it is possible to identify a range of additional factors that reconfigured the world of associations and associational networks. These developments were not the consequence of immediate changes in the economic and political environment. They resulted from changes that were long-term in nature. Connected to wider structural processes of modernization at work everywhere in the West, they acted to transform the function that associations played within the wider social universe. These developments encouraged, on the one hand, association fetishism (Vereinsmeierei) or the "cult of associations" (Rudy Koshar) and, on the other, a certain narrowing of the scale of self-organization so that in general, public perception of the scope of self-organization was increasingly limited to leisure time and, perhaps, cultural activities. I can only hint below at some of these developments here; a more substantial discussion might analyze far-reaching influences such as commercialization and reindividualization of lifestyles over the course of the twentieth century, and especially the influence of the mass media.

First, the clubs and associational networks *specialized*. If we take the late eighteenth-century multifunctional middle-class club as an ideal type, then it would be fair to say that by the end of the nineteenth century the form, while still extant and influential, had nonetheless delegated a number of its original pursuits to more specialized societies and associational networks. And by the end of the twentieth century, the form seems to have vanished altogether or cut back its activities to pure socializing, reduced to sponsorship of local wine festivals or anniversary events of one sort or another.[45] Clubs of entrepreneurs in earlier times had wanted to involve themselves in all activities that might be conceived as of common interest. But these organizations grew more specialized, especially in the wake of the economic crisis of the late nineteenth century (the chamber of commerce represented a partial exception). They focused on influencing parliament or the bureaucracy, fighting trade unions, dominating raw materials markets, or fixing prices. Such structural differentiation also affected the labor movement, which fragmented into a number of specialized branches: the party, the trade unions, the cooperative movement, and various ancillary cultural organizations. Physicians had at first concentrated their associational energies on forming scientific academies, but they soon turned to interest-group activity of a more corporate nature. As national health insurance programs got under way, doctors formed special associations of their own to compete with consumer groups in shaping the dispensation of medical services.

Second, clubs not only specialized in function but also at the same time grew more complex in internal organization, establishing associational webs tying locality to region and region to nation. To be sure, many local leisure associations were content to remain just that, local, never making any effort to build up contacts outside the community. Still, the competitive nature of sport created incentives to associate at the regional and, increasingly during the interwar years, at the national level. And as organization grew more complex, hierarchical structures crystallized, delegating decision making to periodic conventions of representatives. Periodicals were formed, and procedures for judging differences of opinion established. Political lobbying was engaged in, and techniques for the expression of opinion and the exercise of majority rule were refined. In many cultural and scientific organizations, most official posts remained honorific. Nonetheless, the larger such organizations grew, the greater the pressure became to find professional leadership and to formalize communications between officers and members via house publications. Take the case of the Ruhr Coal Mining Entrepreneurs Association. At the beginning of the twentieth century, it oversaw formation of a web of loosely affiliated satellite organizations that pursued a wide range of objectives. A handful of industrialists (and their managers), through membership in these various affiliates, maintained strict and effective, though secret, control over their operations. The core association at the same time built up its central organizational apparatus, even staffing a journal and maintaining a library.

Third, the introduction of new techniques of network development, decision making, and lobbying endangered the intimate character of much associational activity. The club had been a kind of "little republic,"[46] catering to the special needs of its members. But it was now more and more turned outward, toward the pursuit of public goals. The professionalization of self-organization created new careers, established new criteria of mutual esteem and respectability, and created new norms of success. But at the same time it led to bureaucratization and all that that entailed: ineffective paper-pushing, stiff-necked functionaries, strategies of manipulation from above, and a hardening of positions. Successful organizational growth was full of perils, and the modern labor movement may be taken as a case in point. It was the growth of labor organization at the turn of the century that provoked the first systematic critiques of the bureaucratizing tendencies of large-scale associationism. And the most pointed critiques were reserved for the most successful labor movement of the lot, the German labor movement.[47]

Fourth, many club activities were over time subjected to such heavy legal regulation that they ceased to appear voluntary in character. The law so constrained shareholder companies and cooperatives, for example, that, to the public mind at least, they came to seem more like administrative bodies than free associations. The same thing happened to fire brigades in large cities. Early in the century, protection against fires (and sometimes floods too) had been a neighborhood affair, organized on a local and informal basis. In small and midsized towns, voluntary associations, with support from local administrations, took over this part of public security. Big city administrations, however, felt the need to go a step further, creating professional fire departments paid for by city funds.

Last of all, many of the functions that associations had once performed were absorbed outright by the state. In the early years of associationism, organizations often performed services touching on the public interest. But as such services loomed in importance, governments felt the need to take them over. This is not quite the same as the process of legalization described above. It might more properly be labeled "governmentalization," and it was of critical importance in the provision of social services, in the domain of what had come to be called the welfare state. Mutual aid societies, for example, had flourished throughout the nineteenth century. The Bismarck government of the 1880s, however, as a "positive" response to the socialist menace, decided to do for itself the job once done by the mutual aid movement. The same thing happened with life, fire, and disaster insurance. Once the purview of private bodies, insurance against risk became more and more subject to state prerogative.

In the field of social policy, Germany was, for reasons too intricate to be discussed here, the first to move ahead. The basic risks of wage-dependent existence, such as accident, sickness, and old age, became regulated, a development that weakened the mutual aid associations and, in the course of just two decades, made them almost obsolete. The provision of unemployment insurance was an exception to this process. The responsibility was at last assumed by the state in the 1920s. Until then though, it was handled by the trade unions and became a source of particular trade-union strength. In any event, the state's drive to monopolize social services was full of consequence, contributing to the construction of an emergent welfare state, of course, but also to a scaling back of civic activity. The role of civic organizations in this area has only become a subject of debate once again in recent years.

THE DEFICIENCIES OF GERMAN CIVIL SOCIETY

The developments outlined here in fact got under way the moment associationism came into being. They exemplify the flexibility of the concept of self-organization and emphasize a well-grounded view that social change in

Western-style societies to a large but changing degree has been managed through self-organization. These developments, moreover, make clear that the function and place of associationism within civil society has changed over time. As a general observation, it may be concluded that the role played by associationism seems to have shrunk across the centuries, such that in modern times, at least on the surface, the domain of associationism is understood to encompass little more than leisure-time; sporting; and, in a broad sense, cultural activities. Much, it seems, has been forgotten about what associational life once meant to society.

In a similar fashion, in the domain of politics, the voluntary association had ceased to be quite so central, ceding pride of place to the political party. In Germany, however, this process was slow to unfold. Until the end of the Kaiserreich, parties were held in low esteem, looked on as necessary evils rather than as decisive channels for participation, conflict management, or self-expression. In part for this reason, legal definition and recognition were not conferred on party life until as late as 1949. Even before 1918, parties had a right to convene, but this was the only concession made on their behalf.

The late-developing character of party life in Germany was shaped in critical ways by the constitutional structure of the Kaiserreich. Governments served at the monarch's pleasure and did not require the approval of parliament. To be sure, they did operate under certain budgetary constraints but were responsible only in this limited sense. Under the circumstances, majority- and consensus-building were not likely to become the central goals of party activity. A party career might lead to parliamentary office, but rarely to positions of great responsibility. For liberal and conservative parties, even into the 1950s, the principal business of party activity remained the organization of election campaigns, not the refinement of a consensus understanding politics. For Social Democrats and increasingly (and not accidentally) Catholics, party life played a somewhat different role. They strove to build up a mass base, and so party life became meaningful in this sense. To a degree, they were successful at this enterprise precisely because the attainment of responsible office remained out of their reach.[48]

The Kaiserreich's constitutional framework devalued parties and parliaments, creating an opening for other kinds of organizations, which would attempt to explore alternative and extra-parliamentary pathways to exert influence, to emerge. Such organizations did in fact evolve, and for a period they had a decisive impact on public opinion and political decision making as well. In particular, the Pan-German League, founded in 1886, provides an example. So, too, do the German Army and Naval Leagues. These were formed in the fin de siècle when the Reich made its bid for world power, under Kaiser Wilhelm II, for a German "place in the sun."[49] From the 1890s, these and similar national associations opened a new chapter in the uses of mass organization for explicitly political ends. Led on the whole by members of Germany's old elites and financed by influential economic interests, they managed to garner mass support, in particular from the lower middle classes (which also lent mass support to veterans' organizations). The membership of these mass societies far outnumbered that of local and regional associations of all kinds. By such means, at the end of the nineteenth century, middle-class organization at last reached the masses. Even a portion of the Protestant working class responded to such appeals, in consequence alienating itself from the labor movement and socialist politics. For Catholic workers, however, there was no contradiction between a Catholic trade unionism and participation, say, in a local veterans' association.

It is sometimes thought that the existence of a vibrant civil society built on a bedrock of middle-class associationism is the surest safeguard of political freedom. But where mass right-wing organization exists, combined with the fracturing of associational life along confessional and class lines, this assumption must be cast into doubt. On the surface of things, the degree, type, and purposes of associational activity do not seem to differ much from Germany, to Great Britain, to the United States. But on closer inspection, certain critical structural differences may be detected. Legal structures (or the lack thereof) vary from one country to the next, straitjacketing or steering the associative efforts of citizens. Constitutional systems vary and party systems vary too, molding the space available and potential objects of collective action. Because of local conditions and traditions, certain forms of association prosper in one country but not in another. And last of all, there is the question of political culture and the limits it places on associational life. Associations are supposed to socialize citizens, but the precise relationship between associationism and citizen-making, between social and political being, is not the same everywhere. In the end, political culture may hem in, in fundamental ways, what can be achieved through self-organization.

In the Tocquevillian scheme of things, associations are meant to function as consensus-building little republics. They did not work this way in Germany. Here, the accelerated growth of associationism was coincident with certain processes, both particular to Germany and general, which produced a different outcome. Enduring feudal traditions and the peculiar constitutional systems of nineteenth-century Germany served to deepen and sharpen confessional barriers and class differences. Nineteenth-century Germany was rife with rivalries that associational activity exacerbated and very nearly set in stone. At the same time, general processes of structural differentiation narrowed the scope of associational life, making the little republic ideal of associationism all the more remote.

From a historical point of view, middle-class (and with some chronological delay, lower-class) associations in Germany played a crucial role in the shaping of a civil society based on individual rights, equal participation, and responsible citizenship. At the same time, it has to be recognized that such a civil society never developed in full, not in 1918 and not under the Weimar Republic. The associational legacy of the Kaiserreich remained too strong, intensified by a series of political and economic crises. And civil society, such as it was, was destroyed altogether by the Hitler regime. Nazi Gleischschaltung (coordination) meant many things, but above all it meant the absolute destruction of a free and voluntary associational life.

NOTES

1. This introductory description is based on the case study by Gertrud Hüwelmeier, *100 Jahre Sängerkrieg: Ethnographie eines Dorfes in Hessen* (Berlin: Reimer, 1997). The author of this important little study decided to code the names of the village and organizations, to safeguard inhabitants and informants against unwelcome questions.

2. See Gerhard A. Ritter and Klaus Tenfelde, *Arbeiter im deutschen Kaiserreich 1871–1914* (Bonn: Dietz, 1992), 219 ff.

3. See Eckart Lohse, article on "Vereinswesen in Deutschland," *Frankfurter Allgemeine Zeitung*, no. 253/30.10.1993, 7. Further information may be found in Friedhelm Kröll et al., *Vereine: Geschichte-Politik-Kultur* (Frankfurt: Institut für Marxistische Studien und Forschungen, 1982) (Jahrbuch des IMSF 4/1981), 123 ff.; article by Heinz Sahner, in *Vereine in Deutschland: Vom Geheimbund zur freien gesellschaftlichen Organisation*, ed. Heinrich Best (Bonn: Informationszentrum Sozialwissenschaften, 1993), 11 ff.

4. *The Works of William E. Channing*, 1882 (reprinted New York, 1970), 138–58.

5. Alphonse de Lamartine, *Du duel*, *Des Caisses d'épargne* (Paris, 1835), 15, my translation.

6. Alexis de Tocqueville, *Democracy in America*, ed. Richard D. Heffner (New York: New American Library, 1956), 194 ff.

7. Karl Immermann, *Briefe*, vol. 1, 1804–1831, ed. P. Hasenbek (Munich, 1978), 99 f., my translation.

8. *Mittheilungen des Centralvereins für das Wohl der arbeitenden Klassen* 1 (1848/49), (reprinted Hagen: von der Linnepe Verlagsgesellschaft, 1980), 171, my translation.

9. A fundamental study has been produced most recently by Wolfgang Hardtwig, *Genossenschaft, Sekte, Verein in Deutschland. Vol. 1: Vom Spätmittelalter zur Französischen Revolution* (Munich: Beck, 1997). A second volume dealing with the nineteenth century will be published soon.

10. There is a rich literature on the history of associations, and government repression, during the first half of the century. As an introduction, the volume edited by Otto Dann may be used: *Vereinswesen und bürgerliche Gesellschaft* (Munich: Oldenbourg, 1984).

11. See, for instance, Heinz Schilling, *Die Stadt in der Frühen Neuzeit* (Munich: Oldenbourg, 1993); the most important empirical study on urbanization has been presented by Horst Matzerath, *Urbanisierung in Preussen 1815–1914* (Stuttgart: Kohlhammer, 1985).

12. Among others, Renate Mayntz, *Soziologie der Organization*, 3rd ed. (Reinbek: Rowohlt, 1968), 15; Kröll et al., *Vereine*, 19f.

13. The standard work on this subject was written by Wolfgang Schieder, *Anfänge der deutschen Arbeiterbewegung: Die Auslandsvereine im Jahrzehnt nach der Julirevolution von 1830* (Stuttgart: Klett, 1963); a comparative study on the role of older artisan organization and their continuity with the modern trade-union movement has been provided by Christiane Eisenberg, *Deutsche und englische Gewerkschaften: Entstehung und Entwicklung bis 1878 im Vergleich* (Göttingen: Vandenhoeck & Ruprecht, 1986).

14. Since the 1980s, as a result of several major research efforts at different places in West Germany, an impressive literature on the history of the German middle classes, and with a comparative perspective to boot, has been published. For a comprehensive presentation of these results, see Jürgen Kocka, "The Middle Classes in Europe," *Journal of Modern History* 67 (1995): 783–806. Dealing especially with the eighteenth century, see Ernst Mannheim, *Aufklärung und öffentliche Meinung: Studien zur Soziologie der Öffentlichkeit im 18. Jahrhundert,* ed. Norbert Schindler (first published 1933) (Stuttgart: Fromann-Holzboog, 1979).

15. My research on one of these is published in "Die 'Gesellschaft Ressource' von 1795: Bielefelder Kaufleute und Vereinswesen im übergang zur Industriegesellschaft," *Jahresbericht des Historischen Vereins für die Grafschaft Ravensberg* 83 (1996): 127–42.

16. See especially James Sheehan, "Liberalism and the City in Nineteenth-Century Germany," *Past and Present* 51 (1971): 116–37; James Sheehan, *German Liberalism in the Nineteenth Century* (New Jersey: Humanities Press, 1995).

17. For a recent comprehensive treatment, see Michael Wetterengel, "Parteibildung in Deutschland: Das politische Vereinswesen in der Revolution von 1848," in *Europa 1848: Revolution und Reform,* ed. Dieter Dowe et al. (Bonn: Dietz, 1998), 701–38.

18. As a sort of exception, economic interest organizations of entrepreneurs, for obvious reasons, clearly tended to be founded during phases of economic recession, whereas employers' associations were founded as a response to trade-union activity, especially from the 1890s.

19. Many social and political scientists have attempted to formulate such a definition for the German literature on the subject. See, for instance, *Vereine in Deutschland,* 23–27; *Vereine,* Kröll et al., 36–40; Peter Raschke, *Vereine und Verbände: Zur Organization von Interessen in der Bundesrepublik Deutschland* (Munich: Juventa, 1978), 19–22.

20. For what follows, I rely to an extent on earlier articles of my own, "Die Entfaltung des Vereinswesens während der Industriellen Revolution in Deutschland (1850–1873)," in *Vereinswesen,* 55–114; "Historische Milieus-Erblichkeit und Konkurrenz," in *Nation und Gesellschaft in Deutschland: Historische Essays,* ed. Manfred Hettling and Paul Nolte (Munich: Beck, 1996), 247–68. Other recent treatments include Christiane Eisenberg, "Arbeiter, Bürger und der 'bürgerliche Verein' 1820–1870: Deutschland und England im Vergleich," in *Bürgertum im 19. Jahrhundert: Deutschland im europäischen Vergleich,* vol. 2, ed. Jürgen Kocka (Munich: Deutscher Taschenbuch Verlag, 1998), 149–86; Michael Sobania, "Vereinsleben: Regeln und Formen bürgerlicher Assoziationen im 19. Jahrhundert," in *Bürgerkultur im 19. Jahrhundert,* ed. Dieter Hein and Andreas Schulz (Munich: Oldenbourg, 1996), 170–90; Lothar Gall, "Adel, Verein und städtisches Bürgertum," in *Adel und Bürgertum in Deutschland 1770–1848,* ed. Elisabeth Fehrenbach (Munich: Oldenbourg, 1993). Within the field, Thomas Nipperdey's essay on "Verein als soziale Struktur in Deutschland im späten 18: Und frühen 19. Jahrhundert," in *Gesellschaft, Kultur, Theorie: Gesammelte Aufsätze zur neueren Geschichte,* ed. Thomas Nipperdey (Göttingen: Vandenhoeck & Ruprecht, 1976), 174–205, is considered a classic. Many types and groups of associations have been investigated more closely; see, for example, *Handbuch literarisch-kultureller Vereine, Gruppen und Bünde 1825–1933,* ed. Wulf Wülfing et al. (Stuttgart, 1998); Joachim Großmann, "Verloste Kunst: Deutsche Kunstvereine im 19. Jahrhundert," *Archiv für Kulturgeschichte* 76 (1994): 351–64. There is an abundant literature on Catholic and working-class associations, some of which will be quoted later on in this article.

21. See *Geheime Gesellschaften*, ed. Peter Christian Ludz (Heidelberg: Schneider, 1979); Richard van Dülmen, "Die Aufklärungsgesellschaften in Deutschland als Forschungsproblem," *Francia* 5 (1977): 251–75; a comprehensive study is Monika Neugebauer-Wölk, *Esoterische Bünde und bürgerliche Gesellschaft: Entwicklungslinien zur modernen Welt im Geheimbundwesen des 18. Jahrhunderts* (Göttingen: Wallstein, 1995). A comparative perspective may be found in *Freimaurer und Geheimbünde im 18. Jahrhundert in Mitteleuropa*, 2nd ed., ed. Helmut Reinalter (Frankfurt/M.: Suhrkamp, 1986); see also *Aufklärungsgesellschaften*, ed. Helmut Reinalter (Frankfurt: S. Fischer, 1993).

22. The German notion of Bildung is unique and untranslatable. It means a good deal more than just "education." It suggests an ongoing process of self-development, aimed at the production of an ideal type of cultivated person whose character and mind function in full harmony. As such, Bildung may be a way of life rather than a kind of education. See *Bildungsbürgertum im 19. Jahrhundert*, 4 vols. (Stuttgart: Klett, 1985–92), esp. *Vol. 2: Bildungsgüter und Bildungswissen*, ed. Reinhart Koselleck (1990), introduction 13 ff. In recent studies influenced by "culturalist" approaches, Bildung and the mode of life associated with it (its "habitus"), are considered to have exercised a decisive influence on the formation of middle-class identity in nineteenth-century Germany, the so-called century of the "Bürgertum." As an important example, see Manfred Hettling and Stefan-Ludwig Hoffmann, "Der bürgerliche Wertehimmel: Zum Problem individueller Lebensführung im 19. Jahrhundert," *Geschichte und Gesellschaft* 23 (1997): 334–59. Case studies include U. Döcker, *Die Ordnung der bürgerlichen Welt: Verhaltensideale und soziale Praktiken im 19. Jahrhundert* (Frankfurt: Campus, 1994); P. Sarasin, *Stadt und Bürger: Struktureller Wandel und bürgerliche Lebenswelt. Basel 1870–1900* (Basel, 1990, and Göttingen: Vandenhoeck & Ruprecht, 1997).

23. See Otto Dann, ed., *Lesegesellschaften und bürgerliche Emanzipation: Ein europäischer Vergleich* (Munich: Beck, 1981).

24. For more information on this, see Helmut Reinalter, ed., *Lexikon zu Demokratie und Liberalismus 1750–1848/49* (Frankfurt/M.: Suhrkamp, 1993).

25. There is an abundant literature on Burschenschaften; see, for example, the articles published by Wolfgang Hardtwig, some of which are reprinted in Wolfgang Hardtwig, *Nationalismus und Bürgerkultur in Deutschland 1500–1914: Ausgewählte Aufsätze* (Göttingen: Vandenhoeck & Ruprecht, 1994).

26. See above, note 3.

27. See Jürgen Reulecke, *Sozialer Frieden durch soziale Reform: Der Centralverein für das Wohl der arbeitenden Klassen in der Frühindustrialisierung* (Wuppertal: Hammer, 1983).

28. See the voluminous study by Petra Wilhelmy, *Der Berliner Salon im 19. Jahrhundert (1780–1914)* (Berlin: de Gruyter, 1989); also Verena von der Heyden-Rynsch, *Europäische Salons: Höhepunkte einer versunkene n weiblichen Kultur* (Munich: Artemis & Winkler, 1992).

29. See especially Tenfelde, "Entfaltung des Vereinswesens."

30. As an important example, see Ursula Krey, *Vereine in Westfalen 1840–1855: Strukturwandel, soziale Spannungen, kulturelle Entfaltung* (Paderborn: Schöningh, 1993). Older studies include Herbert Freudenthal, *Vereine in Hamburg* (Hamburg, 1958); Heinz Schmitt, *Das Vereinsleben der Stadt Weinheim a. d. Bergstrasse* (Weinheim, 1963); Ingo Tornow, *Das Münchner Vereinswesen in der ersten Hälfte des 19. Jahrhunderts, mit einem Ausblick auf die zweite Jahrhunderthälfte* (Munich: Stadtarchiv, 1977).

31. See Theo Schiller, *Stiftungen im Gesellschaftlichen Prozess: Ein politikwissenschaftlicher Beitrag zu Recht, Soziologie und Sozialgeschichte der Stiftungen in Deutschland* (Baden-Baden:

Nomos, 1969); Arno Lustiger, ed., *Jüdische Stiftungen in Frankfurt a. M.* (Frankfurt, 1988; reprint Sigmaringen: Thorbecke, 1994).

32. See Michael Prinz, *Brot und Dividende: Konsumvereine in Deutschland und England vor 1914* (Göttingen: Vandenhoeck & Ruprecht, 1996).

33. A recent comprehensive study has been provided by Andreas Biefang, *Politisches Bürgertum in Deutschland vom 1857–1867: Nationale Organizationen und Interessen* (Düsseldorf: Droste, 1994).

34. Documented in Shlomo Na'aman and Hans-Peter Harstick, eds., *Die Konstituierung der deutschen Arbeiterbewegung 1862/63: Darstellung und Dokumentation* (Assen: Van Gorcum, 1975).

35. See above, note 3.

36. See Jürgen Kocka, *Arbeitsverhältnisse und Arbeiterexistenzen: Grundlagen der Klassenbildung im 19. Jahrhundert* (Bonn: Dietz, 1990), 73 (and the subsequent chapter, 76ff.); *Arbeiter im Deutschen Kaiserreich*, 163ff.

37. See Gustav Mayer, "Die Trennung der proletarischen von der bürgerlichen Demokratie in Deutschland, 1863–1870," 1912, reprinted in *Radikalismus, Sozialismus und bürgerliche Demokratie*, ed. Hans-Ulrich Wehler (Frankfurt/M.: Suhrkamp, 1969), 108–94.

38. The organizational culture of the lower classes has been richly documented during the past two decades; see for instance, Gerhard A. Ritter, ed., *Arbeiterkultur* (Königstein: Athenäum, 1978). As an English introduction, see Lynn Abrams, *Workers' Culture in Imperial Germany: Leisure and Recreation in the Rhineland and Westphalia* (London and New York: Routledge, 1992).

39. While historians of the Kaiserreich maintain that organized workers' culture was rooted in the constitutional and social framework of the political system of the Kaiserreich, and that the workers' associational life peaked under the Kaiserreich, others argue that mass membership reached a peak only in the 1920s and that these organizations became truly important only then. An abbreviated version of the latter view is presented in Peter Lösche and Franz Walter, "Zur Organisationskultur der sozialdemokratischen Arbeiterbewegung in der Weimarer Republik: Niedergang der Klassenkultur oder solidargemeinschaftlicher Höhepunkt?" *Geschichte und Gesellschaft* 15 (1989): 511–36; see the discussion by Hartmann Wunderer, *Geschichte und Gesellschaft* 18 (1992): 88–93. Secondly, many social historians would maintain that the strength of the German labor movement derived to a large degree from its roots in the labor movement culture and that in Great Britain the strength of labor was weaker because of a different cultural base. This view is challenged by Stefan Berger, *The British Labour Party and the German Social Democrats, 1900–1931* (Oxford: Clarendon, 1994).

40. M. Reiner Lepsius, "Parteiensystem und Sozialstruktur: Zum Problem der Demokratisierung der deutschen Gesellschaft," reprinted repeatedly, for instance in Gerhard A. Ritter, ed., *Deutsche Parteien vor 1918* (Cologne: Athenäum, 1973), 56–80; my translation.

41. Abundant evidence has been presented on this point since the 1880s. Much of this has been offered by American scholars. See, e.g., Jonathan Sperber, *Popular Catholicism in Nineteenth-Century Germany* (Princeton: Princeton University Press, 1984); a comprehensive discussion has been presented by Josef Mooser recently: "Das katholische Milieu in der bürgerlichen Gesellschaft: Zum Vereinswesen des Katholizismus im späten Deutschen Kaiserreich," in *Religion im Kaiserreich*, vol. 2, ed. Olaf Blaschke and Frank-

Michael Kuhlemann (Gütersloh: Kaiser, 1997), 59–92. Catholic lower-class associations have stimulated research interest; among several thoroughly researched studies published recently we still find conceptually narrow examples such as Winfried Halder, *Katholische Vereine in Baden und Württemberg 1848–1914* (Paderborn: Schöningh, 1994); and Ansgar Krimmer, *Der katholische Gesellenverein in der Diözese Rottenburg 1852–1945* (Paderborn: Schöningh, 1994); broadly conceptualized, see Antonius Liedhegener, *Christentum und Urbanisierung: Katholiken und Protestanten in Münster und Bochum 1830–1933* (Paderborn: Schöningh, 1998).

42. See my article on "Historische Milieus-Erblichkeit und Konkurrenz," in *Nation und Gesellschaft in Deutschland: Historische Essays*, ed. Manfred Hettling and Paul Nolte (Munich: Beck, 1996), 247–68. See also Klaus Tenfelde, "Die Arbeiterbewegung in der bürgerlichen Gesellschaft," *Mitteilungsblatt des Instituts zur Erforschung der europäischen Arbeiterbewegung* 18 (1997): 181–98.

43. Examples are presented in Heidi Rosenbaum, *Proletarische Familien: Arbeiterfamilien und Arbeiterväter im frühen 20. Jahrhundert zwischen traditioneller, sozialdemokratischer und kleinbürgerlicher Orientierung* (Frankfurt/M.: Suhrkamp, 1992). In her recent article on "Civil Society and the Collapse of the Weimar Republic," *World Politics* 49 (1997): 401–29, Sheri Berman correctly realizes that "however horizontally organized and civic-minded these associations may have been, they tended to hive their memberships off from the rest of society" and contributed to "ferociously jealous 'small republics,'" the latter being a quotation from Peter Fritzsche, *Rehearsals for Fascism: Populism and Political Mobilization in Weimar Germany* (New York: Oxford University Press, 1990), 232. Berman continues that Germany "was cleaved increasingly into distinct subcultures or communities, each of which had its own, separate associational life" (426). As I shall argue later on, it is basically this observation that questions neo-Tocquevillian views, which all too closely relate associationism to civil society. I do not agree with the other pillar of Berman's argument, that middle-class associationism was vulnerable to National Socialist invasion. So far, Berman argues on the basis of the excellent study by Rudy Koshar, *Social Life, Local Politics, and Nazism: Bourgeois Marburg, 1880 to 1935* (Chapel Hill: University of North Carolina Press, 1986). Though doubtlessly National Socialists managed to invade many middle-class associations, there are as many examples contrary to that, and in addition, as a Protestant university town, Marburg provided extraordinary preconditions.

44. See the article by Thomas Ertman in this volume.

45. In the course of two wars and two inflations, most of such clubs lost their properties. In those few cases in which considerable real estate was maintained, members were no longer willing to pay increased upkeep costs via high membership fees. In addition, the hereditary nature of club membership was interrupted by National Socialism (be they adherents or not) and by the other fundamental system changes of German history. To my knowledge, there is no comparative investigation of the British and German club systems.

46. See Helmut Cron, "Niedergang des Vereins," *Merkur* 13 (1959): 262–69.

47. See Robert Michels, *Zur Soziologie des Parteiwesens in der modernen Demokratie: Untersuchungen über die oligarchischen Tendenzen des Gruppenlebens*, reprint of the 2nd ed. (1925), ed. Werner Conze (Stuttgart: Kröner, n.d. [1957]).

48. As a recent introduction into German constitutional history, see Hartwig Brandt, *Der lange Weg in die demokratische Moderne: Deutsche Verfassungsgeschichte von*

1800–1945 (Darmstadt: Wissenchaftliche Buchgesellschaft, 1998); for the following paragraph, see Hans-Peter Ullmann, *Das Deutsche Kaiserreich 1871–1918* (Frankfurt/M.: Suhrkamp, 1995).

49. See especially Roger Chickering, *We Men Who Feel Most German: A Cultural Study of the Pan-German League, 1886–1914* (Boston, 1984); G. H. Eley, *Reshaping the German Right* (New Haven, Conn.: Yale University Press, 1980); Marilyn S. Coetzee, *The German Army League: Popular Nationalism in Wilhelmine Germany* (New York: Oxford University Press, 1990).

II

PRELUDES TO
DURABLE DEMOCRACIES

6

CIVIL SOCIETY, SUBSCRIBER DEMOCRACIES, AND PARLIAMENTARY GOVERNMENT IN GREAT BRITAIN

Robert J. Morris

THE CIVIL SOCIETY DEBATE AND THE BRITISH EXPERIENCE: THE IMPERFECT FIT

The growing debate around the concept of civil society presents the historian, especially the historian of Britain/the United Kingdom with a variety of problems. The first emerges from the number of distinct but interacting levels at which the debate is being conducted. At a normative level "civil society" is clearly a good thing. Almost without question, it is an attribute of a good society, which is sought by all.[1] Secondly, the debate has a major descriptive function. The task of simply defining and mapping out the nature and extent of civil society is a massive and continuing one. There is a hunger and enthusiasm among intellectuals and commentators on all sides to know how they and others fare and compare in the civil society experience. Thirdly, the debate is analytical, although attempts to model situations that create, have created, and are created by civil society seem very underdeveloped.

The current revival of the concept originated in the challenge and subsequent destruction of a variety of totalitarian regimes in Eastern Europe, the former Soviet Union, and Latin America and the concern for the establishment of stable pluralistic democracies in their place.[2]

It is natural that attempts to establish historical references for such a debate should turn to the British case. The history of nineteenth-century Britain, or to be more precise, the United Kingdom of England, Wales, Scotland, and Ireland was in many ways a "success" in the creation of a stable, tolerant, and pluralistic democracy. One of the most important master narratives of British history is the slow but insistent and successful struggle for democracy. The Reform Act of 1832 gave votes to the middle class; that of 1867, votes for the skilled working man; of 1884, for agricultural laborers; of 1918 for women and the remainder of the adult male population; and, finally, in 1927 for young women. Equally important, though often given less emphasis, was the granting of civil rights to Protestant nonconformists, Catholics, and Jews between 1820 and 1870. This narrative was embellished in a variety of ways with accounts of the rise of labor and the welfare state. Asides were added to the effect that the British had reforms and not revolutions like the French; that they were patriotic rather than being nationalistic or, even worse, fascist like Germany or Italy; and that they respected traditions (like the Royal Family) instead of the money-seeking of the Americans. Such naive self-satisfaction may be considerably tarnished in the late twentieth century, but can an understanding of the historical experience behind that narrative make a contribution to the debates around civil society in the 1990s, especially in light of the growing knowledge of the rich associational culture that characterized the public sphere of British Society?[3]

This chapter will emphasize that the success of the slow British march to democracy and any linkage this may have with associational activity depended upon a number of key features. Most important was the culture and practice within that associational activity. Second was the long period of development of such activity. This chapter will focus on a key phase of that development which saw a decisive move from main force to associational modes of conflict resolution and from the dominance of closed forms of association to more open and transparent ones. The third feature was the willingness and ability to overcome a series of disruptive religious, status, and class divisions within that society. In this respect, Ireland was the notable exception. All three aspects will be linked to divisions within the political and social structures of both the aristocratic elite and the urban middle classes.

British society in the late eighteenth and in the nineteenth century had, in varying and increasing degrees, most of the key features that the modern literature requires of a civil society. Social and economic relationships of all kinds were regulated by a jealously guarded rule of law. This law was wholly derived from Parliament without the limitation of any extra parliamentary constitutional forms, but once established had considerable autonomy. In England, trial by jury provided some mediation between the individual and the state. Economic relationships were structured by the sustained spread of the market economy. Price regulation such as the Assize of Bread had gone by 1800. Attempts to legislate for minimum wages or to limit the introduction of machinery failed in the 1830s.[4] Trade monopolies were demolished, and the quasi-monopolies created by protective tariffs were removed between 1820 and 1870.[5] The most important was the repeal of the Corn Laws in 1846. Fragments of communal and feudal rights were commuted into cash or parceled out into individual property rights that could be freely bought and sold. The rich associational culture, which forms the focus of this contribution, had its origins in the late seventeenth and early eighteenth centuries.[6] In the later part of the eighteenth century this culture became more public and more open in its structure and between 1810 and 1850 entered an assertive and expansive phase. The legal space within which free association took place came after a period of often violent and repressive conflict extended rapidly to the point where the controls on association characteristic of countries like France were totally absent. The period between 1790 and 1819 was one in which trade unions and political associations not sanctioned by the ruling authorities were banned through the Six Acts and by legislation against trade unions. In the British case, war and the spectacle of revolution in France initially provided motivation for inventive associational activity by the governing and property-owning classes and repression of activity from other social classes. Peace and the economic revival of the 1820s brought further expansion and a reduction in state repression. By the mid-1820s, trade unions were no longer illegal, and a variety of legislative provisions directed by the Registrar General of Friendly Societies supported and regulated a wide range of mutual societies, notably for burial and sick insurance, and the precommercial form of building societies. Savings banks were also supported by legislation.[7] In the early 1830s, small amounts of government subsidy were offered to a limited number of societies concerned with working-class education.

The period saw the creation of a major area of public space outside the prescriptive relationships of the family and the state—between the tyranny of cousins and the tyranny of the state.[8] Any easy analogy between the situation in Britain between 1800 and 1850 and the developments of the late twentieth century needs to be tempered by two features.

First there are major differences in the focus of the debate. The late twentieth-century debate is dominated by an interest in civil society as a form of mediation between the individual and the state. In Britain, the philosophical debate begun by the Scottish Enlightenment thinkers of the mid/late eighteenth century was more concerned with gaining and sustaining a stable and ethical relationship between the individual and a coherent and orderly wider society. The practices of the early nineteenth century described in this chapter showed a concern for the relationships of the individual to the social group and of social groups to each other, as well as relationships with the state. Both periods were interested in the autonomy of the self-directed individual, but the early nineteenth-century British debate and practice also contained a major interest in social order.[9]

By the 1820s debate over the proper conduct of civil society was increasingly concerned with what is now called pluralism, notably in the relationships between religious groups. Such pluralism was bounded. Tolerance of the non-English languages of the British state declined rapidly, and concepts of race exhibited increasing degrees of closure not just to non-white but often to non-Saxon peoples. Citizenship was a contested part of the debate. This had less to do with ethnicity and language than with property, maleness, education, and the ability to take an informed part in political debate. Religion played an initial and declining part in the debate. The concept of citizenship was widened to include skilled trades and the ability to take part in the economy.

Secondly, the structure of power in the eighteenth century makes it difficult to make a clear distinction between the prescriptive relationships of family and those of the state. Power in the British state rested with an executive that was responsible to representative parliamentary institutions, which were effectively controlled by a limited number of landowning families in association with the dwindling but still useful power of the crown. Party was a concept often used in political contest, but parties were essentially loose alliances of family and quasi-family relationships. The contest for state power took place between a changing selection of family compacts and their supporters. These supporters might be sons, cousins, tenants, servants, tradesmen, and others who recognized the obligations of patronage. The twentieth-century notion of client politics has some analogy with this situation.

Many of the concepts involved in the modern literature relate very imperfectly to the experience of Britain in the eighteenth and early nineteenth centuries. Party was a form of social organization directed to the contest for state power, but it had little of the formal, rule-based, clearly defined nature of a twentieth-century political party. Those involved in the politics of this period would have understood the notion of "interest." They talked of the corn interest, the East India interest, the woolen interest, and many more and sought to ensure that they were represented in Parliament through MPs, petitions, and witnesses before parliamentary committees. Finally, any attempt to use the notion of "democracy" is not appropriate. The British experience was one of "representative" government.

The slow dance of the British historical process might be summarized as follows:

1. The civil wars of the seventeenth century led to a permanent destruction of the monopolistic power of the crown.
2. The settlement of 1688 created a representative form of government based upon property, mainly landed property and urban "interests."
3. Constitutional changes in the 1820s and 1830s created a more liberal and pluralistic form of representative government by the extension of the franchise and recognition of a legal place for dissenters and Catholics in public life.
4. The progressive enlargement of the franchise created full democracy by 1927.

This chapter focuses on the context provided by a particular form of civil society for the developments of the third period. This was the period that established the nature of associational culture in Britain and initiated a period of representative government with increasing numbers of voters who needed to organize and be organized.

Civil society as presented in the current literature seems to be a concept, normative, descriptive, and analytical, but it is not yet at least a narrative. Civil society does not seem to have acquired a stages theory like the 1960s account of "economic growth." Civil society does have a before and an after. It is the goal of the "good society." The British narrative, which takes some 150 to 200 years to unwind, sits uneasily with the speed of post-1989 developments. The historian may appear to slip with ease into the so-called historical path analysis, although there is a need to show why the historical actors made certain choices at key points in the narrative. That being said, it is hard to envision simple and direct models of the type civil society creates democracy under conditions x, y, and z or democracy creates civil society under conditions r, s, and t. It is easier to envision a model in which socioeconomic development produces cultural and institutional resources and creates conditions for both civil society and representative government and the sustenance and expansion of both.

Hence this chapter will give attention to key features in the rich associational culture that came to dominate public life in Britain, namely those that seemed likely to support and expand stable, pluralistic, and eventually democratic government in Britain. Such features were not inevitable or self-evident. The openness and transparency of the associations that came to dominate this period were very different from the closed "club" culture of the earlier period. Equally, the particularist cultures of nationality, race, language, and religion that came to dominate other parts of Europe played a small part in the British structure.

Two features dominated the civil society of Britain in the first half of the nineteenth century, the public meeting and the open voluntary association. They were notable not only in themselves but also because of the practices they embodied. They were also important because they effectively replaced other means by which interests and identities could be articulated and conflict legitimately furthered and resolved. Two incidents that took place in the commercial and industrial town of Leeds in the north of England illustrate the nature of this change. They were both ones in which established authority was challenged. In the second the matter was resolved by main force. The important features of the first incident were the manner in which legitimacy was claimed through the public and open nature of the meetings, the practice of speaking to formal motions upon which votes could be taken, and the claim to hear "the other side" before taking the vote. The rhetoric of this meeting was of informed, rational, self-directing individuals hearing the evidence and arguments and then taking a decision. This was the basis of the claim for legitimacy, not main force and the threat of violence.

TWO INCIDENTS IN NORTHERN ENGLAND;
CIVIL SOCIETY AND MAIN FORCE

In early September 1839, the British and Foreign School Society[10] announced a public meeting in the Commercial Buildings with Edward Baines, Whig evangelical MP for the borough, in the chair and Lieutenant Fabian, RN agent of the society, to give an address. The meeting had been announced the previous week as a "public meeting." When the meeting opened the organizers found the hall packed with supporters of the Charter.[11] George White, who had recently been committed to York [12] Castle for demanding money from Leeds shopkeepers for the Chartist organization, stood up: "I move an amendment that Mr. Joshua Hobson take the chair." (Hobson was the publisher of the *Northern Star*.) A vote was taken. There was a huge majority for the new chairman as well as mingled cheers and hisses, and Mr. Hobson came onto the platform.

> Hobson. I have been elected by this meeting to act as Chairman, and therefore it will be your duty to vacate (Loud Cheers).
>
> Mr. Baines. Have you paid for this room?
> Hobson. No.
>
> Mr. Baines. Then you have no right to assume the position of Chairman here, and I shall not vacate the Chair unless by force (Great hissing and uproar).
>
> Hobson then challenged the organizers: If the gentlemen who object to my possessing the chair, disagree with the decision already come to, let them put it to the vote again, and let the meeting decide.

What followed among the noise and confusion was a minor debate on the nature of the civil society being created in Britain during those decades.

> Fleming, a socialist lecturer. This I contend is a public meeting called to take certain matters into consideration and consequentially every individual has a right to speak his sentiments. We have acted in accordance with the ordinary rule observed at public meetings and have committed no breach of etiquette in choosing as we have done by an overwhelming majority, a chairman. We are ready to hear all that may be said, and when the other side have done, we shall be prepared in the same spirit of candor and fairness, to deliver the opinions we entertain.
>
> Rev. Thomas Scales (a Congregationalist minister). No person who is not a member of that society has a right to interfere with the arrangements already made for holding this meeting. [13]

The following week the society made another attempt to hold the meeting. Admission was by ticket only, and attendance was, according to the Whig newspaper, "very numerous and respectable." In his introduction, Baines said,

It is a matter of high gratification to me that the buoyancy of public spirit of Leeds shows that it can rise above all detraction.

The major speakers of the meeting made very little reference to events of the previous week, but many in the hall clearly found matters deeply troubling. Rev. J. E. Giles found Wednesday evening

an insult to the great principles of civil and religious liberty . . . a triumph of noise. . . . those who hired this room had a right to dispose of it as they saw fit. . . . let argument be met by argument. . . . we came not here for party purposes, but to promote the great catholic object of enlightening the mind.

Rev. John Ely, congregational minister at East Parade, the chapel of the Baines family, joined in,

Burke once told us that the impotent chirping of a few grasshoppers, while the British cattle were reposing in the field and chewing their cud beneath the British Oak, were not to be regarded as the state of the whole community.[14]

Some three years later in August 1842 the nature of the contest was very different. The Leeds magistrates met to consider reports of disorder in the towns and villages west of the borough.[15] On Wednesday morning a party of "turnouts" were reported in the weaving villages on the southern boundary of Leeds. By midday some twelve hundred to fifteen hundred people had marched from Bradford Moor and stopped the mills in Stanningley and Bramley.[16] The Whig *Mercury* skillfully represented them as outsiders, "marching from Bradford" and "the itinerant body of Lancashire turnouts . . . strangers, ill dressed and dusty." This was less plausible for the events of the afternoon when after a public meeting on Hunslet Moor attended by persons from Hunslet and Holbeck "generally of the lowest class," attacks were made on a number of local mills such as that of Edward and George Tatham where the plug of the boiler was forced, thus draining the water and stopping the mill with minimal damage. Within a few hours order was restored by the energetic action of the army and special constables. His Royal Highness Prince George of Cambridge led the Seventeenth Lancers and a troop of horse artillery, whilst Lieutenant Colonel Beckett, a member of a long-standing local gentleman merchant family, now firmly established in land and banking, led the yeomanry of the Yorkshire Hussars. The military were supported by local police and special constables and soon reinforced by units brought in on the new railway.[17] There was initial relief, but after a few weeks complaints grew. Noisy crowds gathered to watch the troops parade. Soldiers were accused of fighting, accosting women, and interrupting the respectable middle classes of west and north Leeds on their way to religious worship. By January, the *Mercury* wanted them gone; "with an orderly population and a police force of 128 men, the inhabitants of Leeds require no resident military force. . . . Our Ancestors, in their jealousy for the maintenance of public liberty, were accustomed to consider a standing army in time of peace as a public grievance."[18]

It was the "civil" behavior of the first incident that came to dominate the way in which British society created opinion, interests, and identities and came to express and resolve the conflicts involved. These practices were an important aspect of social stability and integration. They were embedded in a culture of voluntary societies and public meetings that had evolved since the late seventeenth century. The impact of this culture was not just in the density of such organizations, which was formidable and increasing, but in the practices of open debate and open rule-based membership involved in both. Three phases may be identified in this long process.

ASSOCIATIONAL CULTURE: FROM CLOSED TO OPEN FORMS

There was a close link between early eighteenth-century associational activity and the growing civic consciousness of the "middling sort."[19] In the main, the eighteenth century was a world of clubs, lodges, and trusts. Entry was controlled by a variety of means. There were the rituals of the Masonic lodges, the friendly societies, and quasi–trade union craft associations. In some groups, members had to be sponsored and could be rejected by the votes of existing members.[20] In others, the association was a closed group of trustees who were self-selecting, choosing replacements for those who died or left. The Leeds Charity School originated in a subscription in 1705. The position of trustee was consolidated in a closed circle of Tory Anglican families, Cooksons, Sheepshanks, Wilsons, Becketts, and Blaydes; clergymen; merchants; and bankers whose task was to sustain the initial objective. The records in the Leeds City Archives noted,

> A subscription was entered into for the purpose of establishing a charity school in Leeds for the maintenance and education of 40 poor children in the knowledge and practice of the Christian religion as practiced and taught in the Church of England, for the teaching of them to read and write English, and a competent skill in Arithmetic and other necessary qualifications for honest trades and professions.[21]

These organizations ensured identity and continuity for charitable endeavor. They gave discipline and structure to the debates and meetings of the coffeehouse and tavern. Objectives ranged widely from politics, trade and neighborhood interests to literature, collective insurance, savings, or just simple sociability under a structure of rules and chairmen guided by the developing code of polite society, with its notions of disciplined, elegant, and sometimes mannered interaction between individuals.[22]

In the last quarter of the eighteenth century, there was an increasing number of associations whose task was to organize oppression and social discipline:

Societies for the Suppression of Felons; Watch and Ward Societies; and, in the late 1780s and 1790s as a response to political instability, the Proclamation Society, the Association Movement, and the Society for the Suppression of Vice. These societies were not closed in a formal sense, but they were designed to limit the autonomy of others. Above all, the various volunteer yeomanry regiments provided ostensibly to defend against French invasion but equally important for internal security duties were a collective voluntary embodiment of physical force identified with nation and property.[23] In terms of the development of civil society, these volunteer regiments have a very equivocal place. They involved rule-based cooperation by large numbers of the middle classes and some of the more deferential members of the lower classes, but their purpose was to impose social order by the aggressive and repressive use of force.

By the 1810s, one form of association, and in its full development a relatively new one, had begun to dominate, namely the subscriber democracies of the urban middle classes.[24] This label has been derived from their open and accountable nature. They were greedy for public support. Membership was gained by the payment of a cash subscription, which implied support for the objectives of the society and agreement to obey published rules.[25] Members organized themselves in public space through public meetings with their ritual of motions proposed and "debated." They published annual reports with accounts and lists of subscribers as part of the relationship of accountability between committee and member subscribers. An increasing number had their own public building, such as the Philosophical Hall, the Mechanics Institution, the General Infirmary, and the Zion Schoolroom. Others used the public space of the town hall, the commercial buildings, or the dissenting chapel. In Leeds, the Benevolent or Stranger's Friend Society, dedicated to poor relief, was an early success in 1798. The Religious Tract Society arrived in 1804 and was followed by other bible and missionary societies. The Philosophical and Literary Society and the Mechanics Institution were established in the 1820s with the Temperance Society following in the early 1830s. These societies were based upon urban communities. In meetings the leaders of these societies often presented themselves as "the people of Leeds." They used the language of class sparingly to assert responsibility and interest rather than exclusion.

This development was encouraged by new and national systems of media and transport. By the 1830s, these societies were using a wider range of media. Print had always been important, but in the 1820s the reduction in the cost of printing and the wider range of newspaper and periodical presses increased the exposure of the activities of these societies. Provincial papers often gave apparently verbatim accounts of the public meetings of the leading societies, although these accounts were clearly filtered through reporter's shorthand, memories, and the willingness of participants to give written versions of speeches. The public display of the procession exploited the growing number of improved streets. Public dinners in the new urban locations of halls and institutions were fully reported. In the 1830s, improved roads and then the completion of the major network of intercity railways made the delegate meeting and the annual assemblies at national level easier to sustain. Easier communication created a sense of local civic and urban movements being part of greater national movements, which was at its most powerful in the Anti–Corn Law League and the Chartist movement but equally important for the bible and education societies and the antislavery movement. Individuals could read about societies like theirs in other towns and hear visitors like Lieutenant Fabian who came from the national society.

The growth of these societies moved at a different pace in different places. Some responded to particular crises of disease or disorder, others followed fashion. Early developments were stronger in large towns with a significant dissenting middle class. The subscriber democracy was often the public expression of social claims by those who felt excluded by state and earlier associational forms. A strong Unitarian congregation, usually composed of a small number of high-status elite families often, as in Manchester, played a disproportionate part in initiating these open voluntary societies. The Unitarians comprised an economically powerful minority that had until the early nineteenth century been excluded by law and prejudice from much of public life. In the early 1790s, their houses had been the targets of rioters in Birmingham.[26] Smaller towns with a low percentage of professional and commercial people experienced later development.[27]

Those involved saw these organizations as important, coherent, and new. Edward Baines, junior MP, evangelical, newspaper editor, and protagonist at the Chartist invasion of the 1839 meeting, summed up what the development of these voluntary societies meant to him.

> I might dwell upon many institutions and associations for the diffusion of knowledge, and for the dispensing of every kind of good, which have arisen within the present or last generation and which have flourished most in the manufacturing towns and villages—such as mechanics institutes, literary societies, circulating libraries, youth's guardian societies, friendly societies, temperance societies, medical charities, clothing societies, benevolent and district visiting societies—forty-nine fiftieths of which are of recent origin.[28]

The importance of these developments had been realized by 1820 when Thomas Chalmers, a Scottish evangelical minister, advocated voluntary associations as a means of stabilizing industrial society.[29]

Baines was not just listing societies. This group was seen as a coherent whole. In 1846, a handbill advocating the Leeds Permanent Building Society (then in its origins as a voluntary and mutual association) related these societies to a wider vision.

> Young men especially are recommended to join this society and thus lay the foundation for future comfort and ease. The Temperance movement has removed temptation out of the way of thousands, and the Mechanics Institutes and Reading Rooms have taught them many useful lessons. Let these advan-

tages be further improved by securing a comfortable habitation. The means are now within their reach and they are invited to embrace them.[30]

RESOURCES FOR A CIVIL SOCIETY

The British brought a wide range of historical resources to the decisions they made in the first half of the nineteenth century regarding the conduct of public meetings and voluntary societies and the manner in which they derived the legitimacy of authority and public opinion. Since the late seventeenth century, local government had involved collective decision making by a local elite under chairmen chosen by rule. During the eighteenth century the self-selecting nature of these municipal corporations meant that an increasing portion of the local elite, usually those not of the established religion, were excluded. The practice of policy making by debate and vote among representatives elected by property owners emerged in a variety of so-called Improvement and Police Commissioners, established by act of Parliament for a variety of local government tasks. The experience of collective debate under rules was also one that was common to many nonconformist religious groups that did not have the support of endowments and taxes as did the established church. Hence they needed to collect cash by subscription and pews rent, create collective forms of ownership, and decide policy if they were to build places of worship and appoint ministers. The nature of Parliament and parliamentary elections and the weakness of the crown also enabled the British to develop habits of collective decision making. The apparent nature of parliamentary debate was often taken as a model for public and voluntary society meetings. Although the selection of members of Parliament often took place through the nomination of a small number of landowners, there were many who were chosen by a substantial number of electors. Finally, there was the increasingly used right to petition Parliament, which was the occasion of many public meetings.[31]

The early nineteenth century also inherited and developed two discourses of public life that were powerful supports to a civil society. The Scottish enlightenment supplied the notion of the ethical, autonomous individual who cooperated and interacted with others through informed rational argument and debate.[32] The middle-class radicals used a version of this discourse, which they identified with seventeenth-century Puritan radicals, notably the poet John Milton. The following quotations are taken from editorials written by Samuel Smiles in 1839 during his period as editor of the *Leeds Times*. They are a powerful expression of the liberal democratic position held by a minority of the middle classes. These editorials were written in bitter opposition to Chartists and government alike.

> We object to the employment of anything like force, either for the propagation of opinion, or the enforcement of political and social reforms. Truth is

strong enough to work in its own way. Government has hitherto been so much a matter of force and so little a matter of utility, that without seeking to remove the causes of discontent by good measures, it has invariably attempted to crush and repress them by the vulgar expedient of brute force.[33]

> The first indispensable preliminary for the adoption of great principles and measures of policy is their bold and uncompromising discussion and agitation. All that is required to enable them to pass into law is that general conviction of their utility which public discussion will sooner or later establish.[34]

He saw education and the extension of "the great market of the suffrage"[35] as the means to achieve these ends and rejected not only violence, but also monopolies of political and economic power.

There was nothing inevitable about the manner in which these historical resources assisted in the development of the culture of meetings and voluntary societies outlined here. There were many social forces that created difficulties for this process and for the link between the civil society that emerged and the creation of a liberal democracy in Britain. The concept of liberal democracy implies that state power was regulated and legitimated by some form of representative selection, usually through the votes of adult citizens, and that free, rational, and informed decisions rather than force or influence should direct the allocation of those votes. Liberal democracy requires provision for a change of government and policy direction without violence.

Individuals and groups operated under the rule of law, and authority went to the majority. There was and is a tension between the "democratic" notion of the rule of the majority and the pluralistic notions of tolerance and integration, which were implied in the practice of the associational culture of the period.

Even after reform in 1832 British practice was far from this ideal. When Whig leaders Lords Melbourne and Grey justified the changes, they used the language of interests and classes and made no attempt at a balanced democratic suffrage. Only a sixth of adult males had the vote, and dramatic variations in constituency size remained.

THREATS TO STABLE LIBERAL PLURALISM IN BRITAIN

There were several other difficulties. First there was the threat of aristocratic dominance. Their power as landowners, political power, and naked social prestige, together with their ability to profit from the commercial economy and recruit new wealth, made a relatively small number of families a formidable influence. Several authors see their power as an effective barrier to the development of a full capitalist bourgeois society in Britain.[36]

Conflicts derived from tensions over production had always been present in Britain, but they reached a new intensity in the 1820s and 1830s, notably in the textile districts. The "plug plot" riots of the Chartist years were only one of a series of strikes in which main force was met by the military and police action of the state and which diverted the middle classes from the culture of debate and association to that of armed associations.[37] Behind the strikes and disputes were nebulous dreams of general strikes, Owenite socialist utopias, or returns to the state control of wages and prices.

Even in the textile districts, the class identities building around the control of capital and the sale of labor had none of the precise demarcation or unity of social experience that some theorists and contemporary commentators attributed to them. The language of class, especially in the environment of associational culture, was the language of "classes" plural. This reflected a reality in which the interests and social activities of the middle-class elite of merchants, major manufacturers, and their professional allies could be very different from the insecurities of shopkeepers, master craftsmen, and the lesser manufacturers and professional men. The challenge of the radical middle class reflected in the quotations from Smiles in 1839 was part of this tension. Wage earners were equally divided. The elite of male artisans, craftsmen, and supervisory workers had very different interests from casual labor and the groups of female and younger male labor.[38] This lack of coherence in class cultures was a threat to stability but also an important aspect of the context within which associational culture operated.

Equally serious was the actual and potential disruption created by religious and political divisions within the middle classes themselves. The history of both Newcastle and Leeds recorded incidents in the 1790s and 1800s in which philosophical and debating societies had broken up because of political disputes.[39] One reason why many towns were cautious about seeking political representation in the late eighteenth century was the tension and mayhem created by political contest. Essentially, British politics was organized around two loose alliances. The Tories were led by a group of Tory landowning families. They believed in sustaining a strong central government based upon the crown and the established (state) Church of England. The Whigs were led by a group of Whig landowning families who wanted a more diffuse structure of power. They tended to attract urban dissenters who resented the power of the state Church and the closed associational monopolies established in the seventeenth and early eighteenth centuries. In the urban localities, the Tories tended to attract those who believed in a more hierarchical structure of society and attended the established Church. The disruptive power of this contest may be illustrated by the case of working-class education, which most middle-class leaders believed was essential for future social stability. Despite this, progress was delayed by the failure to agree on the relationship between the state, religion, and the supply of education.

Lastly, attention must be drawn to the ethnic and national conflicts within the United Kingdom that had been created by the acts of union of 1707 (Scotland) and 1801 (Ireland). State and nation were not the same. Scotland had experienced the only really effective armed rebellion in eighteenth-century Britain (1745) and a new wave of national consciousness in the first half of the nineteenth century.[40] In Ireland the rebellion of the United Irishmen (1798) had been extensive and threatening, while the Catholic emancipation campaign of the 1820s provided a more subtle challenge to the coherence and stability of civil society in the United Kingdom.[41]

VOLUNTARY SOCIETIES AND SOCIAL INTEGRATION

In the context of these divisions, fractures, factions, and fragments in British society, both potential and actual, associational culture operated in two crucial ways. First it enabled the different elements of British society to assert difference without the need to eliminate "others." While the bitter battle over the nature and control of state education halted progress, the education of working-class children was directed by several voluntary societies, notably the British and Foreign School Societies, which represented evangelical Protestants, and the National Society, which operated within the tradition of the state Anglican Church. The bible and missionary societies each had different associations for different denominations and for different combinations of denominations that would cooperate. Voluntary poor relief enabled the middle classes to act while the political debate over the Poor Law proceeded. In Leeds the Benevolent or Stranger's Friend Society operated in loose association with the Wesleyan Methodist Chapel. As political tension rose in the 1830s the Anglicans felt increasingly uncomfortable about this and formed their own Church District Visiting Society.[42] Even in an apparently tranquil arena like the Flower and Vegetable Societies, this capacity for variety could ease tensions. There were artisan and lower middle-class societies that concentrated on the sort of vegetables and flowers grown behind urban cottages, while others had sections for the precious hothouse flowers grown by the gardeners employed by wealthy town elites. At the same time, all these societies operated within the same culture of public meetings, committees, annual reports, motions proposed, speeches given, and accounts published. Those who walked from the meeting of the British and Foreign Bible Society to the Church District Visiting Society would notice the difference in content but would be immediately familiar with the form and practice of the meeting.

A very specific feature of this period was also important for the impact of this associational culture on British society and political direction. Rule 34 of the Leeds Philosophical and Literary Society stated, "The subjects of all compositions and conversations . . . may be selected from any branch of philosophy or general literature, excluding discussions on politics and religion."

This elite cultural society was responsible for a variety of initiatives in the town ranging from the Mechanics Institution and Infants School to the statistical surveys of the 1830s. Its members consisted of an elite deeply divided by religion and politics. This rule was the basis on which they cooperated. The same rule appeared in the Mechanics Institution and many other organizations. When it failed the result was division, which often compromised the social and cultural objectives of that elite.

Thus the 1820s and 1830s saw a strong associational culture establishing itself for the urban middle classes, notably for its male elite. Its importance lay not so much in density; indeed variety might have been more important. The strategic contribution made by this culture to the progress the British made toward a stable open liberal democracy in the twentieth century lay in key features of ideology and practice within the dominant elements of that culture as it developed from the 1820s onward. An association was open to those who supported its aims, accepted its rules, and paid their subscription. Accountability was a major feature expressed through the election of committees and officials by subscribers and the publication of annual reports and accounts. The ritual of debate and public meeting identified the association with its community. There was an increasing ideology of tolerance in the practice of debate, hearing the other side but eliminating topics that caused division through the "no religion, no politics" rules. The dominant group of urban associations was part of a strategy through which the middle-class elite sought to consolidate the middle classes and to incorporate the working class. It was this strategic desire that gave these key developments in associational culture openness, accountability, and limited tolerance their momentum.

The long-term influence of this culture may be demonstrated by the manner in which two key out-groups gained qualified access to state and political power. The working-class elite of skilled males was drawn cautiously into this open associational form and away from the closed world of lodges and ritual oaths. A few did accept the offer to join Mechanics Institutions. Others were involved in the transformation of the trade unions in the 1860s. The labor party of the early twentieth century was based upon an infrastructure of associations, Socialist Sunday Schools, Clarion Rambling Clubs, ILP (Independent Labour Party) Branches, the Co-operative Movement, and the related Women's Co-operative Guild.[43] For the women's movement in its broadest sense the culture of associations was an area of contest and a means of access to public life.[44] In the 1830s most women were restricted to limited activities such as collecting subscriptions for the Bible Society, while male clerics and treasurers held the platform. Others, notably in the Antislavery Movement, activated the rhetoric of the meeting to claim places for themselves in the delegate meetings of the movement.[45] Both labor and many participants in the women's movement used associational culture to claim a legitimate[46] place in public life. In Edinburgh the Ladies Edinburgh Debating Society met in the drawing rooms of the elite houses of the New Town in the 1860s and 1870s to debate questions of the day in a way that their elders would have thought presumptuous. The Ladies Edinburgh Educational Association prepared members for university examinations a generation before women could legally enter the universities. It was characteristic of both that they ensured that they debated and held meetings in the correct manner. In such an arena the first generation of women to enter the public sphere of local politics used the associational culture of civil society to train themselves.[47]

IRELAND AND SCOTLAND: FAILURE AND SUCCESS

In formal terms the unit of representative cum democratic government under consideration here is that of the United Kingdom, which consisted of four national units. Despite separate religious, educational, and legal systems, and distinctive differences in language and culture, Scotland not only remained within the United Kingdom, but played a creative part in the formation of the associational culture outlined above. Adam Ferguson and Adam Smith were the first to theorize about the importance of civil society. The practice of Mechanics Institutions and Savings Banks originated in Scotland, as did much of the content and style of the Literary and Philosophical Societies.[48] In part this was related to the nature of the state in Scotland, or rather the space left by the lack of an effective state in Scotland. After 1707, Scotland was not so much ruled from Westminster as not ruled at all. Apart from the law courts there were no central state agencies and day-to-day governance lay in the hands of the magistrates, corporations, and parishes.[49]

Ireland proved to be quite different. The 1820s saw the closure of voluntary institutions. The open, liberal Protestant range of institutions never prospered in the same way that they did in the large cities of England, Wales, and Scotland. In Ireland, associational culture was trapped by urban constitutions, which had excluded Catholics through both law and practice.[50] The growth of labor and working-class organizations later in the century was hampered by the divisive nature of religion and debates over the form of the state. There were brief moments of organization across civil society, but in general Ireland, notably in the cities of the north, was a case in which a dense network of associational life served to divide and exclude rather than create true subscriber democracies.[51] There are several reasons why the density of organization in urban Ireland failed to produce a stable liberal democracy. It is unlikely that the division between Protestant and Catholic was in itself a sufficient cause. The answer probably lies in the nature and motivations of the urban elite. In 1837, Leeds elected the first Catholic mayor of an English city since the Reformation, James Holdforth, silk spinner.[52] On the other side of the Atlantic, Montreal, divided by language as well as religion, achieved a stable relationship between francophone and anglophone communities. For a time the two elites provided alternate mayors for the city. In Montreal, both elites held substantial amounts of property; the French tended toward real estate and regional trade while the British were more interested in finance capital and international trade. The result was a mutual interest in a stable society.[53] There is also a hint that an open civil society tends to be urban centered. Ireland had a low level of urbanization, and many of the most divisive organizations in towns like Belfast, notably the Orange Order, were imported from the countryside.[54] Finally, Ireland had no tradition of independent statehood from which to derive resources such as the corporations, trusts, and royal burghs that were so important in Scotland.[55]

LESSONS FROM THE "SLOW" HISTORY OF CIVIL SOCIETY IN BRITAIN

The associational culture of meetings and voluntary societies established in the first half of the nineteenth century played a key part not just in the organization of civil society, but also in articulating relationships between civil society and the state, through pressure groups like the Anti–Corn Law League as well as through the redefinition of the nature of political parties. Local registration associations appeared quite rapidly after the Reform Act of 1832 had expanded the electorate, but the variety of local experience was vast. The Birmingham Caucus was founded in 1865, followed by the National Liberal Federation (NLF) in 1877. Both were designed to give "majorities" a place in policy making and to represent all sections of the party. Both were the inspiration of Joseph Chamberlain, the radical Birmingham manufacturer, but ironically the NLF supported William Gladstone when Chamberlain split from the party over Irish Home Rule.[56] By the 1860s the national state was responding to the growth of trade unions and labor organizations not by repression but by ensuring that trade unions became legal entities, which were then answerable in the courts.

The success of this associational culture was not just in terms of its ability to reproduce itself and spread into all sections of British society, or its tendency to support the practices and ideologies of a liberal democracy. Success must also be measured by the ability to promote stability and integration within a complex and rapidly changing society and to promote a limited pluralism and tolerance. There were several reasons for this success. Britain had urbanized slowly and early and in a manner that retained close links between town and country. Specific "peasant" or even rural movements were rare, and only in the Scottish Highlands did such a movement gain political expression.

In Britain there was a failure of any strong particularist ethnic or confessional movement to gain a dominant position in associational life. There was nothing to compare with the manner in which nationalist and Catholic associational and political formations edged out associations of liberal civic consciousness as tended to happen in the German states and the Austro-Hungarian Empire.[57] In the late nineteenth century, British consciousness, especially in its dominant English form, was fully occupied with its world imperial role. Patriotism was an open invitation to loyalty to the imperial crown. This invitation was dominated, but not restricted, by language, religion, and race and quite different from the particularism of national identity in late nineteenth-century German and Magyar associations. The invitation was widely accepted by Scots, Jews, Catholics, and working-class people. It was only the Catholic Irish who were ultimately to reject.

The spread of market relationships widened the social and economic space between the prescriptive relationships of state and family and the quasi-family or state relationships of the landed estate, the paternalistic employer, and the established religion, which already existed in 1800.

A central place in developing and sustaining the discourse and practice outlined in this chapter was played by the tension between the divided nature of British elites coupled to their need to cooperate to sustain their own privileges and power. The landed national elite was divided between the two major family compacts of Whig and Tory. The Whigs favored a diffusion of power among the major landed families. Their slogan "civil and religious liberty" referred mainly to their own liberty but did imply a limited tolerance. The Tories favored a strong central government of "church and king." The British crown was too weak to ensure dominance of either faction. Hence each group needed to appeal for support through the parliamentary system. By the end of the eighteenth century urban commercial and manufacturing elites were equally divided. In the countryside, patronage and client relationships directed by the great landowners were usually adequate, but in the complex society of the commercial and manufacturing towns the distribution of power was too diffuse, hence the appeal to "opinion." In this competition for influence the major target audience was often the lower-status middle class and "respectable" working class, in other words those groups with most sympathy for open individualistic and accountable forms of social and political interaction.

Running alongside this competition for influence was a further need of the urban elite to cooperate to ensure stable relationships with the rest of society and a secure base for their own power and privilege. Hence the need for a common ground for debate and opinion-forming in the societies that demanded "no religion and no politics." Urban elite motivations were formed by the need to respond to a period of rapid social change and instability. Rural urban migration, the intensification of commercial competition, discontent with aristocratic rule during the war, the Malthusian awareness of the extent and cost of poverty, increased fear of public disorder, the growth of public health fears, and the need for civic and class assertion were all part of this. The subscriber democracies began with groups excluded from state power, in Parliament, and in the older civic trusts and corporations. Dissenters and the evangelicals, overlapping but not identical groups, were especially important. Once the influence of this network became evident the Tory Anglican establishment had to respond.

In practice the aristocracy sought to sustain their influence and compete for power in three ways. Direct coercion was used on rare occasions when tenants were evicted for failing to support landlords. Influence or patronage was more effective. Tenants, employees, and local tradesmen were simply expected to follow the lead of landlord or employer and usually saw nothing wrong in this. Such means of sustaining power were inadequate, especially in urban society, and power was sought through opinion. Thus the landlords were drawn into public meetings and public debate. They joined societies and sat on committees. The survival of aristocratic power in Britain has often been noted, the so-called "gentlemanly capitalism." This happened because the landed families were able and willing to exploit and adapt to the new conditions of civil society in order to sustain their power much in the manner in which former communist party hierarchies have used their skills to sustain power within democratic structures. The major area of failure in civil society for Britain was Ireland. Ireland lacked a divided elite, had weak local government, a weaker associational culture, and a powerful central state.

Thus the rich associational culture of Britain became a powerful resource for the furtherance of the practices of liberal democracy but was equally important as a base for a limited pluralism and a powerful set of integrative social practices. This associational culture was able to prosper and interact with the development of liberal pluralism in British representative government for several reasons. The events of the seventeenth century had left Britain with no monopolistic central focus of power. The divided landed elite of family alliances and their clients were only able to compete for power by seeking the cooperation of local elites and interest groups. These local elites, especially urban elites, were themselves increasingly divided by ideological, religious, and economic interests. The factions of these elites needed to find ways of acting together if they were to gain power and act to solve a wide variety of social and economic problems created by the development of commercial, industrial, and urban society. In turn these local elites fought for power by seeking the support of lower-status social groups, many of whom held a forceful radical ideology of individual autonomy; orderly, well-informed debate; and representative government. All three groups were able to exploit the resources of practice, especially in civic culture and voluntary societies, ideology, and institutions outlined in this chapter. Central to that practice was a culture of rule-based association and informed debate together with a limited pluralism. The process that took place was as much about the integration and stabilization of British social relationship as it was about liberalization or the slow road to democracy.

NOTES

1. Ernest Gellner, *Conditions of Liberty: Civil Society and Its Rivals* (London: Hamish Hamilton, 1994); John A. Hall, ed., *Civil Society: Theory, History, Comparison* (Cambridge: Polity, 1995) both reflect and acknowledge this feature of the use of the concept.

2. For example, the *Ethnic Studies Network Bulletin* 10 (February 1996) reports on the Centre for Democracy, Human Rights, and Development (CEDRIDGE) based in Accra, Ghana. Its aims have an uncanny resemblance to the definitions of civil society in Hall and Gellner.

3. R. J. Morris, "Voluntary Societies and British Urban Elites, 1780–1870: An Analysis," *The Historical Journal* 26, no. 1 (1982): 95–118; "Associations," in *The Cambridge Social History of Britain, 1750–1950*, vol. 3, ed. F. M. L. Thompson (Cambridge: Cambridge University Press, 1990), 395–443.

4. Peter Borsay, *The English Urban Renaissance: Culture and Society in the Provincial Town, 1660–1770* (Oxford: Clarendon Press, 1989); Jonathan Barry, "Bourgeois Collectivism? Urban Association and the Middling Sort," in *The Middling Sort of People: Culture, Society, and Politics in England, 1550–1800*, ed. Jonathan Barry and Christopher Brooks (New York: St Martin's, 1994).

5. E. P. Thompson, *The Making of the English Working Class* (London: Gollancz, 1965), contains accounts of this process.

6. Asa Briggs's *The Age of Improvement* (London: Longman, 1959) is still one of the best accounts of the political developments of this period.

7. P. H. J. H. Gosden, *Self Help: Voluntary Associations in Nineteenth-Century Britain* (London: Batsford, 1973).

8. Gellner, *Conditions of Liberty*, 7.

9. Notably between social classes and between religious sectarian groupings. See Adam B. Seligman, *The Idea of Civil Society* (Princeton: Princeton University Press, 1992).

10. This was a voluntary society based in London with branches in most centers. Subscription income was used to provide elementary education to working-class children in a nonsectarian but Protestant fashion.

11. Chartism was a widely supported campaign for universal adult male suffrage, usually seen as an early expression of working-class consciousness but now increasingly interpreted as part of a wider and longer-running tradition of popular political action; Asa Briggs, ed., *Chartist Studies* (London: Macmillan, 1959); Dorothy Thompson, ed., *The Early Chartists* (London: Macmillan, 1971); James Epstein and Dorothy Thompson, eds., *The Chartist Experience* (London: Macmillan, 1982); Gareth Stedman Jones, *Languages of Class* (Cambridge: Cambridge University Press, 1983).

12. York was a major administrative, legal, and ecclesiastical center in the north of England. Most major regional criminal trials took place there.

13. *Leeds Mercury*, September 7, 1839.

14. *Leeds Mercury*, September 15, 1839.

15. See Mick Jenkins, *The General Strike of 1842* (London: Lawrence and Wishart, 1980), for a general account of this strike. "Turnouts" was the word used to refer to those on strike.

16. Bradford was a rapidly growing center for worsted textile manufacture, while Bramley and Stanningley were important weaving villages south of Leeds. All were experiencing the social tensions created by the spread of factory production in many sectors of cloth manufacture. See Theodore Koditschek, *Class Formation and Urban Industrial Society: Bradford, 1750–1850* (Cambridge: Cambridge University Press, 1990).

17. *Leeds Mercury*, August 20, 1842.

18. *Leeds Mercury*, January 21, 1843.

19. Barry, "Bourgeois Collectivism?" 84–112; Borsay, *The English Urban Renaissance*.

20. R. J. Morris, "Clubs, Societies and Associations," in *The Cambridge Social History of Britain, 1750–1950, Vol. 3*, ed. F. M. L. Thompson (Cambridge: Cambridge University Press, 1990), 395–444.

21. Indenture of the Leeds Charity School (reciting an earlier document of 25 October 1705), Leeds City Archives D B 196/4.

22. John Dwyer, *Virtuous Discourse: Sensibility and Community in Late Eighteenth-Century Scotland* (Edinburgh: John Donald, 1987).

23. J. R. Western, "The Volunteer Movement as an Anti-revolutionary Force, 1793–1801," *English Historical Review* 71 (1956): 603–14; Linda Colley, *Britons: Forging the Nation, 1707–1837* (New Haven, Conn.: Yale University Press, 1992).

24. I use the language of class in its plural form both for theoretical reasons and because the majority of actors among these associations did the same. See Dror Wahrman, *Imagining the Middle Class: The Political Representation of Class in Britain, c. 1780–1840* (Cambridge: Cambridge University Press, 1995), for a survey of this language with a different emphasis.

25. For a fuller account of the subscriber democracies see R. J. Morris, *Class, Sect, and Party: The Making of the British Middle Class, Leeds, 1820–50* (Manchester: Manchester University Press, 1990).

26. John Seed, "Unitarianism, Political Economy, and the Antimonies of Liberal Culture in Manchester, 1830–50," *Social History* 7 (January 1982): 1–25.

27. Richard H. Trainor, *Black Country Elites: The Exercise of Authority in an Industrial Area, 1830–1900* (Oxford: Oxford University Press, 1993).

28. Edward Baines, Jr., *The Social, Educational, and Religious State of the Manufacturing Districts* (London and Leeds: 1843), 28 and 62.

29. Thomas Chalmers, *The Christian and Civic Economy of Large Towns*, 3 vols. (Glasgow: Chalmers & Collins, 1821–26), esp. vol. 1, 23–30 and 59.

30. Leeds Building and Investment Society, handbill issued in 1846. Records of Leeds Building Society.

31. Charles Tilly, *Popular Contention in Great Britain, 1758–1834* (Cambridge, Mass.: Harvard University Press, 1995), notes the increasing use of the petition and public meeting toward the end of the eighteenth century.

32. Seligman, *The Idea of Civil Society.*

33. *Leeds Times,* August 15, 1839.

34. *Leeds Times,* August 3, 1839.

35. *Leeds Times,* July 27, 1839.

36. Perry Anderson, "Origins of the Present Crisis," in *Towards Socialism,* ed. Anderson et al. (London: Fontana Library, 1965); Martin J. Weiner, *English Culture and the Decline of the Industrial Spirit, 1850–1980* (Cambridge: Cambridge University Press, 1981); Harold Perkin, *Origins of Modern English Society, 1780–1880* (London: Routledge and Kegan Paul, 1969); M. J. Daunton, "Gentlemanly Capitalism and British Industry, 1820–1914," *Past and Present,* no. 122 (February 1989): 119–58.

37. The class analysis of this period has lost the assurance it once had in books like John Foster, *Class Struggle and the Industrial Revolution: Early Industrial Capitalism in Three English Towns* (London: Weidenfeld, 1974); emphasis has been placed on the political and populist aspects of mass consciousness: Patrick Joyce, *Visions of the People, Industrial England and the Question of Class, 1840–1914* (Cambridge: Cambridge University Press, 1991). Recent case studies have emphasized the variety of influences and

structures involved in popular action: Peter Taylor, *Popular Politics in Early Industrial Britain: Bolton 1825–1850* (Keele: Ryburn, 1995).

38. Taylor, *Popular Politics*.

39. R. J. Morris, "Middle Class Culture," in *A History of Modern Leeds*, ed. Derek Fraser (Manchester: Manchester University Press, 1980); Eneas Mackenzie, *A Descriptive and Historical Account of the Town and County of Newcastle Upon Tyne* (Newcastle, 1827), 500.

40. Graeme Morton, *Unionist Nationalism: Governing Urban Scotland, 1830–1860* (East Linton, Scotland: Tuckwell Press, 1999); Graeme Morton, "Civil Society, Municipal Government and the State: Enshrinement, Empowerment and Legitimacy. Scotland 1800–1929," *Urban History* 25, no. 3 (December 1998): 348–67.

41. R. F. Foster, *Modern Ireland, 1600–1972* (London: Penguin, 1988), 257–308.

42. See Morris, *Class, Sect and Party*.

43. Mike Savage, *The Dynamics of Working Class Politics: The Labour Movement in Preston, 1880–1940* (Cambridge: Cambridge University Press, 1987); Alan McKinlay and R. J. Morris, eds., *The ILP on Clydeside, 1893–1932: From Foundation to Disintegration* (Manchester: Manchester University Press, 1991).

44. L. Davidoff and C. Hall, *Family Fortunes: Men and Women of the English Middle Class, 1780–1850* (London: Hutchison, 1987), esp. chap. 10.

45. Elspeth King, *Scotland Sober and Free: The Temperance Movement, 1829–1979* (Glasgow: Glasgow Museums and Art Galleries, 1979); F. K. Prochaska, *Women and Philanthropy in Nineteenth-Century England* (Oxford: Clarendon, 1980).

46. "Legitimate" is used here to imply accepted by the dominant modes of thinking and evaluation.

47. Morris, "Associations," 433.

48. R. J. Morris, "Scotland, 1830–1914: The Making of a Nation within a Nation," in *People and Society in Scotland* vol. 2, *1830–1914*, ed. W. H. Fraser and R. J. Morris (Edinburgh: John Donald, 1990), 1–7; also R. J. Morris, "Victorian Values in Scotland and England," in *Victorian Values*, ed. T. C. Smout (Oxford: Proceedings of the British Academy, vol. 78, 1992), 31–48.

49. Lindsay Paterson, *The Autonomy of Modern Scotland* (Edinburgh: Edinburgh University Press, 1994).

50. J. C. Beckett et al., eds., *Belfast, the Making of the City* (Belfast: Appletree Press, 1983); John Killen, A *History of the Linen Hall Library, 1788–1988* (Belfast: Linen Hall Library, 1990).

51. Jonathan Bardon, *Belfast: An Illustrated History* (Belfast: Blackstaff Press, 1982); Alison Jordan, *Who Cared? Charity in Victorian and Edwardian Belfast* (Belfast: Institute of Irish Studies, Queens University Belfast, 1990).

52. Derek Fraser, *Urban Politics in Victorian England: The Structure of Politics in Victorian Cities* (Leicester: Leicester University Press, 1976).

53. Paul André Linteau and Jean Claude Robert, "Montréal au 19e siècle: Bilan d'une recherche," *Urban History Review/Revue d'histoire urbaine* 13 (February 1985): 207–24; Paul André Linteau, *Histoire de Montréal depuis la Confédération* (Montreal: Boreal, 1992).

54. Peter Gibbon, *The Origins of Ulster Unionism* (Manchester: Manchester University Press, 1975); David W. Miller, ed., *Peep O'Day Boys and Defenders* (Belfast: Public Record Office, Northern Ireland, 1990).

55. It is an irony of historical and political discourse that the "former Soviet Union" and the "former Yugoslavia" are debated with great vigor, but nothing is heard of the "former United Kingdom" after the loss of the twenty-six counties of Ireland.

56. D. A. Hamer, *Liberal Politics in the Age of Gladstone and Roseberry: A Study in Leadership and Policy* (Oxford: Clarendon, 1972), 46–56.

57. Jonathan Sperber, "*Bürger, Bürgertum, Bürgerlichkeit, Bürgerliche Gesellschaft*: Studies of the German (Upper) Middle Class and Its Sociocultural World," *The Journal of Modern History* 69 (June 1997): 271–97; Ewald Hieble, "Associations and the Middle Class in Hallein (Austria) from the Nineteenth to the Twentieth Century," and Elena Mannová, "Middle Class Identities in a Multicultural City (Associations in Bratislava in the Nineteenth Century)," both papers delivered to the Fourth International Conference on Urban History, Venice, 1998, to be published under the editorship of Boudien de Vries and Thimo de Nijs.

7

POLITICAL ASSOCIATION IN NINETEENTH-CENTURY FRANCE: LEGISLATION AND PRACTICE

Raymond Huard

When we examine the history of French associations in the nineteenth century, we confront a striking paradox. In France, the right to associate was granted very late in comparison with other European states. It was not until 1901 that this fundamental right was recognized and the government waived its authority to prevent citizens from founding associations. Even in the face of such legal obstacles, however, citizens made repeated efforts to associate, for political purposes or otherwise, efforts that persisted across the entire century from the Revolution of 1789 down to the passage of the 1901 law on associations. This paradox requires further analysis and raises three main questions. First, how did the obstacles that prevented the recognition of the right to associate survive so long and what were the effects of previous historical experiments, ideological reservations and the impact of political circumstances? Second, what were the driving forces behind associational activity? Third, how was the pervasive and long-lasting opposition to associations finally overcome?[1]

If we have chosen to focus on political associations or, as they were named in the early nineteenth century, political societies, it is because they exemplify the case of all associations. Admittedly, political societies were the most feared by the government, but it must be considered that, more or less, all associations could become political in certain circumstances. This was possible because, mainly in the first half of the century, the majority of the French associations were not specialized, and they performed various functions. Each association could be as much a mutual benefit society as a circle in which people gathered every day or several days a week to read the papers, play cards, or share some group activity. Each could become, in electoral periods, a political society in which citizens discussed politics and prepared for elections. As a consequence the authorities wished to be in control of all and not just of some of the associations.

In the French case, the relationship between liberalization and democratization is particularly complex. By liberalization, we mean the ongoing fight for fundamental liberties, such as freedom of the press and freedom of association. Democratization supposed not only that a wide range of people should enjoy these liberties but that the mass of the citizenry should also have a say in the running of public affairs. In France, universal male suffrage, a major democratic victory, was established as early as 1848, before the fundamental liberties of press and association were definitively obtained. In this respect, democratization preceded liberalization in France.

Since, until 1880, political societies were most often founded by opposition forces, they tended to fight less among themselves than against the state, which was their main adversary. All such societies, royalist, liberal, and republican alike, declared themselves pro-liberal inasmuch as they wanted greater freedom to pursue their particular goals. Their respective ideologies, however, were not necessarily liberal. Republican associations, which were perhaps the most active, were indeed pro-democratic, but not legitimist associations, which defended a traditionalist vision of society. Thus, in France, liberalization and democratization were not successive phases in the nation's political development but simultaneous processes that exerted a continuous and ongoing pressure on public life. To make this point clearer, we will first examine the opposition to the right to associate and then track the development of the political associative system over the course of the century.

THE OPPOSITION TO THE RIGHT TO ASSOCIATE

At least until 1848, when political leaders of the nineteenth century discussed the right to associate, their opinions and decisions were shaped by the historical experience of the French Revolution.[2] Between 1789 and 1795, and particularly between 1792 and 1794, "political societies" expanded not only in French towns, but also in villages and rural areas. Approximately 5,500 "political societies"—a considerable number—existed for a relatively long time during the French Revolution. The nineteenth-century liberal bourgeoisie was frightened by three essential features of the political societies of the Revolution. First, instead of remaining mainly bourgeois and aristocratic, these societies became more and more popular over time, enabling the lower classes to take part in political life through the network of societies; second, by the fact that the Montagnard government used the popular societies as weapons against both their aristocratic and Girondin bourgeois opponents. Lastly, the popular political societies backed the Terror, a harsh repression against opponents (1793–94). Thus, after the Revolution, the liberal bourgeoisie was confronted with at least two serious questions: Could associations be regulated so that only the upper and middle classes might benefit from the right to associate? And more generally, how could the disruptive consequences of this right be prevented?

It is meaningful that in all the parliamentary debates about the right to associate on down to 1851, repeated allusion was made to the political societies of the Revolution. Another interesting mark of the influence exercised by the revolutionary experience is the analogy drawn in the early twentieth century by the conservative sociologist and historian Augustin Cochin between the political societies of the revolutionary era and the Masonic lodges and radical committees of the late nineteenth century (although the latter were conceded to be less fearsome than the former).[3]

There were, however, other hindrances besides the memory of the revolutionary experiments. The right to associate, even though it was accepted, did not occupy a central place in the main political ideologies of nineteenth-century France.

As early as 1791 liberal debates in the National Assembly revealed a strong opposition to a widely granted right to associate. The argument used by Isaac Le Chapelier, the main proponent of this stance, was that political societies, especially if they were linked together, exerted an illegal influence upon public powers and disturbed the free expression of national sovereignty.[4] In 1797, Jean-Etienne Portalis and Claude Pastoret, conservative deputies in the Conseil des Cinq Cents, one of the two assemblies of the Directory Regime, also underscored the danger of granting the power of words and speeches to ordinary men—a power liable to make them commit offenses.[5] To be sure, there were some deputies who believed that political societies were a natural consequence of human sociability, helpful and necessary phenomena which, like *beacons*, propagated the values of the new era. Nevertheless, the French Declaration of Rights of 1789 did not proclaim the right to create associations. The Declaration of Rights of 1795, which was more explicit in this respect,[6] set strict limitations on societies, forbidding them to be named *société populaire* (Article 361) or to affiliate and exchange correspondence. (Article 362).

In 1828, Prosper Duvergier de Hauranne, a leading liberal figure, wrote several articles on this issue in *Le Globe*. Even though he spoke in favor of the right to associate, his conception of the association was very restrictive, admitting only private societies that did not expand in the public sphere.[7]

Midcentury, in 1864, Adolphe Thiers, a former minister and now an opponent to the Second Empire, gave his famous speech on the *libertés nécessaires,* which he defined as those permitting the normal functioning of a representative regime. Thus, it was essential that both the press, whose task was to form public opinion, and the electoral process, by which the majority of public opinion could influence the government, should be free. But Thiers did not mention the right to associate as a basic right.[8]

Republicans, even though they acknowledged that associations favoring the emancipation of working men and promoting the advancement of education had a useful role to play in the social sphere, did not hold political societies in the same esteem. They did not forget the warnings of Jean-Jacques Rousseau against factions and intrigues that distorted the general will.[9] They believed that free and open debate would prevent artificial divisions and that, if political societies were necessary, it was only for the short term. François-Vincent Raspail, a republican and socialist doctor, wrote in the *Tribune* (August 29, 1833): "In the future, only agricultural, industrial, and commercial societies will exist. But today, as political privilege is devouring the great social community, it is necessary for generous men to gather and to organize themselves into political societies."[10]

What counted most to republicans was the existence of a republican regime and the honest functioning of universal suffrage. These were judged the essential conditions for a living political democracy. Still, among all the currents of political opinions, it was the republicans who were most amenable to the idea of association. In the 1848 constitution, they proclaimed the right of citizens to associate (Chapter 1: Article 8). But as early as June 1848 this right was strictly regulated by the Assembly and limited even further in the following years. It was eventually abrogated in 1852, immediately after Louis Napoléon's Coup against the Second Republic.

In Bonapartist thought, state authority was much more important than the initiatives of free citizens gathered in associations. None of the various assemblies of the revolutionary era had legislated on the question of associational activity. The Napoleonic Penal Code of 1810 undertook to fill this vacuum, defining new and strict legal regulations that were to survive for almost a century. All associations with more than twenty members, whatever their aim, had to be authorized. Thus the government could potentially supervise the whole of the associative life. And because the police were ever watchful, even the smallest societies were not absolutely free.[11]

The champions of the Ancien Regime monarchy had a very traditional conception of associative life. They mainly supported professional associations (corporations) or religious ones (*congrégations*). Political societies were looked upon with some fear, and it was judged sufficient that the sovereign should be advised by the representatives of the Grands Corps (magistracy, clergy), the main professions of the nation.

Thus in the early nineteenth century, political associations were not popular among the nation's principal political forces, and these ideological prejudices provided little incentive for their creation. Political circumstances nevertheless encouraged the opposition parties, including republicans, Bonapartists, and even liberals and legitimists, to overcome these reservations early in the nineteenth century.

In view of the obstacles that hindered the development of political societies, it is necessary to point out two specific characteristics of French political
life in the nineteenth century. First, opposition forces were not thinking about
gaining power within the existing regime. They wanted to replace the existing
system with another. The government's struggle against the opposition forces
thus was also a struggle for the life of the existing political system. The government could not allow the opposition to use powerful weapons of association
freely. Second, because universal suffrage was granted in France as early as 1848,
the rise of the lower classes as a political force renewed the fears of the liberal
bourgeois, compelling them to oppose the creation of political societies that recruited members from the lower classes. They thought, as a former police minister, Émile de Maupas, declared in the Corps Législatif in May 1868, that thanks
to universal suffrage the people already had enough influence and that adding
other liberties would be dangerous.[12]

As we have said before, the majority of the French associations were not
specialized, and they performed various functions. This feature of the associational system made it difficult to make the differentiations that would allow
some associations to be authorized and others to be banned.

In France, the fear of democratization in political life hampered liberalization. Though it is not surprising that authoritarian governments forbade the
development of associations, the liberals themselves were reluctant to grant this
fundamental right. Despite the restraints, attempts to create political societies or
other associations never ceased throughout the nineteenth century. Given this
curious resistance, what were the driving forces behind the development of associations in the political domain?

THE DRIVING FORCES OF THE ASSOCIATIONAL TREND IN FRANCE DURING THE NINETEENTH CENTURY

The development of associations occurred in three phases: from 1815 to 1848,
from 1848 to 1880, and finally from 1880 through the passage of the 1901 Law
on Associations.

1815–1848

In the first period, Napoleonic restrictions on associational activity remained in effect or were even reinforced. We can, nevertheless, observe the
development of various political associations. Throughout the century, political associations were divided into three main categories: first, associations
that were created to support a legal political activity such as elections or the
publication of newspapers; then, public or secret associations, mainly republican or legitimist, with revolutionary aims; and last, workers' associations or

socialist parties, active mainly in the second part of the century, which fought for the emancipation of the proletariat. During the French Revolution, electoral questions were of little importance to political societies, which were preoccupied with problems of greater urgency. After 1815, during the Restoration (1815–30), circumstances changed. Peace had returned, and elections become a regular feature of the political landscape. Liberals, who were opponents of the dominant royalists, now felt under pressure to organize, the better to supervise voter registration, nominate candidates, and canvas the electorate. Despite the restrictive legislation on the books, it was very difficult for government authorities—who after all wanted free elections—to forbid the creation of societies in which reputable individuals, some of them deputies, took on tasks that were not at all illegal. After some limited attempts, the first major organization, created by François Guizot, a Protestant opponent, and others in 1827, was the Société "Aide-toi le Ciel t'aidera" whose influence expanded over about thirty-five departments.[13] During the July Monarchy (1830-48) the electoral process prompted the development of several associations such as the central committees created before the elections of 1837, 1839, and 1846. Similar to these in organization, but slightly different in their aims, were the reformist committees created in 1839 and 1840 to promote electoral reform and organize meetings. These were unauthorized associations, and in the tense climate of 1847–48, similar committees in order to function at all had to recast themselves as political banquets.[14]

Left-wing liberals or republicans and even legitimists also attempted to create societies to support newspapers whose existence was menaced by prosecutions and fines. As early as 1817, La Fayette, Dupont de l'Eure, and Benjamin Constant founded the Friends of the Press Society. In the first years of the July Monarchy, an association in favor of the patriotic press was created by republicans such as Etienne Arago and A. Marchais. Within a few months, corresponding societies were founded in towns of various regions: Strasbourg, Tulle (Corrèze), Bourg (Ain), and in the southeast of France.[15] These societies were crushed by the antirepublican repression of 1834–35. The legitimists organized several congresses of the press in the last years of the July Monarchy, in which forty to fifty newspaper editors gathered and elected a permanent committee to act between the congresses. Thus, permanent associations came to exist alongside the newspapers and in support of them. All the societies named above were legal or paralegal associations. To a greater or lesser extent, similar societies organized throughout the century, until the entire creation of political parties.

Created at this time were other societies that clearly opposed the existing regime and aimed to overthrow it. Among these were the Charbonnerie established during the Restoration, the Society of the Rights of Man founded at the beginning of the July Monarchy, and smaller societies such as the Société des Saisons des Familles chartered at the end of the 1830s. Following G. Perreux,[16] we define these as *sociétés d'action,* for they attempted to pave the way for a radical change in the political and perhaps the social systems both by ideological training and by material preparations. If the Charbonnerie was close to earlier, more traditional conspiracies in its structure, with its secret ceremonies of initiation and recruitment of officers or noncommissioned officers rather than ordinary citizens, the Society for the Rights of Man was an interesting example of a more modern *société d'action politique.* It was divided into small sections, composed of ten to twenty members, that bore the names of French or foreign revolutionary leaders. Agents periodically visited the sections to supervise their everyday life. Working men were numerous in the society, particularly in Paris, Marseilles, Lyon, Saint-Etienne, and other industrial towns. Though the society did not issue a public call to insurrection, it was clear that its aim was to replace Louis Philippe's government with a republic.

In February 1834, to prevent political societies from evading the provisions of the Penal Code on associations, the government of Louis Philippe submitted a bill to parliament forbidding the subdivision of associations into sections of fewer than twenty members. This practice was used by associationists to circumvent authorization since the Penal Code was inapplicable to associations with fewer than twenty members. The debates showed that many deputies thought that political societies, especially ones that had a popular or working-class rank and file, were a danger to social and political order. Thus, some deputies thought political societies should never be authorized. The law passed by a large majority. The uprisings of Lyon silk-weavers (the *canuts*), Parisian workers, and republican militants against the law and against the government in April 1834 were crushed. The republican movement was severely weakened. As a result, the remaining *sociétés d'action* were reduced in importance, and only under the Second Republic did they find a new vigor.

The two kinds of societies just described shared a common commitment to building a national audience and to the centralization of local efforts in the interests of creating a nationwide organization. Workingmen's associations and so-called *cercles* (which served a middle- or lower-class clientele) represent a third and final type of society. In terms of size of membership, though, they were perhaps the most significant. These societies reflected specific associational trends, which have been outlined in part by the studies of Maurice Agulhon and William Sewell: the spirit of sociability on the side of the *cercles,* or circles, the concern for mutual aid and workers' defense on the side of workingmen's associations.[17] While every circle led its own independent life, workingmen's societies were more closely linked with one another, either through the *compagnonnage* or by way of new societies such as the Société de l'Union, which appeared in the thirties. In the beginning, most of these societies had no political purpose. In an atmosphere of intense politicization, however, such as that generated by a revolutionary upheaval, they proved well adapted to providing a framework for organized political activity.

Given the situation that existed between 1815 and 1848 how were these associations and societies transformed over the next thirty years? What events or circumstances influenced these changes?

Transforming the Network of Associations from 1848 to 1880: Process and Stages

From 1848 to 1880 associational life developed despite the harsh regulations that remained in effect. Associations became increasingly specialized, and at the same time, the structure of the associational system in general evolved. Secret societies declined, and conversely, workers' organizations grew. The existing associations became more and more legitimate, and suspicions about associations on the whole declined. Thus the associational landscape was changing. Even pro-government forces began to create organizations. Without major legislative changes, associations came to occupy a new place in French society. During this period, few legislative reforms were effected, but these few showed that the imperial legislation no longer fit the new conditions

In the aftermath of the February 1848 Revolution, Republicans drafted a new constitution that proclaimed the right of citizens to associate (Chapter I, Article 8). By July, however, parliamentary opinion had reversed course, imposing certain restrictions on the right of association, which were made yet more severe in the following years. Immediately after Louis-Napoléon's Coup of 1851, the regulations of the Napoleonic Penal Code were reinstituted. Nevertheless, in June 1868, by the end of the Second Empire, the Napoleonic state was obliged to recognize the existence of nonpolitical, and in electoral periods, political meetings. On the whole, such concessions were weak, and the fear of liberalization remained high throughout that period. After the Paris Commune of 1871, the legislation governing the associations was toughened with the enactment of a new law (March 14, 1872) aimed against the International Working Men's Association. Thus, it was not through legislative changes (that were minor or unfavorable) that the associations evolved, but through the changes in the French society itself.

The transformations of the associational network were not linear; they alternated between advances and retreats, depending upon political circumstances. The revolutions of 1848 and 1870–71 strongly encouraged the creation of political societies. For brief periods, existing legislation was suspended, as popular movements mobilized and seized control of the situation. All sorts of societies, especially political ones, appeared, the most famous being the "clubs" of 1848 studied by P. H. Amann.[18] There were also electoral committees, workers' associations,[19] and so on. Conversely, after a period of growth, political societies often had to adapt to periods of repression again and again. This was the case between 1849 and 1851, as well as after the 1851 Coup and, later on, after the Paris Commune.

Thus, the history of political societies was anything but linear. The very structures of associational life bore the marks of repression. In particular, repression favored the retention or even the expansion of older forms of organization, which made no clear distinction between political and nonpolitical activities. By the end of the Second Empire and during the first years of the Third Republic, more and more republicans became affiliated with the Masonic lodges in which they could freely discuss political matters.[20]

From 1848 onward, the institution of universal male suffrage extended political citizenship to all male adults. Repeated general elections kept levels of politicization high and prompted political forces to get organized in order to adapt to the new environment. A conflict thereby arose between the requirements of electoral competition and the legal restrictions that prevented political societies from freely expanding. Under these circumstances, state authorities found it even more difficult to obstruct the opposition's efforts.

In the 1860s and 1870s, the increasing specialization of associations came about progressively and affected the whole associative system. The multivalent circles, which had performed a variety of functions, were replaced more and more by associations that carried out a precise activity: workingmen's *chambres syndicales*; the circles of the Ligue de l'enseignement, which promoted education; leisure societies such as the *orphéons* (or band clubs), and political committees. In all likelihood, this specialization was in keeping with a general diversification of social life, which made it harder for the multivalent circles to cope with new and greater demands. In this often very hostile context political societies continued to develop during the thirty years between 1848 and 1880.

The Evolution of the New Political Societies (1848–1880)

Here it is necessary to briefly describe the main features of the evolution of each type of society we have already distinguished: the electoral organizations and societies for the support of the press, the *sociétés d'action*, and finally, the circles and workingmen's societies.

The electoral committees that had gotten their start in the first month of the Second Republic became national in scope during the presidential campaign of December 1848. Eugène Cavaignac's Democratic Association of the Friends of the Constitution, Ledru-Rollin's National Electoral Congress, Louis-Napoléon's Central Electoral Committee, and Raspail's Central Club are cases in point. In the departments, particularly the Seine in 1849 and 1850, electoral organizations became much more structured. They relied on the support of local committees, and even tried to become permanent. This advance was nullified by the Bonapartist Coup of 1851, and the imperial regime attempted to deprive its adversaries of all legal or material possibilities for organization. The use of such means, however, became increasingly difficult as electoral competition was revived. The goal of the *procès des Treize*, a prosecution against republican opponents in 1864, was to prevent republicans from building up a national electoral organization, but in this case, the government's success was short-lived.[21] With the liberalization of the imperial regime in the late 1860s, electoral organizations multiplied. They were founded by both republicans and Bonapartists above all on occasion of the plebiscite in 1870. Thus as early as the last years of the Empire, electoral organizations were conceded the right to exist but only in so far as they promised to be temporary. In the first years of the Third Republic, permanent electoral central committees were founded in several towns (for example in Lyon and Marseilles) to strengthen the Republican Party. But the government obliged them to dissolve, arguing that permanent organizations were illegal. Certain republican leaders and publicists tried to find a way to put together an *organisation électorale* that would not fall afoul of existing regulations. Nothing came of these efforts, but they show that the republican movement was now more acutely aware of the importance of organizing.[22]

As for associations connected to the press, they did not expand much during the Second Republic. They just could not keep up with the remarkable proliferation of the newspapers. Congresses of the Press, however, proved more successful. They in fact played a key part in the fortunes of the so-called Parti de l'Ordre, which relied on press congresses in lieu of more permanent party structures. In the late 1860s, congresses of the press made a reappearance, but this time under the auspices of less reactionary forces. Such was the Congress of Lyon, held in 1869, following the initiative of a conservative newspaper of Lyon, *La Décentralisation*. The republicans followed this example. In May 1871, a congress of the provincial republican press met in Moulins and demanded that the government of Versailles negotiate with the Paris Commune. Nevertheless, though such meetings were generally followed by the formation of a permanent committee, Congresses of the Press did not have enough continuity to play the role of a powerful political organization.

During the same period, the transformations of *sociétés d'action*—the democratic revolutionary societies—were even more dramatic. The changes occurred in two main phases. During the Second Republic, several attempts were made to build up a national organization of the Republican Party. The first attempt came in November 1848 with the founding of the Solidarité républicaine by Martin Bernard and Charles Delescluze, to support the candidacy of Ledru-Rollin in the presidential election.[23] Corresponding committees were set up in departments, arrondissements, and cantons. The Solidarité was more than an electoral organization. Its program supported four main activities: political mobilization through meetings and newspapers, popular education, support for republicans who were imprisoned or fined, and the provisions of mutual aid benefits to members. In January 1849, the government stopped expansion of the Solidarité, arguing that it aimed at forming "a state within the State." It continued to exist, however, after 1849 in the guise of a secret organization, La Nouvelle Montagne (New Mountain), which had the same goals. In addition, it prepared the republican defense against Louis-Napoléon's Coup, and even an insurrection, aimed at establishing "the Good Republic." According to Ted W. Margadant, the membership of New Mountain, which was recruited in seventeen departments in central and southeastern France, numbered between fifty thousand and one hundred thousand, roughly the size of a French political party before World War I.[24] The New Mountain was the last major secret society in French history, but it was already very different from the old secret societies of the Restoration. The failure of the insurrection of 1851 against the Bonapartist Coup—a revolt that had been driven mainly by members of the New Mountain—discouraged the republican party from using secret societies as a political weapon in the future. Not only did the insurrection fail (which was proof that the secret societies were not appropriate weapons) but the republicans also noticed that the new Bonapartist regime found ways to exploit the fear of secret societies to serve its own interest. After 1851, only small minorities such as the Blanquists in the last years of the Second Empire continued to spawn such societies. Thus the death knell seemed to have sounded for *sociétés d'action*. They received, however, a new impetus from the development of the workers' movement during the 1860s. As early as 1848, workers' organizations had started to express political concerns, but this phenomenon was still limited. Thanks to the creation of the First Working Men's International Association in 1864, the *sociétés d'action* started out on a new course. Their goals were not just electoral or legal. Social questions came to be much more important as the new societies' main goal was not so much to establish a new republic as to found a new social order. Lastly, while the members of the earlier societies were recruited mostly from among ordinary people, now members joined the societies as self-conscious working men.[25] Admittedly, the life of the First International was short, but it paved the way for the first socialist parties, which appeared as early as the 1870s and had many of the same concerns.

A third type of organization, the circle, was also affected by the growing specialization of organizations. Especially after the fall of the imperial regime, the names of some circles began to indicate their political nature and their sympathies. The *cercles républicains* multiplied, and later, as the Republican Party itself grew more and more divided, some of those circles specified that they were *cercle républicain radical* or *cercle républicain socialiste*.[26] Thus the political circles began to evolve into what would later become rank-and-file subdivisions of the first political parties. Their lives, however, were still threatened by government repression, similar to that which was inflicted under the Ordre Moral from 1873 until 1877.

So, between 1848 and 1880, even though the legislation upon associations remained in place, both the requirements of political life and the advancement of society made the prevention of the formation of political associations impossible in the long term. Universal suffrage had become a standard practice, and political movements began to understand the necessity for organizing. Beyond this political impulse, however, those who wanted to defend ideological or religious interests or to promote new ideas or reforms became more and more convinced that campaigning through the press was no longer sufficient to garner support for their causes. They had to band together to be effective. The growth of the towns generated various new needs for their inhabitants—for education, entertainment, assistance, and mutual aid—and new forms of communication among individuals. The old rural forms of solidarity had to be replaced by new ones. The needs of citizens could be satisfied through the creation of associations, and state authorities could no longer ignore these needs.

Thus, the development of political associations, though hindered, gained ground, even among those who, like the Bonapartists and, to a lesser degree, the liberals, were cautious about political organizations right from the very beginning. In 1869, one of these liberals, Ernest Duvergier de Hauranne, even defended political parties against their critics, writing in the *Revue des Deux Mondes*, the main liberal review, "There is only one means of maintaining peace within a democratic society and that is by permitting and favouring as much as possible, the organization of large political parties as much as one can."[27]

De Hauranne's assertion was rather significant given that the parties he was advocating were no longer simple currents of opinion nor locally based circles like the old political associations. On the contrary, they were organized structures spreading throughout the national territory.

Political Associations from the Victory of the Republicans to the 1901 Act Governing Associations: The Rise of Political Parties

Beginning in 1880 under governments led by the moderate ("opportunist") republicans, political associations began to expand freely even while the legal restrictions on them remained firmly in place. Only the right to meet was granted by law (as of June 30, 1881). Political circles, trade unions, societies for the development of popular education, and Catholic societies such as the *cercles catholiques* multiplied. Thus, at the grass roots, the network of societies enlarged significantly, but the government retained all the existing legal weapons to squelch them if necessary. Given their principles, the republican leaders did not profess to be against either democratization or liberalization. They thought, however, that the republic was not secure enough and were reluctant to give their adversaries (either monarchists, boulangists, Catholics, or socialists alike) the opportunity to strengthen. The republicans won the 1881 election with a large majority, but were within a hair's breadth of defeat in 1885. Then, in 1887, came the boulangist menace. Thus the republicans, like their adversaries, thought that the party in power had to retain the possibility of using the strength of the state against its opponents.

Republican deputies, (mainly radical, but even some conservatives) hoped, however, that parliament would pass a bill granting the complete right to associate. Many bills were brought forward for consideration, but without success. The most interesting bill was prepared in October 1883 by René Waldeck-Rousseau, then acting as minister of the interior.[28] It conceded the liberty to create associations freely other than those whose essential goal was to earn money. Religious congregations were to be excluded from the ruling; because the bill did not automatically grant such associations the *personnalité civile*, their sphere of action would have been limited. Further, the government was to retain the right to prosecute any association engaging in illegal activities. Thus the bill, which was assuredly more liberal than all previous measures, still did not deprive the government of all its powers. The bill, however, did not become law. Opponents easily criticized the republicans, showing that they were unfaithful to their principles. The somewhat contradictory approach of the republicans was difficult to maintain for long.

Though the government remained reluctant to concede the right to associate, all major political forces came to understand during the 1880s and 1890s that they had to organize to win elections. Whereas in the 1860s, only the opposition had tried to organize, now everyone recognized that association was a necessity. This change had its origins in general and particular causes. In general, the republic modified the conditions of the political fight. Now the fight was not between the opposition and the state, but between the various political forces that competed for power. At the same time, the area covered by political life was now more and more national, thanks to the development of transportation and communications. But each political force also had its particular reason for getting organized. We will briefly describe the cases of the republicans, the socialists, and the Catholics and the case of the Right.[29]

The republicans' primary motive in organizing was to prepare for the elections. From their point of view, organization was linked to the requirements of universal suffrage. They did not immediately succeed, however, because initially they refused to accept the idea that the old united republican party was obsolete and that each faction of the new Republican Party had to organize to serve its own interest. Beginning in 1886, the republicans attempted several times to build a party organization. The centenary of 1789 gave both the moderate and the radicals the opportunity to create two distinct associations.[30] In the 1890s, new organizations arose such as the Grand Cercle républicain, created in 1897 by Waldeck-Rousseau for the opportunists, and the Comité d'action pour les réformes républicaines, created in November 1885 for the radicals. The Dreyfus Affair underscored still further the divisions within the old Republican Party. Eventually, three republican organizations were created at the beginning of the twentieth century, the Parti républicain radical et radical-socialiste in 1901;[31] the Alliance républicaine democratique in 1901–2[32] where center-left republicans gathered, and the Fédération républicaine in 1903 that brought together the center-right Republicans.

The concerns of the socialists were quite different. At first, they were much less interested in electoral competition, considering it a deception from which only the bourgeoisie benefited. In their minds, a party organization was necessary above all to provide a stronger cohesion to the working class and to prepare the social revolution.

To speak of a working-class party is to join workers together into a class party in order to politically and economically expropriate the class of capitalists and to socialize the means of production.[33] Consequently, the socialists thought that instead of admitting just any citizen, the party should recruit first of all among the proletariat. The socialist party tried to be different from the bourgeois parties in its general line and in the goals it pursued, thus retaining some characteristics of the old *sociétés d'action*.

The unification of the working class, however, was slow in coming. Socialists remained divided into numerous factions until the Unity Congress of 1905. Even then, the party never became purely proletarian in composition, recruiting many lower middle-class members such as journalists and small shopkeepers. And in practice, unity proved an elusive goal. The 1905 statutes of the unified Socialist Party promoted the *section* as the basic building block of party organization, but smaller groups within the party, the local circles, still retained a critical measure of autonomy. Not only that, as socialists enjoyed ever greater electoral success at both the national and municipal levels, they paid increasing attention to the problems of vote-getting. Some socialists, such as Jean Jaurès, even believed it possible to achieve the social revolution through the ballot box. Thus, by 1914, the French Socialist Party had become ambivalent in its aspirations, its earlier commitment to revolution now more and more tempered by concerns about winning elections.[34]

Catholics had yet another approach to the problem of organization. Catholic royalists were satisfied with being represented by the administrative staff of the Royalist Party, but others, like social catholic Albert de Mun, thought it necessary to accept the republican regime. For de Mun, self-organization was the only means by which Catholics could influence French government policy. De Mun declared in December 1892, "First of all, it is necessary for the Catholics to be organized. It is the first condition and it must be the first goal of their activity. As long as they will not, neither public opinion, nor the parties will accord them the consideration which they have a right to expect."[35]

To achieve this goal, Catholics had powerful supporters in the network of clerical associations, both those that had existed for a long time and those that were newly created, such as de Mun's *cercles ouvriers*. Catholics were also inspired by the models of their counterparts in Belgium and Germany, who were further along the road to organization than the French. French Catholics wavered between several possible paths, however, in determining the structure of the party to be created and in adopting a clear-cut position toward the republic. They made several attempts to organize, starting such groups as the Union nationale, founded by the abbé Garnier,[36] or the Comités Justice-Egalité, directed by the catholic paper *La Croix*, and the first initiatives of Christian democracy[37] showed that the Catholics were more and more interested in this question. The Dreyfus Affair and the anticlerical policies that resulted from it, however, hindered these attempts, which finally succeeded in 1901–2 with the creation of the Action libérale populaire.[38]

After losing power in 1877, the Right became aware of the necessity of organizing in order to gain it back. The Right, however, was hampered by several weaknesses. (1) Many right-wing local notables were not prepared to work patiently for further organization; they scorned electoral contests and refused to share their authority with committees. (2) For a long time, the forces of the Right had chosen to rely on the influence of the newspapers rather than on associations. (3) The traditionalist Right could hardly continue to rely upon Catholic forces, since some of the Catholics were beginning to question the political authority of the monarchists. (4) The Right was divided into three competing currents, the Bonapartists, the legitimists, and the Orleanists. Thus, the efforts to organize made by the Right for the general election of 1885 were both temporary and, in the long term, fruitless. These failures led the Right to neglect the formation of parties and to act instead through leagues such as the Ligue des patriotes or the Ligue de la patrie française,[39] with the hope that a mighty and temporary movement could upset the republic. After 1898, with the creation of the Action française,[40] a movement halfway between a league and a party, the extreme Right (and only the extreme Right) adopted a durable political structure.

Such was the situation of political associations in France at the dawn of the twentieth century. The republican majority in parliament decided, under the leadership of Waldeck-Rousseau, to pass the bill on associations that the French people had been waiting for since 1870.[41] In the short term, the object of the bill was to make it easier for the government to act against religious congregations and, further, against the nationalist Right. It also sought to realize a long-standing republican commitment to relax associational regulations. For too many years, associational networks had operated without legal sanction. The new law on associations gave expression to an important long-term change in liberal thinking. With the growth of capitalism, the old bonds joining individuals had slackened. Modern liberal society now appeared to be too individualistic, a flaw that some felt to be harmful to the social order. Associations, it was believed, would promote a strengthening of voluntary social bonds, which would in turn improve social harmony.

The 1901 law did not deal separately with political parties, which were placed on an equal footing with other associations, religious congregations excepted. The law was very liberal. Associations could be freely created, and it was not even necessary to declare their founding. But only the declared associations had the *personnalité civile* that gave them various rights such as that of owning

Like the Middle East!

buildings. Only associations composed partly of foreigners or directed by foreigners were subjected to stricter regulation. Still, most ordinary associations were now governed by a common law, and the government's powers were significantly reduced. The government no longer had the right to prevent the founding of an association and could only prosecute in cases where offences were committed. Nevertheless, the law was severely criticized by the Right and by the Catholics because it imposed such strict controls on congregations. These were viewed with great distrust by the republicans because the congregations' influence and wealth revealed at the time of the Dreyfus Affair were thought to be dangerous. Thus the republicans decided that the congregations could be authorized only by a special law, and the enforcement of the 1901 law gave the government the opportunity to dissolve many of them.

Almost one century later, the main dispositions of the 1901 law—a major republican act—are still in effect.

The complex history of France's political associations reveals some major characteristics of French political life in the nineteenth century. For most of the century, the right to create associations freely was considered threatening to the political and even social order, which looked frail in a country where the Revolution had destabilized the power of the state. Memories of the societies of the French Revolution reinforced this opinion among conservatives. Further, the nature of French associations made it difficult to distinguish political societies from other forms of organization. Until the 1901 law, the regulations governing associations, far from liberalizing, became stricter and stricter. Even the republicans, when they were in charge of government, did not immediately liberalize the legislation, fearing that the royalists as well as the Church might grow and strengthen as a consequence.

Nevertheless, these strict regulations did not succeed in preventing the creation of societies, because other forces pushed in the opposite direction. For example, the requirements of a legal political life (mainly the exercise of universal suffrage) caused the creation of new political societies and committees. Republican and left-wing liberal opponents, inspired by the models of the revolutionary societies, created new political organizations such as the *sociétés d'action*; the growing working-class movement tried to organize itself; and finally, in day-to-day social life, citizens needed to meet for various purposes. Associational life never disappeared and was even temporarily boosted by the revolutions of the nineteenth century.

The almost permanent repression of associations had effects upon political societies. Compared with Great Britain or Germany, it slowed down the formation of political parties in France while older forms of organization, such as the multivalent circles, survived until late in the nineteenth century.

After 1880, however, associations were more or less free. The various old forms of organization converged toward the modern political party. However different their various agendas, all political forces, except for the radical Right, adopted the party form of organization. The party was a flexible structure capable of acting on the national stage. It was also well suited to conduct electoral campaigns at a time when elections were becoming more and more important in French public life. Parties, however, never dominated the whole sphere of political organization, and other societies such as the Freemasons continued to exert a political influence alongside them.

The 1901 Act legalized the formation of political organizations, even though it did not deal explicitly with political parties or societies, treating them as associations like any other. Why did this approach prevail? Two explanations are possible. First of all, it may be that the political parties then in existence, undeveloped as they were, did not require specific regulations. But second, when it came to the monitoring of associational life, Republican legislators, much like their Napoleonic forebears, remained preoccupied first and foremost with the preservation of social and political order.

NOTES

1. A more extensive discussion of the subject of this chapter appears in *La Naissance du Parti Politique en France* (Paris: Presses de Sciences Po, 1996). Consequently, I have only given limited references here. The reader will find more extensive developments of my arguments in this text, along with numerous bibliographical and factual references. See also R. Huard, "La Genèse des Partis Politiques Modernes en France, l'expérience du XIXéme Siècle," *La Pensée* 201 (October 1978): 96–119.

2. See J. Boutier, P. Boutry, and S. Bonin, *Atlas de la Révolution Française*, t. 6. (Les Sociétés Politiques, Paris: E.H.E.S.S., 1992), 132 (with a copious bibliography); C. Peyrard, "Les débats de l'an VII sur l'association politique," in *Les Droits de l'homme et la Conquête des Libertés* (Grenoble: Presses Universitaires de Grenoble, 1986), 311–18.

3. A. Cochin, *Les sociétés de pensée et la démocratie, Étude d'histoire révolutionnaire* (1921), reprinted under the title *L'esprit du Jacobinisme, une Interprétation Sociologique de la Révolution Française* (Paris: P.U.F., 1979), 198. F. Schrader, *Augustin Cochin et la République Française* (Paris: Seuil, 1992), 46.

4. A speech by Le Chapelier upon the political societies, September 20, 1791, in F. Furet and R. Halevi, *Les Orateurs de la Révolution Française* (Paris: Gallimand, 1989), 434–35.

5. C. Peyrard, "Les débats sur le droit d'association et de réunion sous le Directoire," *Annales historiques de la Révolution française* 3 (1994): 467.

6. The 1795 constitution only granted citizens "the right to gather peacefully" (art. 7) and did not overtly proclaim the right for them to join in societies or associations, but as it prohibited only particular sorts of societies (art. 360–62), it seemed that all the societies that were not forbidden were legal.

7. *Le Globe*, April 5 and 16, 1828 (Duvergier de Hauranne's articles were signed O).

8. G. Robertet, *Pages choisies des Grands Ecrivains. Ad. Thiers* (Paris: A. Colin, 1894), 631–34.

9. J. J. Rousseau, *Le Contrat Social* (Paris: Burgelin, 1966), livre 2, chap. 3, 67.

10. *La Tribune*, August 29, 1833.

11. Art. 291 of the penal code: "No association bringing together more than twenty persons, the aim of which will be to meet everyday or at some appointed days in order to deal with religious, literary or political or other subjects, can be created unless it has the government's assent and is in accordance with the conditions that the public authorities will be disposed to dictate to these societies."

12. *Moniteur Universel*, no. 168 (May 29): 736–37.

13. Cf. Sherman Kent, *The Election of 1827 in France* (Cambridge, Mass.: Harvard University Press, 1975), esp. 88–96.

14. S. Kent, *Electoral Procedure under Louis Philippe* (New Haven, Conn.: Yale University Press, 1937), 264.

15. I deal more completely with this question in chapter 2 of my book, mentioned above.

16. G. Perreux, *Au Temps des Sociétés Secrètes* (Paris: Hachette, 1931), 68.

17. M. Agulhon, *Le Cercle dans la France Bourgeoise: Etude d'une Mutation de Sociabilité* (Paris: A. Colin, 1977), 106; M. Agulhon, *La République au Village* (Paris: Plon, 1970), 543; W. Sewell, *Work and Revolution in France: The Language of Labor from the Old Regime to 1848* (Cambridge: Cambridge University Press, 1980).

18. Peter H. Amann, *Revolution and Mass Democracy: The Paris Club Movement in 1848* (Princeton: Princeton University Press, 1975), 370.

19. Rémi Gossez, *Les Ouvriers de Paris* (La Roche-sur Yon: Société d'histoire de la Révolution de 1848, 1967), 477; Pierre Chevallier, *Histoire de la Franc-Maçonnerie Française. T. II: La Franc-Maçonnerie Missionnaire du Libéralisme 1800–1877* (Paris: Fayard, 1974), 556.

20. According to the decree on clubs (July 28, 1848) only public political societies could meet without an authorization. The public authorities had the right to keep an eye on the meetings and in some cases to force the meeting to disband.

21. In 1864, thirteen republican leaders, among whom were Louis-Antoine Garnier-Pagès, F. Hérold, C. Floquet, Jean-Jules Clamageran, and J. Ferry, had organized in Paris a committee to prepare the by-elections and had correspondence with republicans in Marseilles, Selestat, and other cities. They were prosecuted and condemned to pay a fine of FF 500.

22. I deal more completely with this point in chapter 5 of my book.

23. Edouard Berenson, *Populist Religion and Left Wing Politics in France, 1848–1852* (Cambridge: Cambridge University Press, 1984), esp. 85–95.

24. Ted W. Margadant, *French Peasants in Revolt: The Insurrection of 1851* (Princeton: Princeton University Press, 1979), esp. 121–37.

25. *La Première Internationale, L'institution, L'implantation, Le Rayonnement*, Colloque C.N.R.S. 1964 (Paris: Editions du C.N.R.S., 1968), esp. 93–127.

26. I have discussed this process in *Le Mouvement Républicain en Bas-Languedoc* (Paris: Presses de Sciences Po, 1982), 333–39.

27. P. Duvergier de Hauranne, "La démocratie et le droit de suffrage," *Revue des deux mondes*, April 15, 1868, 798.

28. "Documents parlementaires," Sénat, annexe la séance du 23 October 1883, no. 4, 1018–20.

29. I have dealt with this question in "Aboutissements préparés et cristallisations imprévues, la formation des partis," in *La France de l'Affaire Dreyfus*, ed. P. Birnbaum (Paris: Gallimard, 1994), 87–119.

30. Association nationale du centenaire de 1789 (opportunist) and Fédération de 1889 (radical).

31. Gérard Baal, *Histoire du Radicalisme* (Paris: La Découverte, 1994), 120; Serge Berstein, *Histoire de Parti radical. T. 1: La recherche de l'age d'or, 1919–1926* (Paris: Presses de Sciences Po, 1980), 486; Jacques Kayser, *Les Grandes batailles du radicalisme, 1829–1901* (Paris: Rivière, 1962), 407.

32. G. La Chapelle, *L'Alliance Républicaine Démocratique* (Paris: Grasset, s.d.), 63; R. Sanson, "Centre et gauche 1901–1914, L'Alliance Républicaine Démocratique," *Revue d'Histoire Moderne et Contemporaine* (July–September 1992): 493–512.

33. Parti ouvrier, Programme et Réglement (Lille, 1893), 15, 19 (this *règlement* was adopted in 1890).

34. Maurice Moissonnier, "La Longue Marche Vers un Parti Ouvrier fin du XIXème Siècle," *in La Classe Ouvrière et la Politique* (Paris: Editions Sociales, 1980), 41–85; Madeleine Rebérioux, "Le Socialisme français de 1871 à 1914," in *Histoire Générale du Socialisme*, ed. J. Droz, t. 2 (Paris: P.U.F., 1974); Claude Willard, *Le Mouvement Socialiste en France, les Guesdistes* (Paris: Editions Sociales, 1965), 722.

35. *Ligue de la propagande économique et sociale: Discours de M. Albert de Mun* (Paris: Saint-Etienne, 1892), 8.

36. Stephen Wilson, "Catholic Populism in France at the Time of the Dreyfus Affair, The Union Nationale," *Journal of Contemporary History* (October 1975): 667–701.

37. Jean Marie Mayeur, "Les congrès nationaux de la démocratie chrétienne, Lyon (1896–1897–1998)," *Revue d'histoire moderne et contemporaine* (July–September 1962): 171–206.

38. B. F. Martin, "The Creation of the Action Liberiale Populaire," *French Historical Studies* 4 (1976): 660–89.

39. Jean Pierre Rioux, *Nationalisme et conservatisme, la Ligue de la patrie française, 1899–1904* (Paris: Beauchesne, 1977), 117; Peter M. Rutkoff, *Revanche and Revision: The Ligue des Patriotes and the Origins of the Radical Right in France 1882–1900* (Athens, Ohio: Ohio University Press, 1980), 182; Zeev Sternhell, *La Droite Révolutionnaire, 1885–1914* (Paris: Ed. du Seuil, 1978), 441.

40. E. Weber, *L'Action, Française* (Paris: Fayard, 1985), 665.

41. A de Faget de Casteljau, *Histoire du Droit d'association de 1789–1901* (Paris: A. Rousseau, 1905), 495; F. Nourrisson, *Histoire de la Liberté d'association en France depuis 1789* (Paris: Sirey, 1920), 2 t., 349, 386; Jean Claude Bardout, *Les Libertés d'association, Histoire étonnante de la loi de 1901* (Paris: Editions Juris Service, 1991), 238.

8

LIBERALIZATION, DEMOCRATIZATION, AND THE ORIGINS OF A "PILLARIZED" CIVIL SOCIETY IN NINETEENTH-CENTURY BELGIUM AND THE NETHERLANDS

Thomas Ertman

Aside from *apartheid*, the only other Dutch word to enter the language of social science is *verzuiling*, or "pillarization." This term refers to a particular pattern of civil society in which self-defined subcultural groups acquire "sovereignty in their own circles" (to use a famous Dutch formulation) by building up separate networks of schools; economic interest organizations; welfare and leisure-time associations; means of mass communication; and, last but not least, political parties. Such a highly developed but segmented form of civil society first began to take shape in the Netherlands as well as in Belgium in the 1870s and reached its apogee between the end of World War I and the mid-1960s. It helped provide the impetus in both polities for the transition from parliamentary government with limited suffrage to full democracy between the late 1880s and 1919–20 and ensured that once democracy had arrived, it would be of the consociational variety with which Belgium and the Netherlands have become so closely identified ever since.

In this chapter, I examine why civil society in these two countries came to be dominated around the turn of the century by thoroughly organized yet isolated Catholic, socialist, liberal, and (in the case of the Netherlands) orthodox Calvinist subcultures. Neither similar patterns of socioeconomic development, common features of their respective populations, nor shared cultural legacies can adequately account for this convergent outcome in Belgium and the Netherlands. Thus while the former was already continental Europe's most heavily industrialized state around 1850, the latter would not even begin the industrialization process in earnest until over four decades later. And while mid-nineteenth-century Belgium was religiously homogeneous (99 percent Catholic) but linguistically divided (55.3 percent Dutch and 41.5 percent French speaking), the Netherlands was linguistically homogeneous but religiously diverse (54.6 percent Dutch Reformed, 38.1 percent Catholic, 4.6 percent other Protestant, 1.9 percent Jewish) during this same period.[1] Finally, although the two states did share a common, city-based commercial culture during the late middle ages, they had developed in opposite directions in the centuries after separation in 1585, when the northern Netherlands became a decentralized, highly urbanized republic, whereas the formerly dominant metropolises of the south (Antwerp, Ghent, Bruges) lost their autonomy and economic dynamism under the rule of the absolutist Habsburgs.

How then can the emergence of quite similarly structured civil societies in such diverse pre-democratic states be explained? I argue below that it was the common existence in both polities during the 1850s, 1860s, and 1870s of hegemonic liberal political and socioeconomic regimes that pushed groups with substantial internal resources (orthodox Calvinists and/or Catholics and, somewhat later, workers) to organize in opposition to liberal policies in the areas of education and the economy and to work toward changes in property-based electoral laws that would benefit their particular subcultures. At the same time, it was precisely the liberal character of the political and social order they were fighting that permitted these groups to mobilize their followers, create their associations, build their schools, and found their critical newspapers without constraint. Faced with such opposition, liberals in the Netherlands and especially in Belgium then adopted the approach of their rivals and attempted, with mixed success, to construct separate, so-called neutral "pillars" of their own built in part around state institutions like schools, which had been all but abandoned by the religious communities.

Thus in the Netherlands it was fundamentalist Calvinists, horrified at the increasingly "nondenominational" character of the state schools, who, led by Reverend Abraham Kuyper, began in the 1870s to build up an organized, cross-class subculture in order to protect themselves from the evil influences of a "pagan" modern world. This subculture, which eventually came to include separate schools, newspapers, unions and employers associations, leisure-time organizations, an extensive social security system, and even a breakaway Reformed Church, was represented in the political sphere by the Netherlands' first modern political party, the Anti-Revolutionaire Partij (ARP). This party was founded by Kuyper in 1879 with the purpose not of overturning the liberal order, but rather of winning the resources from a liberal state necessary to construct an isolated, nonsecular "counterorder." Parallel to the orthodox Calvinists, and for similar reasons, Catholics also embarked on the road to pillarization, to be followed in the late 1890s by socialist workers. Finally, just prior to World War I, the formerly hegemonic liberals also sought to carve out a separate subculture to meet the needs of secularized members of the middle classes, though with much less success. As a result of these efforts, nearly every area of Dutch society from the 1920s through the 1960s was organized around three and sometimes four competing organizations, each linked to one of the four communities mentioned above.

Developments in Belgium closely resemble those in the Netherlands, though with some variations. Thus it was the passage of a liberal Schools Act in 1879, which aimed to undermine the role of the Church in elementary education, that brought a previously divided Catholic community together in a common antiliberal front and swept its leaders into power in 1884. The appearance during this decade of a growing socialist subculture modeled on that of the German social democrats eventually led the Church to found its own workers', farmers', employers', and youth organizations and to expand its social welfare activities in order to meet both the liberal and socialist threats. Finally, as in the Netherlands, the liberals belatedly sought to organize, thus leaving Belgian society divided into three camps until the 1960s, when the language issue finally rent each of the pillars along linguistic–regional lines.

THE EMERGENCE AND CONSOLIDATION OF LIBERAL REGIMES IN THE NETHERLANDS AND BELGIUM, 1815–1870

Belgium and the Netherlands set off down the road toward fully liberal regimes, which in these cases took the form of constitutional monarchies with parliamentary governments and limited suffrage but with a full range of civil liberties, from the same starting point: the United Kingdom of the Netherlands, founded in 1814–15. This new political entity brought together, mainly at the urging of the Dutch Prince of Orange and future king William I, the formerly independent United Provinces of the northern Netherlands and the previously Habsburg-controlled provinces of the southern Netherlands. Great Britain, Prussia, Austria, and Russia were willing to support the reunification of all of the Low Countries—last together in one polity in 1567, prior to the outbreak of the Dutch Revolt against the Spanish Habsburgs—in order to create an anti-French buffer state, and the project finally became a reality following Napoleon's final defeat at Waterloo.[2]

While the United Kingdom possessed the outward trappings of a constitutional monarchy, it was in its actual operation closer to the absolutism of Metternich's Austria. The executive rested firmly in the hands of the king, who named and dismissed ministers at will. The new state did possess a bicameral legislature, the States General, but neither of its chambers was directly elected. Members of the upper house were named for life by the sovereign, and those of the lower house were chosen by the provincial Estates, still organized around the three orders principle. While the States General could withhold its approval from new legislation, the constitution allowed the ruler to make new laws touching upon most areas of life by royal decree, thereby permitting him largely to ignore the assembly. Furthermore, the budget, which did require the assent of the legislature, only had to be passed once every ten years, thus depriving the States General of its greatest source of practical political leverage. Thanks to his extensive prerogatives, William I was able to rule for the most part as he sought fit and did not hesitate to impose extensive controls on the press in order to stifle any nascent dissent.[3]

While William's "enlightened absolutist" policies, which aimed to achieve true national unity through economic modernization and cultural integration promoted by a cautiously secular state, initially enjoyed some success in both north and south, by the late 1820s opposition to his rule had begun to grow within the former Austrian Netherlands. This opposition took concrete form in 1828 with the emergence of a political alliance (the Union Sacrée) that brought together two groups with very different kinds of grievances: liberal, mainly French-speaking intellectuals, lawyers, and other professionals angered both by the dominant role played by northerners in the new state's administrative infrastructure and the efforts of that state to promote the Dutch language in the south and Catholics, fully backed by the Church hierarchy and ironically drawing much support from Dutch-speaking Flanders and Brabant, outraged at the government's attempts to construct a state (i.e., nonreligious) system of secondary education. In 1830, this elite opposition suddenly gained a popular following thanks to the acute economic crisis affecting the south at that time.[4]

It was, however, the French July Revolution of 1830 that provided the spark that set off an uprising in Brussels in August 1830 led by a group of young radical liberals. It is unlikely that this uprising would have enjoyed the success it did had it not been for the confluence of two further fortuitous circumstances: the hesitation of William I in putting down this challenge and the rapid decision of the great powers, fearful of the spread of revolution across the continent, to recognize the new state of Belgium, the independence of which had been proclaimed by radicals within the southern opposition on October 4. Though William did not reconcile himself to this outcome until 1839, the protection afforded Belgium by France and by Holland's traditional ally Great Britain rendered him impotent to reverse it.[5]

Belgium

A constitution for the new Belgian polity was drawn up by a National Congress chosen in November 1830 through direct elections still restricted by property qualifications. Two models provided inspiration for the Congress's members, who were considerably more conservative than the radicals who had first initiated what was to become known as the Belgian Revolution: the new

French constitution of 1830, which provided one third of the text of the new Belgian document, and British bicameralism, the success of which was emphasized in the often heated debates over what form of government the country should adopt.[6] In the end, the delegates opted for a "dualist" constitutional monarchy[7] to be headed by the German prince Leopold of Saxe-Coburg, a relative of the British royal family.

The new political order was based upon a written constitution, which explicitly guaranteed freedom of opinion, religion, assembly, instruction, and the press and which, at least implicitly, carried through a separation of church and state. At the same time, the constitution specified that all power flowed from the nation, and that the nation's will was to be represented through an elected assembly, which, inspired by the British example, was to be bicameral. However, the idea of a hereditary upper house of Belgian peers was rejected in favor of a directly elected senate. By setting the property qualification for candidates exorbitantly high, the Congress in effect ensured that that body would long remain dominated by the nation's wealthiest noble landowners. While any adult male was permitted to stand for the lower house, the electorate remained limited by a property qualification to about 1 percent of the population.[8]

While the Belgian constitution of 1831 had provided explicit guarantees with regard to the classic liberal rights and freedoms, it had left unresolved, as did all such dualist documents, the question of whether it was ultimately to be the ruler or the representative assembly that would have the last word in determining the make-up of the government. While the ministers were to be responsible, in both a criminal and a political sense, to the assembly (art. 63, 64), the right both to name and dismiss said ministers (art. 65), along with the right to command the military and make peace and war (art. 68), lay exclusively with the king. And Leopold I, after having acclimatized himself to his new home, attempted to make full use of these prerogatives in order to keep the upper hand vis-à-vis the elected legislature. Thus he opposed the formation of formal political parties, chose as ministers men who enjoyed his confidence, and refused to grant dissolutions of the assembly requested by the government.[9]

This royal superiority could only persist for as long as the assembly was made up almost exclusively of unionists, a disorganized mass of liberals and Catholics committed to the continuation of the alliance that had brought about the revolution of 1830. By the 1840s, however, many liberals began to feel that the Church had been the main beneficiary of independence and decided to present themselves as a separate political grouping committed to anticlericalism. At the first ever national congress of liberals, held in Brussels in 1846, the delegates representing local liberal electoral associations vowed to combat Catholic control of the education system and to fight for an extension of the right to vote. When the liberals then gained an absolute majority in the legislature following the elections of 1847, the country reached a constitutional crossroads. Rather than contest the will of the voting public,

Leopold decided, in spite of his own preferences, to ask the liberal leader Charles Rogier to form a government. From this moment on, and without any formal change in the constitution, the principle of parliamentary supremacy was established in Belgium, never again to be seriously challenged by the monarch.[10]

Liberals of various stripes led successive Belgian governments for the next twenty-three years, until 1870. In the immediate aftermath of the shock caused by the February 1848 revolution in Paris, Rogier was able to realize some of the most immediate liberal goals. He pushed through a lowering of the property qualification for voting, thus expanding the electorate from 46,436 to 79,076 (still only 1.8 percent of the population), and ended the stamp duty on newspapers, which finally made full freedom of the press a reality. In addition, a series of bilateral treaties negotiated with Belgium's neighbors lowered customs duties on a whole range of products. Most controversially, a government act of 1850 sought to regain state control over secondary education, hitherto firmly in the hands of the Church.[11]

The Netherlands

The process of liberalization in the Netherlands was similar in broad outline to that in Belgium, and indeed was in part directly influenced by it. Thus after the Dutch king William I was finally forced to abandon his resistance to Belgian independence in 1839, pressure mounted both within the previously docile States General and in intellectual circles outside it for reforms that would move the country in the direction of a constitutional monarchy on the Belgian model. Despite sustained opposition from the king, the assembly approved amendments in 1840 that permitted ministers to be prosecuted if they violated the law in the performance of their duties and required them to countersign all royal decrees and orders. Even these very modest changes proved to be too much for the monarch, who abdicated later that year rather than accept these restrictions upon his prerogatives.[12]

Dissatisfied with minor alterations to what remained a semi-absolutist political system, a group of politicians and publicists influenced by Belgian and French doctrinaire liberalism pressed throughout the 1840s for much more substantial constitutional modifications. The most prominent of their number was J. R. Thorbecke, leader of a small group of nine liberals within the second chamber (total membership: fifty-six), which in 1844 published a new draft constitution modeled on that of Belgium. There is little evidence, however, that this proposal enjoyed widespread popular support. Thorbecke's moment arrived in 1848 when William I's successor William II, frightened by the outbreak of revolution in France and Germany and some minor disturbances in Amsterdam, agreed to the establishment of a true constitutional monarchy and asked the liberal leader to head the commission that was to design it.[13]

Not surprisingly, the new Dutch constitution of 1848 closely resembled its Belgian counterpart of 1831. As in that document, the full range of liberal rights and privileges were now legally guaranteed, though a stamp duty still hindered the free circulation of newspapers. The new political system was also to be dualist rather than parliamentary in character, for Thorbecke was critical of the British model of government. In practice, this meant that the sovereign was to retain the right to appoint and dismiss his ministers and in general to direct the work of the executive, though his right to make new laws by decree now disappeared. At the same time, however, the king was declared to be "inviolable," meaning that royal ministers were to assume both criminal and political responsibility for government policy vis-à-vis the States General (legislature), the composition of which was to be substantially altered. Members of the upper house would now be chosen by the (soon to be reformed) provincial assemblies, and lower house deputies were to be directly elected for the first time using the two-round majority system. A property qualification limited the size of the Dutch electorate to seventy-five thousand men, or 10.7 percent of adult males (2.4 percent of the total population), against 8 percent in Belgium (2 percent).[14]

As in Belgium, the inclusion of the principles of the criminal and political responsibility of ministers vis-à-vis the elected assembly was not meant to imply that that body should directly control the composition of government ministries. Within the dualist schema, this was the prerogative of the monarch, and like Leopold I during the 1830s and 1840s, the new Dutch king William III attempted to convert this power of appointment into more than just a formality during the 1850s and 1860s. Again as in Belgium, a significant degree of royal influence remained possible as long as no clear party groupings appeared within the States General.

However, the policies of Thorbecke's liberal government between 1849 and 1853—especially his decision in 1853 to allow the reestablishment of a Catholic ecclesiastical hierarchy in the Netherlands—helped provoke the emergence of a conservative grouping within the assembly. This grouping, which was no more a "party" at this time than were the liberals, brought together on the one hand members of the former regent aristocracy, who still possessed strong economic interests linked to the old Dutch trading system threatened by the government's antiprotectionist policies, and on the other, orthodox Calvinists opposed to equality for the large Catholic minority. While members of the former regent class could draw on intersecting family, business, and local government networks, which dated back to the republic when entering the public arena, both orthodox Calvinists and liberals seem during this period to have made use of the same organizational infrastructure to support their political activities, namely that provided by the Dutch Reformed Church, which contained under its roof both free-thinking latitudinarians and proto-fundamentalists.[15]

As in Belgium, the rise of ideologically distinct factions within the national assembly soon led to a direct confrontation between crown and parliament over control of the executive. This came between 1866 and 1868, when William III attempted to sustain a conservative government in power against the will of a liberal majority in the States General. Following a refusal by the assembly to pass the Foreign Ministry budget and two elections provoked by royal dissolutions in which voters gave their support to the liberals, the king was forced to concede defeat. Thus after a brief but dramatic struggle, (elite) parliamentary government finally replaced dualism in the Netherlands in 1868. This victory was crowned a year later by the disappearance of the stamp tax on newspapers and with it the last restrictions on a free press.[16]

CIVIL SOCIETIES BEFORE PILLARIZATION, 1815–1870

At first glance, one would expect the character of civil society in Belgium and the Netherlands before 1870 to differ quite substantially, given the fact the former was one of Europe's earliest industrializers and had in fact largely completed the industrialization process by 1870, whereas the latter would not even begin that process in earnest until after 1870. As a result, both the size of the industrial workforce and the number and influence of manufacturers was much greater in Belgium than in the Netherlands throughout this period.

Yet despite these variations in social structure, the pattern of civil society found in the two countries was remarkably similar. In both cases, civil society was marked above all by a pronounced vertical stratification, with class-specific patterns of sociability clearly distinguishing old elites (the landed aristocracy in Belgium and the regent patriciate in the Netherlands) from a bourgeoisie of mixed composition (industrialists, merchants, financiers, rentiers, professionals, state officials), a petite bourgeoisie, workers and craftsmen, and the rural population. In addition to these vertical divisions, horizontal divisions within the associational landscape based on religion were already present in both countries (active Catholics versus anticlericals in Belgium; Calvinists of various stripes versus Catholics in the Netherlands), though they were not yet as extensive or pronounced as they would gradually become after 1870.

Belgium

In Belgium as in much of the rest of western Europe, the first half of the nineteenth century was an epoch in which a diverse, ever wealthier bourgeoisie came to take over the leading role within an expanding civil society from an aristocracy now in the grip of gradual decline. Nonetheless, aristocrats continued to exercise much influence throughout this period as large landowners and investors, politically active members of the senate, and cultural trendsetters whom the bourgeoisie often sought to emulate. While the individual bourgeois might not be able to afford the enlightened nobleman's country estate with its extensive library, laboratory, natural history collection, and perhaps even small theater, he could still pursue the ideals of self-cultivation and amateur scientific inquiry by making common cause with others of his class and forming an association to that end.[17]

Thus the local *cercles littéraires*, local cultural societies, arose after 1815 in the southern Netherlands as the successors to the scattered reading groups and literary societies of the late eighteenth century and quickly established themselves as a new, distinctly bourgeois, form of sociability. Modeled on the English club with its permanent library and reading rooms, the *cercle* acted both as a meeting place for intellectuals, artists, businessmen, and politicians and as the umbrella organization for a whole range of more specialized cultural and scientific societies. Its members were also the foremost supporters of the local orchestra and municipal theater and principal consumers of the books, periodicals, and newspapers that now flooded the market. By 1848 the young country could already boast 202 different newspapers and periodicals and over one hundred other journals.[18]

Another bourgeois cultural institution that was fated to play a significant political role in Belgium well into the twentieth century was the Masonic lodge. Freemasonry had established itself in the then Austrian Netherlands during the reign of Maria Theresa (1740–80) and had initially received encouragement from her enlightened son Joseph II, who then, however, attempted to bring the movement under his control through strict regulation from above. Following the outbreak of the French Revolution Joseph ordered all lodges closed, but they were revived under the French occupation, which gave a massive boost to Belgian Freemasonry.[19]

Following the country's independence in 1830, the Masonic leadership attempted to keep politics out of the lodges, but this became increasingly difficult in the face of repeated attacks from the Catholic Church, most notably the Belgian bishops' outspoken condemnation of Freemasonry in a pastoral letter of 1838. As a result, the movement began to develop in an explicitly anticlerical direction, and, especially after the lifting of the ban on political engagement and discussion in 1856, the nationwide network of lodges furnished the country's liberals with an invaluable basis of support. As such the lodges came to form a kind of permanent complement to the liberal electoral associations, which, beginning in the late 1830s, were called into life for each election.[20]

If the *cercle littéraire* and the Masonic lodge stood at the center of urban bourgeois sociability, the neighborhood café with its newspapers and piano fulfilled a similar function for the petite bourgeoisie, craftsmen, and skilled workers. In addition to its other amenities, the café could also offer a headquarters for the mutual aid societies that former guild members had founded following the dissolution of their organizations after 1818. The new class of industrial workers soon began to form similar self-help and mutual aid societies, and in 1857 the cotton spinners and weavers of Ghent founded the first industrial trade union in Belgium. Finally, during the 1860s the first consumer cooperatives were inaugurated, a form of working-class self-organization that was later to carry great weight within the Belgian socialist movement.[21]

While the influence of the Catholic Church over the lower classes within the cities was weakening due to the inadequacies of the ecclesiastical infrastructure in the face of explosive urbanization, its hold over the countryside—and especially over largely agrarian Flanders—remained as strong as ever. For the three-quarters of the population that continued to live outside of the cities, the local parish remained the center of social as well as religious life. Between the 1840s and 1860s, however, as relations between Catholics and liberals became ever more strained, the Church began to found or encourage a new range of associations outside the parishes in order to counter the growing organizational power of anticlericalism.[22]

Foremost among these were the St. Vincent de Paul Society (1842), which performed charitable works; the Brotherhood of St. Francis Xavier (1853), which focused on moral education and fellowship among the craftsmen and farmers of Flanders; and the Federation of Catholic Workingmen's Circles (1867), an umbrella organization for a variety of sickness funds, and benevolent, leisure-time, and youth associations. During this same period, a Catholic press came into being, and so-called Catholic Circles, the Church-sponsored counterparts to the *cercles littéraires*, also began to spread among those bourgeois who remained faithful Catholics. In 1868, they were united in the Federation of Catholic Circles.[23]

Finally, it was during the 1850s that Catholic electoral associations arose at the local level to counter the influence of liberal associations. Yet, as Righart together with van Isacker has emphasized, the appearance of such associations did not represent the first step toward the creation of a Catholic political party, because liberal Catholics still remained firmly opposed to such a move, as they repeatedly stated at the Catholic Congresses held in Mechelen in 1863, 1864, and 1867. Rather, such men as Edouard Ducpétiaux were hoping to create a liberally minded (*vrijheidsgezinde*) political force of the center, which, by acting as an effective counterweight to liberal anticlericalism, would remove religious issues from the political agenda altogether. As we shall see, this vision was doomed to failure, a failure that would bring pillarization in its wake.[24]

The Netherlands

As noted above, the pattern of civil society found in the Netherlands before 1870 was similar in many respects to that found in Belgium. As in the latter, a variety of associational forms with their roots in the Enlightenment of the late eighteenth century stood at the center of bourgeois sociability.

The nearest equivalent to the *cercles littéraires* were the *leesgenootschappen*, or reading societies, of which there were over three hundred by the late 1700s and as many as nine hundred during the early 1800s. In addition, more specialized associations devoted to various kinds of scientific research and literary production had sprung up across the country from the 1750s onward. Freemasonry established itself earlier in the northern Netherlands, in 1734, than in the Austrian Netherlands to the south, but during the nineteenth century, the Dutch Masonic lodges do not seem to have involved themselves to any significant degree in politics, though as in Belgium many of their members were associated with political liberalism.[25]

More significant than reading groups, scientific associations, or Masonic lodges as a forum for bourgeois engagement was a uniquely Dutch organization, the Maatschappij tot Nut van 't Algemeen, or Society for Public Welfare, formed by Baptist minister Jan Nieuwenhuyzen in 1784 and still in existence today. The Nut, which had already attracted close to four thousand members by the turn of the nineteenth century and by 1870 could boast nearly fifteen thousand adherents organized in 309 local "departments," was active in a wide range of areas. It founded primary and infant schools and "people's libraries," published improving literature, organized lectures and courses of instruction, and helped set up savings banks and insurance schemes for the poor. Unlike many other associations of the time, its membership was open to adherents of all religious denominations rather than just those of the Dutch Reformed Church.[26]

Sociability among the lower classes seems to have been less developed in the Netherlands than in Belgium in the period before 1870. Thus unlike the former, the latter did not possess much of a café culture, and though typographers founded the first Dutch trade union in 1866, it was not until the 1880s that a significant union movement began to appear. This is hardly surprising considering the late onset of industrialization in the Netherlands and the continued validity there of the 1791 Le Chapelier law banning combinations (repealed 1872). Prior to the last few decades of the century, then, the primary form of organization among both workers and petits bourgeois alike was the mutual aid or self-help society, often set up, as in Belgium, by craftsmen to replace the former guilds.[27]

Far more important than any of these associations to the lives of the common people were the churches, whether Protestant or Catholic. Not only did the churches remain, at least through the end of the century, at the center of local social and intellectual life, especially in the countryside, but they were also primarily responsible for the extensive system of poor relief that had already existed in the Netherlands under the republic. A new Poor Law of 1854 confirmed and even strengthened the primacy of the local parishes within this area.[28]

Until 1848, the Dutch Reformed Church (Nederlands Hervormde Kerk), representing 54.6 percent of the population, remained the official state church, just as its predecessor the Reformed Church (Gereformeerde Kerk) had been during the republic. Traditionally, however, this body had always contained within it a wide variety of theological currents as well as the full range of social classes, and this remained true throughout the nineteenth century. After 1815, adherents of the so-called Groningen School, which adopted a latitudinarian position on the interpretation of the Bible in the interest of maintaining the unity of all Dutch Calvinists, held sway within the hierarchy, but from the 1840s onward came under increasing attack from two directions.[29]

On one side stood the "modernists" led by J. H. Scholten of the University of Leiden, rationalists who called into question the divinity of Christ, biblical accounts of miracles, and the divine inspiration of the Scripture. On the other stood the "antirevolutionaries" or "Christian historicals," adherents of scriptural orthodoxy who saw just this brand of rationalism, with its roots in the Enlightenment and French Revolution (hence "antirevolutionary"), as the major threat to Christian—by which they meant orthodox Protestant—civilization in the Netherlands. While the modernists found most of their adherents among members of the upper bourgeoisie, the "antirevolutionary" camp contained a strange alliance of aristocrats from the old patriciate, such as their most prominent spokesman Groen van Prinsterer, and "little people" (*kleine luyden*), members of the popular classes who were largely excluded from the governance of the nominally participatory Reformed Church until 1867 (see below). It was precisely elite control over the appointment of ministers and deacons that permitted first the Groningen School and then, increasingly, the modernists to set the tone within the Church because, as would become evident after 1867, the majority of parishioners were firmly orthodox, if not fundamentalist, in their beliefs.[30]

Just as the separation of church and state in the 1848 constitution spelled the end of the Hervormde Kerk's privileged status, it also laid the groundwork for the restoration of a Dutch Catholic hierarchy, absent since the late sixteenth century. This occurred in 1853 with the support of Thorbecke's liberal government and unleashed a storm of protest from orthodox Calvinists under the leadership of Groen. This popular, anti-Catholic mobilization, known as the April Movement, succeeded in collecting over two hundred thousand signatures on a petition presented to William III asking him to block the return of the Catholic bishops, a request the king denied. The movement was able, however, to bring down the Thorbecke government in the wake of the 1853 elections and replace it with a more conservative one. During this and subsequent elections through the late 1860s, local liberal and conservative electoral associations, which had appeared sporadically from the late 1840s, spread across the country, with candidates and their supporters on both sides looking for support from different factions within the Dutch Reformed congregations. As in Belgium, such associations were not permanent bodies, but were called together before each election campaign and dissolved thereafter.[31]

Not surprisingly, the newly emancipated Catholic Church, which represented about 38 percent of the population, was initially hesitant to expand its associational infrastructure in the manner of its Belgian counterpart lest it arouse the suspicions of an already irate Calvinist majority. Even those Catholics active in politics rejected the formation of separate electoral associations, and the Church instead urged those of its members who possessed the right to vote to examine the views of local liberals and conservatives toward their religion and support the candidate least likely to prove harmful to Roman Catholic interests, which almost invariably meant the liberal. Thus emerged during the 1850s and 1860s a common liberal–Catholic front in opposition to Calvinist conservatism.[32] The battles of Thorbecke and Groen—the Dutch Gladstone and Disraeli—seemed by the late 1850s to have laid the groundwork for a bipolar division of Dutch politics and society into liberal and conservative camps on the British model. Yet, as we shall see, the political struggles of the next decades were in fact to push both society and politics in a very different direction, toward pillarization.

ANTILIBERALISM AND THE ORIGINS OF PILLARIZED CIVIL SOCIETIES, 1870–1914

By the late 1860s, the process of liberalization had been successfully completed in the Netherlands and in Belgium. Both states now possessed fully parliamentary governments, though property qualifications limited the suffrage to a small percentage of the adult male population. Written constitutions in both countries guaranteed equality before the law for all citizens as well as freedom of the press, assembly, and worship, and the doctrines of free trade and fiscal responsibility guided economic policy. Furthermore, the liberals who had largely created this new order remained the dominant force on the political scene.

It was this liberal dominance—and its perceived connection to a growing "ungodliness" within Dutch and Belgian society—which first led religious communities in both countries to seek to shield themselves from liberal influences by organizing and segregating their respective milieus. Somewhat later, socialist workers followed the same strategy as a way of combating the depredations of the liberal economic order. From a religious point of view, however, the appearance of a new socialist subculture merely added to the forces of the ungodly, and hence quickened the resolve of Catholics and Calvinists to complete the construction of their own self-contained life-worlds.

The Netherlands

The origins of the process of "pillarization" that eventually reshaped Dutch civil society into four major self-contained subcultures (orthodox

Calvinist, Catholic, socialist, "neutral" or liberal) can be traced to a number of policies that liberal-dominated governments introduced during the 1850s and 1860s. In 1857 the liberals had passed a new education law, which called for state schools to be religiously neutral and at the same time forbade state aid to private, specifically, Catholic and Calvinist, educational institutions. Five years earlier, in 1852, another law had carried through the division of church and state decreed in the 1848 constitution by introducing full participation by the Dutch Reformed Church's (male) membership in the selection of elders and ministers in place of the previous authority of the sovereign. This democratization of the former state Church did not come into force until 1867, however, and in the meantime many important leadership positions within it had been taken over by modernist clergy who were seen as casting doubt on the literal truth of the Bible. Finally, in 1870 a liberal government, against strong conservative opposition, abolished the death penalty in the Netherlands.[33]

It was these liberal trends within the political and religious spheres that called forth the resistance of the young "antirevolutionary" Calvinist minister Abraham Kuyper (1837–1920). Kuyper believed that the fundamental cleavage line of the age was not that between capitalist and worker or even Catholic and Protestant, but rather the "antithesis" (*antithese*) between true Christians of whatever denomination and non-Christians or "pagans" inspired by the secular humanist ideology of the French Revolution. His response to this, in the most general sense "liberal" threat, was to call for the construction of a separate orthodox Calvinist life-world that would remain free from all the evils of modern secularism. Hence Kuyper's famous battle cry of *souvereiniteit in eigen kring* ("sovereignty within one's own circle"). His practical aim was to gain "equality" for his fundamentalist subculture by securing government funding for its activities on par with that received by official, liberal-sponsored state institutions. The means he would use to achieve this aim was the mobilization of Holland's God-fearing, Calvinist *kleine luyden* (little people) against elitist, modernizing liberals.[34]

Despite the deeply conservative if not reactionary nature of his worldview, Kuyper made use of thoroughly modern methods to promote his cause. First, he encouraged the creation of "antirevolutionary" electoral associations at the local level and himself unsuccessfully stood for parliament for the first time in 1871. The following year he formed the "Anti-School Law Association," modeled on the British Anti-Corn Law League, which aimed to reverse the liberal School Law of 1857. At the same time he founded a mass-circulation daily, *De Standaard*, a step only made practicable by a liberal government's abolition of the stamp duty on newspapers in 1869. In 1877, Calvinist workers called the Workingman's Association "Patrimonium" (Werkliedenverbond Patrimonium) into being.[35]

Finally, after a left liberal government under Johannes Kappeyne van de Coppello sponsored a new School Law in 1878, which strengthened the secular character of the state system, reaffirmed the ban on subsidies to private schools, and imposed new standards on the latter that they were in no financial position to meet, Kuyper founded (1879) the Anti-Revolutionaire Partij (ARP), the first truly modern mass political organization in the Netherlands. This was followed one year later by the creation of an independent orthodox university, the VU (Free University) in Amsterdam, and in 1886 by the withdrawal of Kuyper's followers from the increasingly latitudinarian Dutch Reformed Church, a move that would eventually lead to the emergence of a separate, fundamentalist Gereformeerde Kerk (Reformed Church) in 1892.[36]

Meanwhile, only nine years after its founding, the ARP achieved a major political breakthrough when, in 1888, it was able to form its first (coalition) government. This government, which was led by A. E. MacKay, promptly replaced van Kappeyne's hated School Law of 1878 with a new Education Act that permitted one-third of the costs of private schools to be met by the state. In so doing, it saved the Calvinist and Catholic school systems from extinction and made possible a rise in the percentage of pupils educated outside the state sector from 25 percent in 1880 to 38 percent in 1910.[37]

The ARP's partners in their first government were none other than the Catholic members of the States General—hardly, one would think, the natural allies of fundamentalist Calvinists. Yet parallel to Kuyper the Catholic hierarchy in the Netherlands had also taken the first steps toward the construction of their own separate pillar within Dutch society, and for many of the same reasons. During the 1840s and 1850s the Catholic community was led by bourgeois notables who made common cause with the Protestant liberals who had, after all, carried out a separation of the Dutch Reformed Church and the state in 1848 and allowed the restoration of an independent Roman Catholic hierarchy in 1853. That new hierarchy was staffed, however, by many prelates imbued with ultramontane ideas that were quite close in many respects to those of Kuyper. Thus the ultramontanes also viewed the French Revolution and the secularizing liberalism it had spawned as the source of most modern evils, and their *subsidiariteitsbeginsel*, or principle of subsidiarity (not coincidentally the touchstone of today's EU), which held that whenever possible political and social tasks should be carried out by local organizations, clearly possessed an elective affinity with the notion of *soevereiniteit in eigen kring*.[38]

By the late 1860s the Dutch hierarchy had largely succeeded in winning its internal struggle against liberal Catholic notables who opposed a policy of community isolation and could hence begin with their campaign against the liberal political and social order. In 1868, eleven years after its passage, the Dutch bishops rejected the School Law of 1857 and called for the strengthening of a separate Catholic educational system. At the same time, they encouraged the creation of independent Catholic electoral associations in the constituencies without any ties to those of the liberals. Furthermore, it was in 1868, four years before the first appearance of *De Standaard*, that the daily *De Maasbode* was founded in Rotterdam as an organ of Catholic antiliberalism.[39]

During the late 1870s and early 1880s, however, Catholic leaders remained ambivalent about taking the nascent process of pillarization still further by building confessionally segregated organizations for workers and farmers or by expanding the Church's role in the sphere of social welfare. What pushed them inexorably in this direction was the appearance from the 1880s onward of a growing socialist subculture among Holland's expanding industrial workforce, many of whose members were Catholic in origin. Though the country's first trade union was formed in 1866 by typographers, the very slow pace of Dutch industrialization meant that a significant trade union movement did not arise until the 1880s. It was also not until 1881 that a Social Democratic Federation (SDB) was founded under the leadership of a charismatic Lutheran minister, Ferdinand Domela Nieuwenhuis. This nascent socialist party remained very weak, however, and in 1894, following a shift toward anarchism, many of its members seceded and formed the Social Democratic Workers Party (SDAP), modeled on the German SPD. Thirteen years later, the growing number of social democratic unions grouped themselves into the Dutch Confederation of Trade Unions (NVV), which saw its membership increase from nineteen thousand (1906) to nearly eighty-five thousand on the eve of World War I. As in Germany, the expanding socialist milieu came to include not only a political party and trade unions, but also newspapers and women's, free time, sport, and youth organizations. Adherents of this pillar made use almost exclusively of the nondenominational state education system.[40]

It was in the wake of these developments that both Catholics and Calvinists moved to expand and complete the organization of their own communities in the face of a double liberal/socialist threat. Thus the first Catholic trade unions were founded in 1888, and their number increased rapidly throughout the 1890s. Around the turn of the century, however, Catholic and Calvinist workers began to make common cause in a union known as Unitas. In 1906, the Catholic hierarchy put an end to this nascent interconfessionalism, forcing their coreligionists to withdraw and forming the Office of Roman Catholic Unions in 1908. Unitas, now left with only Calvinist members, was brought together in 1907-8 with other Calvinist Unions to create the National Christian Union Federation (CNV). The latter numbered about eleven thousand members in 1914, compared to about twenty-nine thousand in its Catholic counterpart. Church intervention to end grassroots interconfessionalism among farmers' organizations led in 1912–13 to the emergence of separate Catholic and Calvinist associations to represent that social group as well. Finally, in 1911, the Church also ended cooperation between Catholic and liberal employers and instead created, in 1915, the General Catholic Employers Association. The last step in the pillarization process came in 1925, when local Catholic electoral associations were united into a formal political party, the Roman Catholic State Party (RKSP).[41]

In the face of this feverish organization building on the part of their ideological and political opponents, the response of liberals was noticeably weak. Rather than a proper pillar, the liberal camp was and remained, at least until after World War II, a loose collection of "neutral" or nondenominational newspapers, charity organizations, women's and youth groups, employers' and farmers' associations, and two small trade unions. In the political sphere, the liberals remained divided into three groupings—left liberals, moderate liberals, and right-wing liberals, each of which possessed its own political party.[42]

Belgium

There are many parallels between the origins of pillarization in the Netherlands and in Belgium. As in the former, it was a liberal education law (van Humbeeck's School Act of 1879) that provided the impetus for a religious community, in this case the Catholics, to begin to organize and isolate their subcultural milieu. Also, as we have seen, some of the raw materials for the construction of the future Catholic pillar were already in place well before the late 1870s in the form of a growing network of Catholic social work, instructional, and leisure-time bodies and the electoral associations that had arisen during the 1850s.

However, as Hans Righart and others have pointed out, these organizations did not yet represent the beginnings of a "pillar" because a significant portion of the Catholic bourgeoisie, the so-called liberal Catholics, remained firmly opposed to the idea of a separate, isolated Catholic sociopolitical community advocated by ultramontanes within the church hierarchy. They preferred instead to act as a conservative but loyal opposition to the dominant liberals, so long as the policies of the latter remained relatively moderate. What altered the position of the liberals and led them to make common cause with the ultramontanes in defense of the Church was liberal Pierre van Humbeeck's School Law of 1879 and its companion act on secondary education of 1881, both of which sought to build a truly secular system of public instruction by imposing state control on those local school authorities inclined to leave education firmly in the hands of the Church. The bitterness of the ensuing "school war," during which parents who remained loyal to the state schools were often denied communion and socially ostracized, left Belgium divided between loyal followers of the Church and deeply anticlerical liberals (and later socialists) for generations to come.[43]

In the political sphere, its most immediate effect was to mobilize voters through the newly formed Federation of Catholic Circles and Conservative Associations in order to oust the liberals at the 1884 elections. From this election onward Catholic governments were to rule Belgium with absolute majorities until the end of World War I. At the same time, the return of the Liberal Catholics to the arms of the Church opened the way to a further solidification and expansion of the Catholic associational landscape so as to create a lasting bulwark against liberal secularism.[44]

Just as in the Netherlands, what lent this project added urgency was the appearance of a growing socialist subculture, which was as anticlerical as its liberal counterpart, if not more so. Though the first Belgian trade union appeared on the scene in 1842, and several abortive attempts were made to found durable workers' parties in the 1870s, it was only in the 1880s that the socialist movement took firm root in the country. In 1885, the Belgian Workers' Party (BWP/POB) was founded, modeled on the German SPD. Representatives from twenty trade unions as well as many of the local cooperatives that had spread across the industrial regions since 1881 were present at the party's founding congress. As in the Netherlands, the socialist subculture then grew rapidly, creating youth and women's organizations and newspapers and sickness funds. It even attempted to expand into the countryside, but remained centered around the trade unions and, to a much greater degree than in Holland, the cooperative movement.[45]

And as in the Netherlands, it was this socialist expansion that gave the final push to Catholic pillarization. From the late 1880s onward, the Church began to expand its social welfare activities, and Catholic workers founded cooperatives and trade unions as well. The latter were in fact able to compete much more effectively with their socialist rivals than were their Dutch denominational counterparts. Though the socialist trade unions numbered 125,000 members on the eve of World War I, the Catholic unions organized in the General Christian Union (known as the ACV-Confédération) could also claim about one hundred thousand members. In addition, Catholic farmers', women's, and middle-class associations were all founded between 1890 and 1914, and a Catholic employers' association in 1925. And of course the Church possessed an all-encompassing private education system, the fruit of the battles of the late 1870s and 1880s, now subsidized by generous grants from the state.[46]

Finally, as in the Netherlands, it was the liberal pillar that remained the most diffuse in Belgium. Politically, liberals were divided into two camps, the progressives and the doctrinaires, though they finally agreed to cooperate in 1900. In addition to the liberal circles and other organizations like Masonic lodges that had survived from the earlier part of the century, the liberal subculture was built around various pressure groups (especially those for universal suffrage), the nondenominational school system, and various business organizations. Though a liberal union movement existed, it remained very weak.[47]

How, then, can we account for the fact that in the Netherlands it was the orthodox Calvinists and Catholics and in Belgium the Catholics and socialists who were able to organize their communities most thoroughly? The rapid success of all three groups in realizing the pillarization project can be explained in good part by their superior access to a range of resources: in the case of socialist workers, the organizational advantages derived from the high concentration of large industrial plants within very small areas in both countries and in that of the religious communities both the organizational and material resources already present within an extensive network of local parishes, as well as ideological resources derived from a glorification of past victories won by each of the religious groupings (for Dutch Calvinists, successful resistance to Habsburg absolutism; for Dutch Catholics, successful resistance to Calvinist hegemony; for Belgian Catholics, successful resistance to the enlightened absolutism of Joseph II and William I). Finally, the importance of exceptional leaders like Kuyper should not be overlooked. It is a telling fact that liberals in both countries, who enjoyed none of these advantages, experienced the greatest difficulties in institutionalizing their own separate subcultures when they finally set about doing this after the turn of the century.

EPILOGUE: NASCENT PILLARIZATION AND DEMOCRATIZATION, 1887–1920

As was mentioned at several points above, there exists an intimate relationship between the emergence of highly organized, segmented civil societies in the Netherlands and Belgium and the transition from elite parliamentarism to full democracy in these two countries between the late 1880s and 1920. In Belgium, it was during the last decade of liberal dominance in the 1860s that young, left-wing members of that movement began to agitate for further reductions in the property qualification leading to universal manhood suffrage, and the first bill to revise the constitution in this direction was introduced—and defeated—in 1870.[48] In 1881, radical liberals formed the Ligue nationale pour la réforme électorale (National League for Electoral Reform), and they were supported in their efforts by members of the nascent socialist movement. Following its formation in 1885, the Belgian Workers' Party then lent its full support to the cause of political democratization and called four general strikes to this end in the period leading up to World War I.[49]

It was following a period of popular mobilization for electoral reform organized by socialists, radical liberals, and progressive Catholics culminating in the general strike of 1893 that the dominant Catholic parliamentary group finally compromised with the opposition on a constitutional change that introduced universal manhood suffrage, but with plural voting (three vote maximum per person).[50] Six years later, after it became clear that the combination of universal (if unequal) suffrage and majority voting was threatening to destroy the liberals and polarize the country between a Catholic Flanders and a left-wing Wallonia, Belgium became the first state in Europe to adopt proportional representation when the Catholic parliamentary group split and its more progressive members voted with the liberals and the socialists to replace the traditional two-round majority electoral system.[51] Despite much agitation (including two further general strikes), the next step toward universal and equal manhood suffrage was only taken in the aftermath of the country's traumatic wartime occupation, and, even then, it would require thirty years of waiting and another war before women received the vote (1948).[52] With this one caveat in mind, Belgium, which had nearly achieved full parliamentary democracy in the early 1890s, finally reached this goal in 1919.

As in Belgium, it was left liberals and socialists who were in the forefront of the fight to democratize the Dutch parliamentary monarchy by extending the right to vote. In 1876 and again in 1879 liberals founded organizations devoted to electoral reform, and in 1883 a League for Universal Franchise (Bond voor Algemeen Kiesrecht) brought together both liberals and socialists. Indeed, despite its revolutionary rhetoric, the socialist SDB proved to be a tireless campaigner for universal manhood suffrage. In 1885, the first mass demonstration was held in The Hague in support of the expansion of the franchise, and the States General responded two years later by lowering the property qualification so as to more than double the electorate, from 122,000 to 292,000 men (6.4 percent vs. 13.9 percent of the adult population). As mentioned above, the elections of 1888 that followed favored the religious parties, and the result was the formation of the MacKay government uniting for the first time the Catholics and the orthodox Calvinists of the ARP.[53]

It was to be another twenty years, however, before demands for universal manhood suffrage were finally heeded. In 1892–93, the left liberal Tak van Poortvliet introduced a bill to enfranchise all men except the illiterate and those on poor relief, but a coalition of right liberals, Catholics, and some antirevolutionaries opposed the measure. Indeed this issue split the ARP in 1894 when Kuyper's aristocratic rival Savornin Lohman quit the party because he (Savornin Lohman) refused to support such a radical suffrage extension, a move that eventually led to the founding of the Christelijk Historisch Unie (Christian Historical Union) in 1908. Nevertheless, a compromise on a further expansion of the electorate was finally reached in 1896. The result was an increase in the number of male voters from 295,570 (13.9 percent of the adult population) in 1890 to 854,539 (30.7 percent) in 1910.[54]

As in Belgium, it was World War I that provided the final impetus to full democratization. In 1917, the "Pacificatie" (Pacification) was negotiated, a grand compromise in which the Catholic and Protestant school systems were finally placed on an equal footing with their state counterpart, while the conservatives within the religious camp finally agreed to universal manhood suffrage and the simultaneous introduction of proportional representation. Unlike in Belgium, however, women were also granted the right to vote three years later, in 1920.[55]

As will be clear from the above narrative, the processes of pillarization and democratization in Belgium and the Netherlands clearly advanced side by side from the 1870s onward, though the relationship between them was complex. On the one hand, it is obvious that the organizational capacities of the socialist movements in both countries played a key role in mobilizing mass support for electoral reform of the kind that liberals, due to their lack of such capacities, would have been hard pressed to generate alone. In addition, in the Netherlands the pro-democratic forces at the disposal of the ARP helped compensate for the relative weakness of the Dutch socialist movement before the turn of the century.

Yet on the other hand, pillarization also increased the ability to resist universal suffrage on the part of those forces opposed to it. In a curious parallel to the situation in the progressive camp, the Catholic milieu, though internally divided on the issue, provided needed support to the right-wing liberals whom they opposed on so many other issues. What can be said without qualification, however, is that the emergence as early as the 1880s of regular top-level bargaining among the leaders of all of the pillars, and their ability for the most part to impose the compromises they reached upon disciplined followings, inaugurated a pattern of democratic politics, which allowed both countries to weather the upheavals of this century without serious challenge to their respective democratic orders.

NOTES

1. E. H. Kossmann, *The Low Countries 1780–1940* (Oxford: Clarendon, 1978), 170; Theo Luykx, *Politieke Geschiedenis van Belgie*, 2 vols. (Amsterdam/Brussels: Elsevier, 1977), 1:100; Robert Dahl, ed., *Political Oppositions in Western Democracies* (New Haven, Conn.: Yale University Press, 1966), 425.

2. J. Roegiers and N. C. F. van Sas, "Revolutie in Noord en Zuid (1780–1830)," in *Geschiedenis van de Nederlanden*, ed. J. C. H. Blom and E. Lamberts (Rijswijk: Nijgh & Van Ditmar, 1993), 242–44; Kossmann, *Low Countries*, 103–11.

3. Horst Lademacher, *Geschiedenis van Nederland* (Utrecht: Het Spectrum, 1993), 269–70; Roegiers and van Sas, "Revolutie," 244–46; Kossmann, *Low Countries*, 112–16; J. A. Bornewasser, "Het Koninkrijk der Nederlanden 1815–1830," in *Algemene Geschiedenis der Nederlanden*, 15 vols., ed. D. P. Blok et al. (Haarlem: Fibula-Van Dishoeck, 1977–1983), 11:233–39.

4. Lademacher, *Geschiedenis*, 282–86; Roegiers and van Sas, "Revolutie," 246–50; Kossmann, *Low Countries*, 118, 121–52.

5. Roegiers and van Sas, "Revolutie," 250–51; Kossmann, *Low Countries*, 151–55, 158–59.

6. John Gilissen, *Le Régime représentatif en Belgique depuis 1790* (Brussels: La Renaissance du Livre, 1958), 87–88.

7. A "dualist" constitutional monarchy is one in which the constitution assigns all executive power to a hereditary monarch, but calls for legislative powers to be shared between that monarch and a directly elected representative assembly, the approval of which is necessary in order for new laws to be valid. On the concept of "dualism" as it relates both to constitutional monarchies in general and the Belgian case in particular, see Klaus von Beyme, *Die parlamentarischen Regierungssysteme in Europa* (Munich: Piper, 1970), 30, 124–26.

8. E. Lamberts, "België sinds 1830," in *Geschiedenis*, 253; Gilissen, *Régime représentatif*, 88–94.

9. A. Simon, "België van 1840 tot 1848," in *Algemene Geschiedenis der Nederlanden*, 12 vols., ed. J. A. van Houtte et al. (Utrecht: De Haan, 1949–58), 10:2–3; E. Witte, "De politieke ontwikkeling in België 1831–1846," in *Algemene Geschiedenis*, 11:336–38; Val Lorwin, "Belgium: Religion, Class and Language in National Politics," in *Political Oppositions*, 151.

10. Simon, "België," 19–21; Lamberts, "België," 255; Lorwin, "Belgium," 152–53.

11. Gilissen, *Régime représentatif*, 94–98, 188; Lamberts, "België," 255–56; Kossmann, *Low Countries*, 232–37.

12. G. J. Hooykaas, "De politieke ontwikkeling in Nederland 1830–1840," in *Algemene Geschiedenis*, 11:310–14; Kossmann, *Low Countries*, 179–80.

13. J. C. Boogman, "The Dutch Crisis in the Eighteen-Forties," in *Britain and the Netherlands*, ed. J. S. Bromley and E. H. Kossmann (London: Chatto & Windus, 1960), 193–96; Boogman, "De periode 1840–1848," in *Algemene Geschiedenis*, 12:321–23, 329–32; Kossmann, *Low Countries*, 188–93.

14. J. C. H. Blom, "Nederland sinds 1830," in *Geschiedenis*, 312–14; Kossmann, *Low Countries*, 191–95.

15. Kossmann, *Low Countries*, 274–82.

16. Von Beyme, *Parlamentarische Regierungssysteme*, 282–83; Blom, "Nederland," 314–15; Kossmann, *Low Countries*, 285–88.

17. J. Art, "Sociocultureel leven in de Zuidelijke Nederlanden 1815–circa 1840," in *Algemene Geschiedenis*, 11:145–46.

18. Art, "Sociocultureel leven," 11:145–46, 150–51; J. Rogiers, "Sociocultureel leven in de Zuidelijke Nederlanden 1794–1814," in *Algemene Geschiedenis*, 11:75.

19. Michel Dierickx, *De Vrijmetselarij: De Grote Unbekende 1717–1967* (Antwerp: Uitgeverij De Nederlandsche Boekhandel, 1972), 54–56; Rogiers, "Sociocultureel leven," 76–77; Margaret Jacob, *Living the Enlightenment: Freemasonry and Politics in Eighteenth-Century Europe* (Oxford: Oxford University Press, 1991), 157.

20. Dierickx, *Vrijmetselarij*, 80–84, 85–86; Lamberts, "België," 346–47, 351.

21. Art, "Sociocultureel leven," 146; D. de Weerdt, "Arbeidersbeweging 1844–1873," in *Algemene Geschiedenis*, 12:123–24, 129–30; Léon Delsinne, *Le Parti Ouvrier Belge des Origines à 1894* (Brussels: La Renaissance du Livre, 1955), 105.

22. Art, "Sociocultureel leven," 147–48, 152; Art, "Kerk en religie 1844–1914," in *Algemene Geschiedenis*, 12:169–70.

23. Hans Righart, *De Katholieke Zuil in Europa* (Amsterdam: Boom Meppel, 1986), 137–41; Rudolf Rezsohazy, *Origines et Formation du Catholicisme Social en Belgique 1842–1909* (Louvain: Publications Universitaires du Louvain, 1958), 48–58; Art, "Sociocultureel leven," 153.

24. Righart, *Katholieke Zuil*, 138; K. van Isacker, *Werkelijk en Wettelijk Land: De Katholieke Opinie tegenover de Rechterzijde 1863–1884* (Antwerpn: Uitgeversmaatschappij N.V. Standaard-Boekhandel, 1955), 10–18.

25. Jan de Vet, "Verlichting en christendom in Nederland," in *Het Onstaan van het moderne Nederland*, ed. Wantje Fritschy and Joop Toebes (Nijmegen: SUN [1996]), 103–9; W. van den Berg, "Literary Sociability in the Netherlands, 1750–1840," in *The Dutch Republic in the Eighteenth Century*, ed. Margaret Jacob and Wijnand Mijnhardt (Ithaca, N.Y.: Cornell University Press, 1992), 256 and passim; Dierickx, *Vrijmetselarij*, 57–59, 118–22.

26. De Vet, "Verlichtung," 111–12; Wijnand Mijnhardt, "The Dutch Enlightenment: Humanism, Nationalism and Decline," in *Dutch Republic*, 220–22; Wijnand Mijnhardt and A. J. Wichers, eds., *Om het Algemeen Volksgeluk* (Edam: Maatschappij tot Nut van 't Algemeen, 1984), 7–65, 359–60.

27. Ger Harmsen, "De Arbeiders en hun Vakorganisaties," in *De Nederlandse samenleving sinds 1815*, ed. F. L. van Holthoon (Assen: Van Gorcum, 1985), 262–65; Jos Leenders, *Benauwde Verdraagzaamheid, Hachelijk Fatsoen: Families, standen en kerken te Hoorn in het midden van de negentiende eeuw* (The Hague: Stichting Hollandse Historische Reeks, 1991), 203–6.

28. F. L. van Holthoon, "De Armenzorg in Nederland," in *Nederlandse samenleving*, 176–78; Blom, "Nederland," 430.

29. Dahl, *Political Oppositions*, 425; Blom, "Nederland," 431–32; Kossmann, *Low Countries*, 290.

30. Kossmann, *Low Countries*, 289–91, 294–96; Blom, "Nederland," 431–32.

31. Kossmann, *Low Countries*, 277–80; Theo van Thijn, "The Party Structure of Holland and the Outer Provinces in the Nineteenth Century," in *Vaderlands Verleden in Veelvoud*, 2 vols., ed. C. B. Wels (Den Haag: Martinus Nijhoff, 1980), 2:109–13; Leenders, *Benauwde Verdraagzaamheid*, 22–28.

32. Righart, *Katholieke Zuil*, 197–99; van Thijn, "Party Structure," 110–17; Blom, "Nederland," 432–33.

33. Theo van Tijn, "Op de Drempel van de Nieuwe Tijd," in *Vaderlands Verleden*, 2:150–51, 153; Blom, "Nederland," 435.

34. Kossmann, *Low Countries*, 302–5; van Tijn, "Op de Drempel," 151.

35. J. C. Boogman et al., *Geschiedenis van het Moderne Nederland* (Houten: De Haan, 1988), 239–40; Blom, "Nederland," 434–35; Kossmann, *Low Countries*, 308.

36. Boogman, *Moderne Nederland*, 240–41; D. Th. Kuiper, "Christen-Democratie," in *Driestromenland*, ed. A. P. M. Lucardie, M. Brinkman, and D. Th. Kuiper (Leiden: Stichting Burgerschapskunde, 1993), 148–49, 151–52.

37. Kossmann, *Low Countries*, 354; Dahl, *Political Oppositions*, 425.

38. Righart, *Katholieke Zuil*, 197–202; J. W. van Deth and J. C. P. M. Vis, *Regeren in Nederland* (Assen: Van Gorcum, 1995), 38–39.

39. Righart, *Katholieke Zuil*, 202–9.

40. Righart, *Katholieke Zuil*, 212–14; Harmsen, "Arbeiders," 265; Ger Harmsen and Bob Reinalda, *Voor de Bevrijding van de Arbeid* (Nijmegen: Socialistieke Uitgeverij, 1975), 430. On the origins and development of the socialist youth organizations, see Ger Harmsen, *Blauwe en Rode Jeugd* (Assen: Van Gorcum, 1961).

41. Righart, *Katholieke Zuil*, 222–36; Harmsen and Reinalda, *Voor de Bevrijding*, 430–31.

42. Paul Lucardie, "Liberalisme," in *Driestromenland*, 38–43, 45.

43. Righart, *Katholieke Zuil*, 143–46; Lamberts, "België," 356–58; Kossmann, *Low Countries*, 361–63.

44. Kossmann, *Low Countries*, 363–68; Righart, *Katholieke Zuil*, pp. 154–56.

45. Delsinne, *Le Parti Ouvrier*, 106–9, 119 and passim; Lamberts, "België," 361–62, 368–69; J. J. De Jong, *Politieke Organisatie in West Europa na 1800* (Den Haag: Martinus Nijhoff, 1951), 195–99.

46. Righart, *Katholieke Zuil*, 161–69; Lamberts, "België," 369, 371–72.

47. Lamberts, "België," 371–72; De Jong, *Politieke Organisatie*, 199.

48. Gilissen, *Régime représentatif*, 120–21; L. Wils, "De politieke outwikkeling in België 1847–1870," *Algemene Geschiedenis* 12: 298.

49. Kossmann, *Low Countries*, 327–28, 341–43; Wils, "Politieke ontwikkeling," 298–302; Lamberts, "België," 266–67; Lorwin, "Belgium," 156.

50. Lamberts, "België," 270–71; Kossmann, *Low Countries*, 372–74; Gilissen, *Régime représentatif,* 121–26. Under the plural voting system, heads of household aged thirty-five and older meeting certain qualifications were granted a second vote, and owners of property valued at a certain amount enjoyed yet another vote. Furthermore, holders of higher educational degrees were entitled to two extra votes regardless of their wealth and family status, but the total number of votes any one person could accumulate was limited to three. Out of a total electorate of 1,370,687 following the passage of the constitutional amendment, 850,000 possessed one vote, 290,000 two, and 220,000 three. For these and many others details of the various electoral systems employed in Belgium since 1790, see Gilissen, *Régime représentatif,* 124–25.

51. Lamberts, "België," 271; Gilissen*, Régime représentatif,* 126–32; Lorwin, "Belgium," 157.

52. A constitutional amendment calling for women's suffrage was defeated in 1921 by a vote of ninety to seventy-four, with the Catholic Right voting in favor and the liberals and socialists voting against. As a form of compensation, all women were granted the right to vote in local elections, and the widows and mothers of fallen soldiers were enfranchised at the national level as well. In addition, a further constitutional stipulation stated that female suffrage could pass into law without further formalities as soon as two-thirds of the legislature was willing to support it. All efforts to find such a majority failed, however, until 1948. Gilissen, *Régime représentatif,* 133–41.

53. Kossmann, *Low Countries*, 326–28, 350–52.

54. Kossmann, *Low Countries*, 355–61.

55. Kossmann, *Low Countries*, 555–56.

III

THE MEANING OF THE
NINETEENTH CENTURY TODAY

9

BETWEEN THE STATE AND NETWORKS OF "COUSINS": THE ROLE OF CIVIL SOCIETY AND NONCIVIL ASSOCIATIONS IN THE DEMOCRATIZATION OF POLAND

Jan Kubik

Discussions on the relationship between civil society and democracy are often marred by conceptual imprecision.[1] The social arrangements found huddling under the umbrella of "civil society" are so diverse that the danger of conceptual stretching becomes very real. For example, there are many forms of self-organization (outside of the state) that either facilitate or impede liberalization or democratization. Although they often are referred to as "civil society," they rarely posses the full range of attributes usually associated with this concept's conventional, Western understanding.[2] In this chapter I will examine how various forms of such "imperfect civil society" influenced the fall of state socialism and the subsequent democratization efforts in Central Europe, particularly Poland. Before 1989, the domain of associations in Central Europe differed considerably from the ideal, "Western" model of civil society that began to be realized in such countries as Poland only after 1989. Nonetheless, those pre-1989 associations (constituting imperfect civil society) played a significant role in the liberalization of the old regime, paradoxically often due to their "imperfections."

DEFINITIONS

I believe there are three basic types of definitions of civil society, one normative and two analytical.

Civil society as a normative idea. The concept of "civil society" is frequently used in reference to a historically evolved and/or normatively (un)desired vision of the "proper" form of associationism in a modern Western society.[3] It is used in (philosophical) debates on the *ideal* self-organization of society *outside* of the state's control. The concept has tremendous emotional and intellectual appeal to the people living under authoritarian and (post)totalitarian regimes, which programmatically attempt to destroy or limit the sphere of independent associations.[4] In the writings utilizing this version of the concept, emphasis is placed on how people think about a desired social arrangement, not on how public life is actually organized.

Civil society as a public space, institutionally protected from the state's arbitrary encroachment, within which individuals can freely form their associations. This understanding of civil society is perhaps most eloquently developed by Jürgen Habermas, who defines a public sphere as "a sphere which mediates between society and state, in which the public organizes itself as the bearer of public opinion."[5] Geoff Eley writes about "the structured setting where cultural and ideological contest or negotiation among a variety of publics takes place."[6]

Civil society as a set of social groups, whose members deliberate or act collectively to accomplish common goals.[7] Additionally, groups belonging to this set share several characteristics, usually including the following:

- civil society's groups are secondary, not primary (e.g., family)
- they are open and inclusive
- they are tolerant and moderate in their claims and methods;
- their activities are transparent (not hidden from public scrutiny; they are publicly accountable)
- they are willing to protect the independent public space and tend to be antiradical, reformist, moderate
- their members are able to dissociate themselves from influences exerted by their primary (e.g., familial) associations (Gellner's modular man)

Utilizing the basic insights of these three approaches I will propose a more precise definition of an ideal type of civil society.

First, I will include in my ideal model only *secondary* groups composed of individuals who join *voluntarily* on the basis of a (written or not) *social contract.* By making this distinction I want to preserve an opposition of "ascriptive" and "attained" group membership.[8]

Second, I will further narrow my definition by considering only those secondary groups that are transparent. Informal discussions in "smoke-filled backrooms" have been long recognized as a very important mode of programmatic deliberations, policy formation, personnel selection, and decision making in all political systems. It seems that most, if not all, secondary associations routinely engage in such actions. The critical question is whether such informal gatherings serve as the most important source of policy formation, recommendation, and implementation or rather that they represent merely a fraction of the group's actions, which—as far as they influence the wider public—take place in the "public square," are transparent and may be subjected to public scrutiny by other groups (the press), individuals, or some authorized public or governmental agency. I propose the following definition:

There exists a subset of groups belonging to *secondary society* (operating within the public domain) whose (a) internal activities, as a matter of routine, are available for some form of external "inspection" in order to determine its compliance with existing laws and regulations; (b) policy recommendations, which may influence people outside of the group, are accessible to "outsiders" for discussion and scrutiny; and (c) proposed policy changes that will influence others are publicly announced so they can be (dis)approved through a process of wider public deliberation. This is *transparent secondary society*, "inhabiting" the official public space.

In the third analytical move I will isolate a subset of groups belonging to the transparent secondary society that are characterized by (1) a horizontal rather than vertical interpersonal network; (2) a democratic, deliberative rather than authoritarian "authority" structure; and (3) the tolerance for other similar groups and readiness to collaborate or compete with them according to a specified *set of rules* and on the basis of mutual respect.

This operation weeds out both hidden and transparent autocratic clientelistic networks as well as Führer-type cults.[9] I will call the resulting subset *transparent civil society* (TLS). I suspect most analysts proposing a positive correlation between civil society and democracy have this meaning of civil society in mind.

The final distinction needed to produce an effective taxonomy of groups aspiring to the name "civil society" deals with the *legal status* of the relationship between civil society and the state (government, rulers, etc.). There are three variants of this relationship: (a) illegality, a situation whereby the government defines the state in such a way that it has no room for any independent organizations or groups—the totalitarian solution; (b) selective legality, whereby the government selectively legalizes certain groups—the authoritarian solution; and (c) full legality, whereby the government creates and protects a social space within which any group fulfilling required legal criteria may operate—the democratic-liberal solution characterized by the rule of law. The full-fledged, "classic" civil society emerges only when transparent civil society and the legally protected social space coexist. I will call this arrangement *legal transparent civil society* (LTCS).[10]

It must be also noted at the outset that the institutional arrangement most conducive to democratic development seems to be a combination of civil society's autonomy and its connectedness to other domains of the polity, such as the economic system, the state, and the political society.[11] For many authors, civil society is inconceivable unless it is anchored in a market economy based on private (or at least nonstate) property.[12] This formulation is too restrictive: civil society is seriously impaired when its organizations do not have some economic base independent from the state, but this base does not need to be the (private) enterprises of a market economy. Other nonstate agents may provide civil associations with the necessary funds and material base. Various churches and informal networks of "friends" often provide such support, as was the case in Eastern Europe. In some cases, civil society organizations may even access state resources, thus becoming "parasites" of sorts. The dependence of civil society on external sources of material support poses a larger question of its independence and will be dealt with later in this chapter.[13]

It is also useful to distinguish civil society from political society, defined thereby as an intermediate realm within which the double process of translation and mediation takes place. It is composed of political parties and other explicitly political organizations, such as lobbying groups, that provide channels through which various societal interests and claims are aggregated and translated into generalized policy recommendations.[14]

IMPERFECT CIVIL SOCIETIES UNDER STATE SOCIALISM

In contrast to most works on civil society under state socialism I will not focus my analysis on the history of the concept of civil society, which served as a normative ideal of many (if not all) oppositional activities. Instead—proceeding *modo sociologico*—I will identify various types (or forms) of imperfect civil society and analyze their role in the politics of authoritarian breakdown and democratic consolidation in Poland.

Pseudo-Civil Society: Official Associations

One of the understudied legacies of state socialism is the dense network of organizations and movements that were created during the consolidation of communist regimes in order to colonize public space and extend the party-state's penetration into all segments of society. These state-run organizations simulated the functions of organizations existing in democratic societies and performed vital political, ideological, and social tasks within the institutional design of the party-state. Especially in the earlier period of communist rule, they were nothing more than communist fronts with mandatory membership. As a result, the organizational density of state socialist regimes was higher than in democratic countries. More people belonged to various formal organizations and movements (trade unions, youth and professional associations, etc.) than under any other type of political regime. Moreover, these organizations and movements provided their members with an entire range of benefits and services—the same as would be supplied by the marketplace, family, or local civic organizations under most other regimes.[15]

The dependent status of these organizations, initially created as de facto state agencies and instruments of control, changed over time. Beginning in the late 1950s, some of them were able to wrestle a degree of autonomy from the party-state bureaucracy, accumulate considerable resources, secure ever expanding benefits for their members, and even occasionally defy party-state policies. During political crises some of these organizations (at least in certain countries) achieved considerable autonomy. The collapse of state socialist regimes in 1989 left them free and entirely responsible to fend for themselves. Some were significantly compromised by years of political servility and ideological rigidity while others enjoyed limited credibility due to their long-standing tradition of promoting specific groups' interests. Thus, there were those groups that disappeared almost instantaneously (e.g., the Society for the Polish–Soviet Friendship) and other groups that swiftly adapted to the new situation. In fact, those that did adapt had distinct advantages over the newly emerging organizations and movements. They controlled sometimes sizable resources accumulated over the years; had legally defined functions; monopolized certain services; and had cadres of bureaucrats, organizers, and activists.[16]

Networks Anchored in Informal Economic Activities

One of the fundamental tasks of the communist project was the elimination of civil society. This task was conceptually developed in classic communist writings and vigorously pursued during the early stages of the project's implementation. The abolition of civil society as public space, however, proved to be easier than the suppression of people's proclivity to organize their life through secondary associations, independent of the state.

In East Central Europe around 1956, the dream of the total reconstruction of society according to the tenets of Marxism-Leninism died. The system entered its post-totalitarian phase with most Leninist institutions intact but possessing diminished ideological zeal. The economy was still centrally coordinated, politics was completely monopolized by the communist party, and culture was carefully guarded by preventive censorship. And yet here and there independent groups and organizations emerged.

As political economists demonstrated, state socialism's own institutional design made its economic system inefficient in the long run, hostile to innovation, and tremendously wasteful.[17] In order to meet its own plan targets, the official system needed informal institutional crutches in the form of supplementary and complementary economic mechanisms that would make up for its increasingly crippling deficiencies. Such mechanisms emerged gradually, as many state employees who had to fulfil official plans but wanted also to improve their standard of living developed alternative nonofficial strategies of economic behavior. These strategies, which eventually formed complex systems of shadow and second economies, not only allowed people to cope with chronic shortages, but also made the sluggish socialist economy survive as long as it did.[18] As Ogrodzinski observed, the "unofficial" economy was both parasitic and symbiotic in relation to the official one.[19]

While engaging in these nonofficial strategies of economic behavior, people created a complex network of mutual relationships, which came to be known as "the unplanned" or "second" society.[20] This unplanned society had many sectors, some of which were structured as patron–client hierarchies, with communist party officials frequently serving as "informal" patrons. But there existed also another pattern, more egalitarian and "democratic" *srodowisko* (milieu), in which horizontal reciprocal exchanges were dominant.[21] Within their milieus people exchanged goods, services, and information. Some of these activities were public though unofficial; some became semi-official because they influenced official policy-making processes, but were never carried out within the official public domain.[22] Most milieus were structured as egalitarian, leaderless networks with clear though flexible boundaries, but some of them, particularly those which intersected with the world of politics, could be hierarchical.

There is a fair amount of controversy surrounding two critical questions: To what degree did these unofficial economic activities constitute political opposition to the official system, and to what degree did they contribute to the development of the civil society? They definitely emerged through spontaneous organizing, outside of the state's direct supervision, and formed a *non-state* self-organized system of networks and organizations. For some authors they did therefore form a sector of the "distorted" civil society:[23] "civil" for they were spontaneously created by individuals, yet "distorted" for they often were unofficially public and did not enjoy full constitutional protections.

In Hungary, the sector of the informal economy became so extensive that it led to qualitative changes in social stratification and pushed the Hungarian rural population on a path toward "socialist embourgeoisement."[24] What was slowly emerging was a Bürgerliche Gesellschaft, but initially it was rather a "bourgeois society" than a "civil society."[25] Gradually, however, the Hungarian state began recognizing and authorizing various secondary associations, particularly within the economic domain. After 1982, they operated openly within the official public space, constituting therefore a sector of the legal civil society.

Anna Seleny argues that Hungarian "goulash communism," where people were relatively free to engage in independent economic activities while abstaining from open participation in politics, produced a specific political climate of pragmatism and gradual reformism.[26] The Polish unofficial economic sphere never achieved a degree of institutionalization and official authorization comparable to Hungary's, but it did allow people to take care of themselves and their families outside of the state-controlled redistributive system.

The informal economic networks that people formed through independent activities were sometimes hierarchical and always unofficial. They often led to intense rivalry and engendered a divisive cultural pattern of "amoral familism," which was not conducive to the creation of procivic social capital.[27] Since they were clandestine, informal economic networks did not constitute a transparent civil society (as defined in this chapter). Yet, despite all these shortcomings, by the very fact of their existence, informal milieus defied the rules of the post-totalitarian system (whose ambition was to control most if not all human interactions) and thus should be construed as one of the forms of *imperfect civil society.*[28]

Clandestine and Open Anti-Communist Resistance and Independent Circles (Milieus) of "Talkative Opposition"

Since the beginning of communist rule (1944 in Poland), various segments of Polish society resisted the Soviet-type system. Little is known about how the networks of resistance were created and how they operated. Occasionally, they developed into clandestine organizations, which managed to survive longer periods of time. Ekiert lists six domains in which resistance networks and organizations emerged: (1) peasant resistance against collectivization; (2) religious groups and churches opposing official secularization; (3) dissident intellectuals; (4) youth subcultures; (5) everyday resistance of workers on the shop-floor; and (6) the unofficial economy (analyzed in the previous section).[29]

The most dramatic form of resistance against communism was armed struggle, which continued, with diminishing fervor, until 1956.[30] Due to their clandestine character and hierarchical (military-like) structures, however, the resistance organizations do not fulfil my criteria for civil society. But they constituted a very important source of independent networks, which continued either directly (through the surviving members and their families) or indirectly (through mythologies of martyrdom and resistance).

The tradition of armed resistance began to function as an ideology/mythology of many informal networks, milieus, and organizations, which taken together form a phenomenon of "talkative opposition," without which "there could not have been a movement of practical social activity."[31] Discussions in these informal clandestine networks served as unofficial public fora where many ideas, later implemented by "open" dissident organizations, were forged. They also served to establish a network of connections that later facilitated organizing efforts of dissident groups. None of these social groupings can be properly categorized as civil society, for they existed only in the unofficial public domain and the private domain (family, kinship networks). However, they prepared many people for open oppositional activities, erupting on the official public scene in 1976.

"Opposition" or "Dissidence": The Anti-Communist Illegal Transparent Civil Society

In Poland, the post-Stalinist "thaw" of 1956 produced not only the relatively well-known periodicals and organizations of intellectuals, but also the first truly independent trade union.[32] For a brief moment in 1956–57, several independent organizations formed a legal transparent civil society, but they were soon delegalized and dissolved by the communist authorities. Clandestine dissident activities continued for years, but they lacked two defining features of civil society: transparency and legally guaranteed access to the official public space. Instead, they constituted the "talkative opposition."[33] Their situation changed dramatically in 1976.

On September 23, 1976, the people involved in helping the workers persecuted for participating in the June strikes formed the Workers' Defense Committee, known under its Polish acronym KOR. This was the first oppositional group in communist Poland that went public, established working contacts with the workers, and developed an extensive network of collaborators and sympathizers throughout the country. The circle of people who cooperated with KOR in such activities as distributing KOR publications, collecting money, and gathering and transmitting information grew steadily, reaching several thousand by the end of the 1970s.[34] The formation of KOR proved to be a social catalyst: "By the time of Solidarity's formation in 1980, more than twenty different oppositional committees and associations had come into existence in Poland."[35]

Solidarity was born during the massive strikes that erupted all around Poland in the summer of 1980 as the culmination of a complex process of social mobilization initiated in the mid-1970s. It was the first massive, self-governing "social entity" ever to emerge in any communist state. I conceptualize this entity as a cultural-political class in statu nascendi, which was formed in confrontation with the entrenched political-economic cultural class and was made up not of workers or intellectuals but of all those who subscribed to a system of principles and values, usually referred to as counter-hegemonic, unofficial, independent, or alternative. They were people who visualized the social structure as strongly polarized between "us" ("society," "people," etc.) and "them" (authorities," "communists," etc.).[36]

Solidarity was a complex entity: it was and it was not "civil society."[37] Its political power resulted primarily from the effective mobilization of a large number of employees/dependents of the communist state, united by their allegiance to a specific cultural framework (a set of "a-political" symbols and discourses). Solidarity strove, then, to mobilize people against communist authorities on the basis of a definite vision of "moral order," whereas—as Gellner forcefully argues—"civil society is an a-moral order": it is based on respect for such formal principles as mutual tolerance as well as diversity.[38] Solidarity lacked, therefore, what are, for several authors, defining features of civil society:

economically engendered social diversification, individualism, and the lack of an overarching moral/ideological vision.[39] At the same time, however, Solidarity was organizationally diversified: Some of its units had considerable autonomy, and its registration paved the way for many related, independent organizations.

When Solidarity was delegalized in December 1981, hundreds of thousands of its members went "underground" and initiated thousands of independent oppositional groups and organizations. The network of underground organizations was enormous; it comprised trade union cells, educational institutions, university seminars, publishing houses, political think tanks, daily newspapers, magazines of opinion, news services, radio stations, discussion clubs, theater companies, video-production units, and charity organizations. Physical space for all these activities was provided in private apartments and by the Roman Catholic Church. This underground society was kept together by the myth of Solidarity, but the inevitable process of organizational diversification set in. The basic ideological division was between "those who in their public behavior followed moral or solidaristic anti-politics, and those who were driven by liberal or legally technocratic antipolitics."[40] For the final confrontation with the communist authorities in 1989, Solidarity emerged symbolically united (for the last time), but with increasingly visible political cracks.

From the foundation of KOR in 1976 to the final Solidarity victory in 1989, Polish organized anticommunist opposition underwent many changes. It was a complex, constantly evolving, social entity. It is therefore not easy to itemize its main features and determine to what degree it met the standards of civil society, as defined in this chapter. It should be pointed out, however, that like the rest of the pre-1989 civil society in Eastern Europe, the oppositional civil society was also "distorted" or "imperfect." There were several sources of its imperfection.

Throughout most of the pre-1989 period, most of these groups were illegal, and therefore, harassed and persecuted. In 1976, some of them decided to go public. This was an event of enormous historical significance, but the combination of transparency and illegality put tremendous pressures on the members of the transparent groups. In order to survive and continue their activities, these people needed an extensive system of support. The only institutions that provided such support were the Roman Catholic Church and the networks of family, kinship, and friendship. This inevitably led to the loss of "purity": in order to act effectively within the official public domain but without legal guarantees, one had to rely on extensive contacts within the unofficial public domain and private domain, but sometimes even with "the world of real socialism." In fact, oppositional official public activities would be inconceivable without nontransparent support networks. Oppositional civil society had to become a part of a larger "second society,"[41] which, particularly in the domain of economy, relied often on "uncivil" strategies and structures.

Oppositionists operated in several sectors of the imperfect civil society. The great revolutionary innovation occurred in 1976, when many of them decided to go public and thus constitute a new sector: *illegal transparent civil society.* The emergence of this sector could not however lead to the Weberian routinization of dissident associations. Dissident networks did not become examples of singlestranded, business-like Gesellschaft; they continued to operate as a specific Gemeinschaft.[42] An important consequence of dissidents' complex existence, which demanded from them that they were both public figures and conspirators, made practicing such civil virtues as inclusiveness and egalitarianism almost impossible. In fact a closer look at oppositional groups reveals their elitism and status hierarchy. Wojciech Arkuszewski described his experiences in the following way:

> The entrance into the opposition *srodowisko* (milieu) was not easy and was little dictated by political beliefs alone: one had to have the right contacts to be accepted by the right people. . . . When I first met people of the Opposition, I was shocked at the hierarchical quality of its relationships. Its structure and activities resembled those of a closed religious sect.[43]

This exclusive, nonegalitarian character of dissident organizations resulted primarily from the necessity to keep at least part of their activities secret. But it may have been also related to another important feature of oppositional civil society: it constituted a surrogate political society. Under the conditions of state socialism, such organizations by the very fact of their existence were political— they reshaped the power calculus within the polity, which was supposed to be ruled exclusively "from the top." The politics of oppositionists, in their own self-conceptualizations, were often "apolitical" or "ethical"; they were nonetheless engaged in "politics" and consequently their networks tended to be hierarchical (to increase efficiency) and exclusive (to increase security).

The coexistence of these various "societies" and the nondemocratic, prerogative state calls for a brief comment on a distinction between democratization and liberalization. Systematic analysis of state socialism suggests that another distinction is equally important: between de facto liberalization or humanization and de jure liberalization.[44] The former refers to situations in which previously oppressive authorities relax their control and become more tolerant of oppositional activities, without, however, authorizing or selectively legalizing such activities. The fact that KOR members in Poland were not permanently imprisoned indicates humanization only; KOR was never legalized. By contrast, the legalization of Solidarity in 1981 marks an important threshold: a massive independent organization was authorized, but a legally protected space, formally open for all independent organizations meeting the procedural criteria (a feature of democratization), was not created. Such a space emerged in Poland only after the fall of state socialism, when the de facto liberalization was combined with a thorough democratization. The de facto liberalization means tolerance for the illegal transparent civil society; the de jure liberalization makes the selectively legalized civil society possible. But it seems that only after the collapse of the old system, when liberalization is amplified by thorough democratization, can the full-fledged *legal transparent civil society* emerge.

Selectively Authorized NGOs of the 1980s: A Forgotten Sector of Civil Society

After the delegalization of Solidarity in 1981, independent social activity moved underground. Illegal civil society, which formed almost overnight, was diversified but also strongly unified by a common symbolic umbrella in the myth of Solidarity. It continued its existence in the unofficial public domain until April 1989, when Solidarity was officially reregistered.

During the 1980s, however, the "humanization" of the regime (de facto liberalization) progressed as it began to tolerate increasing numbers of independent initiatives. Some organizations and Solidarity agencies, following the KOR pattern, went public and entered the official public domain, although they were defined as illegal by the state. Moreover, in the second half of the 1980s, communist authorities began authorizing selected independent civil initiatives: the process of de jure liberalization commenced. For example, in 1983, various local branches of the Polish Ecological Club (PEC) were officially registered. It was an important event, for the PEC was founded as an independent organization in 1980 under the protective umbrella of Solidarity. After 1983, the local branch of the PEC in the town I study not only was allowed to produce very critical reports on the dismal state of the local environment but also became a training facility of independently minded activists. Many of them supported underground Solidarity, were active in the local Citizens' Committee, and became leading politicians after the first independent elections for local self-government in 1990.

The progressing liberalization of the regime, occurring several years before it collapsed, is clearly reflected in the data collected by Klon (figure 9.1). The peak of "organizational frenzy" came in 1991, but the trend was detectable from 1983, two years after Solidarity was crushed by Wojciech Jaruzelski's martial law.

Semi-Civil Society: Organizations Sponsored by the Catholic Church and Other Religious Institutions

Paralleling Latin American experiences,[45] semi-independent spaces for grassroots organizing were created under the protection of the Roman Catholic Church almost since the imposition of state socialism in Poland. The relationship between the Catholic Church and the state socialist regime and the role of religion in anticommunist opposition have been analyzed many times.[46] Here I

Figure 9.1   Number of organizations by founding year (Source: Urszula Krasnodebska, Joanna Pucek, Grzegorz Kowalczyk and Jan Jakub Wygnanski. 1996. Podstawowe statystyki dotyczace dzialan organizacji pozarzadowych w Polsce. Warsaw: Program PHARE-Dialog Spoleczny.)

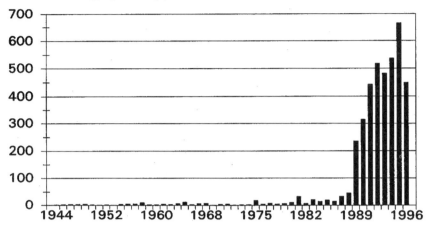

will just enumerate the most important elements of the Catholic semi-independent sphere: (1) clubs of Catholic intelligentsia; (2) "Znak," the Cracow publishing institute, which issued a monthly journal and constituted an independent milieu; (3) "Wiez," the Warsaw publishing institute, which also constituted an independent milieu; (4) *Tygodnik Powszechny,* the Cracow weekly and independent milieu; (5) pilgrimages, which often included discussion groups and seminars; (6) weeks of Christian culture (started in 1974), often including educational sessions and lectures on topics ranging from the social doctrine of the Church to the ethics of politics, (7) "Sacrosong," festivals of religious songs initiated in 1968, and (8) the Oasis Movement,[47] which was responsible for motivating and organizing thousands of young Catholics.

During the 1981–89 period, Church-sponsored independent activities intensified. Countless lectures, discussions, seminars, art exhibits, theater performances, movie screenings, and massive charity actions were organized around the country. In many cases the participants in this "Catholic" civil society were also active in other illegal societies of the oppositional underground. It is also striking that during the period of martial law, beginning in 1982–84, there was a veritable explosion of Catholic publications.

Imperfect Civil Society under State Socialism: A Summary

State socialism was not uniformly totalitarian throughout its existence. Particularly, during its post-Stalinist phase, incomplete civil society emerged and assumed several organizational forms. Its development was especially dynamic in Poland for a number of historical reasons, analyzed elsewhere.[48] Polish incomplete civil society was diversified, composed of several sectors of varying degree of autonomy vis-à-vis the state. Networks, organizations, and associations, existing in the restricted and arbitrarily controlled public space provided by the party-state, can be classified as pseudo-autonomous, semi-autonomous, and illegally autonomous. Accordingly, three basic sectors of "socialist" civil society can be identified. Each of these sectors played a different political and social role, ranging from economic support for oppositional activists, offered by (semi)clandestine trade networks of the shadow economy, to direct political action carried out by dissident organizations.

The speed and quality of civil society's institutionalization during democratic consolidation depended on legacies left by the preceding nondemocratic system. In Poland, various imperfect civil societies developed long before the collapse of the nondemocratic regime. This development seems to be the main factor explaining the quick consolidation and vibrancy of legal transparent civil society after 1989. In turn, the existence of well-developed civil society contributes to the relative strength of democracy in Poland. In contrast, in places where civil society has been weak, for example, in Croatia or Romania, democratic consolidation is slow and feeble.

CITIZENS COMMITTEES: CIVIL SOCIETY DURING THE TRANSFER OF POWER

The 1989 transfer of power in Poland was not a straightforward intra-elite deal nor was it a clear-cut case of "pacted transitions." Lech Walesa, representing the partially transparent, massive social movement, arrived in Warsaw in August 1988 to begin negotiations with the representatives of the communist government.[49] The Solidarity strikes continued until the negotiations ended in April 1989 and immediately afterwards became a permanent fixture in Polish public life.

This wave of mobilization continued as Solidarity began hasty preparations for the first semi-free elections of the postcommunist period. In order to overcome the state's tremendous advantage in resources and media access, Solidarity facilitated the creation of Citizens' Committees (CCs). Earlier, on December 18, 1988, Walesa officially convened the Citizens' Committee of the Chairman of Solidarity. It was an elite group of intellectuals and activists conceived mostly as an advisory board to the chairman but also as a shadow cabinet of sorts.[50] On April 8, after deciding to form a united electoral front, Solidarity leaders called for the formation of regional and local Citizens' Committees. Thousands of such committees were formed, and during the next two months, they organized Solidarity's electoral campaign with the help of primitive homemade propaganda materials. The elections of June 4 saw the stunning success of the just re-legalized movement and the unanticipated, thorough defeat of the communist bloc: Solidarity candidates won all of the mandates they were allowed to contest, except for one.

After this victory, Walesa authorized a very controversial move: the dissolution of the CCs at the provincial level. "The CCs at the local level were allowed to continue, but without the Solidarity logo and union financing."[51] This not only severed the links between the CCs and Solidarity but also led to the tremendous diversification of local civil patterns of activization, which by now constituted the full-fledged legal transparent civil society. The "golden age" of this massive set of local CCs came between September 1989 and May 1990, when they prepared the free election to local self-governments. "They became the main force behind the wide-ranging changes at the local level: from the revival of associational life to the assault on local communist networks to the promotion of the local administrative reform."[52] And once again the CCs achieved spectacular electoral success. Their candidates came in first among all the organized forces.

No other postcommunist country had anything resembling Citizen Committees. They mobilized local communities throughout the whole country and produced, almost overnight, viable local counterelites that effectively challenged the ex-communist incumbents. They also provided organizational structure for those who were ready to go to work for their municipalities but would not be associated with the organizations left behind by the outgoing regime. Moreover, they even began elaborating their own social-political philosophy, based on the rejection of political partisanship and a vision of "the third way" between the suffocating uniformity of state socialism and "empty" procedural diversity of Western democracy. What eventually destroyed the CC movement was a tension between this apolitical, civic, and organic philosophy and the growing politization of the local public arenas as well as the furious assault by political parties, who wanted to co-opt CCs as their base and component.

THE ROLE OF CIVIL SOCIETY DURING THE CONSOLIDATION OF DEMOCRACY

Although the communist constitutions guaranteed the freedom of association and expression, in practice permissions to form independent organizations were granted sparsely and arbitrarily. The situation changed dramatically in 1989. In Poland, for example, the Law on Associations was adopted in April 1989 and the Law on Foundations was amended in 1991 to eliminate existing barriers. What followed was a virtual explosion of associational activity. It is therefore puzzling that some authors complain about postcommunist apathy or the decline of civil society.[53]

Obviously, the postcommunist civil society differed considerably from its imperfect predecessor that existed either illegally or due to arbitrary decisions of the authorities. After 1989, civil society as a social space, protected by constitutional guarantees, was reinstitutionalized. Citizens became free to organize themselves according to their wishes, as long as they followed existing procedures and laws. As a result, thousands of new organizations and movements sprang up locally and nationally. The civil society space was immediately filled with three types of organizations: (1) reformed organizations inherited from the communist period, (2) spin-off organizations, specifically, those that broke away from their communist-era parent organizations, and (3) newly formed organizations.

The somewhat unexpected organizational continuity was most noticeable in the sector of professional associations. For example, in 1985, fourteen organizations represented the Polish artistic community with a combined membership of 16.9 thousand. In 1992, the same fourteen organizations remained unscathed with an increased membership of 19.3 thousand. Similarly, the Statistical Office listed 105 nationwide scientific and professional associations that survived the regime transition intact. Although overall membership in these associations declined by some 50 percent (approximately one million members in 1987 and 404 thousand in 1993), the membership losses were confined to a few organizations that had artificially inflated their membership numbers in the past.[54] Only those organizations that represented different professional groups of engineers had significant membership losses (on average 50 percent), due in part to the dramatic transformation of the Polish state industry. At the same time, a large number of new professional associations appeared, such as these organized under the auspices of the Church. Their memberships were usually small, however, and they lacked the resources of the older, established associations.

Counting the number of new organizations and analyzing their activities is not an easy task. In Poland, however, the Klon/Jawor research team, operating since 1991, produced some reliable estimates. According to their studies, by the end of 1994 there were 29,580 registered associations and 12,216 regional affiliates of these organizations. Moreover, by the end of 1996 there were about five thousand foundations registered in the district court in Warsaw and nine hundred local foundations (see figure 9.1).[55] Altogether, civil society in Poland was comprised of about 48,000 organizations, while before 1989 there were only several hundred large, centralized organizations.[56]

The Klon/Jawor database provides comprehensive information on 4,515 organizations in 1993. A year later, they listed 7,000 associations and 4,500 foundations and estimated that two million Poles were active in these organizations. They had some 53,000 full-time employees, and 64 percent of their budget came from private and foreign sources while only 26 percent came from the state budget. Their activities concentrated mainly in large urban centers (68 percent).[57] New organizations were rapidly emerging in all sectors of civil society, especially where existing organizations were unsuccessful in adapting to the new conditions or where new spaces and issue-arenas opened after the collapse of the party-state.

The development of the trade union sector after 1989 exemplifies both the continuity and innovativeness of Polish postcommunist civil society. The new postcommunist labor sector emerged as a result of several mergers of old and new organizations. In April 1989, as a result of the "Round Table Agreements," Solidarity was relegalized in its trade-union formula. The postcommunist All-Poland Alliance of Trade Unions (OPZZ) and Solidarity became two major competitors within a highly pluralistic, competitive, but politically divided trade-union sector. Solidarity had 1.7 million members, while the OPZZ boasted a membership of around four million. The OPZZ lost some two million members since 1989, and several unions left the organization, including the powerful Federation of Miner Unions with some 350,000 members. It became a key element of the ex-communist coalition and its activists ran for the parliament on the SLD ticket (Union of Democratic Left).

Solidarity never regained its 1980 strength and position. Not only was its membership a fraction of what it had been in 1980–81, its salaried staff was also largely new. Solidarity was organized in thirty-eight regions and sixteen national industry secretariats and nearly one hundred industry branch secretariats. There were a number of smaller and usually more radical federations such as Solidarity '80 with approximately half a million members. The smaller, newly funded unions were critical of both Solidarity and the OPZZ for their cooperation with the government and became more prominent in organizing protest actions in Polish industry.

In short, the trade-union movement was (1) highly fragmented and decentralized, by comparison with other East European states; (2) competitive and politically divided on both national and local levels; and (3) organizationally mixed, with interlocking regional and industrial structures.

This brief overview illustrates the impressive recovery of Polish civil society after 1989. Yet, across all sectors of the newly reconstituted civil space there emerged significant organizational continuity with the past as well as serious fragmentation, political divisions, and intense struggle for resources and members. Some observers noted also excessive personalization and exclusiveness of several influential organizations, particularly those that have extensive contacts with Western sponsors.[58] The most striking feature of this new civil society was, however, its lack of systematic linkages with the party system (political society). As the Klon/Jawor data base demonstrates (see figure 9.1), NGO relationships with political parties were much worse than their relationships with any other institutional sector.

In short, from 1989 to 1993, the development of the legal transparent civil society in Poland was well underway. This new LTCS was composed of myriads of spontaneously created associations and many reconstituted organizations that had been formed under state socialism. In many sectors (for example, labor unions) several old and new organizations competed with each other for resources, members, and access to policymakers, and therefore the whole domain was highly contentious and fragmented. At the same time the party system (political society) did not effectively fulfill its function of interest aggregation, representation, and articulation;[59] there existed a lack of strong linkages between the people and political parties.[60] As a result, many of civil society's organizations and actors played an increasingly visible and vocal role in the country's politics, often confronting through protest actions both the parliament and the government. Such a prominence of contentious collective action in the activities of civil society organizations combined with weak linkages to political actors and the low responsiveness of political institutions could have serious destabilizing consequences for a newly established democratic regime. In the Weimar Republic, a combination of a vibrant, contentious civil society with the "weak and poorly designed political institutions"[61] destabilized democracy, an ominous sign for Polish postcommunist politics. Is, however, such a combination of robust civic society and anemic political society always threatening to democracy? Or, perhaps, do other factors also need to be considered?

Clearly, the German predicament demonstrates that a dense and vigorous civil society by itself does not guarantee the robustness of democracy. Thus it seems that when it comes to civil society's impact on democratic consolidation or survival, its "nature" is more important than its "density." The nature of civil society depends on the predominant normative orientation (ideology) of its constituent organizations, its sectoral composition, the intensity of intrasectoral fragmentation and competition, and the viability of its links with the party system and the state. In particular, if civil society is dominated by free riders and enemies who subscribe to antidemocratic ideologies and use protest to challenge the legitimacy of the political system (as was increasingly the case in Weimar Germany), the entire independent public sphere and democracy are in jeopardy. If, by contrast, civil society's organizations use protest as a means of bringing forward demands for reforms and do not aim to challenge the legitimacy of the government, that is, their methods are predominantly nondisruptive and their goals moderate, civil society thrives and contributes to the strengthening of democracy, particularly when political society is weak. My research with Ekiert indicates that such is the case with post–1989 Poland: Polish postcommunist civil society was often contentious, but this contentiousness was accepted by the majority of the populace; channeled through well-known strategies; coordinated by established organizations; and usually framed through nonaggressive, moderate rhetoric and symbolism. In brief, Polish postcommunist contentiousness was well-institutionalized, indicating that Poles were mostly dissatisfied with the existing "conventional" channels of interest articulation (such as parties and the parliament), but not with democracy itself.[62] As a result, vigorous—but also pro-democratic in its orientation—civil society was contributing to democracy's consolidation.

CONCLUSION

Historically, *legal transparent civil society* (LTCS) is a rarity.[63] There exist, however, other types of social arrangements that resemble it in one respect or another; they do not possess all of its characteristics and yet effectively limit the state's power and allow citizens to work out their problems without the state's participation. Such forms of *imperfect (incomplete) civil society* can function as allies, precursors, or even enemies of LTCS, depending on the historical circumstances. In this chapter I identified and described several forms of imperfect civil society, and analyzed the conditions under which LTCS may emerge out of them, as well as clarified and assessed the way these forms facilitate or hamper liberalization and democratization.

In authoritarian and post-totalitarian systems where there is no rule of law, a set or system of social networks develops. Some of them constitute the transparent but illegal or selectively legalized civil society, made possible within the confines of the arbitrary autonomy allowed either deliberately or inadvertently by the rulers. Totalitarian regimes allow very little, if any, autonomy; authoritarian and post-totalitarian systems are more open and often tolerate some independent associations, whose existence is, however, unprotected by the law and subject to the arbitrary interference by the authorities. This situation can be called *uninstitutionalized autonomy*: selectively authorized civil society, as a set of groups, exists but there is no full legal protection of a universally accessible official public domain. Moreover, some organizations may be arbitrarily protected by the authorities, while others are ruthlessly persecuted.

Under state socialism the principle of uninstitutionalized autonomy (de facto liberalization) allowed the existence of three types of organizations, possessing various degrees of autonomy: (1) pseudo-autonomous (for example official trade unions); (2) semi-autonomous (e.g., the Roman Catholic Church in Poland); and (3) "illegally" autonomous (e.g., dissident groups, black-market networks). In authoritarian or post-totalitarian systems where the elite political actors reserve for themselves an almost complete monopoly of "doing politics," any independent action of the "illegally" autonomous civil society becomes inadvertently political. On the other hand, mobilizing for action within dissident groups is unthinkable without the support of familial, kinship, and friendship networks. For these two reasons, the borders among political society, civil society, and domestic society are very porous. In fact, civil society cannot exist without a base in domestic society: Gellnerian "cousins" are not civil society's greatest enemies (as in liberal-democratic systems), but rather its necessary benefactors.

In polities based on the rule of law, the situation is different. First, the system of laws makes possible the establishment and protection of an autonomous official public domain. Thus the vitality of civil society groups depends (1) on the comprehensiveness and durability of this autonomy, (2) on their degree of separation from traditional communities (primary groups), and (3) on their ability to depend on "civil economy."[64] It is a situation that is the opposite of authoritarian systems, where civil society's strength depends on its interpenetration of traditional communities and "uncivil economies." Second, in lawful polities, the sectoral diversification of civil society is functional. All associations are formally equal, in the sense that they enjoy (more or less) equal expectations of institutional survival, as long as their actions remain within an existing legal framework. Such an institutionally guaranteed freedom of association produces a multitude of organized collective actors and civil society sectors, each characterized by a different institutional structure, functions, and political influence. The configuration, relative strength, and institutionalization pattern of these sectors differ from country to country, producing various types of civil society.

In societies initially controlled by authoritarian regimes, civil society often develops through a sequence of three stages. In a post-totalitarian regime it emerges first as *illegal transparent civil society* out of nontransparent activities (the KOR's foundation in 1976). One of the conditions of its emergence and survival is the humanization (de facto liberalization) of the regime; another is a set (or system) of links with nontransparent networks, which are the major provider of resources for actors undertaking open civil actions. For both processes—the formation of the first islands of transparent civil society and the humanization of an authoritarian (or post-totalitarian) regime—external pressure and assistance are very important, if not decisive. It is hard to imagine the KOR's successes in 1976–80 without the multiple ties its members established with their Western allies. The KOR's survival rested on the external pressure created by the Helsinki process, initiated in 1975. In its essence, this process was based on a simple deal: Western economic assistance in exchange for a more lenient treatment of dissident groups and the increased openness of the country's borders.

The second phase is selective *de jure legalization of some organizations* by the rulers. Polish examples include Solidarity in 1980 or ecological clubs in the 1980s. Here again, Western recognition and assistance proved to be critical. Also, Solidarity's years in the underground (1981–88) would not have been possible without massive aid programs, equipment transfers, steadfast moral support, and political pressure. This phase ends with the collapse of the "ancient" regime. I would list three major factors that contributed to this collapse in 1989. Two were internal: (a) the ruling elite's realization that their economic policies were a failure and the growing sense of the necessity for a more radical change and (b) the unyielding pressure of the initially clandestine and then increasingly transparent civil society (Solidarity and other organizations). The external factor was Mikhail Gorbachev's abandonment of the Brezhnev doctrine and his repeated signals to the Polish elites (particularly in 1988) that they were on their own in any dealings with domestic problems.

During the first two phases, people's activities within various imperfect civil societies effect both liberalization and democratization. They *directly* facilitate liberalization of the nondemocratic regime, by challenging the state's monopoly on power, creating islands of independent activism, and forcing the authorities to selectively authorize some forms of societal self-organizing. They also *indirectly* influence the upcoming democratization by training future "democrats," preparing activists for viable counterelites, and forging links to and accessing democratic "know-how" from Western democracies.

Finally, during the third stage, a legal space is created, and the fully fledged, *legal transparent civil society*, may develop. The depth and quality of this civil society is shaped, however, by the legacies of the imperfect civil society that existed earlier. The ten years of East European democratic consolidations are clear testimony that the scope and depth of self-organizing as well as the strength of pro-civic and pro-democratic ideologies developed by dissidents under state socialism are positively correlated with the quality of postcommunist democracy. Poland, Hungary, and the Czech Republic had the most extensive imperfect civil societies under communism; it was also only in these three countries that dissidents most consistently "dreamed" their future in terms of civil society, not nationalism. After 1989 these same three countries managed to build the most solid liberal democracies in the postcommunist world.

Yet, the negative legacies of the earlier times are also discernible. Some organizations of the postcommunist civil society are plagued by excessive secrecy and frequently semitransparent practices; others tend to be exclusive and cliquish. Self-reliance is sometimes lacking, as if some activists had been pampered by the earlier generosity of their Western sponsors. The three-stage model I am proposing here is a generalization of the Polish developments, but it approximates Hungarian, Czech, and Russian experiences as well.[65]

In different political systems the center of political gravity can be found in civil society, political society, or the state. In authoritarian and statist regimes the state is the most important arena of politics, and state actors have an almost exclusive capacity to structure political outcomes. Autonomy, political resources, and freedom of action in the other two realms are seriously restricted if not abolished altogether. The state often attempts to substitute a network of corporatist arrangements for autonomous activities of civil and political society. In corporatist institutions, however, the variety of interests and claims that are allowed to be articulated and represented is narrow. In some types of nondemocratic regimes political and civil societies are almost completely destroyed or incapacitated. This is the case with communist and neopatrimonial regimes.[66] In contrast to neopatrimonial regimes, the destroyed organizations under communist regimes are replaced by a wide range of state-dependent, highly centralized, and fully controlled mass organizations, which penetrate the entire sociopolitical order. Gradually, however, society's ability to self-organize is restored, and various imperfect civil societies emerge. This process is, however, unthinkable without gradual humanization and liberalization of the Soviet-bloc regimes. When organizations whose goal is to challenge or limit the state's power monopoly go public an *illegal transparent civil society* emerges. It becomes the locus of independent political power and thus constitutes also a nucleus of autonomous political society outside of the ruling party-state apparatus.

In contemporary liberal democracies, political society with its party system, legislative assemblies, and elections plays the dominant political role. It selectively structures and channels claims advanced by the actors in civil society as well as controls the expansion of bureaucratic politics and the coercive capacity of the state.

(Imperfect) civil society organizations become the locus of (alternative) political power in two basic types of circumstances: (1) in authoritarian and post-totalitarian regimes, when they functions as a *surrogate political society*, and (2) during the periods of dramatic sociopolitical change, revolutions, civil wars, or foreign invasions, when the national-level political institutions collapse. One type of dramatic sociopolitical change is the democratization of authoritarian or post-totalitarian regimes. The first phase of this process, the deconstruction of the old regime, entails the weakening of the state's coercive capacity through the mobilization of various organizations and movements within, necessarily imperfect, civil society. The strengthening of civil society and the simultaneous weakening of the state and the (old) party system, facilitate democratization.

However, when this high "civil" mobilization, accompanied by the weakening of the state and political parties, continues during the transfer of power and consolidation of democracy, an anarchic transitory polity may result. For example, the disintegration of the state and political society leads to the (over)politization of civil society, producing aggressive mobilization and seeming to delay the consolidation of the institutions of representative democracy.[67] The disintegration of the former Soviet Union and Yugoslavia provide some examples of the possible consequences of what happens when the bulk of political power shifts to the realm of the amorphous and poorly institutionalized (proto)civil and/or noncivil society.[68]

It seems, therefore, that constructing a viable and stable democratic polity entails the *simultaneous* rebuilding of civil and political societies as well as increasing the state's administrative efficiency and its capacity to enforce the rule of law.[69] Thus, the successful crafting of democracy requires not only the elites' capacity to negotiate intra-elite pacts but also the ability of social groups to build the three public realms (the state, political society, civil society), make predictable and stable links among them, and reduce the level of mutual antagonism between collective actors in these realms.

NOTES

1. I greatly benefited from the other papers and discussions at the Princeton conference Civil Society before Democracy. My gratitude goes primarily to Nancy Bermeo and Philip Nord, the conference organizers. Much of the material covered in this chapter is a result of my collaboration with Grzegorz Ekiert; our collaboration produced the best formulations, and remaining weaknesses are mine alone. I am also grateful to Richard Rose for his comments. Tomek Grabowski shared his very insightful criticisms, which allowed me to clarify several points. Finally, the most important credit: without Martha Kubik's many substantive and editorial inputs, this paper could not be written.

2. Chris Hann and Elizabeth Dunn, *Civil Society: Challenging Western Models* (London: Routledge, 1996).

3. See, for example, Adam Seligman, *The Idea of Civil Society* (New York: Free Press, 1992); and Dominique Colas, *Civil Society and Fanaticism: Conjoined Histories,* trans. Amy Jacobs (Stanford: Stanford University Press, 1997).

4. David A. Kideckel, "Us versus Them: Concepts of East and West in the East European Transition," in *Cultural Dilemmas of Post-Communist Societies,* ed. Aldona Jawlowska and Marian Kempny (Warsaw: IFiS Publishers, 1994), 137–43; John Hall, "In Search of Civil Society," in *Civil Society: Theory, History, Comparison,* ed. John A. Hall (Cambridge: Polity, 1995), 1–31.

5. Geoff Eley, "Nations, Publics, and Political Cultures: Placing Habermas in the Nineteenth Century," in *Habermas and the Public Sphere,* ed. Craig Calhoun (Cambridge, Mass.: MIT Press, 1992), 290.

6. Eley, "Nations, Publics," 306. Nancy Frazer brings out an important issue of the multiplicity of public spaces in the context of her discussion on women's exclusion from many of them. Her analysis helps in developing a more nuanced understanding of both public spaces and civil society, which, on many occasions, should be reconceptualized as the multiplicity of civil societies. See Nancy Frazer, "Rethinking the Public Sphere: A Contribution to the Critique of Actually Existing Democracy," in *Habermas and the Public Sphere,* 109–42. It is important to remember that in most conceptualizations both "civil society" and "public space" denote public accountability and the rule of law.

7. For a similar distinction between "space" and "mode of organizing secondary groups" see Marcia Weigle and Jim Butterfield, "Civil Society in Reforming Communist Regimes: The Logic of Emergence," *Comparative Politics* (October 1992): 1–23.

8. Tester and Schmitter define civil society in a similar, "narrower" manner. The former talks about "formal, voluntary associations." See Keith Tester, *Civil Society* (London: Routledge, 1992), 8. The latter about groups that "agree to act within pre-established rules of 'civil' or legal nature." By contrast Cohen and Arato, Keane and Habermas offer much more general definitions, comprising several different "societies. Keane writes about "an aggregation of institutions whose members are engaged primarily in a complex of non-state activities—economic and cultural production, household life and voluntary associations." See John Keane, ed., *Democracy and Civil Society* (London: Verso, 1988), 14. Habermas includes in his definition all "voluntary unions outside of the realm of the state and the economy." See Jürgen Habermas, "Further Reflections on the Public Sphere," in *Habermas and the Public Sphere,* 454. Cohen and Arato include in civil society "above all the intimate sphere (especially the family)." See Jean L. Cohen and Andrew Arato, *Civil Society and Political Theory* (Cambridge, Mass.: MIT Press, 1992), ix.

Such general definitions make a distinction between transparent and democratic civil society and the hidden, hierarchical networks of "amoral familism" impossible. See Elzbieta Tarkowska and Jacek Tarkowski, "Social Disintegration in Poland: Civil Society or Amoral Familism," *Telos* 89 (Fall 1991): 103–9. On a related point, concerning various types of "social trust," see Margaret Levi's critique of Putnam in "Social and Unsocial Capital: A Review Essay of Robert Putnam's *Making Democracy Work*," *Politics and Society* 24, no. 1: 45–55; and Martin Krygier's comments in "Virtuous Circles: Antipodean Reflections on Power, Institutions, and Civil Society," *East European Politics and Societies* (Winter 1997): 67–72.

9. Putnam observes that the basic difference in Italy has not been between the atomized, asocial south and the civic, organizationally rich north. "The relevant distinction is not between the presence and absence of social bonds, but rather between horizontal bonds of mutual solidarity and vertical bonds of dependency and exploitation," Robert D. Putnam, *Making Democracy Work: Civic Traditions in Modern Italy* (Princeton: Princeton University Press, 1993), 144.

10. As Colas argues, "The demand for a 'law-governed state' on the one hand and a 'civil society' on the other are one and the same demand. In its very essence civil society is a society composed of individuals endowed with civil rights." See Colas, *Civil Society and Fanaticism*, 348.

11. I follow here a tradition of distinguishing between civil society and political society. Stepan, for example, argues that "it is conceptually and politically useful to distinguish three important arenas of the polity: civil society, political society, and the state. Obviously, in any given polity these three arenas expand and shrink at different rates, interpenetrate or even dominate each other, and constantly change." Alfred Stepan, *Rethinking Military Politics* (Princeton: Princeton University Press, 1988), 3. For similar conceptualizations see Ernest Gellner, *Conditions of Liberty: Civil Society and Its Rivals* (New York: Allen Lane/Penguin, 1994); Paul G. Lewis, "Introduction," *Democracy and Civil Society in Eastern Europe*, ed. P. G. Lewis (New York: St. Martin's Press, 1992), 3–4; Douglas A. Chalmers, Scott B. Martin, and Kerianne Piester, "Associative Networks: New Structures of Representation for the Popular Sector," in *The New Politics of Inequality in Latin America: Rethinking Participation and Representation*, ed. D. A. Chalmers et al. (Oxford: Oxford University Press, 1997), 569; Philip D. Oxhorn, *Organizing Civil Society: The Popular Sectors and the Struggle for Democracy in Chile* (University Park: Pennsylvania State University Press, 1995), 27–34; Martin Myant and Michael Waller, "Parties and Trade Unions in Eastern Europe: The Shifting Distribution of Political and Economic Power," in *Parties, Trade Unions and Society in East-Central Europe*, ed. M. Waller and M. Myant (Portland: Frank Cass, 1994), 161. Dryzek notes that civil society associations "do not pursue power as interest groups or through electorally oriented parties; yet, they are, of course, concerned with public affairs." See John S. Dryzek, "Political Inclusion and the Dynamics of Democratization," *American Political Science Review* 90, no. 3 (1996): 481.

12. See Gellner, *Conditions of Liberty*, 87; Zbigniew Rau, "Introduction," in *The Reemergence of Civil Society in Eastern Europe and the Soviet Union*, ed. Z. Rau (Boulder: Westview, 1991), 4–5; Miroslawa Grabowska, "Civil Society after 1989—Rebirth or Decease," in *After Communism: A Multidisciplinary Approach to Radical Social Change*, ed. Edmund Wnuk-Lipinski (Warsaw: ISP PAN, 1995), 192; Edmund Wnuk-Lipinski, *Demokratyczna Rekonstrukcja* (Warsaw: Wydawnictwo Naukowe PWN,

1996), 100; Krygier, "Virtuous Circles," 86; Murray Yanowitch, *Controversies in Soviet Social Thought: Democratization, Social Justice, and the Erosion of Official Ideology* (Armonk, N.Y.: Sharpe, 1991), 62–66.

13. It should be also noted that several authors object to reducing civil society to economic relations alone. See Wnuk-Lipinski's criticism of Charvet in *Demokratyczna Rekonstrukcja*, 173 and 177.

14. For an elaboration of these concepts, see Grzegorz Ekiert and Jan Kubik, *Rebellious Civil Society: Popular Protest and Democratic Consolidation in Poland, 1989–1993* (Ann Arbor: University of Michigan Press, 1999).

15. "Although these bodies unquestionably aided the regime's efforts at social control and indoctrination, they also often became the basis of useful social networks. Sports clubs, community centers, summer camps, youth groups, pensioners' clubs and the like filled a certain void, albeit one that the communist system itself had created by suppressing all autonomous versions of such institutions." Alexander Smolar, "From Opposition to Atomization," *Journal of Democracy* 7, no. 1 (1995): 34.

16. On this point see also Smolar, "From Opposition," 35.

17. Particularly Janos Kornai, *The Socialist System: The Political Economy of Communism* (Princeton: Princeton University Press, 1992); and Ed A. Hewett, *Reforming the Soviet Economy: Equality versus Efficiency* (Washington, D.C.: Brookings, 1988).

18. "The shadow economy evolves from the enterprise directors' search for ways to meet their plan; it is the consequence of an effort to achieve the most important targets set in the formal system. . . . In the second economy the motivation is to make money. Enterprises are simply making goods on the side, outside the planning system, which they sell for profit." *Reforming the Soviet Economy*, 179.

19. See also Elemer Hankiss, *East European Alternatives* (Oxford: Clarendon Press, 1990), and Hewett, *Reforming*.

20. Janine Wedel, ed., *The Unplanned Society: Poland during and after Communism* (New York: Columbia University Press, 1992); and Hankiss, *East European Alternatives*.

21. Hankiss introduces here a distinction between the "informal, latent, and non-legitimate sphere . . . characterized by client-patron relationships, oligarchic and nepotism mechanisms, corruption, informal bargaining between state agencies" and the "second society . . . characterized by the slow re-emergence of social networks, the incipient regeneration of local communities, interest mediation through informal channels." Hankiss, *East European Alternatives*, 107.

22. The Chilean *vecino* organizations (based on the neighborhood) function socially and politically as an equivalent of East European milieus. See Oxhorn, *Organizing Civil Society*, 113ff.

23. Piotr Ogrodzinski, *Piec tekstow o spoleczenstwie obywatelskim* (Warsaw: ISP PAN, 1991); Piotr Ogrodzinski, "Civil Society and the Market under Real Socialism," in *From the Polish Underground: Selections from "Krytyka," 1978–1993*, ed. Michael Bernhard and Henryk Szlajfer (University Park: Penn State University Press, 1995); and Piotr Ogrodzinski, "For Models of Civil Society and the Transformation in East-Central Europe," in *After Communism*.

24. Ivan Szelenyi, *Socialist Entrepreneurs: Embourgeoisement in Rural Hungary* (Madison: University of Wisconsin Press, 1988); and Chris Hann, "Civil Society at the Grass-Roots: A Reactionary View," in *Democracy and Civil Society in Eastern Europe*, ed. Paul G. Lewis (New York: St. Martin's, 1992).

25. Hankiss contrasts "citoyennization" to "embourgeoisement." See Hankiss, *East European Alternatives*, 134–35.

26. Anna Seleny, "Old Political Rationalities and New Democracies: Compromise and Confrontation in Hungary and Poland," *Pew Papers on Central Eastern European Reform and Regionalism*, no. 9 (Center for International Studies, Princeton University, 1996), 37.

27. "Internal ties frequently degenerate because of the rivalry of consumers caused by economic shortages. Microstructures tend to compete with other microstructures, thus creating aggression, social pathology and all the features of an 'unfriendly society,'" Elzbieta Tarkowska and Jacek Tarkowski, "Social Disintegration in Poland: Civil Society or Amoral Familism," *Telos* 89 (Fall): 104. See also Levi, "Social and Unsocial Capital."

28. "Political authoritarianisms, even totalitarianisms, which tolerate an autonomous economy, thereby unwittingly also create a Civil Society, or at least the social potential for the emergence of Civil Society." Gellner, *Conditions of Liberty*, 146.

29. Grzegorz Ekiert, "Rebellious Poles: Cycles of Protest and Popular Mobilization under State-Socialism, 1945–1989," *Working Paper* Series, no. 5, Advanced Study Center, International Institute (Ann Arbor: University of Michigan, 1996).

30. Zdzislaw Szpakowski, "Zbrojne podziemie antykomunistyczne," in *Polacy wobec przemocy, 1944–1956*, ed. Barbara Otwinowska and Jan Zaryna (Warsaw: Editions Spotkania, 1996).

31. Wojciech Arkuszewski, "The Elitist Opposition," in *The Unplanned Society*, 237.

32. Robert Zuzowski, *Political Dissent and Opposition in Poland: The Workers' Defense Committee "KOR"* (Westport: Praeger, 1992), 28.

33. For the details of the pre-1976 oppositional activities in Poland, see Michael Bernhard, *The Origins of Democratization in Poland* (New York: Columbia University Press, 1993); Zuzowski, *Political Dissent*; Roman Laba, *The Roots of Solidarity: A Political Sociology of Poland's Working-Class Democratization* (Princeton: Princeton University Press, 1991).

34. For details, see Jan Jozef Lipski, *KOR: A History of the Workers' Defense Committee in Poland, 1976–1981* (Berkeley: University of California Press, 1985), 124; and Bernhard, *The Origins of Democratization*, 124–30.

35. Bernhard, *The Origins of Democratization*, 76.

36. See Jan Kubik, *The Power of Symbols against the Symbols of Power: The Rise of Solidarity and the Fall of State Socialism in Poland* (University Park: Pennsylvania State University Press, 1994).

37. Krygier's analysis in "Virtuous Circles," 73–77, is basically identical with mine.

38. Gellner, *Conditions of Liberty*, 137.

39. Gellner, *Conditions of Liberty*; Rau "Introduction"; Ogrodzinski, *Piec tekstow*; Krygier, "Virtuous Circle." See Jerzy Szacki, *Liberalizm po komunizmie* (Warsaw: Znak, 1994), 104–6 and 138–45, on "collective individualism." Staniszkis and Kubik write about the "symbolic unity" and its political functions. See Jadwiga Staniszkis, *Ontologia socjalizmu* (Warsaw: In Plus, 1989), 116; and Kubik, *The Power of Symbols*.

40. Marcin Krol, *Liberalizm strachu czy liberalizm odwagi* (Krakow: Znak, 1996), 80.

41. Hankiss, *East European Alternatives*; Gordon H. Skilling, *Samizdat and an Independent Society in Central and Eastern Europe* (Columbus: Ohio State University Press, 1989), 160–62.

42. "Bürgerliche Gemeinschaft" as Jasiewicz called it (private conversation). On the complex intertwining of private and public domains ("second" and "civil" societies) in

oppositional activities, see Wedel, ed., *The Unplanned Society*; Skilling, *Samizdat*, 160–66; Hankiss, *East European Alternatives*.

43. Arkuszewski, "The Elitist Opposition," 235–36.

44. Hankiss in *East European Alternatives*, 56, contrasts liberalization (my de facto liberalization) with democratization (de jure liberalization): "The essence of the latter is the creation of an institutional system, based on real power, that guarantees the rights stipulated in the constitution of the community. Liberalization, on the other hand, works without rights. . . . This is the political acrobatics of giving people more or less leeway without releasing the leash."

45. Susan Eckstein, ed., *Power and Popular Protest: Latin American Social Movements* (Berkeley: University of California Press, 1989); Oxhorn, *Organizing Civil Society*; Daniel H. Levine, "Popular Groups, Popular Culture, and Popular Religion," in *Constructing Culture and Power in Latin America*, ed. Daniel H. Levine (Ann Arbor: University of Michigan Press, 1993).

46. Maryjane Osa, "Resistance, Persistence, and Change: The Transformations of the Catholic Church in Poland," *East European Politics and Societies* 3, no. 2 (1989): 268–99; Kubik, *The Power of Symbols*; Barbara Lewenstein and Malgorzata Melchior, "Escape to the Community," in *The Unplanned Society*.

47. Initiated in 1954. See Janusz Mucha, "Religious Revival Movement in Changing Poland: From Opposition to the Participation in the Systemic Transformation," *The Polish Sociological Bulletin* 2 (1993): 139–48.

48. See Ekiert and Kubik, *The Rebellious Civil Society*. For a detailed analysis of the imperfect Russian civil societies, see Steven M. Fish, *Democracy from Scratch: Opposition and Regime in the New Russian Revolution* (Princeton: Princeton University Press, 1995), esp. 52–79.

49. It is estimated that the August 1988 strikes engulfed thirty major enterprises and involved one hundred, fifty thousand people. See Jerzy Holzer and Krzysztof Leski, *Solidarnosc w podziemiu* (Lodz: Wydawnictwo Lodzkie, 1990), 155. For an excellent analysis of the 1988 strikes, see Tomasz Tabako, *Strajk 88* (Warsaw: NOWA, 1992).

50. Tadeusz Borkowski, "Komitety Obywatelskie. Proba Generalizacji," in *Komitety Obywatelskie: Powstanie, Rozwoj, Upadek*, ed. T. Borkowski and Andrzej Bukowski (Krakow: Universitas, 1993), 196.

51. Tomek Grabowski, "The Party That Never Was: The Rise and Fall of the Solidarity Citizens' Committees in Poland," *East European Politics and Societies* 10, no. 2 (1996): 225.

52. Grabowski, "The Party," 227.

53. Michael Bernhard, "Civil Society after the First Transition: Dilemmas of Post-Communist Democratization in Poland and Beyond," *Communist and Post-Communist Studies* 29, no. 3 (1996): 309–30.

54. A comparison of the 1987 and 1993 GUS data on professional organizations shows that the Federation of Regional Clubs Technology and Technical Improvement lost 118,000 members, Polish Economics Association lost 37,000 members, Association of Management and Organization lost 21,000, and Polish Association of Nurses with 60,000 members in 1987 disappeared from the list.

55. *Non Governmental Sector in Poland: Basic Information and Reports Gathered by Information Center for NGOs Bordo* (Warsaw: Civic Dialogue Programme Phare, Cooperation Fund, 1998), 54.

56. The Main Statistical Office reports for 1997 the existence of 32,716 organizations. See *Non Governmental Sector in Poland*, 54.

57. *Jawor 1993: Civic Dialogue NGOs* (Warsaw, 1993). According to another source, by the end of 1992, there were more than two thousand nationwide voluntary associations registered in the Warsaw District Court, a majority of which existed before 1989. See *Polska '93* (Warsaw: Polska Agencja Informacyjna, 1992), 148. This number did not include associations whose activities were limited to the regional or local level and were registered by provincial courts. See Grazyna Prawelska-Skrzypek, "Citizen Activism in the Life of Local Communities: Polish Experiences during the Period of Transformations," ms.

58. See Janine Wedel, *Collision and Collusion: The Strange Case of Western Aid to Eastern Europe 1989–1998* (New York: St. Martin's, 1998); and Kevin F. F. Quigley, *For Democracy's Sake: Foundations and Democracy Assistance in Central Europe* (Washington, D.C.: Woodrow Wilson Center Press, 1997).

59. For definitions of these three terms, see Fish, *Democracy from Scratch*, 54.

60. Wlodzimierz Wesolowski, "Formowanie sie partii politycznych w postcomunistycznej Polsce," *Studia Polityczne*, 4 (1995): 7–28.

61. Sheri Berman, "Civil Society and the Collapse of the Weimar Republic," *World Politics* 49 (April 1997): 424.

62. See Ekiert and Kubik, *Rebellious Civil Society*.

63. See Gellner, *Conditions of Liberty*.

64. On the concept of "civil economy," see Richard Rose *Toward a Civil Economy? Centre for the Study of Public Policy* (Glasgow: University of Strathclyde, 1992); and Krygier, "Virtuous Circles," 86–87.

65. For Russia see Fish, *Democracy from Scratch*, and Yanowitch, *Controversies in Soviet Social Thought*, 57–87.

66. For the distinction between authoritarian, totalitarian, and neopatrimonial regimes, see Juan J. Linz and Alfred Stepan, *Problems of Democratic Transition and Consolidation* (Baltimore: Johns Hopkins University Press, 1996). The concept of incapacitation is developed by Jan Gross, *Revolution from Abroad* (Princeton: Princeton University Press, 1991), 232–40.

67. On this point, see Nancy Bermeo, "Myths of Moderation: Confrontation and Conflict during Democratic Transitions," *Comparative Politics* (April 1997): 305–22; and Samuel J. Valenzuela, "Labor Movements in Transitions to Democracy: A Framework for Analysis," *Comparative Politics* (July 1989): 450.

68. In regard to Gorbachev's Soviet Union, this phenomenon is analyzed by Fish, *Democracy from Scratch*, 73–75; and Marc R. Beissinger and Lubomyr Hajda, "Nationalism and Reform in Soviet Politics," in *The Nationalities Factor in Soviet Politics and Society*, ed. L. Hajda and M. Beissinger (Boulder: Westview, 1990), 316.

69. On this point, see Larry Diamond, "Civil Society and the Development of Democracy," Estudios/Working Papers 1997/101 (Madrid: Instituto Juan March, 1997); "In Search of Civil Society," 23; and Joel Migdal, "The State in Society: An Approach to Struggles for Domination," in *State Power and Social Forces in the Third World*, ed. J. S. Migdal, Atul Kholi, and Vivienne Shue (Cambridge: Cambridge University Press, 1994), 28.

10

THE HISTORICAL ORIGINS OF THE EAST–WEST DIVIDE: CIVIL SOCIETY, POLITICAL SOCIETY, AND DEMOCRACY IN EUROPE

Valerie Bunce

> History may not repeat itself, but it certainly rhymes.
>
> —Mark Twain

There has never been a time such as this when the idea of a single Europe—and a single and singular European experience—has rung more true. With the collapse of state socialism in the eastern half of the continent, a European Union in the process of both deepening and widening, and a NATO expanding eastward (while intervening southward), the distinct possibility exists that the Europe of the future will be united, not just by geography, but also by markets, democracy, and collective security.

Does this mean the triumph of the European idea? And do these developments constitute, as a result, the final chapter in the long European story? There are reasons to be doubtful. Perhaps the most persuasive one is the analogy that can be drawn between recent developments in Europe and developments during the interwar period.[1] At that time, the end of a European war, like the end of the Cold War, produced in its wake a virtually continent-wide embrace of liberal politics and capitalist economics. Moreover, then as now, the eastern half of the continent featured a number of new states that had emerged from the wreckage of empires. However, within a decade of these experiments, the seeming unity of Europe and the consensus around liberalism had given way to increasingly protected economies spanning the entire continent (of which the Soviet Union under Joseph Stalin represented the extreme case of import substitution); the rise of competitive, if not hostile, alliances; growing conflicts along ethnic, class, and spatial lines, particularly within the new states of the east; the rise of extreme leftist and rightist parties that rejected the liberal consensus; the breakdown of democracy in both southern and Eastern Europe; and the rise of fascist regimes in central and southern, as well as Eastern, Europe. What then followed was World War II—testimony, among other things, to the pervasiveness, power, and dangers of a Europe divided along economic and ideological lines.

After the war, these differences took on clear-cut institutional forms, with Europe split along north–south and east–west axes with respect to political, economic, and security regimes. While this was in some sense both politics and business "as usual" in Europe, the postwar era was marked by one innovation: the "long peace."[2] However, even that resonated with Europe's past, given a similarly long episode of peace in the nineteenth century,[3] and given the tendency of western Europeans to presume that their history was Europe's history. For example, neither the Czechs nor the Slovaks, eyeing 1968, nor the Hungarians, eyeing 1956, would find it easy to concur with the argument that postwar Europe was distinguished by the absence of military aggression of one European state against another.

Whether the long peace was a reality or just imagined by international relations theorists in order to extol the benefits of bipolarity and nuclear weapons, however, does not detract from the more general point: the presence today in Europe of some of the very factors that contributed to the diversification, if not the disintegration, of Europe during the interwar period. As then, the continent today is divided between rich and poor capitalist states; well-established, stable democracies and democracies that are new, incomplete, and uncertain; and old and well-established states and states just formed. There is, in short, a European core and a European periphery, with the states in the north and west occupying the core and states in the east and south functioning as the periphery. Envy and inequality—whether defined in political, economic, social, or cultural terms—seem to describe contemporary Europe, then, far better than the more familiar terminology of European integration.

The purpose of this chapter is to look more closely at the core–periphery distinction within Europe by comparing the long-term historical evolution of Europe along its east–west axis—or what was termed during the Cold War era "Western Europe" versus Eastern Europe and the Soviet Union.[4] Our particular concern will be with how long-term differences in the development of the state, economy, and society shaped civil and political society in eastern versus western Europe, and how these differences have affected in turn the establishment and the sustainability of democracy.

The analysis will focus on four time frames: the differences between eastern and western developmental trajectories from Roman times to World War I; the contrasts between interwar eastern and western Europe; the impact of the divide after World War II between capitalist liberal democracy in the west and state socialism in the east; and, finally, the consequences of the collapse of state socialism for the development of democracy in Eastern Europe. This brief historical survey leads to three conclusions.

First, the east–west divide long predates the postwar era and speaks to differences in not just the timing, pace, and sequencing of political, social, economic, and cultural developments, but also in their very content. This was particularly important with respect to civil and political society and democracy. To give a brief example: in the west, political society (or unions, parties, and interest groups) grew out of civil society, and both were foundational for democratic development. By contrast, in the east, political society arose later and largely in reaction to oppressive states and western ideas (including the nation). This meant in turn that political society predated civil society; democracy, when eventually tried, had little societal grounding; and the democratic project, for these and other reasons, was fatally flawed.

Second, just as the west played a crucial role in shaping developments of the east, as has been repeatedly observed, so, less commonly remarked, was the east influential in the development of the west. Indeed, most of the institutions we associate with the rise of the west—for instance, the invention and, later, the export of the nation, the state, capitalism, civil society, and democracy—were made possible in part by what happened in the east. Put simply, the east, by virtue of its geopolitical location, allowed the west to do what the east was never allowed to do; that is, evolve. Later, the east provided the west with opportunities for experimentation and expansion—two projects central to western state-building and economic growth.

Finally, the differences between these two regions of Europe have been remarkably durable and still influence Europe today—in part because of the ways the state socialist experience exaggerated certain themes in Eastern Europe's past and in part because of the turbulence created by postcommunist transformations. However, the socialist experience itself and the collapse of the system have nonetheless provided to Eastern Europe some of the crucial building blocks for the formation of vigorous civil and political society and the sustainability of democracy. This has been particularly the case for the northern tier of Eastern Europe, or Poland; Hungary; the Czech Republic; the Baltic states; and, to dip a bit southward, Slovenia.[5]

CAVEATS AND DEFINITIONS

Before we work through the differences in eastern versus western European historical experiences, we need to pause for a moment over the premise underlying this chapter that it makes sense to divide Europe into an eastern and a western half. It is fully recognized that this distinction, like most distinctions that are drawn for purposes of analysis, is, to some extent, arbitrary. "Europe," like the "nation" and other core concepts tapping identity and power relations, is constructed—not just by historians and cartographers, but also by politicians, armies, intellectuals, and administrators following their own particular agendas.[6] To draw on some recent examples from the politics of the "east": while Mikhail Gorbachev spoke of a common European home and clearly included the Soviet Union within that imagined and quite self-serving community, so the very different interests of many political leaders in the Baltic states, Poland, Hungary, the Czech Republic, and the like during the postcommunist period have led them to argue that their countries are returning to Europe (rather than joining it) and have tended to concur, despite the competition over which country is more European than the other and more deserving of getting to Europe first, that Russia falls outside the boundaries of Europe.[7] As one Lithuanian member of parliament so baldly put it: "Was ist Europa? Europa ist nicht Russland."[8]

Moreover, there is nothing fixed about the particular European divide that serves as the focus of this chapter. One can, for example, make a good case for dividing Europe into three and even four regions, concentrating on a core, a semi-periphery, and a periphery or targeting intersecting north–south and east–west axes that produce four European quadrants.[9] To this we can add two more complications. One is that the countries abutting these various dividing lines evidence, not surprisingly, mixed historical profiles. Germany, Austria, Poland, and the Czech and Moravian lands are obvious cases in point. The other is that there are always differences within clusters. For instance, the Scandinavian historical experience deviates in important ways from, say, the British or French stories of the rise of capitalism and democracy.[10]

However, there are nonetheless two very good reasons to select the east–west divide as the basis for analysis. Most obviously, this is a divide that shaped the European political economy of the entire postwar period. It shaped as well the structure and the stability of the postwar international order, and that, by most accounts, lives on in "post-wall" Europe, defining, among other things, the haves and the have-nots; the established and the new democracies; the sources of European stability and the threats to that stability; and, more generally, the dominant players versus the "wannabes." At the same time, the east–west distinction, while important in itself, considerably predates communist revolutions and Stalin's commitment to protecting socialism in one country. It captures, in many respects, the variance masked by the notion of a European historical experience,[11] and it points to a remarkable continuity in the poles of that experience. As Jeno Szucs has observed in his majesterial study of European history written during the Cold War era,

> A very sharp line of demarcation that was in fact to cut Europe into two parts from the point of view of economic and social structure after 1500, divided off the far larger, more easterly part (of Europe) as the scene of the second

serfdom. Moreover, Europe in our own times, another 500 years later still, is divided more clearly than ever before into two "camps" almost exactly along that same line. . . . It is as if Stalin, Churchill and Roosevelt had studied carefully the "status quo" of the age of Charlemagne on the 1130th anniversary of his death.[12]

Indeed, if our concern is, as here, with the development of and the relationship among capitalism, civil society, political society, and democracy, and if we take note of other chapters in this book on Germany, southern Europe, and Russia in particular, then a, if not *the*, most striking contrast in European historical evolution is between the east and the west. This is most apparent if we compare the geographical extremes along this divide; that is, Great Britain, with its sequencing of feudalism, the state, the nation, capitalism, civil society, political society, and democracy, versus Russia, with its history, for instance, of serfdom; a hybridized empire-state and an equally hybridized Russian nation; authoritarianism followed by state socialism; and a "sudden" capitalism that arises at nearly the same time as the nation, civil and political society, and democracy.

Another issue that requires some discussion is the definition of the European idea. This is an extraordinarily contested concept, not just because its origins are complex and thus hotly debated, but also because one's position on this question depends heavily on controversial choices made about core concepts, core time periods, and core geographical areas.[13] For the purposes of this chapter, the European idea as a concept will refer to those innovations that took root in both theoretical debates and in political-economic practice in the northwest quadrant of Europe from the Middle Ages to the end of the nineteenth century and that spread eventually to much of the rest of the world, albeit in revised, if not compromised form, through the diffusion of ideas, armies, capital, and political authority structures. The essential components include the nation as a political community invested with sovereignty and the state as a durable administrative and territorial entity defining borders, monopolizing the legitimate use of coercion, extracting compliance, and, more generally, setting boundaries on political interactions; separation of church and state, the state and the society, and the economy and the polity; individual freedom; rule of law; a rational bureaucracy controlled by elected officials; limited government, political representation, civil liberties, and political pluralism; competition as the primary determinant of *provisional* political and economic outcomes; private property, markets, and enforceable contracts as the backbone of the economy; and a political culture that defines politics primarily as the pursuit of the "profane"—or interests—rather than the pursuit of "paradise"—or idealized outcomes.[14]

Embedded in this rather long list, however, are five core concepts: the nation-state, individual freedom, societal autonomy, regime accountability, and competition among interests as the driving force of politics and economics. It is these guiding principles, moreover, that help us define civil and political society and their relationship in turn to capitalism and democracy. "Civil society" is legally protected freedom of associational life, with associations understood to be independent of the state and to exist in the space between the family and the state. It refers, for example, to such staples of democratic life as an independent media, church groups, bowling leagues, employee and employer associations, retirement clubs, parent–teachers' associations, vegetarian societies, and the like. The less commonly used term, "political society," which will be central to the discussion below since it provides an important contrast between east and west, refers to the organized activity of citizens in common pursuit of selecting who rules and influencing the agenda and the decisions of the rulers.[15]

Civil and political society are understood as necessary conditions for the development and the sustainability of democracy, as well as the overall quality of democratic life.[16] This is because they empower citizens while constraining the state; they inform decision makers; and they limit the reach and the power of the regime (but without, it must be emphasized, compromising state capacity).[17] However, they are not, it must be emphasized, a sufficient condition.[18] For example, just as Germany featured a vibrant civil society on the eve of the collapse of democracy (as Klaus Tenfelde argues in this volume), so, to take a more recent example, the two republics within Yugoslavia that featured the richest civil society on the eve of that state's collapse—that is, Serbia and Slovenia—subsequently moved in strikingly different political directions, with Serbia a stubborn, if thin, dictatorship and Slovenia well on the way to democratic consolidation.[19] This was despite, moreover, the similar role of nationalism in both cases as the constructor and the conveyor of civil and political society.

With these definitional considerations in mind, let us now look more closely at the historical evolution of the "two" Europes. We will begin with an extended inquiry into the development of east and west from Roman times to World War I. This is necessary, because it helps us understand many of the themes that long defined—and that continue to define—the eastern versus the western evolutionary model, and it helps identify as well the sources of and the relationship among civil and political society and democracy.

GEOPOLITICAL LOCATION AND EUROPEAN EVOLUTION UP TO WORLD WAR I

The origins of the two Europes can be traced to their different geopolitical locations. In the western portion of the continent, separation from Asia, thanks to geography and the shield provided by Eastern Europe, allowed for a series of developments that proved to be foundational for what later came to be known as the European idea. Key to this story was, first, the early and durable consolidation of authority under the Roman Empire. This created a remarkable stability in politics, borders, and composition of the population. This also brought to the fore (albeit in varying degrees of specification) a series of ideas, such as citizenship, private property, rule of law, rational bureaucracy, separation of state and society, and coincidence of political authority and geographical boundaries, that were developed in part by the Greeks, which were to resurface in the thirteenth century and in the Enlightenment and were to function as the basis for the eventual rise of the west and its distinctive profile.

A second factor of crucial importance was the collapse of the Roman Empire and the failure of the Germans by the eighth century to construct a durable political alternative. This resulted in the fragmentation of central political authority and a radical decentralization of both politics and economics. When combined with the existence of increasingly stable communities of increasingly homogenized people and the proliferation of nooks and crannies available to peasants and lords to engage in independent but also some intersecting activity, the stage was set for the rise of a new type of economic and political order—that is, feudalism.

What was distinctive about feudalism—both in terms of developments elsewhere and with respect to the western European past—was that it was built largely from the bottom up and not from the top down. That fact, along with the equally distinctive characteristics of the contractual basis of feudal relationships; the retreat of the proto-state and the rise of the Church; the variability and decentralized character of feudal structures; and, finally, the dense networks of political, social, economic, and cultural interactions that were encouraged by the evolving structure of feudal systems, imparted experience with and legitimacy to what eventually became the hallmarks of the Western idea—freedom, popular sovereignty, limited government, political equality, pluralism, and separation between state and society, church and state. For many of the same reasons, moreover, feudalism also laid the foundation in the west for the rapid expansion of the population and the rise of cities, the market, and the nation. Where there was a rough balance between the crown and the aristocracy, where there was a revolutionary break with the past, where commercialized agriculture freed labor, and where the bourgeoisie was autonomous, these earlier developments could in time translate into democratic governance.[20]

The final piece to the puzzle of the west was the development of the modern state. As Charles Tilly[21] has persuasively argued, the state evolved in the west because, in order to finance wars, kings needed to regularize and guarantee their access to revenues and warriors. To achieve that, kings needed to "capture" populations by establishing a geographically defined and bureaucratically controlled political monopoly. This could assure them of long-term control over the population, long-term access to the resources they needed, and the guarantees that these resources would be transferred to state coffers. Thus enters the age of absolutism and the rise of the modern state. However, because of feudalism, state-building was constrained—by the independence, diversity, and normative foundations of feudal systems and by their empowerment of society in general and the landed aristocracy in particular. The states that formed in the west, then, were in many instances limited in their powers. They built nations as a by-product of greedy elites, and were combined with regimes that were forced to be inclusive—initially of the aristocracy and thereafter of other groups positioned, due to the socioeconomic and political changes produced by feudalism, commercialization of agriculture, and capitalism, to become sought-after members of political coalitions and powerful political forces in their own right. These constraints both reflected and produced competition in politics and economics within the confines of the state, and this competition functioned over time to further limit the state, separate the state from the economy, and liberalize the regime. In the process, political society came into force and contributed to both further political liberalization and the formation and consolidation of democracy.

The long-term development of the east, however, followed a different trajectory. With its flat terrain in the north running westward to the Urals, its mountains in the south and its proximity to Asia, the development of the east was far more influenced by the tribes, armies, ideas, belief systems, and institutions of that contiguous continent. Thus, while western Europe was, by comparison, relatively isolated in its development before and during the Middle Ages, Eastern Europe was subjected to repeated invasions from the south and the east and thus to constant wars, changing ideas and institutions, new populations bases, and repeated shifts in political and economic jurisdictions. As a result, Eastern Europe, in contrast to its western counterpart, featured, even before the first millennium, a far more diverse, competitive, and ever changing ideological, political, social, cultural, and economic landscape. If the west moved toward a certain homogenization, then, the east remained a complex and ever changing mosaic. While France represents in the extreme form the western model as presented here, the Balkans and Russia provide the best and extreme example of the eastern variant.

Second, the difficulty of access to and control over Eastern Europe meant that much of the region was incorporated only sporadically, if at all, into the Roman Empire. What is defined today as Russia, of course, remained entirely outside the Roman administrative net. At the same time, the political messages of Rome (and Greece before that) were not just removed in a geographical sense from the Eastern European experience; they were also, when diffusing eastward (as they tended to do in subsequent centuries), forced to compete with the very different set of political, cultural, and economic messages of Islam, Constantinople (after the schism), the princes of Muscovy, the Tatars, and the like.

It is therefore not surprising that a key distinction between Russian and British history—to take the most extreme contrast—was the absence in the former of a tradition of law (and natural law), rational bureaucracy, private property, separation of church and state, and separation of state and society.[22] For instance, the first law in Russia—the law on succession—was promulgated (or, more accurately, declared) by Peter the Great during his campaign to westernize Russia. It is a telling comment that this law fell quickly to the wayside when Peter actually died, and the ensuing succession struggle reverted back, easily and quickly, to the court intrigues so typical of the princes of Muscovy.[23] It is also telling that Peter's understanding of westernization was highly instrumental. He did not want Russia to become the west and sever its connections to the past. Rather, he argued that "we need Europe for a few decades, so that we can turn our backs on it later."[24] Also implied in Peter's comments and actions was another message that would underline east–west interactions for centuries. The "outcomes" of the west could be both imported and imposed; their "causes," on the other hand, could and should be ignored.

If a key difference between east and west during Roman times was the fluidity of the former versus the stability of the latter, then after the collapse of Rome their situations tended to reverse. While the west made a sharp break during the Middle Ages with the integrative political authority of the past, and this, along with some other factors, set in motion a train of developments that eventually led to the rise of liberal orders (albeit sooner and more easily in some places than in others), the situation in the east was one of *continuity* with the past, wherein a divided, weak, and thinly populated society was joined with a continuing struggle over the course of the Middle Ages (and after) on the part of warlords and princes to extend and to consolidate political authority. The opportunities for societal autonomy in the east, then, as well as for the autonomy of the economy from political authority, were limited and, in fact, declined over time as the population base of the region eventually settled and as political and economic integration was forged by the rise of absolutist political entities. Indeed, rather than following a sequence of aggregation of political authority, collapse of authority, feudalism, and reimposition of authority (albeit compromised), as in the west, we find in the east far slower and more uneven aggregation of authority that eventually took hold by combining elements of absolutism with elements of feudalism—one consequence of which was the imposition in the sixteenth century of the second serfdom. [25] As a consequence, feudalism in the east came late, as did states, and this stripped feudalism in that context of all those characteristics that linked the feudal order in the west to the rise of civil and political society, limited government, and the like.

A final difference between eastern and western historical paths—and one that, likewise, grew out of differences in geopolitical location—was in the area of socioeconomic development. The instability and sparseness of the population and the fragmentation and instability of authority structures in the east translated into a much later development—by several centuries at least—of stable communities and the widespread use of the plow. This created a gap by the late Middle Ages that was never to be closed and, indeed, grew larger over time between east and west in rates of urbanization; population growth and population density; technological innovation; marketization; and, thus, overall economic expansion. Less obviously, this, plus the sheer diversity of the population and the highly competitive forms of organizing political, economic, and cultural life, slowed down the development in the east of dense economic, political, social, and cultural networks. This undermined social integration and the formation of nations, as well as economic development.

This also, in combination with continued competition over political boundaries originating in the region and to its east, west, and south, led to the rise of empires, not states in Eastern Europe; that is, to authority structures that enclosed highly diverse populations and that were unusually despotic; uneven in their political and ideological penetration; ever changing in their boundaries; and premised on spatially and culturally defined political, social, and economic inequalities.[26] While different from some other empires in the sense of featuring contiguous rather than geographically removed colonies, the empires of the east were in all other respects, therefore, typically imperial—for example, their lack of legitimacy, their political inequality, their fluid boundaries, and their radial administrative structures. Thus, they were contested from without and contested from within and as a result failed to achieve the political monopoly that defines the modern state and that assures a compliant citizenry. Rebellious publics were in evidence especially where distinct cultural groupings were spatially concentrated and had once resided in a sovereign unit; where the western ideas of nation and sovereignty had penetrated the most; and where imperial control had been undermined by economic and administrative inefficiency, intra-elite divisions, political liberalization at the core, and expanding competition from other states and empires. The Poles in particular were prone to rebel against their various imperial masters, and so were the Serbs. While these rebellions only began to produce imperial leakage by the mid-nineteenth century, most notably within the weakening Ottoman Empire, they did not succeed in redefining the core distinction between east and west. Until World War I, then, the contrast in Europe was one between democracies, states, entrenched capitalism, and economic vitality in the west and authoritarianism, empires, early and uneven capitalism, and lower growth in the east.

This overview of eastern versus western European historical development from Roman times until World War I has been all too brief. Moreover, it has slighted the undeniably variable trajectories within the two "camps." However, the advantage has been to leave us with a clear sense of a sharply contrasting historical ledger along the east–west axis. Phrased succinctly, the eastern story is one of costs, and the western story is one of benefits. This is the case, whether our normative standard is democracy, growth, or stability. However, implied in that observation are several points of contrast that help us understand variations in Europe in the development of civil and political society and democracy. First and too rarely noted is the fact that Eastern Europe, given its geopolitical location, provided western Europe with the political, economic, social, and cultural space—or, more succinctly, the stability in context—that proved to be so crucial for the rise of the state, the nation, and liberalism as theory and as practice. While it is common to think of European development in terms of the west's impact on the east, since, among other things, the west became more dynamic in economic and military terms and used the east as preparation for its imperial expansion into the rest of the world, it is also the case that the arrow of influence worked in the opposite direction. By functioning as a "sponge," the east allowed the west to become the west, while appropriating for itself, in the process, the term "Europe."

Another and more familiar contrast is that many of the characteristics that are associated with the European idea came far later, if at all, to eastern than to western Europe. This is the case, whether we focus on when populations settled and engaged in regularized interactions with each other; when political authority consolidated; when feudalism developed; when cities, markets, the state, and the nation developed; or when civil and political society and democracy made their appearance. Geopolitical location, therefore, consigned Eastern Europe to a developmental trajectory that was slower than the west.

This leads us to a third and final conclusion. It would be a mistake to reduce the historical experiences of the east to that of the west, albeit at a much slower cadence. Like modernization theory, [27] this interpretation presumes, erroneously, that the paths of the east and the west were similarly linear; that the east faithfully followed a trail first blazed by the west; and that the political economy of the east, as a result, was a simple story of struggling to catch up with the west. This is not just objectionable from the normative standpoint of a Slavophile, who would quickly object to the use of the west as *the* standard for comparison and who would point out, among other things, the distinctive virtues of the eastern way. It is also problematic, because it misrepresents a key contrast between east and west. That contrast is between the *deviation* involving a sharp break with the legacies of the past—as in the west with the rise of feudalism and what followed—versus the far more common practice of linear historical development—as in most of the world, including Eastern Europe. [28] It was this contrast, in combination with the influences of Asia and the regionally segmented, but, beginning with the Middle Ages, increasingly intertwined character of European development, that produced in the east a *distinctive* set of economic, political, social, and cultural experiences. One key difference between east and west was in the sequencing of developments. As argued above, this was evident in the historical pattern of consolidating political authority. In the east, we see a slow and linear aggregation of political authority that fused absolutism and feudalism, that eventually produced despotic empires with continuously contested boundaries and rebellious populations and that failed for the most part to produce either states or liberal regimes—until the international system intervened decisively in the twentieth century to support that outcome. In the west, by contrast, the story is one of early political integration, followed by collapse and then slow reconstruction through the sequencing of feudalism and absolutism and through the interplay, as a result, of greedy elites and resourceful societies. It was this interaction—a leveling of the political and economic playing field—that was central to the rise in the west of capitalism, civil society, and democracy. The importance of balance and autonomy is central to Barrington Moore's account of the origins of democracy, with the absence of such balance and autonomy foundational to dictatorship.[29]

Another contrast in sequencing—and one that speaks directly to what happened when western ideas mixed with eastern contexts—was that in the east the rise of the nation tended to go along with the rise of political society and capitalism, and all three preceded the development of either the state or much associational life independent of the state—or what we have defined as civil society. By contrast, the western path featured—in rough order—the rise of the state,[30] then civil society, and then political society and democracy.

This contrast produced very different political dynamics in the east versus those in the west. In the east, the nation tended to be defined in ethnolinguistic and not the civic terms of the west, and the national project became one of rebelling against an empire-state and building a new and modern state, and not one, as in the west, of pressing for political equality, political influence, and regime change within the context of an existing and durable state. To put the matter simply, the natural affinity between nationalism and a liberal project in the west was, in the eastern context, both unnatural and infrequent.

The sequencing in the east also meant that political society there tended to exist separately from a civil society base and came into being prior to much elaboration of civil society—which was testimony to the existence in the east of intellectuals, bureaucrats, and military officers who had been influenced by western ideas and who functioned as societal "surrogates" within a distinctly nonwestern context that combined authoritarian politics, fused political and economic hierarchies, the uneven development of capitalism, and a weak and divided society. Typical of contexts peripheral to the west, then, Eastern Europe exhibited what might be termed "precocious" politics—or, in this case, a political society that tended to stand above and separate from a civil society far less in evidence. Like the state's relationship to society in eastern Europe, so political society in this region tended to "float above" its social base.

Finally, the relationship between civil and political society and the nation in the eastern context led to a "nationalization" of the agenda of political society and, therein, to a tendency to define political action and organization as "us" versus "them" or society versus the regime-state. This was in contrast, again, to the west, where political society evolved as a by-product of the development of capitalism and civil society and represented a response, therein, to the differentiation of political interests within a larger context of a single national community and a modern state.

If the sequencing of developments was different, and this shaped a distinctive eastern versus western path of development, so politics itself assumed different forms in the two regions of Europe. The most obvious contrast, evident by the eighteenth century, was between the increasingly democratic regimes of the west and authoritarianism in the east. This, along with the sequencing differences between east and west, imparted a certain urgency to Eastern European politics and (reversing Marx and embracing Leninist revisionism) the domination of the superstructure over the base. The centrality of politics and political authoritarianism in the east can be seen in a brief comparison between Great Britain and Russia in the nineteenth century. It was Russia, and not the international hegemon, Great Britain, that functioned as the "gendarme" of Europe, and the Reform Bill of 1867 in Britain paled considerably in its radical character when compared with the Great Reforms introduced by Alexander II.

What was also different about the politics of the two Europes was their contrasting political spectrums as they took shape in the nineteenth century. In the east, there arose an extraordinarily complicated and multidimensional political spectrum that was defined by varying combinations of class position, position on the national and state questions, and spatial location. This cluttered spectrum meant that eastern European politics tended to feature simultaneously all those political cleavages that in the west had tended to be resolved in sequential fashion and that had produced by the nineteenth century (at least where cleavages had not been frozen) a far more simple anchoring of political conflict along class lines.[31] In this sense, Eastern European politics became in effect a "museum" of western and eastern development. It managed to collect in one time and place all the political artifacts produced by the two developmental experiences. This undermined the subsequent development of democracy in Eastern Europe, because it undercut the development and the power of civil society; produced an extraordinary range of political movements and parties, interests, *and* values that fragmented political society; favored the polarization and paralysis of politics; and left the national and state questions unresolved by the time democracy appeared on the agenda of political possibilities.[32]

A final contrast was between the political cultures of the two Europes.[33] In the west, an instrumental culture took form, reinforced by capitalism and nascent democracy, that valued pluralism; competition based on interests; limited government; and separation between state and society, economy and state, and church and state. In the east, the dominant culture was transcendental. Uniformity, not pluralism was valued, because the costs of diversity were so high; competition was seen as disruptive and the interplay of interests as both demeaning and destabilizing; values, preferably widely shared, were seen as the proper currency of political debate and struggle; and state intervention in the economy, the society, and religious affairs were all seen as desirable and necessary in order to provide order, consensus, and morality amidst the natural and highly destructive tendency toward chaos, conflict, and immorality—a tendency that would necessarily reappear, if the state should retreat and society be allowed to dominate. From this perspective, the state in the east was a savior; in the west, a referee.

By the end of the nineteenth century, then, it was evident that there were two Europes, long separated by their histories and, thus, by their politics, economics, social structure, and culture. With the collapse of empires during and after World War I, however, an opportunity presented itself for the two Europes to become one. As in the past, what proved pivotal was a change in the international system.

THE INTERWAR PERIOD

Following World War I, the political boundaries of Eastern Europe were changed radically through the establishment of new states, the reconstitution of an old one (Poland), the folding of another into a larger and new entity (Serbia into Yugoslavia), and a redefinition of those state boundaries that already existed (with Romania expanded and Hungary contracting). At the same time, the new regimes that formed throughout the region committed themselves to democratic politics, land reform, and rapid and state-directed socioeconomic development. Thus, the interwar period seemed to provide that crucial break with the past that had long eluded Eastern Europe and that had cramped, as well as complicated, the development there of states and capitalism and their familiar, though hardly guaranteed, offshoots of civil and political society and democracy.

However, by the end of the 1920s, the great experiment had failed. Throughout the region (with the exception of Czechoslovakia[34]) democracy gave way to dictatorship; the rate of economic growth plummeted; peasants suffered and landlords in most cases remained powerful in terms of both land ownership and political influence; and state boundaries were increasingly subjected to challenges from within and outside the perimeters of the state.

There are a number of reasons why Eastern Europe failed during the interwar period in its quest to catch up with and become the west.[35] There were two obvious problems. The first was the collapse of the world grain market followed by the Great Depression. As grain exporters, these economies were particularly hard-hit by the global economic downturn and market contraction. With these economic difficulties, moreover, came considerable social conflict and less confidence, especially among those groups with considerable political influence, such as political leaders, landed aristocrats, the military, and intellectuals, in the capacity of democracy to deliver either good politics or good economics. At the same time, there was the flawed design of the democratic institutions that were established throughout the region—for instance, the political fragmentation and paralysis that came from strictly proportional representation systems in diverse societies; the limits on civilian control over the military and the control of elected officials over the bureaucracy; and the various emergency clauses in the constitutions that allowed political leaders to suspend democratic politics.[36]

However, perhaps the major reason for this failure was in fact the absence in many respects of a sharp break with Eastern Europe's past. The changes introduced in Eastern Europe after World War I were largely cosmetic and lacked the grounding in the society, economy, polity, and culture that was necessary if these new institutions were to survive and function effectively.[37] Thus, state boundaries bore little relationship to either national boundaries or the boundaries of earlier proto-states within the region and instead testified in large measure to the desire and the capacity of external actors to punish certain states and to create what they saw as a stabilizing regional balance of power; parliaments and parties were detached from the social structure and, when captured by it, tended to exaggerate the tensions among national communities and among classes that had long defined and polarized Eastern European politics, The banking system was separated, in part because of redefined political boundaries, from well-established patterns of economic interactions on the ground. All this reflected, of course, the limits intrinsic to the enterprise of political and economic engineering and the power of the past to reassert itself, despite institutional innovations.

But this experiment also failed, it must be emphasized, because of the very approach to change that was used. Indeed, what is striking about this attempt to remake Eastern Europe in the image of the west is that it exhibited certain features that were not just anti-western in their conception and practice, but that were also in close keeping with the eastern and not the western European historical tradition. One was the power of the international system in general and the west in particular to dictate developments in the region. It was the agenda and the power of the victors of World War I, then, and less the interests and the influence of Eastern European elites-to-be, that were largely responsible for state and regime construction. Society, moreover, was exhausted and watched from the sidelines. Another was the tendency to merge, rather than sequence, the development of the nation, the state, capitalism, civil society, political society, and democracy. The interwar experiment, therefore, constituted a "big bang," rather than an evolutionary approach, to the construction of liberal orders. Third, as in the past, so in interwar Eastern Europe the state and the regime were to function as a substitute for what was missing in politics, economics and society. Thus, the regime-state was to create a bourgeoisie, build capitalism, and promote rapid growth; it was to claim and then defend sovereignty; and it was to promote freedom, build political parties, and construct civil societies. And all of this was to happen, moreover, within a larger goal of building an accountable and constrained regime. Thus, to anticipate the socialist period and to echo the Eastern European past, politics was in command. While the ostensible logic of the west in this exercise was to defend the region against socialism, the methods used to accomplish such an objective were, to some degree, closer to Leninist than liberal practices. Finally, as in the past, the cart was placed before the horse. Democracy was established prior to the rise of either a vigorous capitalist economy or a vigorous civil society, and political society was created prior to the establishment of either a strong civil society or a rooted, capitalist economy, and in tandem with democratic politics and political institutions.

In this sense, then, the interwar experiment in Eastern Europe testified in three ways to the power of the past. With so many holes, the past had ample room to reassert itself; the experiment featured the familiar sequencing and forms of earlier Eastern European development; and the interwar architects deployed the familiar tools of the past to force political, social, economic, and cultural change. The contrast between revolutionary and evolutionary development, therefore, continued to be a fundamental distinction between the eastern and the western European idea. This was a distinction, moreover, that was most obvious when focussing on developments in Russia after the revolution. It was in the Soviet Union, following the Bolshevik Revolution *and*, usually forgotten, the collapse of the world grain market and the transformation thereafter of the Stalinist developmental agenda, where the eastern historical model assumed its most extreme form as the boundaries between state and society, state and economy, state and religion, and the public and the private were obliterated; as a single ideology took root and counterideologies and their proponents and representatives were destroyed; and as an extraordinarily despotic and penetrative party-state was constructed that eliminated and then took the place of civil society and the bourgeoisie. If so many ideas of the Russian revolution were western in origin, what followed was modernization in the eastern style.

STATE SOCIALISM

After World War II, the Soviet model was exported to the rest of Eastern Europe—even where the socialist revolution was homegrown and had generated widespread popular support, as most notably in Yugoslavia. State socialism was based on five principles: rapid socioeconomic development, state ownership of the means of production, central planning, authoritarian rule by a Leninist party, and isolation from and competition with the west. The result was the creation of a centralized and fused economic, political, and social monopoly in the hands of the party-state.[38]

When viewed from the perspective of the region's history, the socialist experiment in Eastern Europe exhibited three competing strands. One was an exaggeration of those characteristics that had defined Eastern Europe's past—for example, authoritarian rule; the erasure of the boundary between the state and society, the state and the economy, and the public and the private; the resulting contrast to the extreme in state socialism between a strong regime-state and a weak society; the radial structure of the political system (both at the regime and the Soviet bloc level) and its resemblance to imperial structures; the rejection of an interest-based, pluralist, and competitive politics and legitimization of a value-based and consensual politics that denied both the existence and the value of diverse interests under socialism; the overriding commitment to catch up with the west and to do so quickly, even at high human costs; and, for most of the region, given the structure of the Soviet bloc, the dominance of international over domestic forces as the determinant of state, regime, and societal behavior.

A second strand, however, involved a dramatic break with the past. Especially in the early decades of socialism, there was extraordinarily rapid urbanization, expansion of the educational and health care systems, and economic growth. Stalinism, in short, was a system bent on modernization. At the same time, at the state level the region broke with the enormous diversity of its past, as Stalinism emerged "in ready-to-wear fashion" in one state after another throughout Eastern Europe by the end of the 1940s.[39] This homogenization of Eastern European political economies was joined, moreover, in the 1950s with the introduction at the regional level of the Soviet bloc and its core components of the Warsaw Treaty Organization and the Council for Mutual Economic Assistance. All of this forced regional political, economic, and cultural integration while removing the east in a decisive way from western contact and western influence.

The final strand combined the past with new elements. Here, we can point to the complex approach taken to the national question. On the one hand, socialist identity was to supplant nationalist identity—and this notion of an ideological basis for identity was new to the region. On the other hand, national differences were encouraged—most notably in the multinational states of Yugoslavia, Czechoslovakia, and the Soviet Union with their multiple officially recognized languages; their representation at the center of national groupings; and, more generally, their ethno-territorial federal structures that allowed for a coincidence among nationality, administration, and geography.[40]

When combined, these three strands of the Soviet model produced several long-term and unexpected consequences for the eastern half of Europe.[41] One was that state socialism—understood as both a domestic and an international system—turned out to be self-destructive. In practice, it undermined over time the very economic and political foundations of state socialism and the bloc. In particular, the structure of the system functioned to divide the party into factions, to reduce the control of the center over the periphery, and to limit its control over society in the domestic arena. At the same time, the parallel structures within the bloc undercut Soviet control over its client states, and the governing parties in the periphery were, as a result, caught between the demands of the party faithful and society versus the demands of the Soviet Union. These parties were, of course, weakened by that tug-of-war. The structure of the system also sabotaged economic performance and regional economic integration. This in turn forced these economies to open up to the west as a way of importing what they were lacking—that is, efficiency and capital—while avoiding, in the process, the destabilizing consequences of needed reforms that would anger the public, deregulate the party's economic and political monopoly, and destabilize the system. Rather than enhancing economic performance, bloc integration, and political stability, however, trade liberalization (which carried the cost, imposed by the west, of liberalization in the movement of people and ideas) had quite the opposite effects. Exposing these highly inefficient economies to a global economy in recession and rich in capital, but at a high price, translated into even more rapid economic decline; a reduction in the center's control over the economy; an angry public resentful of periodic attempts at domestic austerity measures; a party sorely divided horizontally and vertically on the issue of reform; and, more generally, party-states in the Eastern European periphery that were more and more dependent on the Soviet Union for political and economic capital and thus for their very survival. For the Soviet Union, all this carried one clear cost. Eastern Europe had become a burden, not an asset, not just because it was a financial drain, but also because its political problems could easily travel eastward.

Finally, the very design of the system worked—again, by accident and over time—to empower society. This reflected the growing resources and anger of society as a consequence of, for instance, the weakening of the party-state, which gave society and its allies within the party greater room for maneuver; the decline of Soviet control over the region and growing Soviet resentment over its subsidization of its client states, both of which undercut the power of those regimes located in the bloc's periphery; and the growing tension between the premises and promises of socialism versus the reality of dictatorship, a slowdown in social mobility, economic decline, rising political corruption, and a standard of living far inferior to that of the west. What was particularly important in empowering society, however, was a homogenization of interests, reflecting the absence of pluralism, the remarkable similarities among the public forged by the party-state's economic and political monopoly, and the ability of the public, given the party-state's political-economic monopoly, to identify a common enemy. The stage was set, in short, for mobilization against the regime. Anger, resources, and opportunity had come together—in spite of and, indeed, because of the system.[42]

Mobilization against the regime, moreover, was particularly easy to mount in Poland. This was because Stalinization there was painful enough to alienate, but not painful enough to destroy the Polish nation; because Polish history had been such as to nurture the ties among the nation and civil and political society; and, finally, because Poland lacked (for tragic historical reasons) the cultural divisions that were characteristic of much of the rest of Eastern Europe and that allowed communists to divide and conquer.

These complex and long-term developments in politics, economics, and society, in the domestic and in the international arenas of socialism, can be put in relatively simple terms. The essence of state socialism—and what distinguished it from other forms of dictatorship—was the construction through Stalinization of an economic and political monopoly. The workings of state socialism, however, generated a series of developments that deregulated that monopoly. What was left, as a consequence, was a weak, sometimes liberalized, and, in every case, vulnerable dictatorship and an assertive and increasingly autonomous society. All that was needed to save the system and yet end it, then, was liberalization from above—an approach that is, we must remember, fully in keeping with eastern historical traditions. And that was provided by Gorbachev, first in the Soviet Union and then throughout the bloc; by Enver Hoxha's successors in Albania; and by the political and economic stalemate that destroyed what little was left of the center in Yugoslavia following Josip Broz Tito's death.

The other consequence of the very structure of the system was to build, sometimes from scratch and sometimes with the aid of the presocialist past, nations and states within each of the three federalized socialist systems and to do the same among states composing the Soviet bloc. With the decline of the system and the bloc and the dependence of the state on the regime and the periphery on the Soviet core, the stage was set for the rise of nationalist movements; the collapse of the bloc; and, in the federal cases, the multiplication of states. Thus, the very structure of the system decentralized political authority by redistributing, accidentally and over time, economic, political, and social resources—from the party to the society; from the Soviet Union to its client states; and, in the federations, from the center to the republics.

The contribution of state socialism to the historical evolution of Eastern Europe, then, was the following. It modernized these economies and these societies; it built nations and states and facilitated a realignment between the two; it empowered society and laid the groundwork for the rise of civil and political society; and it delegitimized authoritarian politics and socialist economics. State socialism was designed to separate the east from the west, but its impact, ironically, was to bring the two blocs closer together—in an even more fundamental way than similar developments in the west, with its more orchestrated and humane capitalism. With the collapse of state socialism, the Eastern European tradition of bully states, cowed societies, and authoritarian regimes was succeeded by a new development: limited states, assertive publics, and regimes in transition to capitalism and democracy. State socialism, therefore, seemed to complete in many respects the break with the past that had been started during the interwar period.

CONCLUSION: AFTER STATE SOCIALISM

The collapse of state socialism—with its mobilized publics, its fragmented political authority structures, and its decoupling of politics and economics—could be construed, then, as a replay in the east of the break with the past that had oc-curred in the west some twelve hundred years earlier. This parallel seems par-ticularly apt for the northern tier of central and Eastern Europe, where homo-geneous populations combined with sabotaged revolutions and liberalized politics during the socialist period to produce the makings of a civil and, espe-cially, a political society; the establishment of effective democratic institutions; a clear break with the socialist past through the victory of the liberal opposition in the first competitive elections; and, finally, a rapid transition to capitalism. In this sense, the revolutions of 1989, already deviant because they were peaceful, were unusual in another respect—at least in the northwest corner of the region. They were not as revolutionary as they might have seemed. The actions of 1989 formalized what had been long in the making: societies that existed separate from the state. Indeed, this is precisely why we can speak confidently today—a mere ten years after the collapse of communism—about democratic capitalism in one-fourth of the postsocialist region.

However, the path to a liberal order has been far more complicated and more easily derailed in the Balkans, Russia, Belarus, and Ukraine. This was be-cause these countries represent the extremes of the eastern developmental ex-perience. Moreover, in part because of those earlier developments, they had di-verged from the northern tier of Eastern Europe in lacking a history during the socialist period of revolutionary protest (though Slovenia and Serbia were ex-ceptional in this regard). At the same time, political and economic liberalization in those parts of the east had come after and not before the collapse of the com-munist party monopoly. Finally, the populations in the south and in Russia and Ukraine are more diverse (featuring, to borrow from Engels, "bits and scraps of peoples"), and nationalism was more tightly linked to two projects that could threaten the consolidation of liberal orders: that is, state-building and the search for power by communists in a context that no longer guaranteed them a mo-nopoly, but that lacked a strong liberal opposition.[43]

However, common to the entire region was the fact that state socialism and its aftermath managed in certain ways to reinforce the dominant messages of Eastern Europe's past. Again, a struggle unfolded in much of the region over how to define the nation and its relationship to the state, and this struggle led at times—most notably, in Serbia, Croatia, and many of the new states formed in the rubble of the Soviet Union—to authoritarian and not democratic politics.

Second, the struggle against the regime had produced an emphasis on con-sensus, rather than conflict, and an emphasis as well on values, rather than in-terests. Thus, the political cultural tradition of the region that emphasized unity and the politics of values was thereby reinforced. Indeed, what happened after 1989 in much of the postsocialist region was the substitution of liberalism for socialism as the reigning ideology. This in turn, along with an extraordinarily fluid class structure and the atomization of the socialist experience, constrained the development throughout much of Eastern Europe of a robust political society: that is, a party system rooted in a dense network of associational life, anchored by well-defined interests, and therefore shaped by class-differentiated voting. What was weakly articulated in postcommunist Europe, then, was the notion of democracy as a product of civil and political society and as a system of governance that is distinctive in tolerating conflicting interests while facilitating their peaceful resolution.

The end of socialism, in addition, was the onset of yet another revolution where the cart was placed before the horse. Again, the key was catching up with the west, and what had been sequenced in western development was fused in the east. This time, the agenda was to build, simultaneously and in a hurry, capitalism, a new social structure, democracy, the nation, civil society, political society, and new relations between the state and the international system of power and money—and, if that were not enough, new states in the territories that once made up the Soviet Union, Yugoslavia, and Czechoslovakia. Central to this ambitious project, moreover, was the regime-state, substituting once again for the missing factors of economic, political, and social production. As Richard Sakwa put it for the Russian case: "Russia has once again become the site for reforms 'imposed on' rather than 'emerging through' politics, and the imposition becomes doubly burdensome because the current transformation is based on values generated abroad. The country is apparently once again trapped between 'is' (sein) and 'ought' (sollen)."[44]

The enormity of these tasks can be captured in two brief examples. One is the humorous definition of socialism, circulating in Eastern Europe, that socialism is the long road between capitalism and capitalism. The other is a comment made by a nominee, in the fall of 1989, for an economic cabinet post in the first Solidarity-led government in Poland. In response to the question from a member of the parliament as to whom he would represent, his reply was that he would represent a class that did not yet exist: the bourgeoisie.

Finally, postcommunism resonated with the past by making painfully clear the diversity within the purported unity of Europe. There was a core Europe that was stable, democratic, and prosperous and a peripheral Europe that wanted all of those things, but that was, by comparison, less stable, new to democracy, and poor. Indeed, eastern Europe has become more impoverished over the course of the postcommunist experience. By early 1999, only two countries in the region (out of a total of twenty-seven) had economies as large as they had been ten years earlier: Poland and Slovenia. Postcommunism, therefore, has been a story of economic contraction, with the war-ravaged economies of Bosnia and Georgia, for example, now one-third of their original size in 1989. [45] Just as the economic gap within the east has grown sharply, so have two other gaps—between rich and poor within these states and between the east and the west.

Thus, postcommunist Eastern Europe is attempting to emulate the west but is still defined in part by its divergent historical trajectory. Does this mean that democracy, growth, and stability will elude Eastern Europe again and that the contrasts between the histories of the two Europes will reassert themselves? While no one can answer this question and the collapse of state socialism should have made us all wary of engaging in such predictive exercises, there is, nonetheless, an answer that follows from what has been argued throughout this chapter. For a good long while, there will be two Europes, but the defining difference will not be so much regime type. Rather, what we will see are lasting differences in the quality of democracy and in the form and the performance of capitalism—differences that will distinguish among the west, the northeast, and the southeast. While this is often characterized as a destabilizing aspect of the postcommunist experience, the reverse might very well be the case. To borrow from the arguments made by Bela Greskovits, the match in Eastern Europe between a low equilibrium democracy and a low equilibrium capitalism may nurture the survival of both.[46]

NOTES

1. Observers of the contemporary Russian scene have been particularly interested in the Weimar analogy. See Stephen E. Hanson and Jeffrey S. Kopstein, "The Weimar/Russia Comparison," *Post-Soviet Affairs* 13, no. 3 (1997): 252–83; Stephen D. Shenfield, "The Weimar/Russia Comparison: Reflections on Hanson and Kopstein," *Post-Soviet Affairs* 14, no. 3 (1998): 355–68; Jeffrey S. Kopstein and Stephen E. Hanson, "Paths to Uncivil Societies and Anti-Liberal States: A Reply to Shenfield," *Post-Soviet Affairs* 14, no. 3 (1998): 369–75. For an analysis of the breakdown of democracy in another interwar regime, see Michael Bernhard, "Institutional Choice and the Failure of Democracy: The Case of Interwar Poland," *East European Politics and Societies* 13, no. 1 (Winter 1999): 34–70.

2. John Lewis Gaddis, "The Long Peace: Elements of Stability in the Postwar International System," *International Organization* 10, no. 3 (Spring 1986): 99–142.

3. Valerie Bunce, "Domestic Reform and International Change: The Gorbachev Reforms in Historical Perspective," *International Organization* 47, no. 2 (Winter 1993): 107–38. The parallels between these two periods are striking. Consider, for example, that they began with the rise of Russia as a major power; that they rested on the Russian role as the stabilizer in the east; and that they came to a close with a Russia undergoing massive reforms. To this we can add several other similarities: the introduction of *glasnost* (which was invented during the Alexandrine reforms) and, with the termination of the long peace, the unification of Germany.

4. There are endless debates, of course, about where to draw the eastern boundary of Europe. In this chapter, Russia (along with the corridor of countries situated between Russia and east-central Europe) will be considered part of Europe. This decision to include Russia reflects not just geography, but also the central role of Russia in European affairs since at least their defeat of Sweden at Poltava at the beginning of the eighteenth century. To put the issue in a different way: with the defeat of Napoleon, Russia was widely recognized as a major European power. Russia was, after all, a member (and a

leading member) of the Concert of Europe in the nineteenth century and not a member, say, of the Concert of Asia. On Russia's ties with Europe and the European tradition, see Martin Malia, *Russia through Western Eyes: From the Bronze Horseman to the Lenin Mausoleum* (Cambridge, Mass.: Harvard University Press, 1999).

5. For a comparison and explanation of postcommunist economic and political trajectories, see Valerie Bunce, "The Political Economy of Postsocialism," *Slavic Review* 58 (Winter 1999): 756–93.

6. See, most generally, Benedict Anderson, *Imagined Communities* (London: Verso, 1991). Also see Larry Wolff, *Inventing Eastern Europe: The Map of Civilization on the Mind of the Enlightenment* (Stanford: Stanford University Press, 1993); Larry Wolff, "The Idea of Eastern Europe," *Slavic Review* 54, no. 3 (Winter 1995): 932–42; Maria Todorova, "The Balkans: From Discovery to Invention," *Slavic Review* 53, no. 2 (Summer 1994): 453–82; Milica Bakic-Hayden, "Nesting Orientalisms: The Case of Yugoslavia," *Slavic Review* 54, no. 4 (Winter 1995): 917–31.

7. Valerie Bunce, "Regional Cooperation and European Integration: The Visegrad Group," in *Mitteleuropa: Between Europe and Germany*, ed. Peter Katzenstein (Providence: Berghahn Books, 1998), 240–84.

8. As quoted in Timothy Garton Ash, "Journey to the Postcommunist East," *New York Review of Books*, June 23, 1994, 18.

9. See, for instance, Jeno Szucs, "The Three Historical Regions of Europe: An Outline," *Acta Historica Revue de L'academie des Sciences de Hongrie* 29, 2–4 (1983): 131–84; Andrew Janos, "The Politics of Backwardness in Continental Europe," *World Politics* 41, no. 2 (April 1989): 325–58; Robert Brenner, "Economic Backwardness in Eastern Europe in Light of Developments in the West," in *The Origins of Backwardness in Eastern Europe: Economics and Politics from the Middle Ages until the Early Twentieth Century*, ed. Daniel Chirot (Berkeley: University of California Press, 1989), 15–52; Perry Anderson, *Lineages of the Absolutist State* (London: New Left Books, 1974); Perry Anderson, *From Antiquity to Feudalism* (London: New Left Books, 1974); Hugh Seton-Watson, *Eastern Europe between the Wars, 1918–1941* (Hamden, Conn.: Archon Books, 1962).

10. Compare, for example, Barrington Moore, *Social Origins of Dictatorship and Democracy: Lord and Peasant in the Making of the Modern World* (Boston: Beacon, 1966) and Timothy Tilton, "The Social Origins of Liberal Democracy: The Swedish Case," *American Political Science Review* 68 (1974): 561–71.

11. Refer to note 9. Also see Brian Downing, *The Military Revolution and Political Change: Origins of Democracy and Autocracy in Early Modern Europe* (Princeton: Princeton University Press, 1992); R. N. Berki, "State and Society: An Antithesis of Modern Political Thought," in *State and Society in Contemporary Europe*, ed. Jack Hayward and R. N. Berki (New York: St. Martin's, 1979), 1–22.

12. Szucs, "The Three Historical Regions," 133.

13. See, for example, Robert Bartlett, *The Making of Europe: Conquest, Colonization, and Cultural Change, 950–1350* (Princeton: Princeton University Press, 1993); William McNeill, *The Rise of the West: A History of the Human Community* (Chicago: University of Chicago Press, 1963); William McNeill, *The Pursuit of Power: Technology, Armed Forces and Society since A.D. 1000* (Chicago: University of Chicago Press, 1982); Eric Hobsbawm, *Nations and Nationalism since 1780* (Cambridge: Cambridge University Press, 1990); Eric Hobsbawm, *Industry and Empire from 1750–Present* (New York: Penguin, 1969); Malia, *Russia through Western Eyes*.

14. On this last observation, see Michael Ignatieff, "On Civil Society," *Foreign Affairs* 74, no. 4 (March/April 1995): 128–36.

15. On the distinction between civil and political society, see Grzegorz Ekiert, "Democratization Processes in East Central Europe: A Theoretical Reconsideration," *British Journal of Political Science* 21, no. 3 (1991): 285–313; Grzegorz Ekiert, *The State against Society: Political Crises and Their Aftermath in East-Central Europe* (Princeton: Princeton University Press, 1996); Bronislaw Geremek, "Civil Society, Then and Now," *Journal of Democracy* 3, no. 2 (April 1992): 28–44; M. Steven Fish, *Democracy from Scratch: Opposition and Regime in the New Russian Revolution* (Princeton: Princeton University Press, 1995).

16. Robert Putnam, *Making Democracy Work: Civic Traditions in Modern Italy* (Princeton: Princeton University Press, 1993).

17. See, for instance, Ernest Gellner, *Conditions of Liberty: Civil Society and Its Rivals* (London: Penguin, 1994); John Keane, ed., *Civil Society and the State: New European Perspectives* (London: Verso, 1988); John Hall, ed., *Civil Society: Theory, History, Comparison* (Cambridge: Polity Press, 1995).

18. Nancy Bermeo, "Civil Society, Good Government and Neo-Liberal Reforms," in *Good Government and the Law*, ed. Julio Faundez (New York: St. Martin's, 1997), 77–90; Sheri Berman, "Civil Society and the Collapse of Weimar Germany," *World Politics* 49, no. 3 (April 1997): 401–29.

19. On civil and political society development in Serbia, see *Nove stranke Srbije: Dokumenti novih politickih stranaka i grupa u Srbiji* (Belgrade: Institut za politicke studije, 1990).

20. See, especially, Moore, *Social Origins*. Also see Anderson, *Lineages*; Brenner, "Economic Backwardness"; Jack Goldstone, *Revolution and Rebellion in Early Modern Europe* (Berkeley: University of California Press, 1991); Gail Stokes, "The Social Origins of Eastern European Politics," in *The Origins of Backwardness*, 210–52.

21. Charles Tilly, ed., *The Formation of National States in Western Europe* (Princeton: Princeton University Press, 1975).

22. See, for instance, Anatole Leroy-Beaulieu, *The Empire of the Tsars and the Russians* (New York: Putnam and Sons, 1898); Martin McCauley and Peter Waldron, *The Emergence of the Modern Russian State, 1855–1881* (New York: Barnes and Noble, 1988); Richard S. Wortman, *The Development of a Russian Legal Consciousness* (Chicago: University of Chicago Press, 1976); George Yaney, "Law, Society, and the Domestic Regime in Russia in Historical Perspective," *American Political Science Review* 59, no. 1 (March 1965): 379–90; Iu. Feofanov, "Demokratiia i pravoi," *Izvestiia*, July 10, 1988, 2.

23. B. H. Sumner, "Peter's Accomplishments and Their Historical Significance," in *Peter the Great Changes Russia*, ed. Mark Raeff (London: Heath, 1972), 188–94.

24. Quoted in Szucs, "The Three Historical Regions," 167.

25. See, especially, Anderson, *Lineages*.

26. On the distinction between state and empires, see, especially, Mark Beissinger, "The Persisting Ambiguity of Empire," *Post-Soviet Affairs* 11, no. 2 (April–June 1995): 149–84; Veljko Vujacic, "Historical Legacies, Nationalist Mobilization, and Political Outcomes in Russia and Serbia: A Weberian View," *Theory and Society* 25, no. 3 (December 1996): 763–801.

27. This is also true for some recent theories of democratization. For a review, see Valerie Bunce, "Should Transitologists Be Grounded?" *Slavic Review* 55, no. 3 (Spring 1995): 111–27.

28. See, in particular, Brenner, "Economic Backwardness."

29. Moore, *Social Origins.*

30. Which the state later elaborated—see Eugen Weber, *Peasants into Frenchmen: The Modernization of Rural France, 1870–1914* (London: Chatto & Windus, 1979).

31. See, for example, Seymour M. Lipset and Stein Rokkan, eds., *Party Systems and Voter Alignments: Cross-National Perspectives* (New York: Free Press, 1976).

32. And, as Dankwart Rustow observed nearly thirty years ago, this made the sustainability of democracy unlikely. See his "Transitions to Democracy: Towards a Dynamic Model," *Comparative Politics* 2, no. 1 (April 1970): 337–63.

33. See, especially, Berki, "State and Society."

34. Interwar Czechoslovak democracy, however, was not without its flaws. See Carol Skalnik Leff, *National Conflict in Czechoslovakia: The Making and Remaking of a State, 1918–1987* (Princeton: Princeton University Press, 1988).

35. See, for example, Seton-Watson, *Eastern Europe.*

36. On the importance of these considerations for all of Europe, see Nancy Bermeo, "Democracy in Europe," *Daedalus* 123 (Spring 1994): 159–78.

37. This is an argument that has also been made in a compelling way for Germany. See Ralf Dahrendorf, *Society and Democracy in Germany* (Garden City, N.Y.: Doubleday, 1967).

38. For elaboration, see Valerie Bunce, "The Empire Strikes Back: The Transformation of the Eastern Bloc from a Soviet Asset to a Soviet Liability," *International Organization* 39, no. 2 (Winter 1985): 1–46.

39. Wlodzimierz Brus, "Stalinism and the People's Democracies," in *Stalinism: Essays in Historical Interpretation*, ed. Robert Tucker (New York: Norton, 1977), 121–51.

40. See Valerie Bunce, *Subversive Institutions: The Design and the Destruction of Socialism and the State* (New York: Cambridge University Press, 1999).

41. For elaboration of these arguments, see Bunce, *Subversive Institutions*; Jan Kubik, *The Power of Symbols against the Symbols of Power: The Rise of Solidarity and the Fall of State Socialism* (University Park: Pennsylvania State University Press, 1994); Ekiert, *State against Society.*

42. Sydney Tarrow, *Power in Movement* (New York: Cambridge University Press, 1994). Also see "Korrenoi vopros perestroiki: Beseda s akademikom T. Zaslavskaya," *Izvestiia*, June 4, 1988, 3.

43. On these constraints, see Vesna Pusic, "Mediteranski model na zalasku autoritarnih drzava," *Erasmus* 20, no. 4 (1997): 2–18. Also see Janina Frentzel-Zagorska, "Civil Society in Poland and Hungary," *Soviet Studies* 42, 4 (1990): 759–78.; Michael Bernhard, "Civil Society after the First Transition: Dilemmas of Postcommunist Democratization in Poland and Beyond," *Communist and Postcommunist Studies* 29, no. 3 (1996): 309–30; Andras Bozoki and Miklos Sukosd, "Civil Society and Populism in the Eastern European Democratic Transitions," *Praxis International* 13, no. 2 (October 1993): 224–41; Sharon Wolchik, "The Repluralization of Politics in Czechoslovakia," *Communist and Postcommunist Studies* 26, no. 2 (December 1993): 412–31.

44. Richard Sakwa, "Subjectivity, Politics and Order in Russian Political Evolution," *Slavic Review* 54, no. 4 (Winter 1995), 950.

45. Bunce, *Subversive Institutions.*

46. Bela Greskovits, *The Political Economy of Protest and Patience* (Budapest: Central European University Press, 1998).

REFERENCES

Anderson, Perry. *From Antiquity to Feudalism*. London: New Left Books, 1974.
————. *Lineages of the Absolutist State*. London: New Left Books, 1974.
Ash, Timothy Garton. "Journey to the Postcommunist East." *New York Review of Books*, June 23, 1994.
Bakic-Hayden. "Nesting Orientalisms: The Case of Former Yugoslavia." *Slavic Review* 54 (Winter 1995): 917–31.
Bartlett, Robert. *The Making of Europe: Conquest, Colonization and Cultural Change, 950–1350*. Princeton: Princeton University Press, 1993.
Bassin, Mark. "Russia between Europe and Asia: The Ideological Construction of Geography." *Slavic Review* 50 (Spring 1991): 1–17.
Berki, R. N. "State and Society: An Antithesis of Modern Political Thought." In *State and Society in Contemporary Europe*, ed. Jack Hayward and R. N. Berki. New York: St. Martin's, 1979, 1–22.
Bermeo, Nancy. "Civil Society, Good Government and Neo-Liberal Reforms." In *Good Government and the Law*, ed. Julio Faundez. New York: St. Martin's Press, 1997, 77–90.
————. "Democracy in Europe." *Daedalus* 123 (Spring 1994): 159–78.
Bernhard, Michael. "Civil Society after the First Transition: Dilemmas of Post-communist Democratization in Poland and Beyond." *Communist and Post-Communist Studies* 29, no. 3 (1996): 309–30.
————. "Civil Society and Democratic Transition in East Central Europe." *Political Science Quarterly* 108 (Summer 1993): 307–26.
Bessinger, Mark. "The Persisting Ambiguity of Empire." *Post-Soviet Affairs* 11 (April–June 1995): 149–84.
Bozoki, Andras, and Miklos Sukosd. "Civil Society and Populism in the Eastern European Democratic Transitions." *Praxis International* 13 (October 1993): 224–41.
Brenner, Robert. "Economic Backwardness in Eastern Europe in Light of Developments in the West." In *The Origins of Backwardness in Eastern Europe: Economics and Politics from the Middle Ages until the Early Twentieth Century*, ed. Daniel Chirot. Berkeley: University of California Press, 1989, 15–52.
Brus, Wlodzimierz. "Stalinism and the Peoples' Democracies." In *Stalinism: Essays in Historical Interpretation*, ed. Robert Tucker. New York: Norton, 1977.
Bunce, Valerie. "Regional Cooperation and European Integration: The Visegrad Group." In *Mitteleuropa: Between Europe and Germany*, ed. Peter Katzenstein. Providence: Berghahn Books, 1998, 240–84.
————. *Subversive Institutions: The Design and the Destruction of Socialism and the State*. Cambridge: Cambridge University Press, 1999.
————. "Should Transitologists Be Grounded?" *Slavic Review* 55 (Spring 1995): 111–27.
————. "Sequencing Economic and Political Reforms." In *East-Central European Economies in Transition*, ed. John Hardt and Richard Kaufman. Washington, D.C.: Joint Economic Committee, U.S. Congress, 1994, 49–63.
————. "Domestic Reform and International Change: The Gorbachev Reforms in Historical Perspective." *International Organization* 47 (Winter 1993): 107–38.
————. "The Empire Strikes Back: The Transformation of Eastern Europe from a Soviet Asset to a Soviet Liability." *International Organization* 39 (Winter 1985): 1–46.
Davies, Norman. *Europe: A History*. Oxford: Oxford University Press, 1996.

Downing, Brian. *The Military Revolution and Political Change: Origins of Democracy and Autocracy in Early Modern Europe.* Princeton: Princeton University Press, 1992.

Ekiert, Grzegorz. *The State against Society: Political Crises and Their Aftermath in East Central Europe.* Princeton: Princeton University Press, 1996.

————. "Democratization Processes in East Central Europe: A Theoretical Reconsideration." *British Journal of Political Science* 21, no. 3 (1991): 285–313.

Feofanov, Iu. "Demokratiia i pravoi." *Izvestiia,* July 10, 1988, 2.

Fish, M. Steven. "The Determinants of Economic Reform in the Postcommunist World," ms., University of California at Berkeley, Department of Political Science, March 1997.

————. "The Predicament of Russian Liberalism: Evidence from the December 1995 Parliamentary Elections." *Europe-Asia Studies* 49, no. 2 (1997): 199–220.

————. *Democracy from Scratch: Opposition and Regime in the New Russian Revolution.* Princeton: Princeton University Press, 1995.

Frentzel-Zagorska, Janina. "Civil Society in Poland and Hungary." *Soviet Studies* 42, no. 4 (1990): 759–78.

Gellner, Ernest. *Conditions of Liberty: Civil Society and Its Rivals.* London: Penguin, 1994.

Geremek, Bronislaw. "Civil Society, Then and Now." *Journal of Democracy* 3, no. 2 (April 1992): 28–44.

Goldstone, Jack. *Revolution and Rebellion in Early Modern Europe.* Berkeley: University of California Press, 1991.

Greskovits, Bela. *The Political Economy of Protest and Patience: Eastern European and Latin American Transformations Compared.* Budapest: Central European University Press, 1997.

Hall, John, ed. *Civil Society, Theory History, Comparison.* Cambridge: Polity Press, 1995.

Hobsbawm, Eric. *Nations and Nationalism since 1780: Program, Myths, Reality.* Cambridge: Cambridge University Press, 1990.

————. *Industry and Empire from 1750–Present.* New York: Penguin, 1969.

Ignatieff, Michael. "On Civil Society." *Foreign Affairs* 74 (March–April 1995): 128–36.

Janos, Andrew. "The Politics of Backwardness in Continental Europe, 1780–1945." *World Politics* 41 (April 1989): 325–58.

Keane, John, ed. *Civil Society and the State: New European Perspectives.* London: Verso, 1988.

"Korrenoi vopros perestroiki: Beseda s akademikom T. Zaslavskoi." *Izvestiia,* June 4, 1988, 3.

Kubik, Jan. *The Power of Symbols against the Symbols of Power: The Rise of Solidarity and the Fall of State Socialism.* University Park: Pennsylvania State University Press, 1994.

Lapidus, Gail. "State and Society: Toward the Emergence of Civil Society in the Soviet Union." In *Politics, Society and Nationality: Inside Gorbachev's Russia,* ed. Seweryn Bialer. Boulder: Westview, 1989, 121–48.

Leroy-Beaulieu, Anatole. *The Empire of the Tsars and the Russians.* New York: G. P. Putnam and Sons, 1898.

Lipset, Seymour Martin, and Stein Rokkan, eds. *Party Systems and Voter Alignments: Cross-National Perspectives.* New York: Free Press, 1976.

McCauley, Martin, and Peter Waldron. *The Emergence of the Modern Russian State, 1855–1881.* New York: Barnes and Noble, 1988.

McNeill, William. *The Pursuit of Power: Technology, Armed Forces and Society since A.D. 1000.* Chicago: University of Chicago Press, 1982.

————. *The Rise of the West: A History of the Human Community.* Chicago: University of Chicago Press, 1963.

Moore, Barrington. *Social Origins of Dictatorship and Democracy: Lord and Peasant in the Making of the Modern World.* Boston: Beacon Press, 1966.

Morawski, Witold. "Economic Change and Civil Society in Poland." In *Democracy and Civil Society in Eastern Europe,* ed. Paul G. Lewis. New York: St. Martin's, 1992, 91–112.

Nove stranke Srbije: Dokumenti novih politickih stranaka i grupa u Srbiji. Belgrade: Institut za politicke studije, 1990.

Pusic, Vesna. "Mediteranski model na zalasku autoritarnih drzava." *Erasmus* 20 (1997): 2–18.

Putnam, Robert. *Making Democracy Work: Civic Traditions in Modern Italy.* Princeton: Princeton University Press, 1993.

Rustow, Danwart. "Transitions to Democracy: Towards a Dynamic Model." *Comparative Politics* 2 (April 1970): 337–63.

Sakwa, Richard, 1995. "Subjectivity, Politics and Order in Russian Political Evolution." *Slavic Review* 54, no. 4 (Winter 1995): 950.

Seton-Watson, Hugh. *Eastern Europe between the Wars, 1918–1941.* Hamden, Conn.: Archon Books, 1962.

Stokes, Gale. "The Social Origins of Eastern European Politics." In *The Origins of Backwardness in Eastern Europe,* ed. Daniel Chirot. Berkeley: University of California Press, 1989.

Sumner, B. H. "Peter's Accomplishments and Their Historical Significance." In *Peter the Great Changes Russia,* ed. Marc Raeff. London: D. C. Heath, 1972, 188–94.

Szucs, Jeno. "The Three Historical Regions of Europe: An Outline." *Acta Historica: Revue de L'academie des Sciences de Hongrie* 29, nos. 2–4 (1983): 131–84.

Tarrow, Sidney. *Power in Movement.* Cambridge: Cambridge University Press, 1994.

Tilly, Charles, ed. *The Formation of National States in Western Europe.* Princeton: Princeton University Press, 1975.

Todorova, Maria. "The Balkans: From Discovery to Invention." *Slavic Review* 53 (Summer 1994): 453–82.

Vujacic, Veljko. "Historical Legacies, Nationalist Mobilization and Political Outcomes in Russia and Serbia: A Weberian View." *Theory and Society* 25 (December 1996): 763–801.

Weber, Eugen. *Peasants into Frenchmen: The Modernization of Rural France, 1870–1914.* London: Chatto & Windus, 1979.

Wolchik, Sharon. "The Repluralization of Politics in Czechoslovakia." *Communist and Postcommunist Studies* 26 (December 1993): 412–31.

Wolff, Larry. "The Idea of Eastern Europe." *Slavic Review* 54 (Winter 1995): 932–42.

————. *Inventing Eastern Europe: The Map of Civilization on the Mind of the Enlightenment.* Stanford: Stanford University Press, 1993.

Wortman, Richard S. *The Development of a Russian Legal Consciousness.* Chicago: University of Chicago Press, 1976.

Yaney, George. "Law, Society and the Domestic Regime in Russia in Historical Perspective." *American Political Science Review* 59 (March 1965): 379–90.

11

CIVIL SOCIETY AFTER DEMOCRACY: SOME CONCLUSIONS

Nancy Bermeo

Centuries, like sages, leave wisdom for those who follow, and the nineteenth century has left valuable lessons for those who study more contemporary times. This is especially true for those of us who puzzle about the relationship between associational life and political democracy for, despite striking changes in scenery and staging, the political dramas of the nineteenth and twentieth centuries share important similarities in both characterization and plotline.

Their most obvious similarity is their swift expansionary dynamic. Despite differences in class composition, *zeitgeist*, and state context, the rapidly expanding and ideologically varied nature of civil societies in nineteenth-century Europe parallels today's awakening civil societies in important ways. In both periods, new forms of associational life emerged and entered highly competitive battles for popular support. Sometimes, these new associations were champions of expanding freedoms. Sometimes they served the interests of freedom unwittingly. Often they were formed to restrict whatever freedoms existed and thus to promote intolerance. In all the national dramas, however, the political coloration of the organizations that gained ascendancy helped determine which nations would consolidate political democracy and which would not.

Contemporary social scientists sometimes overlook the heterogeneity of civic life. Robert Putnam's seminal work on social capital has caused many scholars to emphasize the strength rather than the composition of civil society and to assume a positive association between strong civil societies and sustainable democracies. Yet, the general faith in the power of civil society to effect

237

democratic change and sustain democratic regimes may be misplaced if the historical diversity of civil society is overlooked.

Debates about the consolidation of new, more open regimes loom large in public discussions as the twenty-first century begins, and whether the focus is on Eastern Europe, Latin America, Asia, or Africa, the probabilities of consolidation are increasingly linked to the strength of civil society. The ongoing nature of the cases that political scientists use for theorizing today gives their work a vitality and practical importance that should not be undervalued, but the fact that these cases are still unfolding makes the conclusions we can draw from them especially tentative. The advantage of studying the nineteenth century is that it is no longer a work in progress. At least one act in the drama of civil society's emergence has run its course. We can identify losers, winners, and also-rans and construct explanatory theory by working backward. Our understanding of which sorts of groups will gain ascendancy in emerging civil societies today will be better informed if we understand how the battles for position and ascendancy were waged in the past.

Our concern with analyzing the dynamic of ascendancy and defeat structured this collection of essays. It led us to compare four nations where the nineteenth-century dramas ended fairly happily with four nations where the dramas ended tragically instead. Despite intense conflict and complexity, associational life in Great Britain, France, Belgium, and the Netherlands eventually took on a democratic hue and grew, in the twentieth century, to complement lasting electoral democracies. In Russia, Italy, Portugal, and Germany, the associations that might have been the foundation of lasting liberalization and enduring democracy lost the battle for ascendancy with deadly results. Contrasting these two sets of cases enables us to begin some answers to the very difficult question of how a pro-democratic civil society comes into being. I present the beginning of these answers below—starting with an overview of what we can learn from looking backward and then moving on to a speculative discussion of what the lessons of the nineteenth century might mean for democracies today. The sweep of the argument is deliberately broad but still confined primarily to third wave democracies in Latin America and Eastern Europe.

Before I begin, I must clarify my terms. "Civil society," for me, is a shorthand term for the vast network of associational life that lies between the individual political actor and the state. Though other scholars, including other authors in this book, may use the "civil society" to connote a particularly laudable set of associations, I use the term in a neutral sense. The associations in civil society can be good or evil or something else. A pro-democratic civil society is one in which groups promoting intolerance are outnumbered and overpowered by groups of other sorts. In antidemocratic civil societies, groups promoting intolerance become hegemonic. Since societies do not fit unproblematically into dyadic categories of any sort, I follow Philip Nord's lead and use language that conveys a sense of spectrum. Some societies take on a more democratic hue than others. What sorts of factors affect the coloration of civil society?

LESSONS FROM LOOKING BACKWARD

Some New Light on Old Assumptions

Several of the most important lessons brought to light by historical comparison are about explanations for the coloration of civil society that we should reject. Neither the density of associational life, the timing and extension of voting rights, the level of urbanization, nor the extension of education seem to affect the nature of civil society in the positive ways we might expect.

The idea that a dense organizational landscape is more likely to be a democratic one appears highly questionable. Admittedly, Russian civil society was largely a dream (as Englestein describes it), and Portuguese civil society thrived only in urban areas but, all told, our negative and positive cases do not seem to differ much on the density dimension. On the contrary, both Banti and Lyttelton illustrate the "considerable associative density" of Italy [1] and the "broad spectrum" of organizational life among Italy's middle classes.[2] Germany's civil society was also very densely organized. Indeed, Germany had one of the most densely organized societies in Europe. But this did not prevent the eventual rise of the Nazi party.[3] Nor did the rich associational life in Italy's north prevent the rise of fascism. Ironically, the fascists gained ground fastest in precisely those regions where civil society was best developed.

Variations in voting rights, like variations in organizational density, are also surprisingly poor predictors of civil society's coloration. Franchise laws varied as much within our sets of cases as between them. France adopted universal male suffrage relatively early (in 1848), but suffrage laws in Great Britain, Belgium, and the Netherlands were remarkably restrictive. The 1832 voting reform act in Great Britain enabled only 2.7 percent of the population to vote, and as late as 1886, only 12.1 percent of the population had the franchise.[4] In the Netherlands, means tests kept the male franchise to 2.5 percent in 1850, 6 percent in 1887, and only 12 percent at the century's end. In Belgium, the picture was equally bleak. Only 1.8 percent of the population was eligible to vote as late as 1847,[5] and the most progressive extension of the franchise (in 1893) left a long-standing system of discriminatory voting intact whereby people with a certain amount of property, a certain level of education, or certain professions could cast as many as three votes instead of one.

A look at franchise history in our other, more negative set of cases leads to other surprises. The movement for a democratic franchise in Russia was stillborn, and Italy had enfranchised only 9.4 percent of its population by the 1890s; but Germany had universal manhood suffrage as early as 1871, and Portugal had enfranchised over 70 percent of the male population by 1878.[6] These four cases are obviously very different from one another, but seen in comparative perspective they highlight the same lesson. Voting rights—in themselves—have very little to do with the creation of a democratic civil society or with the longevity of democracy itself.

Density and the extension of the suffrage are not the only seductive explanations that prove disappointing on closer examination. There is probably no single structural or contextual quality that seems to distinguish our cases of success and failure in an unambiguous way. Linear variables (and linear thinking) lead us only into a tangle of new and knotty questions. One might assume for example, that the democratic elements of civil society would be more likely to gain hegemony in states with higher levels of urbanization and education, but neither of these hunches proves helpful. The contrasts between Great Britain and Russia are dramatic along these and a whole host of other structural dimensions (as Valerie Bunce makes clear), but if we look at all the nations in the success and failure categories, the contrast withers away. Great Britain, France, the Netherlands, and Belgium were not more urbanized than their less fortunate counterparts. Nor were their populations better educated.

In 1850 for example, Portugal was nearly as urbanized as the Netherlands and (by some measures) even more urbanized than Belgium or France.[7] In 1870, Germany and Italy were only 1 percentage point behind France in their proportions of population living in towns with over ten thousand inhabitants.[8] By 1890, Germany was far more urbanized than either state with a full 43 percent of its population in cities of over one hundred thousand inhabitants.[9] Highlighting the variations in urbanization across Europe does not undercut the idea that urban life enhances the *growth* of civic life. Virtually all of our essayists drew this conclusion—but the patterns of variation show quite clearly that urbanization does not produce any particular *kind* of civil society. Proximity lowers the cost of starting and maintaining associations, but it has no constant effect on what associations will actually do.

The same conclusion holds for education. High rates of literacy, widely accessible primary and secondary schools, and extensive university communities might increase the likelihood that democratic forces will dominate civil society, but this outcome is far from guaranteed. In fact, the case of Great Britain illustrates how a civil society supportive of political democracy can emerge despite a relatively weak commitment to popular education. English elites were not among Europe's leaders in the push for literacy.[10] Approximately one-third of the population in England was illiterate as late as 1850,[11] and there was no universal system of public education until the twentieth century.[12] The German case presents a very different picture. The states that would eventually unite and become Germany made six to seven years of schooling mandatory in the late eighteenth century.[13] By the middle of the nineteenth century, the German states had one of the highest literacy rates in Europe with nearly 75 percent of the adult population able to read and write.[14]

In the realm of secondary and university education, we see a similar pattern. Educational access was not more restrictive in the states in which democratic forces eventually lost the battle for hegemony. At least one comparative history reports that some of these states were even less restrictive. In Prussia, for example, the ratio of population to pupil in the 1860s was 249:1, while in France it was 570:1. In Italy, the ratio was 1,058:1, while in England it was 1,300:1.[15] A second source puts the Italian system in an even more favorable light, arguing that the percentage of the Italian population attending secondary schools in the late 1870s was greater than that of Great Britain, Germany, or France. The same source argues that the Italian system was so open that in the early twentieth century fees were charged to discourage the poor.[16]

University access was notoriously restricted in Great Britain at midcentury. In the 1860s only 1 in 5,800 got any university education in England and Wales. The comparable figures for Italy and Germany are 1 in 2,200 and 1 in 2,600 respectively.[17] On this score, even Russia may have temporarily outpaced the countries that would eventually become democracies. Pamela Pilbeam writes that in the early 1800s the Russian university system was "more democratic in intake than . . . any modern state," that anyone who passed one of two exams was free to enter, and that the Russian state was "the most generous in Europe in scholarship provision."[18] The state reversed these progressive policies by the end of the century—but the fact that they existed at all shows just how complex the relationship between the provision of education and the creation of a democratic civil society actually is.

Looking backward at the nineteenth century helps us refine our thinking about the negative as well as the positive correlates of the democratic civil society. A review of the nineteenth century makes us question, for example, if the failure of democratic associational life can be attributed to the machinations of an autonomous and powerful aristocracy. Engelstein reminds us that the Russian aristocracy had little autonomy from the Czarist state and Costa Pinto and Tavares de Almeida point out that Portugal's aristocracy waned in influence long before the republic failed.[19]

Casting the Catholic Church—or Catholicism—in a universally villainous role seems unwarranted too. Leaders of the Catholic communities in Belgium and the Netherlands took on a centrist hue in the nineteenth century, and though they shunned alliances with groups that were openly anticlerical, they proved willing to align with a broad range of democratic forces that were not. The church "played a cooperative though subordinate role in the building of the new liberal state" in Portugal,[20] and in Italy, the Catholic movement "had an extremely heterogeneous character" including "real reactionaries," "courageous trade-unionists who fought against landowners in the name of the Gospel," and "many intermediate groups in between."[21]

The discussion of religious identity brings us naturally to a discussion of the explanatory weight of social heterogeneity. The common wisdom holds that democratic civic life is more likely to thrive in homogenous societies and that serious and overlapping ethnic divisions will hamper the forces of consensus and civility. Yet, Thomas Ertman's essay on Belgium and the Netherlands shows us how democratic forces can become hegemonic in civil societies that are sharply divided by religion and language. Likewise, Robert Morris draws our attention to the deadly ethnic and national conflicts that accompanied the growth of a democratic civil society in the United Kingdom.[22]

The chapters on Portugal and Italy lead us in the same direction—though from opposite starting points. In looking at Catholic Italy, Banti points out how a "common religious identity" might have been a source of "particular strength" but was instead "the cause of a deep split in opinion."[23] Italy became an "extremely fragmented civil society,"[24] and a shared religious identity seems to have exacerbated rather than ameliorated its divisions. These historical cases illustrate that both heterogeneity and homogeneity are contextually defined and that only local constructions determine their effects.

What Costa Pinto and Tavares de Almeida argue for Portugal appears true of all our cases. The contours, potential, and limits of civil society are shaped in each country by "*conflicting* trends."[25] Associations usually fight their battles for support in the face of strong social and economic crosswinds. The environmental factors that might enhance the growth of democratic associational life emerge willy-nilly and not in a linear way. What are these factors? What does explain the difference between the sets of civil societies we have examined here?

Some Alternative Explanations

As Philip Nord points out in the introduction to this volume, the key differences between our sets of cases may lie in the relationship between individual associations and the state. At least two aspects of this relationship have special relevance for contemporary times. The first concerns the state as a coercive agency. The second concerns the state as a legitimated maker of laws.

LEGAL SANCTIONS VERSUS TOLERANCE

A state's coercive agencies (its police, armed forces, and judiciary) can relate to any given voluntary association in one of three ways. It can provide legal sanction; it can attempt to repress the association outright; or it can simply tolerate the group, ignoring the letter of the law. The histories recorded here, including Jan Kubik's work on Poland, point to some surprising ironies about the implications of these three options.

Legal sanction was a blessing for associational life in all our cases but a mixed one in most. There is little doubt that state sanctions (plus state funds and officials) contributed to the growth of civil society across nineteenth-century Europe. State support proved essential, for example, in Russia, where the "dream" of civil society took hold only after the state's Great Reforms in 1861;[26] in Italy, where "the conditions for the growth of a true civil society" often had to be created by deliberate state action;[27] and in Portugal, where associational life in rural areas was "largely state induced."[28]

Yet, in these and all our other cases, state legal sanctions often meant state control. Once state officials got involved in sanctioning any associations, they were faced with the task of deciding what organizations should and should not do. The French state was especially astute in recognizing the multifaceted nature of associational life. As Raymond Huard explains, state authorities in France recognized that the "majority of French associations . . . performed *various* functions." As a consequence, they "sought control of *all* of the societies they sanctioned."[29] Just as the terrain between legality and subordination proved to be a slippery slope, the desire to control associational life led easily to outright repression. But this option brought its own surprises. Open coercion certainly had stultifying effects, but throughout nineteenth-century Europe, people were remarkably courageous in defying the repression around them and in making surprisingly creative use of whatever public spaces repression left vacant. Whether as dissidents in the dockets of Czarist courtrooms, as exiles in the Piedmont after 1848, or as Freemasons in France and the Low Countries, citizens petitioning for greater freedoms spoke from whatever platform they were allowed. When these actors were repressed outright and taken out of public space, their martyrdom often inspired more, rather than less, dissent—especially as the century wore on. Fissures within the ruling elite often opened up just as pressures from below intensified, for a state's willingness to coerce only selectively often undermined the coalitions on which it rested. This pattern of response—so frequent in nineteenth-century Europe—repeated itself in Poland in the 1980s as Jan Kubik's essay makes clear.[30]

Looking over all our cases, Philip Nord concludes that formal, legal guarantees played a surprisingly small role in the expansion of civil society.[31] The surprises and ironies outlined above suggest why. What seemed to be more important than de jure legality in all the stories told here was de facto toleration. Pro-democratic groups emerged from legal landscapes that were both remarkably diverse and constantly changing. Yet these groups survived and grew only where they were tolerated—in the legal realm in some cases, in the semilegal realm in others, and outside the legal realm in still others. What mattered was not whether a group's activities were sanctioned by the state but whether the state's forces of coercion actually tolerated the numerous things that the group did. In an ideal setting, this state toleration might come from strongly democratic elite convictions—but elite divisions, elite ignorance, and elite weakness can serve as wellsprings of state toleration too. Kubik's essay on Poland illustrates precisely this.

CONSTITUTIONS VERSUS CONNECTEDNESS

The constitutional structures of the states in which associations operated were important components of their environments. If associations demanding the expansion of freedom emerged where there was already a formally functioning parliament, they were at a decided advantage. But, as these chapters remind us, a functioning and sovereign parliament was no guarantee that groups supportive of democracy would gain hegemony. What was most important was not the formal existence of a working parliament but parliament's ability *to connect* with civil society.[32] This sense of connectedness, defined as the internalized link between the citizenry and the formal arenas of representation, was decisive in determining whether groups would be supportive of democracy or not. The greater the mass of groups that felt disconnected from allegedly "representative" institutions, the weaker the foundations of representative government itself.

Class divisions made the creation of connectedness especially problematic. These divisions were profound in all our cases and therefore do not provide a simple means of sorting cases of success and failure. But the extent to which parliamentary government was constructed as being "captured" by one class or another marked the boundaries around who was likely to feel connected and who was not. Whether strong or weak, the sense of connectedness was forged from two related elements: the political parties that were supposed to link citizens to representative institutions and the public policies that emanated from the representative institutions themselves.

The case studies collected here are filled with leads on how a sense of connectedness might be hindered or helped. The experiences of Germany, Italy, Portugal, and Russia set the hindrances in relief. In Portugal, connections and loyalties to parliament were hindered by the "undifferentiated parties and programs" that emerged from "a relatively closed social structure."[33] The closed nature of social structures had a negative effect in eastern Europe and Russia as well. As both Bunce and Englestein illustrate, the vast cultural differences between those who were politically active in urban areas and those who labored in the subsistence economies of the countryside made the construction of viable connections between political society and society as a whole extremely unlikely. The fact that so many of the movements to create parliamentary institutions in Russia were of non-Russian inspiration made it easy for opponents to use nationalist discourse to argue against them.[34] Those who dreamed of a civil society in Russia used the civil societies of Paris and other European capitals as their models and quite predictably closed their eyes to Russia's peasant majority. Ironically, even those whose vision of civil society included country folk found their messages lost across a cultural divide—peasants did not connect with the urban forces that sought their mobilization.[35]

Even in parts of eastern Europe where the urban–rural divides may have been more narrow, "parliaments and parties" were still "detached from the social structures" at the base of each society. When political parties did link up with social groups "they tended to exaggerate the tensions" that divided them in the first place. If Portugal's political society suffered at one point from too much homogeneity, east European political society suffered from too little. As Bunce puts it, "the cluttered nineteenth-century political spectrum . . . undercut the development and the power of civil society . . . produced an extraordinary range of political movements and parties," and "favored the polarization and paralysis of politics"[36] The possibility of developing a sense of connectedness to a paralyzed parliament was close to nil, and predictably, malfunctioning parliaments plagued virtually all the states in which civil society failed to take on a democratic hue.

Establishing a sense of connectedness to a parliament that was the product of debased voting was similarly unlikely. Where the struggle to extend the franchise yielded only the ability to participate in fixed elections (as was often the case in Italy)—or to elect leaders to representative assemblies that were rendered powerless by an overly strong executive (as was the case in Germany until the Weimar Republic) the meaning of voting and of the electoral process was debased. Even if parliamentary elections and institutions actually managed to become more representative over time, the legacies of cynicism that a history of debased voting leaves behind continued to hamper connectedness.

What prevented the expansion of associations that might have strengthened this sense of connectedness? Part of the answer seems to derive from what Lyttelton describes as "the asymmetry between local and national politics." If there was a broad disjuncture between political life at the local level and political life at the national level, citizens faced a dilemma regarding which institutions represented them best. Laboring under what Lyttelton aptly calls "the illusion of self-sufficiency" local elites often undercut the legitimacy of national (and at least potentially democratic) parliamentary institutions by arguing that local governments had "organic links to civil society while the national parliament did not."[37] The "tendency to criticize parliament as poorly representative of civil society" afflicted local elites on both the Left and the Right.

The effects of this criticism were doubly pernicious. On the one hand, and most obviously, it eroded connectedness. But it also increased the likelihood that parliament would actually *be* dysfunctional by feeding whatever polarities and whatever antidemocratic forces the national parliament contained. Local elites would tolerate or even mobilize collective actions that were "unlawful" in the eyes of the national government; parliamentarians of the opposite camp would point to these actions as evidence of the local elite's lawlessness and disloyalty; parliamentarians of the local's camp would be put on the defensive; and strident debates about law and order would crowd out the task of lawmaking itself. Thus the fissures that were early on only dangerously wide at the local level, eventually expanded upward through the hierarchy of political institutions and cracked the structures at the top. The effects of this asymmetry were undoubtedly magnified by a second set of hindering factors. These related to nationalist sentiments. Nationalist sentiments were a serious barrier to a sense of connectedness wherever parties or associations succeeded in arguing that local governments, or national parliamentarians, were somehow dominated by "foreign" forces. The legacies of military defeat or relative weakness enabled antidemocratic forces to play the sovereignty card to great advantage. The "patriots" game was played with tragic consequences in Italy, Germany, and Russia, but in the lesser-known case of Portugal, we see that nationalist sentiment undercut the credibility of parliament too. Capitulation with the British Ultimatum of 1890 provoked a broad and disruptive "civic mass movement" against the country's liberal rulers at a critical time in Portugal's political development.[38]

The image of parliamentary institutions as "foreign" and even "traitorous" had to be disseminated, of course, and for this, antidemocratic forces needed access to the media. If antidemocratic groups succeeded in muting the media voices of parliament's defenders, through the use of law, intimidation, or physical coercion, a third, very serious hindrance to connectedness came into play. It is not coincidental that all of our positive cases have a longer and stronger history of press diversity than their opposites. Great Britain was the first state in all of Europe "to have a free and responsible press."[39] France, despite sporadic censorship, had a press that "was as varied as the British."[40] Belgium had twenty-three years of "free press" even before 1847, and the Netherlands, despite its small population, was producing over three hundred different newspapers, magazines, and journals by midcentury.[41]

In Russia, Italy, Portugal, and Germany, access to the media for the defenders of parliament proved much more problematic. Where state censorship and coercion were absent, access to funding for newspapers was key. If the local–national asymmetries discussed above resulted in assaults on property, those who feared further assaults could easily be convinced that funding the antidemocratic media was in their interests. Thus, the factors that hindered the development of a sense of connectedness to national parliaments were closely connected to one another. If local–national asymmetries combined with nationalist and militarist struggles in a setting where access to the media was still contested, the chances for creating a sense of connectedness and for promoting the democratization of civil society were minimal.

CIVIL SOCIETY IN TODAY'S NEW DEMOCRACIES

Relating the lessons of the nineteenth century to the democracies of contemporary times yields a mixture of consolation and concern. It is consoling that democracy, as a system of rule, has no truly popular competitor today. In the nineteenth century, monarchical power sanctioned by divine authority provided a powerful alternative. In the twentieth century, communism and fascism provided alternatives for millions in Europe and elsewhere. Today, these visions of how power relations should be organized and legitimated are no longer in vogue. The United States, precisely because it is less threatened by communism, seems more willing to assist weak democracies. Each of these factors works to the advantage of democracy, as does the fact that the legal barriers to free association in third wave democracies are lower now than ever before. Our current, more internationalized civil society includes an extensive network of human rights groups and professional associations that promote the legal guarantees of associational freedom with great effect. The nineteenth century teaches us, however, that legality sometimes leads to control, and it is not coincidental that debates about the autonomy of formally "private" organizations flare up with frequency in a wide range of states.[42]

More important than the ambiguities of legality are the distinctions between legality and toleration. It is toleration that the democratic civil society requires, and our new democracies are, alas, much less tolerant than their constitutions and legal codes would lead us to believe. The problem is partially rooted in the coercive agencies of the new democracies themselves. The elections that mark a transition to democracy have direct effects on the composition of governments, but they usually have very little effect on the composition of the police and military. Continuities in personnel and practice dilute the impact of new laws. Even when reformists within coercive agencies seek to enforce the rule of law, they often lack the required resources: Years of dictatorship leave behind judicial systems that are often too weak to prosecute those who infringe on the associational rights of others and, more often than not, the police lack either the will or the resources to find and arrest the actively intolerant in the first place. In a broad range of third wave democracies, police find themselves outmanned and overpowered by armed gangs. Far too many new democracies find themselves unable to "monopolize" the use of coercion and therefore unable to enforce the rule of law.[43]

The inability to guarantee toleration is closely related to a troubling inability to guarantee the free use of the media. Official press censorship is probably at an historic low as the century draws to a close, but we should be concerned that the intimidation and murder of journalists has become its replacement. In Russia, the murder of investigative reporters has reached epidemic proportions. Murders and beatings of media personnel plague a variety of other states ranging from the Philippines to Mexico to the Ukraine.[44] States with elected governments are less likely to criminalize media dissent, but they seem unable (or unwilling) to protect dissenters from the most grievous forms of intimidation. To the extent that the problem is related to material resources, the austerity budgets that are now nearly ubiquitous will make the problem worse. If Russian dissident Vladimir Buckovsky was right in believing that "a free press is more important than free elections" we would do well to recognize that press freedom is not synonymous with the absence of state censorship.[45]

Press freedom is synonymous with the privatization of the media, for some, but here too the lessons of the nineteenth century give us cause for concern. The privatization of radio and television that has accompanied so many third wave democratizations has the great advantage of ensuring that state elites will not monopolize the flow of public information, but its disadvantage is in giving privileged access to the already monied. Television networks control today's most valuable political currency, but access to their use is often restricted by single individuals in charge of media conglomerates. The effects of this uneven access are already making people question the legitimacy of the electoral process in a variety of states.[46]

As we deliberate about communications policy in the future, we should recall that what hindered the growth of democratic civil societies in the nineteenth century was not state control of the media but control by actors who were fearful of the implications of democracy. Whether the media act as a hindrance or a help to the growth of democratic civil societies in the future depends, to an unsettling degree, on the political ideologies of the individuals who control them in marketized economies.

Global communications groups may help to counterbalance the weight of antidemocratic national media, just as global civic associations may help to protect freedom of association and a free press. These elements of our internationalized civil society have their counterparts, however, in an internationalized economy and in a related set of international agencies that may affect the growth of democratic civil society in less salutary ways. The history of nineteenth-century Europe suggests that elected governments with questionable sovereignty are a poor base for the development of connectedness and easy prey for nationalists of all sorts. Unfortunately, the sovereignty of many third wave democracies is being questioned in a variety of ways as the new century begins.

The current sovereignty problem is rooted in the etiology of the regimes themselves. Most third wave democracies emerged on the swells of economic crises. This meant that newly elected leaders were forced to redirect their often frail ships of state on the high seas of oil shocks and international debt crises. More often than not, newly elected leaders turned to international lending agencies for support—not just for the resources to keep their states afloat but for fundamental navigational advice.[47] The coincidence of intense economic crisis and new electoral freedoms produced severe crowding on the captain's bridge—for it meant that powerful international actors were invited to take a role in decision making just as hordes of citizens expected a meaningful role in shaping the direction of their new democracy after years of authoritarian exclusion. Wherever the crowding problem was resolved by strengthening executive power and weakening the restraints exercised by the elected legislature, questions of sovereignty were raised.[48] The fact that international actors played a very public role in policy making through structural adjustment programs, and the fact that so many of the nationals connected with the implementation of these programs were, in fact, foreign-trained, gave fuel to those who questioned the sovereignty of new democracy's top leadership.

The challenge of developing a sense of connectedness with elected legislatures is greatly increased by the sense that executive policymakers are as likely to be responsive to international lending agencies as to the mandates of their own electorates. This sense emerges when candidates for presidential office campaign with promises to slow the advance of market-oriented reforms and then embrace market reforms anyway, as soon as they gain office. These spectacular policy reversals have occurred in a wide range of countries in both Europe and Latin America. For many, these policy reversals have debased the meaning of the electoral process and contributed to a profound skepticism about the nature of party politics and of politicians more generally.[49] This skepticism has deep historical roots in many if not most third wave systems. (After all, these states are "new" rather than "old" democracies precisely because party politics have been so problematic in the past.) Yet, there is much evidence to suggest that political parties are weaker now than ever before.[50]

It is ironic and troubling that weakened party systems and strengthened executives have diminished the role of legislatures at precisely the time when a record number of people have the right to vote. Given what the nineteenth century shows us regarding the dangers of debased voting, this is a cause for real concern. If the freedom to vote and to express one's opinions at the polls were adequate measures of representation we might conclude that representation has never been so widespread. Yet hoards of people do not feel represented in contemporary democracies. Even in places like Guatemala, where the costs of democratization have been horrific, abstention rates are at an all-time high.

Though the chances of linking citizens to parties seem weak, the chances of linking citizens to one another through associations are less so. Trade unions have been hurt by deindustrialization, and other civic groups born of dictatorship are being forced to disband or recraft themselves; but overall, the opportunity to create associational life has probably never been so widespread. The formal commitment to freedom of association is only the first of four factors explaining why. Global communication technology is the second. Television makes it easier for citizens to be inspired by the successes and the failures of organizations in other regions and to model their own associational life accordingly.[51] The Internet enables people to communicate faster, farther, and less expensively than ever in history. From China to Chiapas dissidents have sought sympathy and support on the Internet with great success. Cyberspace provides unprecedented political space and political resources for associational life in new democracies and nondemocracies alike.[52]

A third and related set of changes contributing to growth opportunities comes from international agencies and associations in the older democracies of the advanced industrial societies. Although civil society was already partially internationalized in the nineteenth century, unprecedented amounts of human and material resources are being dedicated to developing associational life in regions with weak associational life today.[53] The Commission on Global Governance (CGG) reports that there were some twenty-nine thousand international nongovernmental organizations (NGOs) registered in the Organization for Economic Cooperation and Development (OECD) countries in 1993. Though it would be difficult to quantify the amount of resources all these groups dedicate to promoting associational life in the less advanced states, estimates of such funding coming from official government agencies run from between $5.7 and 8.7 billion U.S. dollars.

The worldwide celebration of civil society is a predictable by-product of the widespread disenchantment with the state and the consequent embrace of marketization. Marketization offers a fourth and very powerful set of incentives to further associational development. The incentives are both positive and negative. On the positive side, the state's retraction from the tasks of production, pricing, sales, and distribution decentralizes material and human resources and thus, in theory at least, makes key requisites for associational life more widely accessible.[54] To the extent that marketization actually creates wealth, its benefits go beyond the decentralization of existing resources and to the expansion of the resource base itself.[55]

The negative incentives that marketization offers for the development of civic life are less widely discussed but at least as powerful. The nineteenth-century experience illustrates that negative incentives were the origin of much associational life. Civil society everywhere was rooted in fears and conflicts. Landowners were mobilized by threats from mobilized workers. Catholics were mobilized by threats from socialists. Protestants were mobilized by threats from Catholics. Threats, insecurities, and the voids left by collapsed institutions are still powerful incentives for civic organization today, and the process of marketization has exacerbated all of these.[56]

If the density of associational life were key to democratization, we might find consolation in the patterns of expansion described above, but we know from the nineteenth-century experience that a dense organizational landscape is not in itself a sign that civil society is becoming more democratic. We also know that today's political landscapes lack many of the qualities that made the growth of democratic civil societies possible in nineteenth-century Europe. Co-

ercive agencies in many third wave democracies lack either the will or the capacity to guarantee the toleration of diversity. Important, pro-democratic constituencies are blocked from truly free access to the most influential media by
current patterns of ownership and extraordinary costs. The sovereignty and representative qualities of newly democratic legislatures are increasingly questioned
as foreign actors and foreign models play more salient roles in economic policy
making. Finally, political parties, a key means for connecting civic associations
to the democratic state, are growing weaker and less legitimate.

CONCLUSION

Does this long litany of problems mean that many of the civil societies in third
wave states are destined to be dominated by antidemocratic groups? This is an
extremely difficult question, not simply because political scientists are very poor
at prognosis but because the answer depends to a large degree on how one defines (and recognizes) an antidemocratic group. Associations play such a multitude of roles that fitting any single group into one of two dichotomous categories is necessarily distorting.[57] If we confine our definition to the least
ambiguous cases, that is, to associations that are openly hostile to the democratic
order and to the tolerance embodied in the term "polyarchy," the bleakest outcome is certainly possible but not inevitable.

That it is not inevitable is illustrated by the histories of the third wave
democracies thus far. Antidemocratic groups have made inroads on the organizational terrain of many of these regimes, but they have succeeded in gaining
broad national followings in only a few. The instances in which antidemocratic
groups have actually *toppled* a third wave democracy and succeeded in dominating civil society are even more rare. Overall, third wave democracies have
been remarkably durable. The few that have collapsed did so at the hands of
their own militaries (as in Thailand) or their own executives (as in Peru). With
a few exceptions in the newly independent states of the postcommunist world,
the advance of antidemocratic groups and associations in Europe and Latin
America has been confined to certain regions within certain states. National
popularity and national governmental control have proved illusive.

What explains why overtly antidemocratic groups have not made more
headway? Four factors seem especially influential. First, there are currently no
ideological equivalents to fascism or communism that might serve to legitimate
mass mobilization or dictatorship. Religion and ethnicity sometimes serve the
same mobilizing role (with the same dictatorial outcome) but being based on
cultural identity and not ideas, they are bounded in a sense that fascism and communism were not. Second, rising consumerism (and its resulting atomization)
distracts many citizens from political associations of any sort. The political dis-
engagement of the young is bemoaned in a wide variety of new democracies.[58]

Third and relatedly, a new sort of deference has emerged to legitimate exclusionary forms of policy making. In centuries past, sectors of society rationalized their exclusion from political decision making with the argument that aristocrats were "born to rule." Today, deference is given instead to technocrats and to those "educated to rule."[59]

Deference to technocrats is related to what have been constructed as technocratic policy achievements. These are a fourth set of factors that work to the advantage of the status quo. The nineteenth-century experience showed us that associations could be "connected" to democratic institutions through *policies* as well as political parties. It is in specific realms of policy making that many otherwise deficient third wave democracies have found their salvation. The negative effects of breaking campaign promises, of concentrating economic policy making power in the executive, and of being openly solicitous of foreign agents and agencies have been partially counterbalanced in some countries by dramatic drops in inflation and impressive (though uneven) economic growth. Putting an end to hyperinflation has served to bolster both the legitimacy of certain political leaders and the liberal economic model itself. Restoring economic growth and stimulating investment have helped to do the same.[60] Even when the payoffs of market reforms are not immediately obvious, the fact that the model is seen to have worked elsewhere helps to sustain credibility.

What might tip the balance in favor of antidemocratic groups? The main source of potential disequilibrium comes from the coincidence of democratization and marketization. The latter is generally not as popular as the former.[61] To the extent that market reforms deepen and cause more dramatic disruptions in peoples' daily lives, antisystem associations of all sorts may be advantaged in their competition for popular support. Privatization, austerity budgeting, and decentralization are the reform areas that have the greatest potential for disruption.

The contemporary drives to privatize and cut government spending are closely associated with dramatically rising levels of unemployment. As states privatize more of their services and cut back the number of people employed in government agencies, politicians get directly implicated in rising levels of joblessness. As states privatize industries, and industrial plants either downsize or shut down altogether, elected politicians get blamed as well.[62] Though economic growth rates have improved in many third wave democracies, the ranks of the unemployed far exceed the number of jobs created. To make matters worse, the jobs that are created are often in the skilled service sector. Unskilled industrial workers have little hope of being rehired.[63]

Rising rates of unemployment are an increasingly salient source of dissatisfaction in many third wave regimes.[64] Since these democracies, for the most part, depend on policies rather than political parties as their means of linking associated citizens to the state, this very public policy failure is especially ominous. The nineteenth-century experience provides little consolation. Marketization caused the marginalization and disorientation of vast sectors of society then, too, but because the nineteenth-century states were not formal democracies (because they denied many people suffrage and a whole host of other rights) the economically weak and the politically disenfranchised were often one in the same. The shut out were also the shut up. Today the coincidence of marketization and democratization has produced a vast army of people who are economically marginalized but politically empowered. The political rights of the marginalized are often abused and underutilized, but they have a potential power that is, in national terms, unprecedented. How the two elements of joblessness and formal individual liberties will combine and affect the chemistry of associational life today remains to be seen.

The chemistry will no doubt vary from state to state, but the outcome everywhere is likely to be profoundly affected by how democratic political elites handle the tasks of decentralization. As the twentieth century draws to a close, arguments for the decentralization of political authority ring loudly from various quarters. Sometimes the arguments are made by those who hope to empower or develop ethnic and regional identities.[65] Sometimes the arguments are made by those who hope to promote efficiency and fight the rent-seeking behavior associated with a bloated central state.[66] Almost everywhere, new democracies find themselves under increasing pressure to devolve more authority and responsibility onto regional governments. As this devolution of power occurs, the potential for regional asymmetries grows greater. We know from our histories of nineteenth-century Europe that regional asymmetries can be deeply disturbing to a democratizing state. We know also that many third wave democracies have been plagued by regional asymmetries in the past.

Unfortunately, asymmetries are built on inequalities, and marketization seems to be exacerbating rather than ameliorating regional inequalities, in the short run at least. Unemployment rates vary greatly from region to region, as do the benefits of economic investment and growth. When wide geographic variations in economic and political climate produce regional governments of vastly different political colorations, the possibilities for regional asymmetries grow dramatically. Current moves to decentralize governmental responsibilities may make matters worse for they are very likely to reinforce localism. Decentralization is likely to encourage political elites to prioritize the "close-by and particular" at the expense of the "far-away and national." Yet, as Banti argues persuasively, it is precisely this "inversion of ethical priorities"—this disregard for the national consequences of local activity—which proved detrimental to the growth of a democratic civil society in nineteenth-century Europe.[67] Where localism and the inversion of priorities coincide with highly visible regional inequalities and the easy availability of arms, national-level democratic elites will face not simply regional enclaves of opposition but enclaves of open revolt.

This plotline should sound familiar. Historically, its outcome has turned on the behavior of divided elites and their ability to forge alliances and resolve differences within the context of democratic or at least democratizing institutions. In the nineteenth century, political parties and legislatures provided the backdrops for the scenes in which alliances were forged. Today, these institutions are no longer as prominent. Whether diverse elites will revive them or find alternative political spaces where differences can be resolved remains unknowable.

What we do know is that the shifting sets on which the dramas will be played out are more crowded than ever. International actors are more visible, if not more powerful, and mass actors have formal roles they have never had before. Crowding increases the complexity of associational interaction, and this complexity makes predictions hazardous. Yet complexity also elevates the role of all those who describe and interpret associational life for others. If there is one prediction worth making about the future of civil societies in third wave democracies it is that political "interpreters" in the media and in university communities will have a profound effect on how mass actors use their associational freedoms in years to come. If interpreters in either setting cater to sensationalism, sowing fear and hysteria, antidemocratic forces will be advantaged. Compromise will be made more difficult and the most divisive forms of associational interactions will result.

Because sensationalism sells better than reasoned exchange, the privatized media will likely send out messages of mixed impact (and mixed repute) for years to come. Happily, market considerations should have less effect on the interpretations emanating from universities. In the nineteenth century (and in the beginning of the twentieth century) antidemocratic movements and associations had little difficulty mustering support from university elites. They even recruited academics of great prestige. Today, the ranks of the overtly antidemocratic intellectual elite have dwindled, and the tasks of recruitment will prove more difficult.

This means that universities can play an increasingly positive role in the democratization of the civil societies in which they operate. The importance of universities in the political socialization of national elites is obvious. The role of the university as a political space is less obvious but no less important. Universities have a potential as settings for political dialogue and as venues for the free exchange of information that is often unexploited but probably unmatched. The fact that successful marketization actually requires the *expansion* of university communities provides opportunities that other long-standing institutions lack. As other public spaces become inaccessible or await renovation, universities and university intellectuals have a special obligation to keep their own public spaces open and working in the interest of further civic democratization. To do this, they might learn from the errors of university intellectuals of the past. They should avoid elitism and communicate in the vernacular voice of their fellow citizens. Most important, they should strive to talk across borders, not just across disciplines as we have done here, but across ideological and national divides as well. History suggests no desirable alternative.

NOTES

The author thanks Sheri Berman, Atul Kohli, José Lucero, Philip Nord, and Deborah Yashar for helpful comments on an earlier version of this essay.

1. Alberto Banti, "Public Opinion and Associations in Nineteenth-Century Italy," this volume.

2. Adrian Lyttelton, "Liberalism and Civil Society in Italy: From Hegemony to Mediation," this volume.

3. Klaus Tenfelde, "Civil Society and the Middle Classes in Nineteenth-Century Germany," this volume. Frank Trentmann argues persuasively that the "tidal wave" of expanding associational life was particularly pronounced in Germany. Trentmann, "Introduction: Paradoxes of Civil Society," in *Paradoxes of Civil Society*, ed. Frank Trentmann (New York: Berghahn Books, 1999), 13.

4. Andrew McLaren Carstairs, *A Short History of Electoral Systems in Western Europe* (London: George Allen and Unwin, 1980), 190.

5. Thomas Ertman, "Liberalization, Democratization, and the Origins of a 'Pillarized' Civil Society in Nineteenth-Century Belgium and the Netherlands," this volume.

6. Antônio Costa Pinto and Pedro Tavares de Almeida, "On Liberalism and the Emergence of Civil Society in Portugal," 5.

7. Robert Gildea, *Barricades and Borders: Europe 1800–1914* (Oxford: Oxford University Press, 1987), 8.

8. Gildea, *Barricades and Borders*, 147.

9. Charles Tilly, Louise Tilly, and Richard Tilly, *The Rebellious Century 1830–1930* (Cambridge, Mass.: Harvard University Press), 205.

10. Harvey Graff, *The Legacies of Literacy* (Bloomington: Indiana University Press, 1987), 314.

11. Graff, *The Legacies of Literacy*, 314.

12. Harry Hearder, *Europe in the Nineteenth Century 1830–1880* (London: Longman, 1988), 391.

13. Graff, *The Legacies of Literacy*, 289.

14. Jonathan Sperber, *The European Revolutions 1848–1851* (Cambridge: Cambridge University Press, 1994), 32.

15. Gildea, *Barricades and Borders*, 245.

16. Pamela Pilbeam, *The Middle Classes in Europe 1789–1914* (London: Macmillan, 1990), 190–91.

17. Hearder, *Europe in the Nineteenth Century*, 394. The French fared fairly well on this measure with one student per 1,900.

18. Pilbeam, *The Middle Classes*, 207.

19. Costa Pinto and Tavares de Almeida, "On Liberalism," this volume.

20. Costa Pinto and Tavares de Almeida, "On Liberalism," this volume.

21. Banti, "Public Opinion," this volume. For a more detailed analysis of the relationship between liberalism and Catholicism in nineteenth-century Europe, see Andrew Gould, *Origins of Liberal Dominance: State, Church, and Party in Nineteenth-Century Europe* (Ann Arbor: University of Michigan Press, 1999).

22. R. J. Morris, "Civil Society, Subscriber Democracies, and Parliamentary Government in Great Britain," this volume.

23. Banti, "Public Opinion," this volume.

24. Banti, "Public Opinion," this volume.

25. Costa Pinto and Tavares de Almeida, "On Liberalism," this volume.

26. Laura Engelstein, "The Dream of Civil Society in Czarist Russia: Law, State, and Religion," this volume.

27. Lyttelton, "Liberalism," this volume.

28. Costa Pinto and Tavares de Almeida, "On Liberalism," this volume.

29. Raymond Huard, "Political Association in Nineteenth-Century France: Legislation and Practice," this volume.

30. Jan Kubik, "Between the State and Networks of "Cousins": The Role of Civil Society and Non-Civil Associations in the Democratization of Poland," this volume.

31. Nord, "Introduction," this volume.

32. Nord, "Introduction," this volume.

33. Costa Pinto and Tavares de Almeida, "On Liberalism," this volume.

34. Englestein, "The Dream of Civil Society," this volume.

35. Englestein, "The Dream of Civil Society," this volume.

36. Valerie Bunce, "The Historical Origins of the East–West Divide: Civil Society, Political Society, and Democracy in Europe," this volume.

37. Lyttelton, "Liberalism," this volume.

38. Costa Pinto and Tavares de Almeida, "On Liberalism," this volume.

39. Hearder, *Europe in the Nineteenth Century*, 13.

40. Hearder, *Europe in the Nineteenth Century*, 14.

41. Ertman, "Liberalization," this volume.

42. For evidence of the problem in Chile, see Joel M. Jutkowitz, "Civil Society and Democratic Development in Chile," paper presented to the 1995 Annual Meeting of the American Political Science Association, Chicago. For evidence from the South African case, see Wilmot James and Daria Caliguire, "The New South Africa: Renewing Civil Society," *Journal of Democracy* 7, no. 1 (January 1996). For a more developed version of this argument focusing on what happens when international donors withdraw non-governmental organization assistance, see Larry Diamond, "Civil Society and the Development of Democracy," *Estudios/Working Papers Centro de Estudios Avanzados en Ciencias Sociales* 1997/101, June 1997. Other stimulating critiques of civil society/state relations are available in Brian H. Smith, *More Than Altruism: The Politics of Foreign Aid* (Princeton: Princeton University Press, 1990); and David Hulme and Michael Edwards, eds., *NGO States and Donors: Too Close for Comfort?* (London: Macmillan, 1997).

43. For evidence of the range of new democracies that have proved unable and or unwilling to control violence, see Paulo Sergio Pinheiro, "Democracies without Citizenship," *North American Congress on Latin America Report on the Americas* 30, no. 2 (September–October 1996); Paul Chevigny, *Edge of the Knife: Police Violence in the Americas* (New York: The New Press, 1995); A. W. Pereira, "Elitist Liberalism: Citizenship, Coercion and the Rule of Law in Brazil," in Peter Kingstone and Tim Power, eds., *Democratic Brazil* (Pittsburgh: University of Pittsburgh Press, forthcoming).

44. Philippine journalist Ferdinand Reyes, the editor of the weekly *Press Freedom*, was murdered in his office in February 1996. Another critical journalist, Danny Hernandez, was murdered in the Philippines in the spring of 1997. In January 1997, dissident journalist Natan Pereira Gatinho was murdered in southern Brazil. Igor Grouchetsky, a Ukrainian journalist investigating corruption, was murdered near his home in May 1996 southwest of Kiev. At least four people associated with investigative reporting were mur-

dered between February 1995 and 1996 in Russia, including Dmitry Kholodov, Vladislav Listyev, Oleg Slabynko, and Felix Solovyov. These and other murders and other acts of physical intimidation against investigative journalists are publicized by the International Freedom of Expression Exchange (IFEX) Clearing House on the Internet.

45. Buckovsky is quoted in Adam Michnik and Jay Rosen, "The Media and Democracy: A Dialogue," *Journal of Democracy* 8, no. 4 (October 1997).

46. For more extensive evidence on the costs of gaining access to the media in Latin America, see Hernan Uribe, *Ética Periodista en America Latina* (Mexico City: UNAM, 1984). Historically the legitimacy of Mexican elections has been seriously undermined by bias toward the Partido Revolucionario Institucional in television and other media. Televisa's open endorsement of the PRI and the privileged access given to Carlos Salinas de Gortari in the 1988 presidential elections became notorious on the Right as well as the Left. See Ilya Adler, "The Mexican Case: The Media in the 1988 Presidential Election," in *Television, Politics and the Transition to Democracy in Latin America*, ed. Thomas E. Skidmore. In Brazil, Fernando Collor's privileged access to the GLOBO television network controlled by Roberto Marinho was key to his presidential victory and challenged as unfair both inside and outside Brazil. For more details, see Venicio de Lima, "Brazilian Television in the 1989 Election," in *Television, Politics and the Transition to Democracy in Latin America*.

47. Some of the early crisis cases were Argentina, Bolivia, Brazil, the Philippines, and Uruguay. These cases are nicely detailed in Stephan Haggard and Robert Kaufman, *The Political Economy of Democratic Transitions* (Princeton: Princeton University Press, 1995). For a rich analysis of the connection between economic crisis and the third wave itself, see Karen Remmer, "The Political Impact of the Economic Crisis in Latin America in the 1980s," *APSR* 85, no. 3: 777–800. Detailed overviews of the Eastern European examples are presented in Adrian Karatnycky, Alexander Motyl, and Boris Shor, *Nations in Transition 1997: Civil Society, Democracy and Markets in East Europe and the Newly Independent States* (New Brunswick, N.J.: Transaction Books, 1997).

48. For evidence on the links between neoliberal reform packages and sovereignty critiques, see William C. Smith, Carlos Acuña, and Eduardo Gamarra, eds. *Latin American Political Economy in the Age of Liberal Reform* (New Brunswick, N.J.: Transaction Books, 1994); and "Democracy and the Limits of Popular Sovereignty in South America" in *Essays on the Consolidation of Democracy in Latin America*, ed. Joseph Tulchin and Bernice Romero (Boulder: Lynne Reinner, 1995).

49. For a highly informative analysis of policy reversals and their political consequences, see Catherine Conaghan and James Malloy, *Unsettling Statecraft: Democracy and Neoliberalism in the Central Andes*. For a well-argued and sobering discussion of how insulated policy making affects the likelihood of democratic consolidation, see Atul Kohli, "On Sources of Social and Political Conflicts in Follower Democracies," in *Democracy's Victory and Crisis*, ed. Axel Hadenius (Cambridge: Cambridge University Press, 1997).

50. A recent, careful overview of the political party systems in sixteen Latin American democracies found growing evidence of "upheaval or decay" and concluded that electorates are less linked to parties than ever before. Using the Pedersen index of vote volatility, the authors found that the vote volatility rate in Latin American electoral democracies reached 21.6 in the 1980s and 25.6 in the 1990s. These figures compare very unfavorably with a mean score of 8.6 for European parties between 1885 and 1985. For more details on these points and a well-argued analysis of the crisis of Latin Amer-

ican party systems, see Kenneth Roberts and Erik Wibbels, "Party Systems and Electoral Volatility in Latin America: A Test of Economic Institutional and Structural Explanations," *American Political Science Review* 93, no. 3 (September 1999). For more evidence on the weakness of Latin American party systems, see the essays in Scott Mainwaring and Timothy R. Scully, eds. *Building Democratic Institutions: Party Systems in Latin America.*

51. The importance of television as a stimulus to associational life and to collective action in general was vividly illustrated during the collapse of the Communist bloc in 1989–90. Even in a relatively poor and closed system such as China, television has become increasingly accessible and increasingly important. As early as 1987, there were 130 million sets in the country, approximately one set per ten people. For more on China and a general discussion of television and its mobilizational capacities, see Douglas Gomery and Lawrence W. Lichty, "Television: A New Role around the World?" in *Television, Politics and the Transition to Democracy in Latin America.* For evidence on the stimulating function of television and an important discussion of the connection between technology and transnational civil society, see Sidney Tarrow, "Fishnets, Internets and Catnets: Globalization and Transnational Collective Action," in *Structure Identity and Power: The Past and Future of Collective Action*, ed. Michael Hanagan et al., forthcoming.

52. Wayne Rash reports that in 1996, for the first time in history, the number of computers sold exceeded the number of televisions sold. For a discussion of the importance of computer information networks for a whole range of political associations see Wayne Rask, Jr., *Politics on the Net: Wiring the Political Process* (New York: Freeman, 1997), chap. 6.

53. For more evidence on the "associational revolution" and the funds dedicated toward its expansion in the third world, see David Hulme and Michael Edwards, eds., *NGOs States and Donors: Too Close for Comfort?* (London: Macmillan, 1997). Facts from the CGG and on spending are from p. 4. Larry Diamond presents a helpful discussion of the "unprecedented international cooperation" toward civic education in "Civil Society and the Development of Democracy" in *Estudios/Working Papers*, Instituto Juan March de Estudios e Investigaciones. The CIVITAS initiative beginning in 1996 at United States Information Agency is especially interesting in the context of my argument. See especially pp. 33–36.

54. Well-known arguments about the connection between decentralization and the growth of associational life appear in de Tocqueville, *Democracy in America*, ed. J. P. Mayer (Garden City, N.Y.: Doubleday, 1969) and in Robert Dahl, *Polyarchy* (New Haven, Conn.: Yale University Press, 1971). A more recent argument that points out the governance problems associated with this connection appears in Victor M. Perez-Diaz, *The Return of Civil Society: The Emergence of Democratic Spain* (Cambridge, Mass.: Harvard University Press, 1993). For arguments from and about Poland, see Grazyna Skapska, "Learning to Be a Citizen," ed. Robert Fine and Shirin Rai, special issue of *Democratization* 4, no. 1 (Spring 1997).

55. One of the most influential arguments for the connection between markets, wealth, and associational freedoms appears in Milton Friedman, *Capitalism and Freedom* (Chicago: University of Chicago Press, 1962). For a critical examination of how the market and civil society are connected as "developmental panaceas," see Gordon White, "Civil Society, Democratization and Development (I): Clearing the Analytical Ground," *Democratization* 1, no. 3 (Autumn 1994): 375–90. Interesting critiques and expositions of

the arguments connecting economic liberalization and democracy appear in Laurence Whitehead's special issue of *World Development* 21, no. 8 (1993).

56. Examples of the insecurities and voids associated with marketization are most obvious in the former Soviet bloc. See Secretariat of the Economic Commission for Europe, Economic Survey of Europe in 1995–96, for evidence on rising unemployment. See Richard Rose, "Toward a Civil Economy," *Journal of Democracy* 3 (April 1995): 13–16, for an early discussion of how voids in the legal system were created by rapid marketization in Eastern Europe and the former Soviet Union. For an argument about how the problems associated with marketization helped stimulate the organization of indigenous people's in Latin America, see Deborah Yashar, "Indigenous Politics and Democracy: Contesting Citizenship in Latin America," paper prepared for the Annual Meetings of the APSA, 1996, 12–13.

57. Philippe Schmitter makes a strong case for the mixed qualities of civil society and discusses both its functions and its spread in "Some Reflections about the Concept of Civil Society," ms., Princeton University, October 1996.

58. Evidence that rising consumerism distracts people from political involvement is particularly evident in surveys of those between the ages of eighteen and thirty.

59. For recent evidence on the importance of technocrats and their political support, see Eduardo Silva, *The State and Capital in Chile: Business Elites, Technocrats and Market Economics* (Boulder: Westview, 1996); Benno Galjart and Patricio Silva, eds., *Designers of Development* (Leiden: Research School, 1995); and John Williamson, *The Political Economy of Policy Reform: A Manual for Technopols* (Washington, D.C.: Institute for International Economics, 1994).

60. Impressive drops in inflation have been achieved in Bolivia, Argentina, Peru, and most recently Brazil. In each of these cases, the popularity of the chief executives got a dramatic boost.

61. Juan Linz and Alfred Stepan, *Problems of Democratic Transition and Consolidation* (Baltimore: Johns Hopkins University Press, 1996), 442–44. Marketization and democracy were seen as a package in the early years of postcommunism, but this relationship may be breaking down. For evidence on the first point and a hint of the second, see Geoffrey Evans and Stephen Whitefield, "The Politics and Economics of Democratic Commitment: Support for Democracy in Transition Societies," *British Journal of Political Science* 25 (1995). The point I am making here is that democracy is the preferred form of government—not that citizens evaluate their own national democracies in a positive light. This is clearly not the case in many new (and old) democracies. See Eurobarometer for evidence.

62. Evidence that ruling parties and politicians are blamed for joblessness comes from Michael Lewis-Beck, *Economics and Elections: The Major Western Democracies* (Ann Arbor: University of Michigan Press, 1988). A recent and comprehensive survey of the connections between unemployment and political attitudes in Europe found that unemployment "translates into systematically lower levels of system support." Christopher Anderson, "Desperate Times Call for Desperate Measures? Unemployment and Voter Behavior in Comparative Perspective," in *Unemployment in the New Europe*, ed. Nancy Bermeo (New York: Cambridge University Press, 2000).

63. The old assumptions about economic growth generating jobs no longer seem to hold even in the advanced industrial societies. For an influential discussion of the evidence, see Paul Krugman "Europe Jobless, America Penniless?" *Foreign Policy* 95 (Summer 1994).

64. For evidence that people are extraordinarily fearful of unemployment, see Luiz Carlos Bresser Pereira, José Maria Maravall, and Adam Przeworski, *Economic Reforms in New Democracies* (Cambridge: Cambridge University Press, 1993), 180–81; and various polls summarized in recent issues of *World Opinion Update.*

65. For recent discussions of the connections between decentralization and the reinforcement of ethnic identity in Latin America, see Xavier Albo, "And from Kataristas, MNRistas? The Surprising and Bold Alliance between Aymaras and Neoliberals in Bolivia," and Jesus Avirama and Rayda Marquez, "The Indigenous Movement in Colombia," in *Indigenous Peoples and Democracy in Latin America*, ed. Donna Lee Van Cott (New York: St. Martin's, 1994).

66. The connection between decentralization and efficiency is discussed in Gustav Ranis, ed., *En Route to Modern Growth: Latin America in the 1990s: Essays in Honor of Carlos Diaz-Alejandro* (Washington, D.C.: Inter-American Development Bank, 1994).

67. Banti, "Public Opinion," this volume.

INDEX

accountability, 125
Act Governing Associations, France,
  xix, 146–51
Action française, 149
Action libérale populaire, 149
agrarian societies, in Italy, 64
agriculture: in Italy, 71, 75–78; in
  Portugal, 8, 11
agro-towns, 52
Agulhon, Maurice, 141
Albania, 227
Alexander I, tsar of Russia, 26
Alexander II, tsar of Russia, 24, 30, 221
Allgemeiner Deutscher Automobilclub,
  85
All-Poland Alliance of Trade Unions
  (OPZZ), 196
Amann, P. H., 142
anarchists, in Portugal, 14, 17
Anglican Church, and democratization,
  xxiv–xxv
Anticlericalism: in Italy, 76; in Portugal,
  10
Anti-Corn Law League, 127, 168
antidemocratic associations: factors
  affecting, 251–53; in Portugal, 16
antiliberalism: in Italy, Giolitti and, 74;
  and pillarized society, 167–73
antiparliamentarianism, in Italy, 43–44
Anti-Revolutionaire Partij (ARP), 156,
  168–69, 174–75

Anti-School Law Association, 168
Antislavery Movement, 125
Antwerp, 156
April Movement, 166
Arago, Etienne, 140
Arbeiterbauern, 83–84
aristocracy: in Belgium, 162; in Britain,
  122, 128–29; and development of
  democracy, 241, 253–54; and
  East–West divide, 216; in Germany,
  98; in Portugal, 5; in Russia, 27. *See
  also* elites
Arkuszewski, Wojciech, 190
Army League, Germany, 101
Artisan Brotherhoods, 69–70
artists' associations, 195
Asia, 216
assembly rights, in Portugal, 5
associational life: in Britain, 113; density
  of, and development of democracy,
  239, 250–51; importance of, xiii;
  liberal, character of, xxvii; open versus
  closed forms, 118–20; in Portugal,
  8–12; success versus failure in, 126–27
associational networks: in France,
  142–43; in Germany, 98–99;
  organization of, xxix; in Poland,
  185–87
association fetishism, 98
associations: in Britain, 113, 115;
  definition of, 91; in Germany,

261

ABOUT THE CONTRIBUTORS

Pedro Tavares de Almeida is a professor of politics at the Faculty of Social Sciences and Humanities, University of Lisbon. He has published many books and articles, mainly on Portuguese electoral history and elite recruitment.

Alberto Mario Banti is associate professor of history at the University of Pisa. He has published three books: *Terra e Denaro: Una Borghesia Padana dell'Ottocento* (1989), *Storia della Borghesia Italiana: L'Età Liberale* (1996), and *La Nazione del Risorgimento: Parentela, Santità e Honore Alle Origini dell'Italia Unita* (2000). He has published several articles in English, French, German, and Italian on different aspects of nineteenth-century social and political history.

Nancy Bermeo teaches at Princeton University and writes on the causes and consequences of regime change. Her books include a study of democratization in Portugal titled *The Revolution within the Revolution*, an edited collection on the breakdown of dictatorship in Eastern Europe titled *Liberalization and Democratization*, and two edited books on joblessness titled *Unemployment in Southern Europe* and *Unemployment in the New Europe*. She has just completed a book on the breakdown of democracy titled *Ordinary People in Extraordinary Times*.

Valerie Bunce is professor of government at Cornell University and a longtime specialist in Russian and East-Central European politics and economics. Her most recent book is *Subversive Institutions: The Design and the Destruction of Socialism and the State* (1999). In 2001–2002, she will be serving as president of the American Association for the Advancement of Slavic Studies.

António Costa Pinto is professor of modern European history and politics at ISCTE, University of Lisbon. He has written on fascism, dictatorships, and transitions to democracy in Southern Europe. He recently published *Salazar's Dictatorship and European Fascism* (1996) and edited *Modern Portugal* (1998).

Laura Engelstein is professor of history at Princeton University. She writes on political and cultural themes in late imperial Russia. Among her publications are *The Keys to Happiness: Sex and the Search for Modernity in Fin-de-Siècle Russia* (1992) and *Castration and the Heavenly Kingdom: A Russian Folktale* (1999).

Thomas Ertman is an associate professor in the Department of Sociology at New York University. He is author of *Birth of the Leviathan: Building States and Regimes in Medieval and Early Modern Europe*, which won the 1998 Barrington Moore Prize for best book in historical sociology. He is currently working on a comparative study of liberalization and democratization in nineteenth- and early twentieth-century Europe.

Raymond Huard is professor emeritus at the Université Paul Valéry de Montpellier. He is the author of dozens of articles and six books, including most recently *La Naissance du Parti Politique en France* (1996).

Jan Kubik is associate professor of political science and director of the Center for Russian, Central, and East European Studies at Rutgers University. His work is focused mostly on postcommunist transformations in Eastern Europe and revolves around the relationship between culture and politics and contentious politics. His publications include *The Power of Symbols against the Symbols of Power: The Rise of Solidarity and the Fall of State Socialism in Poland* (1994) and *Rebellious Civil Society: Popular Protest and Democratic Consolidation in Poland, 1989–1993* (with Grzegorz Ekiert)(1999).

Adrian Lyttelton is professor of contemporary European history at the University of Pisa. He is the author of *The Seizure of Power: Fascism in Italy 1919–1929* (1973) and is now at work editing the volume on *Italy 1900–1945* in the *Oxford History of Italy*.

Robert J. Morris is professor of economic and social history at the University of Edinburgh. He is a specialist in nineteenth-century British social and urban history and has authored or edited numerous books and articles in the field, most notably *Class, Sect, and Party: The Making of the British Middle Class: Leeds 1820–1850* (1990).

Philip Nord, professor of history at Princeton University, has authored three books: *Paris Shopkeepers and the Politics of Resentment* (1986), *The Republican Moment: Struggles for Democracy in the Nineteenth Century (1995)*, and *Impressionists and Politics: Art and Democracy in the Nineteenth Century* (2000). He is currently working on a project dealing with conservative elites in France from the 1930s through the 1950s.

Klaus Tenfelde is professor of history and director of the Institute for Social Movements at the Ruhr-Universität Bochum. He is the author or editor of over a dozen books on comparative labor history and industrial relations, including *Sozialgeschichte der Bergarbeitschaft an der Ruhr im 19. Jahrhundert* (1981) and *Proletarische Provinz: Radikalisierung und Widerstand in Penzberg (Oberbayern) 1900–1945* (1982).